# DISCRIMINATIONS:

## Further Concepts
## of Criticism

# DISCRIMINATIONS:
## Further Concepts
## of Criticism

by René Wellek

*New Haven and London, Yale University Press, 1970*

# Prefatory Note

This volume consists of papers and studies written since the publication of my *Concepts of Criticism*. The title *Discriminations* seems to me appropriate, indicating my concern for clarity, coherence, and definiteness in one's thinking about literature. The volume begins with theoretical statements about comparative literature, moves on to studies of two period concepts—classicism and symbolism, which supplement the papers on the baroque, romanticism, and realism in the earlier book—and then proceeds to discuss individual problems and issues in a roughly chronological order. The paper on "Immanuel Kant's Aesthetics and Criticism" greatly expands the incidental treatment of Kant in the first volume of my *History of Criticism;* the piece on "English Literary Historiography in the Nineteenth Century" resumes a topic only marginally discussed in the *History,* though passages from this old paper were incorporated in it, in different contexts; and the paper on "Vernon Lee, Bernard Berenson, and the Aesthetics of Empathy" treats an important strand of aesthetic theorizing, though it starts with the personal history of the conflict between two proponents of the theory. The article on Leo Spitzer is an extended obituary which raises questions of stylistics and literary theory of even greater import than the work of this distinguished scholar. "Genre Theory, the Lyric, and *Erlebnis"* is ostensibly devoted to a criticism of the writings of Käte Hamburger and Emil

Staiger but raises the problem of genre, the nature of the lyric and of sincerity in literature, while "The Poet as Critic, the Critic as Poet, the Poet-Critic" comes back to the central issue: the nature of criticism and its position today in the United States. The following paper, on the Prague School, returns to Europe, discussing theories which under the impact of Russian Formalism and French structuralism have again assumed urgency. "The Sketch of the History of Dostoevsky Criticism" speaks for itself. "Stylistics, Poetics, and Criticism" tries to define the limits of stylistics within the context of a conference held at the Villa Serbelloni, Bellagio, in August 1969. The collection concludes with a bird's-eye view of European criticism of the last two decades, which I do not plan to discuss in detail in the volume of my *History of Modern Criticism* on the twentieth century that I have been preparing for many years. There the cut-off is set at 1950, which will not be observed rigidly but will allow me to concentrate on the great figures and tendencies of the first half of the century rather than on the publications of the last years. Essays on T. S. Eliot, I. A. Richards, F. R. Leavis, Benedetto Croce, Albert Thibaudet, and Friedrich Gundolf, now in print (listed in the Bibliography), will be used in the final volume, which will complete the story of criticism over the last two centuries in many lands.

I want to thank my former student and now my colleague and trusted friend, Lowry Nelson, Jr., for help in reading the proofs. He and other friends—Maynard Mack, Stephen G. Nichols, Jr., and William K. Wimsatt—read individual papers, and I am grateful for their suggestions.

R.W.

*New Haven, Conn.*
*May 15, 1969*

# Acknowledgments

"Comparative Literature Today" and "Leo Spitzer (1887–1960)" first appeared in *Comparative Literature* and are included here by permission of the editors of that journal.

"The Term and Concept of Classicism in Literary History" was included in *Aspects of the Eighteenth Century*, edited by Earl R. Wasserman (Baltimore, 1965) and is reprinted here by permission of The Johns Hopkins Press.

"Immanuel Kant's Aesthetics and Criticism" was first published in *The Philosophy of Kant and Our Modern World*, edited by Charles W. Hendel, and is included here with the permission of The Bobbs-Merrill Company, Inc.

"Vernon Lee, Bernard Berenson, and Aesthetics" appeared in *Friendship's Garland: Essays Presented to Mario Praz on his Seventieth Birthday*, edited by Vittorio Gabrieli (Rome, 1966) and is reprinted here by permission of Edizioni di Storia e Letteratura.

"Genre Theory, the Lyric, and *Erlebnis*" appeared in *Festschrift für Richard Alewyn*, edited by H. Singer and Benno von Wiese (Köln, 1967) and is reprinted here by permission of Böhlau Verlag.

"The Poet as Critic, the Critic as Poet, the Poet-Critic" appeared in *The Poet as Critic*, edited by Frederick P. W. McDowell (Evanston, Ill., 1967) and is reprinted here with the permission of the editor and the Northwestern University Press.

"A Sketch of the History of Dostoevsky Criticism" first appeared as the introduction to *Dostoevsky: A Collection of Critical Essays* (Englewood Cliffs, N.J., 1962) and is reprinted here by permission of Prentice-Hall, Inc.

# Contents

# The Name and Nature
# of Comparative Literature

The term "comparative literature" has given rise to so much discussion, has been interpreted so differently and misinterpreted so frequently, that it might be useful to examine its history and to attempt to distinguish its meanings in the main languages. Only then can we hope to define its exact scope and content. Lexicography, "historical semantics," will be our starting point. Beyond it, a brief history of comparative studies should lead to conclusions of contemporary relevance. "Comparative literature" is still a controversial discipline and idea.

There seem no particular problems raised by our two words individually. "Comparative" occurs in Middle English, obviously derived from Latin *comparativus*. It is used by Shakespeare, as when Falstaff denounces Prince Hal as "the most comparative, rascalliest, sweet young prince."[1] Francis Meres, as early as 1598, uses the term in the caption of "A Comparative Discourse of Our English Poets with the Greek, Latin and Italian Poets."[2] The adjective occurs in the titles of several seventeenth- and eighteenth-century books. In 1602 William Fulbecke published *A Comparative Discourse of the Laws*. I also find *A Comparative Anatomy of Brute*

1. *Henry IV*, I.2.90.
2. *Elizabethan Critical Essays,* ed. Gregory Smith, *2* (2 vols. Oxford, 1904), 314.

*Animals* in 1765. Its author, John Gregory, published *A Comparative View of the State and Faculties of Man with Those of the Animal World* in the very next year. Bishop Robert Lowth in his Latin *Lectures on the Sacred Poetry of the Hebrews* (1753), formulated the ideal of comparative study well enough: "We must see all things with their eyes [i.e. the ancient Hebrews]: estimate all things by their opinions; we must endeavour as much as possible to read Hebrew as the Hebrews would have read it. We must act as the Astronomers with regard to that branch of their science which is called comparative who, in order to form a more perfect idea of the general system and its different parts, conceive themselves as passing through, and surveying, the whole universe, migrating from one planet to another and becoming for a short time inhabitants of each."[3] In his pioneering *History of English Poetry* Thomas Warton announced in the Preface to the first volume that he would present "a comparative survey of the poetry of other nations."[4] George Ellis, in his *Specimens of Early English Poets* (1790), speaks of antiquaries whose "ingenuity has often been successful in detecting and extracting by comparative criticism many particulars respecting the state of society and the progress of arts and manners" from medieval chronicles.[5] In 1800 Charles Dibdin published, in five volumes, *A Complete History of the English Stage, Introduced by a Comparative and Comprehensive Review of the Asiatic, the Grecian, the Roman, the Spanish, the Italian, the Portuguese, the German, the French and Other Theatres*. Here the main idea is fully formulated, but the combination "comparative literature" itself seems to occur for the first time only in a letter by Matthew Arnold in

3. Trans. G. Gregory, *1* (2 vols. London, 1787), 113–14.
4. Vol. 1 (2 vols. London, 1774), iv.
5. Vol. 1 (2nd ed. 3 vols. London, 1801), 58.

1848, where he says: "How plain it is now, though an attention to the comparative literatures for the last fifty years
might have instructed anyone of it, that England is in a certain
sense far behind the Continent."[6] But this was a private letter
not published till 1895, and "comparative" means here hardly
more than "comparable." In English the decisive use was that
of Hutcheson Macaulay Posnett, an Irish barrister who later
became Professor of Classics and English Literature at University College, Auckland, New Zealand, who put the term
on the title of his book in 1886. As part of Kegan Paul,
Trench, and Trübner's International Scientific Series, the
book aroused some attention and was, e.g., favorably reviewed by William Dean Howells.[7] Posnett, in an article,
"The Science of Comparative Literature," claimed "to have
first stated and illustrated the method and principles of the
new science, and to have been the first to do so not only in the
British Empire but in the world."[8] Obviously this is pre-
posterous, even if we limit "comparative literature" to the
specific meaning Posnett gave to it. The English term cannot
be discussed in isolation from analogous terms in France and
Germany.

The lateness of the English term can be explained if we
realize that the combination "comparative literature" was
resisted in English, because the term "literature" had lost its
earlier meaning of "knowledge or study of literature" and
had come to mean "literary production in general" or "the
body of writings in a period, country, or region." That this
long process is complete today is obvious from such a fact
that, e.g., Professor Lane Cooper of Cornell University re-
fused to call the department he headed in the twenties "Com-

6. *Letters,* ed. G. W. E. Russell, *1* (2 vols. London, 1895), 8.
7. In *Harper's Magazine, 73* (1886), 318.
8. In *The Contemporary Review, 79* (1901), 870.

parative Literature" and insisted on "The Comparative Study
of Literature." He considered it a "bogus term" that "makes
neither sense nor syntax." "You might as well permit yourself
to say 'comparative potatoes' or 'comparative husks.' "[9] But
in earlier English usage "literature" means "learning" and
"literary culture," particularly a knowledge of Latin. *The
Tatler* reflects sagely in 1710: "It is in vain for folly to attempt
to conceal itself by the refuge of learned languages. Literature
does but make a man more eminently the thing which nature
made him."[10] Boswell says, for instance, that Baretti was an
"Italian of considerable literature."[11] This usage survived
into the nineteenth century, when James Ingram gave an
inaugural lecture on the *Utility of Anglo-Saxon Literature*
(1807), meaning the "utility of our knowing Anglo-Saxon,"
or when John Petherham wrote *An Historical Sketch of the
Progress and Present State of Anglo-Saxon Literature in
England* (1840), where "literature" obviously must mean the
study of literature. But these were survivals; "literature" had
assumed by then the present meaning of a body of writing.
The *Oxford English Dictionary* gives the first occurrence in
1812, but this is far too late: rather, the modern usage penetrated in the later eighteenth century from France.

Actually, the meaning of "literature" as "literary production" or "a body of writings" revived a usage of late antiquity.
Earlier *literatura* in Latin is simply a translation of the Greek
*grammatike* and sometimes means a knowledge of reading
and writing or even an inscription or the alphabet itself. But
Tertullian (who lived from about A.D. 160 to 240) and

9. *Experiments in Education* (Ithaca, N.Y., 1942), p. 75.

10. *Tatler*, No. 197 (July 13, 1710).

11. *Life of Samuel Johnson*, ed. G. B. Hill, rev. L. F. Powell, *1* (6
vols. Oxford, 1934), 302.

Cassian contrast secular literature with scriptural, pagan with Christian, *literatura* with *scriptura*.[12]

This use of the term reemerges only in the thirties of the eighteenth century in competition with the term *literae, lettres, letters.* An early example is François Granet's series *Réflexions sur les ouvrages de littérature* (1736–40). Voltaire, in *Le Siècle de Louis XIV* (1751), under the chapter heading "Des Beaux Arts," uses *littérature* with an uncertain reference alongside "eloquence, poets, and books of morals and amusement," and elsewhere in the book he speaks of "littérature légère" and "les genres de littérature" cultivated in Italy.[13] In 1759 Lessing began to publish his *Briefe die neueste Literatur betreffend,* where literature clearly refers to a body of writings. That the usage was still unusual at that time may be illustrated from the fact that Nicolas Trublet's *Essais sur divers sujets de littérature et morale* (1735–54) were translated into German as *Versuche über verschiedene Gegenstände der Sittenlehre und Gelehrsamkeit* (1776).[14]

This use of the word "literature" for all literary production, which is still one of our meanings, was in the eighteenth century soon nationalized and localized. It was applied to French, German, Italian, and Venetian literature, and almost simultaneously the term often lost its original inclusiveness and was narrowed down to mean what we would today call "imaginative literature," poetry, and imaginative, fictive

12. Eduard Wölfflin, in *Zeitschrift für lateinische Lexikographie, 5* (1888), 49.

13. Ed. René Groos, *2* (2 vols. Paris, 1947), 113: "Mais, dans l'éloquence, dans la poésie, dans la littérature, dans les livres de morale et d'agrément." Cf. *2,* 132, 145.

14. Reviewed by Herder, in his *Sämtliche Werke,* ed. Suphan, *1* (33 vols. Berlin, 1877), 123.

prose. The first book which exemplifies this double change is, as far as I know, Carlo Denina's *Discorso sopra le vicende della letteratura* (1760).[15] Denina professes not to speak "of the progress of the sciences and arts, which are not properly a part of literature"; he will speak of works of learning only when they belong to "good taste, and to eloquence, that is to say, to literature."[16] The Preface of the French translator speaks of Italian, English, Greek, and Latin literature. In 1774 there appeared an *Essai sur la littérature russe* by N. Novikov in Leghorn, and we have a sufficiently local reference in Mario Foscarini's *Storia della letteratura veneziana* (1752). The process of nationalization and, if I may use the term, aesthetization of the word is beautifully illustrated by A. de Giorgi-Bertòla's *Idea della letteratura alemanna* (Lucca, 1784), which is an expanded edition of the earlier *Idea della poesia alemanna* (Naples, 1779), where the change of title was forced by his inclusion of a report on German novels.[17] In German the term *Nationalliteratur* focuses on the nation as the unit of literature: it appears for the first time in the title of Leonhard Meister's *Beyträge zur Geschichte der teutschen Sprache und Nationalliteratur* (1777) and persists into the nineteenth century. Some of the best known German literary histories carry it in the title: Wachler, Koberstein, Gervinus in 1835, and later A. Vilmar and R. Gottschall.[18]

15. Turin, 1760; Paris, 1776; Glasgow, 1771, 1784. The connection with Glasgow is due to the fact that Denina knew Lady Elizabeth Mackenzie, the daughter of the Duke of Argyle, when her husband was the British Minister at Turin.

16. P. 6: "Non parleremo . . . dei progessi delle scienze e delle arti, che propriamente non sono parte di letteratura . . . al buon gusto, ed alla eloquenza, vale a dire alla letteratura."

17. Naples, 1779; Lucca, 1784.

18. Ludwig Wachler, *Vorlesungen über die Geschichte der teut-*

But the aesthetic limitation of the term was for a long time strongly resented. Philarète Chasles, for example, comments in 1847: "I have little esteem for the word 'literature'; it seems to me meaningless; it is a result of intellectual corruption." It seems to him tied to the Roman and Greek tradition of rhetoric. It is "something which is neither philosophy, nor history, nor erudition, nor criticism—something I know not what: vague, impalpable, and elusive."[19] Chasles prefers "intellectual history" to "literary history."

In English the same process took place. Sometimes it is still difficult to distinguish between the old meaning of literature as literary culture and a reference to a body of writing. Thus, as early as 1755, Dr. Johnson wanted to found *Annals of Literature, Foreign as well as Domestick*. In 1761 George Colman, the elder, thought that "Shakespeare and Milton seem to stand alone, like first rate authors, amid the general wreck of old English Literature."[20] In 1767 Adam Ferguson included a chapter, "Of the History of Literature," in his

---

*schen Nationallitteratur* (1818; 2nd ed. 1834): A. Koberstein, *Grundriss der Geschichte der deutschen Nationallitteratur* (1827); Georg Gottfried Gervinus, *Geschichte der poetischen Nationalliteratur der Deutschen* (5 vols., 1835–42); A. Vilmar, *Vorlesungen über die Geschichte der deutschen Nationalliteratur* (1845); R. Gottschall, *Die deutsche Nationalliteratur des 19. Jahrhunderts* (1881). This term seems to have later disappeared, though note G. Könnecke, *Bilderatlas zur Geschichte der deutschen Nationalliteratur* (1886).

19. *Etudes sur l'antiquité* (Paris, 1846), p. 28: "J'ai peu d'estime pour le mot littérature. Ce mot me parait dénué de sens; il est éclos d'une dépravation intellectuelle"; p. 30: "quelque chose qui n'est ni la Philosophie, ni l'Histoire, ni l'Erudition, ni la Critique;—je ne sais quoi de vague, d'insaisissable et d'élastique."

20. *Critical Reflections on the Old English Dramatick Writers. Extracted from a Prefatory Discourse to the New Edition of Massinger's Works* (London, 1761).

*Essay on the History of Civil Society.* In 1774 Dr. Johnson, in a letter, wished that "what is undeservedly forgotten of our antiquated literature might be revived,"[21] and John Berkenhout in 1777 subtitled his *Biographia Literaria, A Biographical History of Literature,* in which he proposed to give a "concise view of the rise and progress of literature." The Preface to De La Curne de Sainte-Palaye's *Literary History of the Troubadours,* translated in 1779 by Mrs. Susanna Dobson, speaks of the troubadours as "the fathers of modern literature," and James Beattie in 1783 wants to trace the rise and progress of romance in order to shed light upon "the history and politics, the manners and the literature of these latter ages."[22] There were books such as William Rutherford's *A View of Ancient History, Including the Progress of Literature, and the Fine Arts* (1788), *Sketches of a History of Literature* by Robert Alves (1794), and *An Introduction to the Literary History of the 14th and 15th Centuries* (1798) by Andrew Philpot, which complains that "there is nothing more wanting in English literature" than "a history of the revival of letters." But we may be surprised to hear that the first book with the title *A History of English Language and Literature* was a little handbook by Robert Chambers in 1836 and that the first Professor of English Language and Literature was the Reverend Thomas Dale, at University College, London, in 1828.[23]

Thus the change in meaning of the term "literature"

21. Dr. Johnson's Letter to the Rev. Dr. Horne, April 30, 1774, in *Catalogue of the Johnsonian Collection of R. B. Adams* (Buffalo, 1921).

22. James Beattie, *Dissertations, Moral and Critical* (London, 1783), p. 518.

23. On Dale see D. J. Palmer, *The Rise of English Studies* (London, 1965), pp. 18 ff.

hindered in English the adoption of the term "comparative literature," while "comparative politics," prominently advocated by the historian E. A. Freeman in 1873,[24] was quite acceptable, as was "comparative grammar," which appeared on the title page of a translation of Franz Bopp's *Comparative Grammar of Sanskrit, Zend, Greek, etc.,* in 1844.

In France the story was different; there *littérature* for a long time preserved the meaning of literary study. Voltaire, in his unfinished article on *Littérature* for his *Dictionnaire philosophique* (1764–72), defines literature as "a knowledge of the works of taste, a smattering of history, poetry, eloquence, and criticism," and he distinguishes it from "la belle littérature," which relates to "objects of beauty, to poetry, eloquence and well-written history."[25] Voltaire's follower, Jean-François Marmontel, who wrote the main literary articles for the great *Encyclopédie,* which were collected as *Eléments de littérature* (1787), clearly uses *littérature* as meaning "a knowledge of *belles lettres,*" which he contrasts with erudition. "With wit, talent and taste," he avows, "one can produce ingenious works, without any erudition, and with little literature."[26] Thus it was possible early in the nineteenth century to form the combination *littérature comparée,* which was apparently suggested by Cuvier's famous *Anatomie com-*

24. London, 1873. See *The Unity of History* (Cambridge, England, 1872), praising the comparative method as "a stage at least as great and memorable as the revival of Greek and Latin learning."

25. Not published till 1819. In *Oeuvres,* ed. Moland, *19* (52 vols. Paris, 1877–85), 590–92: "Une connaissance des ouvrages de goût, une teinture d'histoire, de poésie, d'éloquence, de critique . . . aux objets qui ont de la beauté, à la poésie, à l'histoire bien écrite."

26. *Eléments, 2* (Paris, 1856 reprint), 335: "La littérature est la connaissance des belles-lettres . . . avec de l'esprit, du talent et du goût, il peut produire des ouvrages ingénieux, sans aucune érudition, et avec peu de littérature."

*parée* (1800) or Degérando's *Historie comparée des systèmes de philosophie* (1804). In 1816 two compilers, Noël and Laplace, published a series of anthologies from French, classical, and English literature with the otherwise unused and unexplained title page: *Cours de littérature comparée.*[27] Charles Pougens, in *Lettres philosophiques à Madame xxx sur divers sujets de morale et littérature* (1826), complained that there is no work on the principles of literature he can recommend: "un cours de littérature comme je l'entends, c'est-à-dire, un cours de littérature comparée."[28]

The man, however, who gave the term currency in France was undoubtedly Abel-François Villemain, whose course in eighteenth-century literature was a tremendous success at the Sorbonne in the late twenties. It was published in 1828–29 as *Tableau de la littérature française au XVIIIe siècle* in 4 volumes, with even the flattering reactions of the audience inserted ("Vifs applaudissements. On rit."). There he uses several times *tableau comparé, études comparées, histoire comparée,* but also *littérature comparée* in praising the Chancelier Daguesseau for his "vastes études de philosophie, d'histoire, de littérature comparée."[29] In the second lecture series, *Tableau de la littérature au moyen âge en France, en Italie, en Espagne et en Angleterre* (2 volumes, 1830), he speaks again of "amateurs de la littérature comparée," and in the Preface to the new edition in 1840, Villemain, not incorrectly, boasts that here for the first time in a French uni-

27. The Bibliothèque Nationale lists *Leçons françaises de littérature et de morale* (2 vols., 1816) and *Leçons latines de littérature et de morale* (2 vols., 1816). *Leçons anglaises de littérature et de morale* (2 vols., 1817–19) has another coauthor, Mr. Chapsal.

28. Paris, p. 149.

29. New ed. 4 vols. Paris, 1873, *1*, 2, 24; *2*, 45; *1*, 225.

versity an attempt at an "analyse comparée" of several modern literatures was made.[30]

After Villemain the term was used fairly frequently. Philarète Chasles delivered an inaugural lecture at the Athénée in 1835: in the printed version in the *Revue de Paris,* the course is called "Littérature étrangère comparée."[31] Adolphe-Louis de Puibusque wrote a two-volume *Histoire comparée de la littérature française et espagnole* (1843), where he quotes Villemain, the perpetual Secretary of the French Academy, as settling the question. The term *comparative,* however, seems to have for a time competed with *comparée.* J.–J. Ampère, in his *Discours sur l'histoire de la poésie* (1830), speaks of "l'histoire comparative des arts et de la littérature"[32] but later also uses the other term in the title of his *Histoire de la littérature française au moyen âge comparée aux littératures étrangères* (1841). The decisive text in favor of the term *littérature comparée* is in Sainte-Beuve's very late article, an obituary of Ampère, in the *Revue des deux mondes* in 1868.[33]

In Germany the word "comparative" was translated *vergleichend* in scientific contexts. Goethe in 1795 wrote "Erster Entwurf einer allgemeinen Einleitung in die vergleichende Anatomie."[34] *Vergleichende Grammatik* was used by August

30. New ed. 2 vols. Paris, 1875, *1,* 187; *1,* 1.

31. Second series, *13* (1835), ii, 238–62. In revised version introducing *Etudes sur l'antiquité* (1840), Chasles does not use the term. See Claude Pichois, *Philarète Chasles et la vie littéraire au temps du romantisme, 1* (2 vols. Paris, 1965), 483.

32. Originally Marseille, 1830; reprinted in *Mélanges d'histoire littéraire, 1* (2 vols. Paris, 1867), 3.

33. Reprinted in *Nouveaux Lundis, 13* (13 vols. Paris, 1870), 183 ff.

34. *Sämtliche Werke, Jubiläumsausgabe, 39* (40 vols. Stuttgart, 1902–07), 137 ff.

Wilhelm Schlegel in a review in 1803,[35] and Friedrich Schlegel's pioneering book *Über Sprache und Weisheit der Inder* (1808) used *vergleichende Grammatik*[36] prominently as a program of a new science expressly recalling the model of "vergleichende Anatomie." The adjective became common in Germany for ethnology, and later psychology, historiography, and poetics. But for the very same reason as in English, it had difficulty making its way with the word "literature." As far as I know, Moriz Carriere in 1854, in a book, *Das Wesen und die Formen der Poesie,* uses the term *vergleichende Literaturgeschichte* for the first time.[37] The term *vergleichende Literatur* occurs surprisingly as the title of a forgotten periodical edited by Hugo von Meltzl, in the remote city of Klausenburg (now Cluj, in Rumania): his *Zeitschrift für vergleichende Literatur* ran from 1877–88. In 1886 Max Koch, at the University of Breslau, founded a *Zeitschrift für vergleichende Literaturgeschichte,* which survived till 1910. Von Meltzl emphasized that his conception of comparative literature was not confined to history and, in the last numbers of his periodical, he changed the title to *Zeitschrift für vergleichende Literaturwissenschaft.*[38] A fairly new term in German, *Literaturwissenschaft,* was adopted early in the twentieth century for what we usually call "literary criticism" or "theory of literature." The new German periodical *Arcadia* is called *Zeitschrift für vergleichende Literaturwissenschaft.*

35. Of Bernhardi's *Sprachlehre,* in *Sämtliche Werke,* ed. Böcking, *12,* 152.

36. *Sämtliche Werke, 8* (15 vols. 2d ed. Vienna, 1846), 291, 318.

37. In a section entitled: "Grundzüge und Winke zur vergleichenden Literaturgeschichte des Dramas." A new edition (Leipzig, 1884) is renamed: *Die Poesie: Ihr Wesen und ihre Formen mit Grundzügen der vergleichenden Literaturgeschichte.*

38. See Á. Berczik, "Eine ungarische Konzeption der Weltliteratur (Hugo von Meltzls vergleichende Literaturtheorie)," *Acta Literaria Academiae Scientiarum Hungaricae,* 5 (1962), 287–93.

There is no need to enter into a history of the terms elsewhere. In Italian, *letteratura comparata* is clearly and easily formed on the French model. The great critic Francesco De Sanctis occupied a chair called *della letteratura comparata* at Naples, from 1872 till his death in 1883.[39] Arturo Graf became the holder of such a chair at Turin in 1876. In Spanish the term *literatura comparada* seems even more recent.

I am not sure when the term is used first in the Slavic languages. Alexander Veselovsky, the greatest Russian *comparatiste,* did not use the term in his inaugural lecture as Professor of General Literature at St. Petersburg in 1870, but he reviewed Koch's new periodical in 1887 and there used the term *sravnitelnoe literaturovedenie,* which is closely modeled on *vergleichende Literaturwissenschaft.*[40] At the University of Prague a chair called *srovnávací literatura* was created in 1911.

Incomplete or even slightly incorrect in its detail, this history of the terms in the main languages could become more meaningful if treated in the context of competition with rival terms. "Comparative literature" occurs in what semanticists have called "a field of meaning." We have alluded to "learning," "letters," and *"belles lettres"* as rival terms for "literature." "Universal literature," "international literature," "general literature," and "world literature" are the competitors of "comparative literature." "Universal literature" occurs in the eighteenth century and is used rather widely in German: there is an article in 1776 discussing *eine Universalgeschichte der Dichtkunst,* and in 1859 a reviewer

39. The chair was created in 1861 and reserved for the German poet Georg Herwegh, who never occupied it.

40. *Sobranie sochinenii 1* (8 vols. St. Petersburg, 1913), 18–29. Veselovsky uses the term *sravnitelnoe izuchenie* (comparative study) as early as 1868; see ibid., *16*, 1.

proposed "eine Universalgeschichte der modernen Littera-tun."[41] "General literature" exists in English: e.g. James Montgomery gave *Lectures on General Literature, Poetry,* etc. (1833), where "general literature" means what we would call "theory of literature" or "principles of criticism." The Reverend Thomas Dale in 1831 became Professor of English Literature and History in the Department of General Litera-ture and Science at King's College, London.[42] In Germany J. G. Eichhorn edited a whole series of books called *Allge-meine Geschichte der Literatur* (1788 ff). There were similar compilations: Johann David Hartmann, *Versuch einer allge-meinen Geschichte der Poesie* (2 volumes, 1797 and 1798), and Ludwig Wachler, *Versuch einer allgemeinen Geschichte der Literatur* in 4 volumes (1793–1801), and Johann Georg Grässe's *Lehrbuch einer allgemeinen Literärgeschichte* (1837–57), an enormous bibliographical compilation.

The term "world literature," *Weltliteratur,* was used by Goethe in 1827 in commenting on a translation of his drama *Tasso* into French, and then several times, sometimes in slightly different senses: he was thinking of a single uni-fied world literature in which differences between the indi-vidual literatures would disappear, though he knew that this would be quite remote. In a draft Goethe equates "European" with "world literature," surely provisionally.[43] There is a well-known poem by Goethe, "Weltliteratur" (1827), which

41. "Über die Hauptperioden in der Geschichte der Dichtkunst," *Gothaisches Magazin der Künste und Wissenschaften, 1* (1776), 21 ff., 199 ff.; a review of Albert Lacroix, *Histoire de l'influence de Shake-speare sur le théâtre français,* in *Jahrbuch für romanische und englische Literatur, 1* (1859), 3.

42. See above, n. 22.

43. Goethe, *Werke, Jubiläumsausgabe, 38,* 97, 137, 170, 278. Cf. discussion and collection of passages in Fritz Strich, *Goethe und die Weltliteratur* (Bern, 1946), pp. 393–400.

rehearses, rather, the delights of folk poetry and actually got its title erroneously from the editor of the 1840 posthumous edition.[44] The history of the concept has been studied well.[45] Today world literature may mean simply all literature, as in the title of many books, such as Otto Hauser's, or it may mean a canon of excellent works from many languages, as when one says that this or that book or author belongs to world literature: Ibsen belongs to world literature, while Jonas Lie does not; Swift belongs to world literature, while Thomas Hardy does not.

Just as the exact use of "world literature" is still debatable, the use of "comparative literature" has given rise to disputes as to its exact scope and methods, which are not yet resolved. It is useless to be dogmatic about such matters, as words have the meaning authors assign to them and neither a knowledge of history nor common usage can prevent changes or even complete distortions of the original meaning. Still, clarity on such matters avoids mental confusion, while excessive ambiguity or arbitrariness leads to intellectual dangers which may not be as serious as calling hot, cold, or communism democracy, but which still hamper agreement and communication. One can distinguish, first, a strict, narrow definition; Van Tieghem, for example, defines it thus: "The object of comparative literature is essentially the study of diverse literatures in their relations with one another."[46] Guyard in

44. *Werke, Jubiläumsausgabe, 3*, 243. Cf. p. 373 for title.

45. Cf. Else Beil, *Zur Entwicklung des Begriffs der Weltliteratur* (Leipzig, 1915); J. C. Brandt Corstius, "De Ontwikkeling van het wereldliteratuur," *De Vlaamse Gids, 41* (1957), 582–600; Helmut Bender and Ulrich Melzer, "Zur Geschichte des Begriffes 'Welt-literatur'," *Saeculum, 9* (1958), 113–22.

46. *La Littérature comparée* (Paris 1931), p. 57: "L'object de la littérature comparée est essentiellement d'étudier les œuvres des diverses littératures dans leurs rapports les unes avec les autres."

his handbook, which follows Van Tieghem closely in doctrine and contents, calls comparative literature succinctly "the history of international literary relations,"[47] and J.–M. Carré in his Preface to Guyard, calls it "a branch of literary history; it is the study of spiritual international relations, of factual contacts which took place between Byron and Pushkin, Goethe and Carlyle, Walter Scott and Vigny, between the works, the inspirations and even the lives of writers belonging to several literatures."[48] Similar formulations can be found elsewhere: e.g. in the volume on comparative literature of Momigliano's series *Problemi ed orientamenti* (1948), where Anna Saitta Revignas speaks of comparative literature as "a modern science which centers on research into the problems connected with the influences exercised reciprocally by various literatures."[49] Fernand Baldensperger, the recognized leader of the French school, in the programmatic article introducing the first number of the *Revue de littérature comparée* (1921), does not attempt a definition but agrees with one implied limitation of the concept: he has no use for comparisons which do not involve "a real encounter" that has "created a dependence."[50] But his article does discuss many wider problems excluded by his followers.

47. *La Littérature comparée* (Paris, 1951), p. 7: "l'histoire des relations littéraires internationales."

48. Ibid. p. 5: "Une branche de l'histoire littéraire; elle est l'étude des relations spirituelles internationales, des rapports de fait qui ont existé entre Byron et Pouchkine, Goethe et Carlyle, Walter Scott et Vigny, entre les œuvres, les inspirations, voire les vies d'écrivains appartenant à plusieurs littératures."

49. *Problemi ed orientamenti: Notizie introduttive* (Milano, 1948), p. 430: "Una scienza moderna rivolta appunto ad indagare i problemi connessi cogli influssi esercitati reciprocamente dalle varie letterature."

50. "Littérature comparée: Le Mot et la chose," *Revue de littérature comparée, 1* (1921), 1–29; p. 7: "Une rencontre réelle . . . crée une dépendance."

In a wider sense "comparative literature" includes what Van Tieghem calls "general literature." He confines "comparative literature" to "binary" relations, between two elements, while "general literature" concerns research into "the facts common to several literatures."[51] It can, however, be argued that it is impossible to draw a line between comparative literature and general literature, between, say, the influence of Walter Scott in France and the rise of the historical novel. Besides, the term "general literature" lends itself to confusion: it has been understood to mean literary theory, poetics, the principles of literature. Comparative literature in the narrow sense of binary relations cannot make a meaningful discipline, as it would have to deal only with the "foreign trade" between literatures and hence with fragments of literary production. It would not allow treating the individual work of art. It would be (as apparently Carré is content to think) a strictly auxiliary discipline of literary history with a fragmentary, scattered subject matter and with no peculiar method of its own. The study of the influence, say, of Byron in England cannot, methodologically, differ from a study of the influence of Byron in France, or from a study of European Byronism. The method of comparison is not peculiar to comparative literature; it is ubiquitous in all literary study and in all sciences, social and natural. Nor does literary study, even in the practice of the most orthodox comparative scholars, proceed by the method of comparison alone. Any literary scholar will not only compare but reproduce, analyze, interpret, evoke, evaluate, generalize, etc., all on one page.

There are other attempts to define the scope of compara-

51. Van Tieghem, *La Littérature comparée,* p. 170: "rapports binaires—entre deux éléments seulement"; p. 174: "les faits communs à plusieurs littératures."

tive literature by adding something specific to the narrow definition. Thus Carré and Guyard include the study of national illusions, the ideas which nations have of each other. M. Carré has written an interesting book on *Les Ecrivains français et le mirage allemand* (1947), which is national psychology or sociology drawn from literary sources but hardly literary history. A book such as Guyard's *La Grande Bretagne dans le roman français: 1914–1940* (1954) is slightly disguised *Stoffgeschichte:* an account of the English clergymen, diplomats, writers, chorus girls, businessmen, etc., appearing in French novels of a certain time.

Less arbitrary and more ambitious is the recent attempt by H. H. H. Remak to expand the definition of comparative literature. He calls it "the study of literature beyond the confines of one particular country, and the study of the relationships between literature on the one hand and the other areas of knowledge and belief, such as the arts, philosophy, history, the social sciences, the sciences, religion, etc., on the other hand."[52] But Mr. Remak is forced to make artificial and untenable distinctions: e.g. between a study of Hawthorne's relation to Calvinism, labeled "comparative," and a study of his concepts of guilt, sin, and expiation, reserved for "American" literature. The whole scheme strikes one as devised for purely practical purposes in an American graduate school where you may have to justify a thesis topic as "comparative literature" before unsympathetic colleagues resenting incursions into their particular fields of competence. But as a definition it cannot survive closer scrutiny.

At one time in history, the time decisive for the establishment of the term in English, comparative literature was un-

52. *Comparative Literature: Method and Perspective,* ed. Newton P. Stallknecht and Horst Frenz (Carbondale, Ill., 1961), p. 3.

derstood to mean something both very specific and very wide-ranging. In Posnett's book it means "the general theory of literary evolution, the idea that literature passes through stages of inception, culmination and decline."[53] Comparative literature is set into a universal social history of mankind, "the gradual expansion of social life, from clan to city, from city to nation, from both of these to cosmopolitan humanity."[54] Posnett and his followers are dependent on the evolutionary philosophy of Herbert Spencer, which today is almost forgotten in literary studies.

Finally, the view has been propounded that comparative literature can best be defended and defined by its perspective and spirit, rather than by any circumscribed partition within literature. It will study all literature from an international perspective, with a consciousness of the unity of all literary creation and experience. In this conception (which is also mine) comparative literature is identical with the study of literature independent of linguistic, ethnic, and political boundaries. It cannot be confined to a single method: description, characterization, interpretation, narration, explanation, evaluation are used in its discourse just as much as comparison. Nor can comparison be confined to actual historical contacts. There may be, as the experience of recent linguistics should teach literary scholars, as much value in comparing phenomena such as languages or genres historically unrelated as in studying influences discoverable from evidence of reading or parallels. A study of Chinese, Korean, Burmese, and Persian narrative methods or lyrical forms is

53. Charles Mills Gayley and Fred Newton Scott, *An Introduction to the Methods and Materials of Literary Criticism* (Boston, 1899), p. 248, summarizing Posnett.

54. H. M. Posnett, *Comparative Literature* (London, 1886), p. 86.

surely as justified as the study of the casual contacts with the East exemplified by Voltaire's *Orphelin de la Chine*. Nor can comparative literature be confined to literary history to the exclusion of criticism and contemporary literature. Criticism, as I have argued many times, cannot be divorced from history, as there are no neutral facts in literature. The mere act of selecting from millions of printed books is a critical act, and the selection of the traits or aspects under which a book may be treated is equally an act of criticism and judgment. The attempt to erect precise barriers between the study of literary history and contemporary literature is doomed to failure: Why should a specified date or even the death of an author constitute a sudden lifting of a taboo? Such limits may be possible to enforce in the centralized system of French education, but elsewhere they are unreal. Nor can the historical approach be considered the only possible method, even for the study of the dim past. Works of literature are monuments and not documents. They are immediately accessible to us today; they challenge us to seek an understanding in which knowledge of the historical setting or the place in a literary tradition may figure, but not exclusively or exhaustively. The three main branches of literary study—history, theory, and criticism—involve each other, just as the study of a national literature cannot be divorced from the study of the totality of literature, at least in idea. Comparative literature can and will flourish only if it shakes off artificial limitations and becomes simply the study of literature.

The meaning and the origin of these distinctions and issues will become clearer if we glance at the history of comparative studies without regard to the name or to definitions. H. H. H. Remak, in a lecture at the Fribourg Congress in 1964, rightly said that there is "no more urgent task than the writing and publication of a thorough history of our discipline."[55] I obviously cannot pretend to fulfill this demand in such a short space, but as I wrote the first and only history of English literary historiography twenty-five years ago[56] and paid constant attention to writings on literary history in the four volumes of my *History of Modern Criticism,* I can sketch the main stages of the development of comparative and general literature with some assurance.

If we glance at antiquity, it will be obvious that the Greeks could not have been comparative students in the early period, as they lived in a closed world to which all the other nations were barbarians. But the Romans were highly conscious of their dependence on the Greeks. In Tacitus' *Dialogue on Orators,* for example, there is an elaborate parallel between Greek and Roman orators where the individual writers are matched or contrasted with some care. In Quintilian's *Institutio* a whole sketch of the history of Greek and Roman literature is provided which consistently pays attention to the Greek models of the Romans. Longinus, or whoever wrote the treatise usually called *On the Sublime,* compares the style of Cicero and Demosthenes briefly and gives as an example of the Grand Style the passage from Genesis: " 'Let there be light'; and there was light."[57] Macrobius, in the much later *Saturnalia,* has a long discussion of Virgil's imitations of Greek poets. Though the experience of the variety of literature in antiquity was limited, and though much of

55. "The Impact of Nationalism and Cosmopolitism on Comparative Literature from the 1880's to the Post World War II Period," *Proceedings of the Fourth Congress of the International Comparative Literature Association* (The Hague, 1966), p. 391.

56. *The Rise of English Literary History* (Chapel Hill, 1941; new ed. New York, 1966).

57. On Longinus, see Allan H. Gilbert, *Literary Criticism: Plato to Dryden* (New York, 1940), pp. 157, 162.

their scholarship was lost—during the Middle Ages it must have been considered ephemeral or local and thus not worth copying—we should not underrate the scope and the intensity of literary scholarship in classical antiquity, particularly in Alexandria and Rome. There was much textual criticism, stylistic observation, and even something which might please a modern comparatist: an elaborate comparison of the treatment of the Philoctetes theme by Aeschylus, Sophocles, and Euripides has been preserved.[58]

The Renaissance revived literary scholarship on a very large scale. There is a clear historical consciousness in the very idea of the revival of learning and the break with the intellectual traditions of the Middle Ages, even though the break was not as complete or sudden as was assumed in the nineteenth century. Still, looking for forerunners of comparative methods or perspectives yields little in that time. The authority of antiquity often rather stifled the concrete variety of the literary traditions of the Middle Ages and imposed, at least in theory, a certain uniformity. Scaliger in his *Poetics* (1561) devotes a whole book, "Criticus" ( a new term then), to a series of comparisons of Homer with Virgil, Virgil with Greeks other than Homer, Horace and Ovid with Greeks, always asserting the superiority of the Romans over the Greeks, using passages on the same subjects from different poets.[59] Scaliger is mainly concerned with the game of ranking and is motivated by an odd kind of Latin nationalism interested in denigrating everything that is Greek. Etienne Pasquier (1529–1615) uses the same method in comparing a passage from Virgil with one from Ronsard.[60] To give an

58. From J. W. H. Atkins, *Literary Criticism in Antiquity, 2* (London, 1924), 187, 331. The treatise on Philoctetes is ascribed to either Dio of Prusa (A.D. 40–120) or Dio Chrysostomos.

59. Geneva, 1561, Bk. V.

60. *Recherches de la France, 7* (Paris, 1643), xi.

English example for the widespread method of rhetorical comparisons: Francis Meres, in "A Comparative Discourse of Our English Poets with the Greek, Latin and Italian Poets," which I have mentioned, quite perfunctorily ranked Shakespeare with Ovid, Plautus, and Seneca.[61] The motivation of most Renaissance scholarship was patriotic: Englishmen compiled lists of writers in order to prove their glorious achievements in all subjects of learning; Frenchmen, Italians, and Germans did exactly the same.

There was also a very occasional awareness of the existence of literature outside of the Western tradition. Samuel Daniel's remarkable *Defence of Rime* (1607) shows that he knew that Turks and Arabs, Slavs and Hungarians use rhyme. For him Greece and Rome are no absolute authority, since even the barbarians are "children of nature as well as they." "There is but one learning, which *omnes gentes habent in cordibus suis,* one and the self-same spirit that worketh in all."[62] But this tolerance and universality in Daniel is still completely unhistorical: men are everywhere and at any time the same.

About the same time, a new conception of literary history was propounded by Francis Bacon in his *Advancement of Learning* (1603). Literary history was to be a "history of the flourishings, decays, depressions, removes" of schools, sects, and traditions. "Without it the history of the world seemeth to me as the *statua* of Polyphemus with his eye out; that part being wanting which doth most show the spirit and life of the person."[63] In the later Latin version (1623) Bacon adds the proposal that from "taste and observation of the argument, style and method" of the best books, "the learned spirit of

61. See above, n. 2.
62. *Elizabethan Critical Essays, 2,* 359, 372.
63. *Works,* ed. J. Spedding, Ellis et al., *3* (14 vols. London, 1857), 329.

an age, as by a kind of charm, should be awaked and raised from the dead."[64] Bacon, of course, did not conceive of literary history as primarily a history of imaginative literature: it was rather a history of learning which included poetry.[65] Still, Bacon's proposal went far beyond the dull lists of authors, collections of lives of authors, and bibliographical repertories which were being assembled at that time in most Western countries.

It took a long time before Bacon's program was carried out in practice. In Germany, for example, Peter Lambeck (1628–80) compiled a *Podromus historiae literariae* (1659) which reprints the passage from Bacon as a kind of epigraph, but the contents show that Lambeck had not understood the idea of Bacon's universal intellectual history at all. He begins with the creation of the world, biblical history, describes the teachings of Zoroaster, compiles data on Greek philosophers, etc. It all remains a mass of inert and undigested uncritical learning.[66] If we want to feel proud about progress in our studies, I recommend looking into Jakob Friederich Reimann's *Versuch einer Einleitung in die historiam literariam antediluvianam d.h. in die Geschichte der Gelehrsamkeit und derer Gelehrten vor der Sündflut* (1727), a display of childish pedantry which shows no sense of evidence or chronology beyond that which can be extracted from the Old Testament accounts.[67]

The accumulation of storehouses of bibliographical and biographical information reached enormous proportions in

64. Ibid., *1*, 502–504.

65. Cf. Ewald Flügel, "Bacon's Historia Literaria," *Anglia, 21* (1899), 259–88.

66. I have seen the Leipzig and Frankfurt 1710 edition. After the passage from Bacon he prints similar statements from Christopher Mylius, *De scribenda universitatis historia,* and from G. J. Vossius, *De philologia.*

67. Halle, 1727.

the eighteenth century. In France the Benedictines started an *Histoire littéraire de la France* (12 volumes, 1733–62) which, in the eighteenth century, barely reached the twelfth century. Girolamo Tiraboschi's *Storia della letteratura italiana* (14 volumes, 1772–81) is still admired for its accuracy and wealth of information. A Spanish Jesuit, Juan Andrés, compiled in Italian one of the most impressive repertories of all literatures, *Dell'origine, progresso e stato attuale d'ogni letteratura* (1782–99), in seven large volumes, where the whole world of books is divided up by genres, disciplines, nations, and centuries with no sense of narrative flow and little of continuity. The English work in literary history which is comparable to those continental achievements, Thomas Warton's *History of English Poetry* (3 volumes, 1774–81), while in the main a repertory of extracts, an account of manuscripts and biographical notices, is, however, permeated by a new spirit. It could not have been written without the idea of progress, without the new tolerant interest in the Middle Ages, and without an idea (however schematic) of literary development.[68]

The idea of progress, also in literature, triumphed in the "Querelle des anciens et des modernes," which in English is usually called The Battle of Books. Charles Perrault's *Parallèle des anciens et des modernes* (1688–97) argues by contrasting and comparing the funeral orations of Pericles, Lysias, and Isocrates with those of Bossuet, Fléchier, and Bourdaloue, or the panegyric of Pliny on the Emperor Trajan with the eulogy of Voiture on Richelieu, or the letters of Pliny and Cicero with those of Guez de Balzac—always preferring the French to the ancients.[69] Progress, in literature as

68. See Giovanni Getto, *Storia delle storie letterarie* (Milano, 1942), and my *Rise of English Literary History* for comments on Warton.

69. Ed. H. R. Jauss (Munich, 1964), e.g. pp. 256 ff., 269 ff., 279.

in other spheres, became the obsessive theme of the whole century, though it is not always naïvely conceived as unilateral and allows for relapses. To give English examples: even the conservative Dr. Johnson conceives of the history of English poetry as a steady advance from the barbaric roughness of Chaucer to the perfect smoothness of Pope, which could not be improved on even in the future; Warton, who had a genuine liking for Chaucer and Spenser, always prefers his own time's ideas of discrimination, propriety, correctness, and good taste to the irregular charms of the Elizabethans.[70] Still, Warton shows a new tolerance for the variety of literature and a curiosity for its origins and derivations. He belongs to a whole group of scholars in the eighteenth century who were interested in the institution of chivalry, in courtly love, and in their literary analogues, the romance and the courtly lyric. But the new interest in the non-Latin literary tradition was still halfhearted. Men like Warton, Bishop Percy, and Bishop Hurd held a point of view which exalted the age of Queen Elizabeth as the golden age of English literature but at the same time allowed them to applaud the triumph of reason in their own "polite" literature. They believed in the progress of civilization and even modern good taste, but regretted the decay of "a world of fine fabling," which they studied as antiquaries pursuing a fascinating hobby. They were animated by a truly historical spirit of tolerance but also remained detached and uninvolved and thus strangely sterile in their eclecticism.[71]

In Warton and his contemporaries another trend had won out which had been preparing for a long time. Literature was conceived in the main as *belles lettres,* as imaginative litera-

70. Cf. my *Rise of English Literary History,* pp. 139, 180 ff.
71. Cf. my *History of Modern Criticism, 1* (4 vols. New Haven, 1955), 131–32.

ture, and not merely as a branch of learning on the same footing as astronomy or jurisprudence. This process of specialization is connected with the whole rise of the modern system of arts and their clear distinction from the sciences and crafts, and with the formulation of the whole enterprise of aesthetics.[72] Aesthetics as a term comes from Germany and was invented by Baumgarten in 1735, but the singling out of poetry and imaginative prose had been accomplished before in connection with the problem of taste, good taste, or *belles lettres,* "elegant," "polite" arts or however they might call it then.[73] With the emphasis on what we would call the art of literature came also the emphasis on nationality, for poetry was deeply embedded in a national language, and the increasing resistance to the cultural leveling accomplished by the Enlightenment brought about a new turn toward the past, which inevitably was medieval or at the most very early modern. The English and Scottish critics of the eighteenth century prepared the way, but it was in Germany that the ideal of literary history on these new terms was stated and carried out most consistently. The decisive figure was Johann Gottfried Herder (1744–1803), who conceived of literary history as a totality in which "the origin, the growth, the changes and the decay of literature with the divers styles of regions, periods, and poets"[74] would be shown and in which the individual national literatures would make up the basic

72. See Paul Oskar Kristeller, "The Modern System of the Arts," in *Renaissance Thought, 2* (3 vols. New York, 1965), 163–227.

73. On aesthetics and taste see, besides general histories of aesthetics, Alfred Bäumler, *Kants Kritik der Urteilskraft, 1* (Halle, 1923), and J. E. Spingarn's introduction to *Critical Essays of the Seventeenth Century, 1* (3 vols. Oxford, 1908).

74. *Sämtliche Werke, 1,* 294: "Den Ursprung, das Wachstum, die Veränderungen und den Fall derselben nebst dem verschiedenen Stil der Gegenden, Zeiten und Dichter lehren."

entities which he wanted to defend in their purity and originality. Herder's first important book, *Über die neuere deutsche Literatur: Fragmente* (1767), attacks imitation, particularly of French and Latin literature, and points to the regenerative powers of folk poetry. Herder recommends collecting it not only among Germans but among "Scythians and Slavs, Wends and Bohemians, Russians, Swedes and Poles."[75] Thus the fervent German nationalism led, paradoxically, to a wide expansion of the literary horizon: every nation does or should take part, with its characteristic voice, in the great concert of poetry. While Herder sketched a new ideal, which was fulfilled only by the romantics, he was still steeped in the concepts of his time. The literary process is seen by him most often in terms of a rather naïve determinism of climate, landscape, race, and social conditions. Madame de Staël's book, *De la Littérature* (1800), with its simple-minded trust in perfectibility and in the contrast between the gay and sunny South with the dark and gloomy North, even in literature, belongs still to the schematic history of the Enlightenment.

Only the two Schlegels developed the forward-looking suggestions of Herder's sketches and became the first literary historians who, on a broad scale and with considerable concrete knowledge, carried out the idea of a universal narrative literary history in a historical context. While they were understandably preoccupied with western Europe, they extended, at least on occasion, their interest to eastern Europe and became pioneers in the study of Sanskrit literature. Friedrich Schlegel's *Über Sprache und Weisheit der Inder* (1808) was a bold program which was later carried out in part by A. W. Schlegel with his editions of the Indian epics. For Friedrich

75. Ibid., p. 266: "Scythen und Slaven, Wenden und Böhmen, Russen, Schweden und Polen."

Schlegel literature forms "a great, completely coherent and evenly organized whole, comprehending in its unity many worlds of art and itself forming a peculiar work of art,"[76] but this "universal progressive poetry" is conceived as being based on national literature as an organism, as epitome of a nation's history: "the essence of all intellectual faculties and productions of a nation."[77] Unfortunately, Friedrich Schlegel's *Geschichte der alten und neuen Literatur* (1815) was written after his conversion to Roman Catholicism, in the atmosphere of the Vienna of 1812, and is thus colored strongly with the spirit of the anti-Napoleonic Restoration. A. W. Schlegel's early Berlin lectures (1803–04), which sketch the whole history of Western literature with the dichotomy of classical versus romantic as an organizing principle, were not published till 1884,[78] and his *Lectures on Dramatic Art and Literature* (1809–11) are limited to one genre and are strongly polemical. Still, they carried, in French, English, and Italian translation, the message of German romanticism to the rest of Europe.[79] The Schlegels' concept of literature, which is definitely comparative both in the narrow and in a wide sense, seems to me still true and meaningful in spite of the deficiencies of their information, the limitations of their taste, and the bias of their nationalism.

Schlegelian literary history was written throughout the

76. *Lessings Geist aus seinen Schriften, 1* (3 vols. 1804), 13: "ein grosses, durchaus zusammenhängendes und gleich organisirtes, in ihrer Einheit viele Kunstwelten umfassendes Ganzes und einiges Kunstwerk."

77. *Sämtliche Werke, 1,* 11: "Der Inbegriff aller intellectuellen Fähigkeiten und Hervorbringungen einer Nation."

78. *Vorlesungen über schöne Literatur und Kunst,* ed. Jakob Minor (Stuttgart, 1884).

79. Josef Körner, *Die Botschaft der deutschen Romantik an Europa* (Augsburg, 1929).

nineteenth century in many lands. It penetrated with Sismondi to France, where Villemain, Ampère, and Chasles attempt it. In Italy Emiliani Giudici, in Denmark Brandes
(with his very different politics), and in England Carlyle share
their concept. When Carlyle says "the History of a nation's
Poetry is the essence of its History, political, economic, scientific, religious," and when he calls literature "the truest
emblem of the national spirit and manner of existence,"[80] he
echoes the Schlegels and Herder. Surprising though this may
appear, even Taine shares their basic insight. Works of art
"furnish documents because they are monuments."[81]

The Schlegelian concept of literary history must be distinguished from the concept I would call peculiarly "romantic": the view based on the idea of prehistory, a kind of
reservoir of themes from which all modern literature is derived and to whose glories it compares only as a dim artificial
light to the sun. This view was stimulated by the new study
of mythology, comparative religion, and philology. The
Brothers Grimm are its main exponents, the early practitioners of comparative research into the migration of fairy
tales, legends, and sagas. Jakob Grimm believed in natural
poetry as composing itself far in the dim past and as gradually
deteriorating with the distance from the divine source of
revelation. His patriotism is panteutonic, but his taste embraces all folk poetry wherever found: old Spanish romances,
French *chansons de geste,* Serbian heroic epics, Arabic and

80. *Works,* Centenary ed. (London, 1896–99); *Essays, 2,* 341–42
*Unfinished History of German Literature,* ed. Hill Shine (Lexington,
Ky., 1951), p. 6.

81. *Histoire de la littérature anglaise, 1* (2nd ed. 5 vols. Paris,
1866), xvii: "Si elles fournissent des documents, c'est qu'elles sont des
monuments."

Indian folk tales.[82] The Grimms stimulated everywhere the study of what later was called *Stoffgeschichte*. It is worth looking at Richard Price's Preface to the new edition of Warton's *History of English Poetry* (1824) to see the changed conception. He pleads for "general literature" as a huge treasure house of themes which spread, multiply, and migrate according to laws similar to those established for language by the new comparative philology. Price believes that "popular fiction is in its nature traditive" and represents an age-old symbolic wisdom.[83] In England scholars such as Sir Francis Palgrave and Thomas Wright pursued these studies systematically with great erudition. In France Claude Fauriel, who had translated Greek folk songs, is a comparable figure, except that what in the Grimms was a dim teutonic past is by him traced back to his own homeland: southern France, Provence.

Around 1850 the atmosphere changed completely. Romantic conceptions fell into discredit, and ideals imported from the natural sciences became victorious, even in the writing of literary history. One must, however, distinguish what might be called "factualism," the enormous proliferation of research into facts or supposed facts, from "scientism," which appealed mainly to the concept of biological evolution and envisaged an ideal of literary history in which the laws of literary production and change would be discovered. The transition can be illustrated strikingly from Renan's *L'Avenir de la science*. Renan looks back to Herder, to the new mythology and the study of primitive poetry. "The comparative study of literature," he tells us, has shown that Homer is a

82. See my *History of Modern Criticism, 2,* 283 ff.

83. Reprinted in Warton, *History of English Poetry,* ed. W. C. Hazlitt, *1* (4 vols. London, 1871), 32–33.

collective poet; it has brought out his "mythisme," the primitive legend behind him. The progress of literary history is entirely due to its search for origins and hence its attention to exotic literatures. The use of the comparative method, that "grand instrument of criticism," is the turning point.[84] Renan, at the same time, is almost intoxicated with hope for the future of the science of philology, which will establish the history of the human mind. But he is still wary (and became more so in his later life) of all attempts to establish laws in literature and history as they were sought for by Comte, Mill, Buckle, and many others before Darwin or Spencer.

The idea of laws, of regularities in literature, goes back to antiquity and was restated in eighteenth-century speculative schemes, but it becomes a dominant concern with the victory of comparative philology, its idea of development, continuity, and derivation. Darwinism and similar philosophical schemes, particularly Spencer's, gave a new impetus to the idea of evolution and genre conceived on the analogy of a biological species in literary history.[85] In Germany Moriz Haupt advocated a "comparative poetics," particularly a natural history of the epic. He studied the analogical development of the epic in Greece, France, Scandinavia, Germany, Serbia, and Finland.[86] Haupt inspired Wilhelm Scherer, who conceived of literary history as a morphology of poetic

84. Paris, 1890, p. 297: "L'étude comparée des littératures"; p. 296: "le grand instrument de la critique."

85. Cf. my "The Concept of Evolution in Literary History" (1956), in *Concepts of Criticism* (New Haven, 1963), pp. 37–53.

86. See Christian Belger, *Moriz Haupt als akademischer Lehrer* (Berlin, 1879), p. 323, for review in 1835. See also W. Scherer, *Kleine Schriften,* ed. K. Burdach and E. Schmidt, *1* (2 vols. Berlin, 1893), 120, 123 130.

forms.[87] Many of these ideas grew out of a Berlin circle around Steinthal, who founded the *Zeitschrift für Völkerpsychologie* in 1864. This circle provided the inspiration for Alexander Veselovsky, who, after his return to Russia in 1870, put out a steady stream of studies on the migration of themes and plots, ranging all over the Western and Eastern world, from the dimmest antiquity to romantic literature. He aimed at a "historical poetics," a universal evolutionary history of poetry, a collective approach which would approximate the ideal of a "history without names."[88] In England the influence of Spencer was felt somewhat differently. John Addington Symonds applied a strictly biological analogy to Elizabethan drama and Italian painting and defended the "application of evolutionary principles" to art and literature also theoretically: each genre runs a fateful course of germination, expansion, efflorescence, and decay. We should be able to predict the future of literature.[89] Posnett's book, which was crucial for the establishment of the term "comparative literature," is another application of Spencer's scheme of a social development from communal to individual life. There are many now forgotten books, some by Americans, which follow this trend. Francis Gummere's *Beginnings of Poetry* (1901) and A. S. Mackenzie's *The Evolution of Literature* (1911) may serve as examples.

In France Ferdinand Brunetière was the theorist and prac-

87. On Scherer, particularly his *Poetik* (1888), see my *History of Modern Criticism, 4* (1965), 297 ff.

88. On Veselovsky, see ibid., pp. 278–80, and V. Zhirmunsky, Introduction to *Istoricheskaya poetika* (Leningrad, 1940).

89. See my *History, 4,* 400–07. Cf. Symonds' "On the Application of Evolutionary Principles to Art and Literature," in *Essays Speculative and Suggestive, 1* (2 vols. London, 1890), 52–83.

titioner of evolution. He treated genres as biological species
and wrote histories of French criticism, drama, and lyrical
poetry according to this scheme. Though he limited himself
to French subjects, his theory led him logically to a concept
of universal literature and to a defense of comparative literature. When in 1900, in connection with the World Exhibition
in Paris, a Congress of Historical Studies was held, a whole
section (sparsely attended) was reserved for "Histoire comparée des littératures." Brunetière opened it with an address
on "European literature" which appealed not only to the
model of the Schlegels and Ampère but also to J. A. Symonds.
Brunetière was followed as speaker by Gaston Paris, the great
French medievalist.[90] He expounded, in a dramatic clash of
viewpoints, the older conception of comparative literature—
i.e. the folklore concept, the idea of the migration of themes
and motifs all over the world. Somewhat later this study received new impetus from Finnish folklore research and has
expanded into an almost independent branch of learning
related to ethnology and anthropology. In this country it is
now rarely identified with comparative literature; but older
nineteenth-century literary journals are filled with such
topics, and in the Slavic countries "comparative literature"
often means just such a study of international themes and
motifs.

With the decline of evolutionism and the criticism launched
against its mechanistic application by Bergson, Croce, and
others, and with the predominance of the late nineteenth-
century aestheticism and impressionism, which stressed again
the individual creator, the unique work of art, and highly

90. "La Littérature européenne," *Annales internationales d'histoire,
Congrès de Paris 1900, 6* (Paris, 1901), 5–28; "Résumé de l'allocution
de M. Gaston Paris," ibid., pp. 39–41.

sophisticated literature, these concepts of comparative literature were either abandoned or were pushed to the margin of
literary studies.

What reemerged was largely the factualism inherited from
the general tradition of empiricism and positivism supported
by the ideal of scientific objectivity and causal explanation.
The organized enterprise of comparative literature in France
accomplished mainly an enormous accumulation of evidence about literary relations, particularly on the history of
reputations, the intermediaries between nations—travelers,
translators, and propagandists. The unexamined assumption
in such research is the existence of a neutral fact which is supposed to be connected as if by a thread with other preceding
facts. But the whole conception of a "cause" in literary study
is singularly uncritical; nobody has ever been able to show
that a work of art was "caused" by another work of art, even
though parallels and similarities can be accumulated. A later
work of art may not have been possible without a preceding
one, but it cannot be shown to have been caused by it. The
whole concept of literature in these researches is external and
often vitiated by narrow nationalism: by a computing of cultural riches, a credit and debit calculus in matters of the
mind.

I am not alone in criticizing the sterility of this conception.
Still, my paper on "The Crisis of Comparative Literature,"
given at the second Congress of the International Association
of Comparative Literature in Chapel Hill in 1958, seemed to
have crystallized the opposition.[91] It formulated the objections to the factualism of the theories and the practices: its
failure to delineate a subject matter and a specific method-

91. Reprinted in my *Concepts of Criticism,* pp. 282–95.

ology. The paper gave rise to endless polemics and, I am afraid, to endless misunderstandings.[92] Particularly distressing is the attempt to create an issue between a supposed American and a French conception of comparative literature. I was, of course, not arguing against a nation or even a local school of scholars. I was arguing against a method, not for myself or the United States, and not with new and personal arguments; I simply stated what follows from an insight into the totality of literature, that the distinction between comparative and general literature is artificial and that not much can be accomplished by the method of causal explanation except an infinite regress. What I, and many others, advocate is a turning away from the mechanistic, factualistic concepts inherited from the nineteenth century in favor of true criticism. Criticism means a concern for values and qualities, for an understanding of texts which incorporates their historicity and thus requires the history of criticism for such an understanding, and finally, it means an international perspective which envisages a distant ideal of universal literary history and scholarship. Comparative literature surely wants to overcome national prejudices and provincialisms but does not therefore ignore or minimize the existence and vitality of the different national traditions. We must beware of false and unnecessary choices: we need both national and general literature, we need both literary history and criticism, and we need the wide perspective which only comparative literature can give.

92. Some of these are discussed in my "Comparative Literature Today," *Comparative Literature, 17* (1965), 325–37; reprinted below, pp. 37–54.

# Comparative Literature Today

At the Second Congress of the International Comparative Literature Association held at Chapel Hill in September 1958, I gave a paper, "The Crisis of Comparative Literature," which excited a lot of comment, much of it dissenting. It was of course designed to elicit such comment. We must imagine the situation and the circumstances. The International Association of Comparative Literature had been founded in 1954. It had held its first Congress late in September 1955 at Venice, with no American participants, since the lateness of the season prevented Americans from coming and since the topic of the Congress, "Venice in Literature" (though not devoid of American association if we think of Howells, Henry James, and even Hemingway), had no American takers. Thus the Chapel Hill Congress was the first occasion at which American comparatists were, officially, able to meet their European colleagues.

Through the generosity of the Ford Foundation and the initiative of Werner Friederich, no less than 43 scholars from Europe made the trip to North Carolina. I am not giving away secrets if I say today that several of us teachers of comparative literature in American universities were, at first, unhappy about the planned composition of the Congress. The visitors were to be largely those who had played a role in the organizing of the International Association and its functionaries; those originally invited to represent the United States were the few American members of the International

Association or those who had some office in the Comparative
Literature Section of the Modern Language Association. It
was, I think, an act of great wisdom and tolerance when the
organizer of the Congress, Werner Friederich, changed the
original scheme and allowed it to become a forum not only
of the specialists expressly committed to the cause of comparative literature but also of a wide variety of literary scholars who had one common purpose—the study of literature
beyond the confines of one national literature. It was thus
appropriate that somebody should question the assumptions
of the methodology which led to the original narrowing in
scope and personnel and that I should be the person—since
I had for years criticized this methodology in various contexts long before the founding of the International Association.

One of my critics quite correctly observed that my objections to the accepted methodology of comparative literature
—an artificial demarcation of subject matter, a mechanistic
concept of sources and influences, motivation by cultural
nationalism—had its beginning in Europe in the 1920s.
While a student at the University of Prague during that
decade, I reacted strongly against the positivistic factualism
of some of my teachers and one dominant tradition of scholarship. In my paper "The Crisis of Comparative Literature" I
refer, in the very first paragraph, to Croce in Italy and Dilthey
and his followers in Germany. I came to this country for the
first time in 1927, to the Princeton Graduate School, where
I found the same discontent become vocal in the neohumanist
movement. I paid a few visits to Paul Elmer More, who lent
me books by the Cambridge Platonists (I still remember
Nathaniel Calderwell's *Candle of the Lord*); and I read the
writings of his friend and ally Irving Babbitt. Babbitt's *Literature and the American College* dates from 1908 and still

remains one of the most powerful blasts against nineteenth-century erudition, which Babbitt then identified with pernicious German pedantry. He predicted that "comparative literature will prove one of the most trifling of subjects unless studied in strict subordination to humane standards."[1] That Harry Levin has been named Irving Babbitt Professor of Comparative Literature is not only a tribute to Irving Babbitt but also a guarantee of a continuity of humane standards at Harvard, even though he might interpret the word "humane" differently from Babbitt's special meaning. The right meaning of "humanism" was the issue at Chapel Hill and is still the issue in comparative literature today.

After my return to Prague in 1930 I was, for a time, a member of the Prague Linguistic Circle and thus came into contact with the teachings of the Russian Formalists. Roman Jakobson, now a professor at Harvard University, then in Prague, was a witty and pungent critic of the expansive and muddled methodology of academic literary history, of its desire to become fused and confused with the totality of cultural history, and of its lack of focus on a separate subject matter—the literary work of art. When I went to England in 1935 I had some contacts with F. R. Leavis and the *Scrutiny* group, who, from different premises, voiced their dissatisfaction with academic scholarship very loudly indeed. When I emigrated to this country in 1939 to join the University of Iowa English Department, I found Norman Foerster, a staunch adherent of the new humanism, as director of the School of Letters, and Austin Warren as a colleague. Austin Warren had been a pupil of Irving Babbitt and had known Paul Elmer More in Princeton, but had since moved to a position rather similar to that of T. S. Eliot and the New Critics.

1. Boston, p. 124.

The conflict between literary history and criticism was very acute and even bitter at Iowa. I still remember vividly how Austin Warren and I met a highly respected member of the department, a good historical scholar, and tried to suggest to him that, in writing about Milton and the English essay in the seventeenth century, he had also written some criticism. He turned red in the face and told us that it was the worst insult anybody ever had given him. I was, by conviction and in the academic constellation of the place and time, classed as a critic, and I collaborated, under Norman Foerster's editorship, on a volume, *Literary Scholarship,* published in 1941 by the University of North Carolina Press, to which I contributed the chapter on "Literary History," which in many ways was a reworking of a much older piece, "The Theory of Literary History," written in 1935 for the *Travaux du Cercle Linguistique de Prague.* Mr. Warren and myself were somewhat dissatisfied with the volume. We felt that we sailed under false colors. We could not endorse the neohumanistic creed of the editor, though we shared most of his objections to current academic practices and enjoyed teaching the humanities courses which he devised. Homer, the Bible, Greek tragedy, Shakespeare, and Milton were taught to freshmen and sophomores in compulsory courses long before the present vogue of far-ranging world literature courses. I myself taught a course in the European novel, which started with Stendhal and Balzac and reached Proust and Mann via Dostoevsky and Tolstoy, but I don't remember that I called it "comparative literature."

Eventually, Mr. Warren and I collaborated on *Theory of Literature,* a book which was written in 1944–46 but for various reasons was not published until January 1949. The last chapter, which first appeared as "The Study of Literature in the Graduate School: Diagnosis and Prescription" in the

*Sewanee Review* (October 1947), reflects the situation at the end of the war and suggests specific reforms for the study of literature in our universities—among them, the establishment of departments of comparative literature, which should become, we said, "Departments of General and International Literature, or simply Literature." We hoped that the Department of Comparative Literature might "become the center for the reform which should, however, be carried out primarily within the departments of English and the other Modern Languages, the reform which, briefly, demands a Ph.D. in literature rather than in English, French, or German Philology."[2]

We were not alone. The New Critics had made the greatest practical impact on the college teaching of literature, particularly with the textbook *Understanding Poetry* (1938) by Cleanth Brooks and Robert Penn Warren, which had begun to catch on in the early 1940s. In Chicago Ronald S. Crane had, since 1935 at least, advocated and institutionalized the study of criticism and its history. In 1939 the English Institute, expressly devoted to an examination of the methods of literary study, had met for the first time in New York. While also concerned with problems of bibliography and editing, the English Institute soon became a forum for the discussion of critical and aesthetic issues. In spite of its name and its original limitation to English scholars, the Institute has had a series of sessions devoted to French and German criticism. As early as 1940 the *Southern Review* and the *Kenyon Review* published a symposium on "Literature and the Professors," to which some of the best known New Critics, J. C. Ransom, Allen Tate, and Cleanth Brooks, as well as Harry Levin, contributed trenchant criticisms and the most varied

2. *Theory of Literature* (New York, 1949), p. 297.

suggestions for a reform of the academic study of literature. Change was in the air and a profound change was actually effected, not overnight and not in all institutions uniformly, but gradually almost everywhere. Present-day students seem completely unable to realize the situation of the early decades of the century in most English departments. Criticism was taboo, contemporary and even American literature was not taught at all, foreign literatures were largely ignored, texts were studied only as philological documents—in short, nineteenth-century positivism reigned unchallenged and supreme.

I have reviewed these developments and my share in them not because I want to indulge in autobiographical reminiscences but because my personal story reflects the history of literary scholarship in these decades, the whole "revolt against Positivism" which I described in my first public lecture at Yale in February 1946—Croce and German *Geistesgeschichte,* the Russian Formalists, American neohumanism and T. S. Eliot, F. R. Leavis, and the New Critics. Thus, when Mr. Friederich, in the first *Yearbook of Comparative and General Literature* (1952), reprinted Jean-Marie Carré's brief introduction to M.-F. Guyard's little handbook *La Littérature comparée* (1951), I felt it as a challenge to all that had been achieved in this country. Carré, the first president of the International Comparative Literature Association, here restates, in the narrowest terms, the old concept of literary study and of comparative literature in particular: comparative literature is a branch of literary history concerned with the "factual contacts" *(rapports de fait)* between the works, the inspirations, and even the lives of writers belonging to several literatures. Carré, in this preface at least, expressly excludes "general literature" from our subject and condemns all comparisons which are not justified by concrete historical contacts as mere rhetorical exercises. I severely criticized the preface and the little book by Guyard in the next *Yearbook* (1953), though I recognized the modest pretensions of a handbook for students and its dependence on a similar earlier booklet by Paul Van Tieghem (1913). Still, it seemed to me a dangerous symptom of the survival of an obsolete methodology and its restrictive legislation. The paper at the 1958 Congress at Chapel Hill merely restated my objections in the presence of the European visitors. It was, regrettably to my mind, understood as a manifesto of an American school of comparative literature and as an attack on the French school, though it was obviously directed not against a nation but against a method. I was and am aware that in France also similar criticisms of academic scholarship had been voiced for many years. One need only think of the attacks against Lanson and *la critique universitaire* before World War I. I know that there are many critics and historians in France who have struck out boldly in many directions opposed to the positivistic factualism advocated by Carré. I am also aware that many American scholars are not in agreement with my point of view, and I have never arrogated to myself the role of spokesman for American scholarship in general. Myself a European by birth, I do not relish being put into the odd position of appearing anti-French or even vaguely anti-European.

I have learned from Harry Levin that Mirabeau is the author of the aphorism that an audience of foreigners constitutes "a living posterity." I can make only melancholy reflections about posterity from the amount of misunderstanding and distortion this polemical paper had to suffer abroad. It was apparently interpreted as a manifesto of American hostility to scholarship, since, after I gave an erudite historical paper on the word "criticism" at the Utrecht Congress in 1961, I was congratulated for being less ignorant and less a defender of ignorance than I had seemed at Chapel Hill.

Marcel Bataillon, in a conciliatory review of the Chapel Hill
*Proceedings,* entitled "Nouvelle Jeunesse de la philologie à
Chapel Hill,"[3] while admitting the justice of some criticisms
against the established theories, misunderstood my position as
being inimical to all literary history and deplored the fact that
Renato Poggioli, Claudio Guillén, and myself, though Eu-
ropeans by birth, had ceased to be interested in the relations
between the rival European nations which the old cosmopolitanism tried to revive after the war. Bataillon regretted the
passing of such a "cosmopolitanism, suspect of bourgeois
idealism by a pseudo-Marxist philosophy of history, or con-
victed of historic vanity by triumphant structuralism."[4] It was
my mistake not to have sufficiently guarded against such mis-
apprehensions in the Chapel Hill speech and to have assumed
that it would be known that I'had defended literary history,
for instance, in the last chapter of *Theory of Literature,*
against the antihistorical tendencies of the New Critics and
that I had for years advocated a proper interplay between a
study of national literatures, their common tendencies, the
totality of the Western tradition—which for me always includes the Slavic world—and the ultimate ideal of a comparative study of all literatures, including those of the Farthest
East.

Far stranger misreadings were made in Russia, where
"comparative literature" was simply a forbidden subject under Stalin. With the thaw its necessity was again recognized
and there was a conference in Moscow in January 1960 which
formally rehabilitated the subject.[5] The Russians pride themselves on having solved all questions on the basis of Marxism,

3. *RLC, 35* (1961), 290–98.
4. Ibid., p. 296.
5. Cf. *Vzaimosvyazi i vzaimodeistvie natsionalnykh literatur,*
Akademiya Nauk SSSR (Moscow, 1961).

and the speakers at that conference discussed us all as poor erring sheep who have not discovered the light of truth. Friederich, who as the organizer of the Chapel Hill Congress assumes in their eyes the role of a "leader," gets a heavy dose of abuse for supposedly making the Congress a "political enterprise,"[6] apparently because Gleb Struve gave a well-informed account of the situation in the Soviet Union. My paper is quoted when it seems to serve as a weapon in the polemics against all Western scholarship, but I am severely taken to task for two sins, Formalism and cosmopolitanism. In all the papers it is assumed that I have never heard of the historical and social implications of literature, that I uphold an abstract Formalism, and that my objections to nationalistic literary history mean advocating the abolishment of national literatures in favor of a colorless superliterature which would serve the aims of American imperialism. I am accustomed to the rigidity of Communist ideology but am often surprised at their complete lack of perspective and understanding of personalities and institutional conditions in this country. They assume that there is, e.g., an Institute of Comparative Literature at North Carolina and that at Yale I plot moves in the cultural cold war, assigning topics and coordinating efforts with my accomplices. Deep designs are seen in the gaps or the chance constellations of papers at the Chapel Hill Congress or in the journal *Comparative Literature*. Even the fact that my paper on "The Crisis of Comparative Literature" was translated into German by Sigurd Burckhardt and published in a West German periodical, *Wirkendes Wort,* seems to N. S. Pavlova most ominous.[7] There would be no point in trying to explain to them that we operate quite differently, that Sigurd Burck-

6. Ibid., p. 106.
7. Ibid., p. 298.

hardt, whom I did not then know personally, happened to be struck by my paper and felt like translating it.

In 1960 in Moscow the Russians were among themselves. The three papers on comparative literature in the West by R. M. Samarin, I. G. Neupokoeva, and N. S. Pavlova were wholesale condemnations of all that we were doing. In October 1962 there was another congress at Budapest on comparative literature in Eastern Europe, which was attended by W. P. Smit, the then president of the International Association of Comparative Literature, by Etiemble, the successor of Carré at the Sorbonne, and by three other Western members of the association (Mortier, Rousset, and Voisine). Madame Neupokoeva repeated there her attack on my paper, accusing me of wanting to "denationalize" literature and linking me and American comparative literature with the reactionary philosophy of history of Arnold Toynbee, apparently only because E. R. Curtius had professed admiration for Toynbee (I never have). Luckily, some of the other participants knew better and tried to correct the Russians: Etiemble, e.g., distanced himself from the view of Guyard and Carré and protested that we are not all adherents of Toynbee. A Polish woman scholar, Maria Janion, saw that I never advocated "denationalization" or rejected all history, and an East German professor, Werner Krauss, who severely criticized our journal *Comparative Literature* for willful and bad contributions, recognized that American comparativism is deeply committed to the task of reconciling the nations.[8] Since then the Hungarian Academy has edited a collective volume of its own, *Littérature hongroise: Littérature européenne,*[9] pre-

8. "Die amerikanische Komparatistik ist zutiefst von ihrer völkerverbindenden Sendung durchdrungen," *La Littérature comparée en Europe orientale* (Budapest, 1963), p. 303.

9. Budapest, 1964.

sented to the Fribourg Congress of the International Association in the summer of 1964. It contains, along with many valuable unpolemical papers, one by Lajos Nyirö ("Problèmes de littérature comparée et théorie de la littérature") which ascribes to me a "metaphysics of the dissociation of content and form,"[10] whatever that may be, a rejection of history, and a confusion between comparative literature and theory of literature. In all my writings I have argued for the unity of form and content, have defended literary history, and have made elaborate distinctions between theory, history, and criticism. A chapter of *Theory of Literature* is expressly devoted to "Comparative, General, and National Literature" and their differences. It is really another world where words mean the opposite of what they mean to us.

In the Netherlands Cornelius de Deugd, in a pamphlet, *De Eenheid van het Comparatisme,* saw the situation correctly. He knows that my position is not specifically American, that Carré has adherents in the United States, and that American comparative literature scholars are by no means "antihistorical New Critics, irrespective of what they may have learned from them. They are literary historians, but touched by the new ideas . . . they demand an aesthetic and critical approach to literature, that is to the literary work *an sich.*"[11]

But this is precisely what is being questioned everywhere in the United States today. To give a striking example, a recent article by Ihab Hassan of Wesleyan University, in the valuable series on contemporary criticism published in the new *Comparative Literature Studies* (edited by A. Owen Aldridge), is called "Beyond a Theory of Literature." There I and, surprisingly enough, Northrop Frye are treated as two old-

---

10. Ibid., p. 511.
11. Utrecht, 1962, pp. 69–70.

timers, survivors from an earlier age who have not understood the new revelation: "The self-destructive element of literature, its need for self-annulment." "Perhaps the function of literature, after all," we are told, "is not to clarify the world but to help create a world in which literature becomes superfluous. And perhaps the function of criticism . . . is to attain to the difficult wisdom of perceiving how literature is finally, and only finally, inconsequential."[12] Ihab Hassan concludes by quoting D. H. Lawrence: "O lovely green dragon of the new day, the undawned day, *come come* in touch, and release us from the horrible grip of the evil-smelling old Logos! Come in silence and say nothing." It would be easy to dismiss Hassan's gospel of silence, which still allows him to write books and articles, and to dub him a ferocious antirationalist, an obscurantist who reflects the mood of our time—its apocalyptic forebodings, its sense of the absurd, its "willing suspension of aesthetic judgment in the interest of right action."[13] But I believe that his extremism is a symptom of something very serious endangering any meaningful literary study. It spells the doom of art and aesthetics.

The whole enterprise of aesthetics and art is being challenged today; the distinction between the good, the true, the beautiful, and the useful known to the Greeks but most clearly elaborated by Kant, the whole concept of art as one of the distinct activities of man, as the subject matter of our discipline, is on trial. The breakup of aesthetics began in the late nineteenth century, when the German aesthetics of empathy (known in English through Vernon Lee and Bernard Berenson) reduced aesthetic experience to physiological processes of inner mimicry, of feeling into the object. It is implicit in

12. *CLS, 1* (1964), 266.
13. Ibid., p. 264.

Croce's theory of intuition, in which aesthetic experience becomes identified with every act of perception of individual quality. The intuition of *this* glass of water, for Croce, does not differ qualitatively from that embodied in a great work of art. John Dewey's *Art as Experience* (1934) denies all qualitative distinction between the aesthetic and the intellectual in favor of unity of experience, which is simply heightened vitality. In the writings of I. A. Richards, more specifically concerned with literary criticism, the distinction between aesthetic and other emotions is abolished, and art and poetry are reduced to means of "patterning our impulses," to tools of mental therapy. Similarly, Kenneth Burke and Richard Blackmur dissolve the concept of literature into action or gesture. More recently has come the onslaught on aesthetics by the analytical philosophers, who dismiss as "non-sense" all traditional problems of beauty and aesthetics. Ihab Hassan echoes this whole trend when he deplores the separation of art "from the continuum of felt life" as the source of the mind's alienation, of what he calls "the Cartesian madness of the West."

Whatever the merits of these criticisms of the great tradition of aesthetics may be—and I am willing to grant much to the critics of its obscurities, verbalisms, and tautologies—the main conclusion, the abolition of art as a category, seems to me deplorable in its consequences both for art itself and for the study of art and literature. We see the consequences today at every step: the new sculptor displays heaps of scrap metal or assembles large grocery boxes, Rauschenberg exhibits clean white canvases as his early works, and an enthusiastic critic, John Cage, praises them as "landing-places for lights and shadows." The composer of "concrete" music produces the noises of machines and the streets, and I hear that there is even a music of silence—three musicians appear on the podium, stand there, and do nothing at all. The dramatist produces the noises of a boys' school lavatory and displays its obscene scribblings. More seriously, Marc Saporta produces a "shuffle novel," *No. 1,* where the pages are loose and unnumbered and can be read in any order. All distinctions between art and reality have fallen. All arts tend toward self-abolition. Some of these acts or works obviously need not be taken seriously. They are elaborate hoaxes as old as Dada or as Marcel Duchamp, who submitted, under the title "Fountain," a hospital urinal to the Independent Show in New York in 1917. I hope I am not suspected of lack of sympathy with modern art, the avant-garde, or experimentation when I judge that art, given these symptoms, has reached the zero point and is about to commit suicide.

It is time for us to return to an understanding of the nature of art. A work of art is an object or a process of some shape and unity which sets it off from life in the raw. But such a conception must apparently be guarded against the misunderstanding of being "art for art's sake," the ivory tower, or asserting the irrelevancy of art to life. All great aestheticians have claimed a role for art in society and thought that art flourishes best in a good society. They knew that art humanizes man, that man becomes fully human only through art. It seems to me time that literary study again recognize the realm of art and stop being all things to all men, that it return to its old task of understanding, explaining, and transmitting literature. Otherwise it will dissolve into the study of all history and all life. I know that students—and not only young students— are often restive with such apparent limitations. Literature for them is simply an occasion or a pretext for the solution of their personal problems and the general problems of our civilization. But literary scholarship, as organized knowledge, needs such limitation. Every branch of knowledge must have a subject matter. Only through the singling out—which does not mean complete isolation—of the object can there be advance in understanding and penetration. The complaints of narrowing are belied by the manifold possibilities of expansion in our chosen field which have increased enormously in the last decades. Recent comments in the *TLS* and the *New York Times,* assuming an exhaustion of dissertation topics, ridiculing the trivialities of literary research which solemnly record W. B. Yeats' liking for parsnips, are wide of the mark.

Just comparative literature offers an almost limitless number of new topics and new problems. We have today—looking back only to the last war—an incomparably greater number of excellent guidebooks, bibliographies, dictionaries, and surveys of literary history which should make it inexcusable for anybody to plead ignorance of authors, names, and problems. Think of the bibliographies beginning with Baldensperger-Friederich and ending with the annual MLA bibliography, which listed 16,089 items for the year 1963. Think of the growing number of well-planned dictionaries of terms and authors. I have just turned the pages of the impressive Alex Preminger *Encyclopedia of Poetry and Poetics,* published by the Princeton University Press. I hear that an English version of the two-volume *Lexikon der Weltliteratur,* published by Herder in Freiburg im Breisgau in 1960–61, is being prepared under the editorship of W. B. Fleischmann. The International Comparative Literature Association is preparing a French-English *Dictionary of Literary Terms,* for which it set up elaborate machinery at Bordeaux and Utrecht, and for which a long series of papers at the Utrecht and Fribourg congresses were written as preliminary exercises. The older Shipley *Dictionary of World Literature* (1943), in spite of many poor articles, the *Columbia Dictionary of Modern Literatures* (1947), edited by the late Horatio Smith, and particularly the enormous *Dizionario letterario Bompiani* (1946–57), which runs to twelve stout volumes in small print, are inexhaustible mines of information. We have worldwide surveys of literary history, including the older and incomplete but generally excellent *Handbuch der Literaturwissenschaft,* edited by Oskar Walzel, and more recently the three volumes of the Pléiade *Histoire des littératures.*

I have reviewed some of these books and am quite aware of their mistakes, lacunae, and disproportions. For example, the second volume of the Pléiade literary history, *Littératures occidentales,* has some excellent chapters by Gaëtan Picon on the main trends of Western literature, but includes also shoddy and willful surveys of individual literatures. German literature is very ill served and Czech literature is discussed by an author, Cyril Wilczkowski, who seems not to know the language and certainly gets many names and all proportions wrong. He spreads such nonsense as that no Czech book appeared between 1620 and the last third of the eighteenth century, that Jaroslav Vrchlický was a Jew, and that Alois Jirásek was president of the Czech government during World War I.[14] But whatever the shortcomings of such collective enterprises may be, they allow us to look at something like a map of literature on an international scale. They suggest that the smaller literatures of Europe and the great wide world of the Orient invite exploration and study. Etiemble, in his pamphlet *Comparaison n'est pas raison: La Crise de la littérature comparée,*[15] may be too sanguine in wanting to change the direction of comparative literature. He wants us all to study Chinese, Bengali, or Arabic. He underrates our inertia and the obstacles to an advanced mastery of Oriental tongues for most of us, but in principle he is clearly right in asking for a com-

14. Paris, 1956, pp. 1231, 1239, 1241.
15. Paris, 1963.

parative poetics, for a genuinely universal study of world literature.

But surely it would be a mistake to think of our studies only in terms of these vistas, of the multiplication of newly accessible documents and unexplored interrelationships. There is another way for many of us, the way into the interior, "der Weg nach Innen," into a fuller and deeper understanding of the great works of art. Here too the last decades have brought about an accumulation of new tools. Methods of analyzing euphony, meter, diction, style, the technique of the novel, metaphor and symbol have been refined enormously. We all can learn also from the discoveries of neighboring disciplines: from psychology, philosophy, the history of art, sociology, and many others. Great practitioners of literary analysis such as Erich Auerbach and Leo Spitzer, Marcel Raymond, Emil Staiger, and Cleanth Brooks offer a choice of methods which allows us to grapple with what, to my mind, still matters most in literary study—the great work which must have moved us and spoken to us before we ever engaged in the professional study of literature.

We have, I conclude, to keep a balance between expansion and concentration, nationalism and cosmopolitanism, the study of literature as art and the study of literature in history and society. The choice will vary with each individual. The variety of methods and views in the Western world is enormous and undoubtedly baffling. The image of the Tower of Babel obtrudes itself insistently. But I do not believe that the dire predictions of exhaustion or the admonitions to silence are justified. Nor can I agree with the criticism coming from the East—e.g. in Robert Weimann's most unfair book, *New Criticism und die Entwicklung bürgerlicher Literaturwissenschaft*[16]—that Western literary scholarship is in a state of

16. Halle, 1962.

complete disarray and decadence. On the basis of thirty-eight years of experience, I can say, I hope quite soberly, that literary studies in this country have come a long way from the factualism, dreary antiquarianism, romantic nationalism, and general provincialism of the 1920s to a much greater awareness of the world around and within us. If we were not suspicious of the word, we could speak of progress not only in quantity and range but also in quality—in refinement, subtlety, and penetration. Comparative literature has played a crucial role as a crystallizing subject for the reform. We must recognize the importance of comparative literature from an organizational point of view and emphasize the function and value of our different common enterprises—associations, periodicals, news letters, and conferences like this one. But we must not, on the other hand, overrate the mere machinery and expect too much from departments, programs, and all the other devices. The men or women struggling in solitude at their desks with their texts and their writings matter most in the long run. But the feeling of a community of scholars is a great stimulus to morale. Such a conference can encourage us—send us, as I hope this one will, "tomorrow to fresh woods, and pastures new."

[The President's address at the meeting of the American Comparative Literature Association held at Cambridge, Mass. in April 1965]

# The Term and Concept of Classicism
# in Literary History

Today it seems impossible to write about English eighteenth-century literature without using the term "classicism" or, possibly even more frequently, "neoclassicism." There are books such as *The Course of English Classicism,* articles called "The Tendency toward Platonism in Neo-Classical Esthetics" or " 'Distrust' of Imagination in English Neoclassicism," chapters in literary histories on the "Rise of Classicism," "The Disintegration of Classicism," etc.[1] But what seems to us a matter of course was not so even sixty years ago, and one hundred years ago the term was not used or hardly used at all. The English classicists or neoclassicists did not, of course, call themselves by that name; they spoke, at most, of the imitation of the ancients, of the observance of the rules, or similarly. When early in the nineteenth century their reputation declined and they were looked upon as belonging to a bygone age, the age was called "The Augustan Age," "The Age of Pope," "The Age of Queen Anne," but not the Age of Classicism. Macaulay in 1828 spoke of "The Critical School of

1. I allude to Sherard Vines (London, 1930); L. I. Bredvold's "Tendency . . . ," *ELH, 1 (*1934), 91–119; D. F. Bond's "Distrust . . ." *Philological Quarterly, 14* (1935), 54–69; and to the chapters by George Sherburn in Albert C. Baugh, ed., *A Literary History of England* (New York, 1948), pp. 699 ff., 967 ff.

Poetry"; some enemies referred to it as "The French School."[2] The issue whether Pope was a poet or not or whether he was a poet of the highest rank, first raised in Joseph Warton's *Essay on Pope* (1756), was debated in terms of a contrast between "natural" and "artificial" poetry or of a distinction between high, imaginative, "pure" poetry and didactic or ethical poetry, but not in terms of a contrast between "classicism" and romanticism.

It took a long time before the term "classicism" was applied to the style of Dryden and Pope. Why was this so? Can we account for it? Is there any significance to the lack of the term? If we believe with Croce that an idea is not there until it is expressed, we must ascribe great importance to the question of terminology. Such terms, I would agree, as Renaissance, romanticism, baroque, and realism crystallize ideas, formulate the problem of periodization and pervasive style, however uncertain and disputable may be the extension, valuation, and precise content of each term. They have become indispensable tools of historiography, and their absence shows a lack of interest in abstraction, in the whole problem of period style, and in the characterization and generalizations implied in these terms. The England of the nineteenth century is a case in point.

It seems significant that during the nineteenth century a whole set of alternative terms to "classicism" was used sporadically: the need for a term was felt, and different words were tried out and dropped. "Classicalism" is now completely out of use, but it occurs—e.g. in a letter by Elizabeth Barrett in 1839. She praises Landor as "the most classical, because the

2. In "John Dryden" (1828), reprinted in *Miscellaneous Works, 1* (New York, 1880), 145. "French School," e.g. in *Edinburgh Review, 207* (July 1828), 1, a review of Bell's edition of Dryden and of Scott's edition of Dryden, referring to the term as customary.

freest from mere classicalism."[3] Ruskin, in the first volume of
*Modern Painters* (1846), refers to "the hybrid classicalism" of
the landscape painter Richard Wilson;[4] Arnold, in his Preface
to *Merope* (1857), complains that people have been "taught
to consider classicalism as inseparable from coldness."[5] Leslie
Stephen, in his *History of English Thought in the Eighteenth
Century* (1876), calls the "classicalism of the time . . . midway between the taste of the Renaissance and that of modern
times."[6] W. J. Courthope, in his *Life of Alexander Pope*
(1889), speaks of the "classicalism which reached its height
in the 'Botanical Garden' of Erasmus Darwin."[7] There was
the alternative term "classicality," which Ruskin used when
he contemptuously referred to the "vile classicality of Canova."[8] Slowly, in the anti-eighteenth-century atmosphere of
Victorian literary studies, the terms "pseudoclassical,"
"pseudoclassicism," and "pseudoclassicalism" emerge. Ruskin referred to Claude Lorrain as "pseudo-classical" in 1856,[9]
and James Russell Lowell, in his essay on Pope (1871), speaks
of a "pseudo-classicism, the classicism of red heels and peri-
wigs."[10] In 1885 the word appears for the first time on the
title page of an English, or rather American, book. Thomas
Sergeant Perry, an early friend of Henry James, wrote *From
Opitz to Lessing: A Study of Pseudo-Classicism in Litera-*

3. Quoted in John Foster, *W. S. Landor, 2* (2 vols. London, 1869),
298.

4. *Modern Painters* I, *Works,* ed. Cook-Wedderburn, *3* (39 vols.
London, 1902–12), 230.

5. In *On the Classical Tradition,* Vol. 1. 2 ed. R. H. Super (Ann
Arbor, Mich., 1960), p. 38.

6. (2 vols. London, 1876), 355.

7. London, 1889, p. 374. Used also on p. 61.

8. *Modern Painters,* I, *Works,* ed. Cook-Wedderburn, *3,* 230.

9. *Modern Painters,* III, ibid., *5,* 224.

10. *Literary Essays, 4* (Boston, 1891), 8.

*ture.*[11] But Leslie Stephen in 1876 used the new term "pseudo-classicalism" to refer to poetry after Pope.[12]

The more neutral term "neoclassical" appeared somewhat earlier. William Rushton, of whom I know nothing, gave a lecture, "The Classical and Romantic Schools of English Literature" (1863), which shows that he was aware of making an innovation. "When we speak of the classical school in English Literature," he says, "we refer to those writers who have formed their style upon the ancient models, and, for the sake of distinction, we might call them the Revived Classical or the Neo-Classical school." Later he refers again to "the development of the neo-classical school" in the works of Dryden and Pope.[13] But as far as I know, the term is exceedingly rare in the following decades. Saintsbury, in his *History of Criticism* (1902), has a chapter "The Neo-classic creed," but the word becomes common only in the 1920s.[14]

The term "classicism" was victorious after all. At first it was definitely an import from the Continent and referred to events on the Continent. Carlyle, in the essay on Schiller (1831), seems to have used the word for the first time in English, complacently and prematurely reflecting that "we are troubled with no controversies on Romanticism and Classicism."[15] Facetiously, in *The French Revolution* (1837), Carlyle enumerates "Catholicism, Classicism, Sentimental-

11. Boston, 1885.

12. *History of English Thought in the Eighteenth Century, 2,* 357.

13. "The Classical and Romantic Schools of English Literature," in *The Afternoon Lectures on English Literature* (London, 1863), pp. 44, 63, 72.

14. "The Crystallising of the Neo-Classic Creed," in *A History of Criticism, 2* (3 vols. Edinburgh, 1902), 240 ff.

15. *Critical and Miscellaneous Essays,* Centenary ed., *2* (5 vols. London, 1899), 172.

ism, Cannibalism; all isms that make up Man in France."[16]
Carlyle's hostility to those abstractions seems somewhat odd,
as he wrote his *History of the French Revolution* very much
in such terms, personifying Constitutional Patriotism, Sans-
culottism, and Monarchism on almost every page. But as
late as 1837 John Stuart Mill had to explain patiently that
"this insurrection against the old traditions of classicism was
called romanticism" in France.[17] I cannot find the term in
English for many years to come, and certainly the standard
discussions of Pope and Dryden get along without it. It
occurs in Arnold's essay on Heine (1863), when he speaks of
his "utter rejection of stock classicism and stock romanticism."[18] Walter Pater, in his essay on "Romanticism" (1876),
which was later reprinted as the Postscript to *Appreciations*
(1889), quotes Stendhal on classicism and romanticism[19] but
otherwise does not use the term even when he discusses
Winckelmann and Goethe. Edward Dowden in 1878, speaking of Landor, is satisfied that "the attempts made . . . to bend
our literature to classicism were not of native origin" and
thus could not succeed for any length of time.[20] Even Edmund Gosse, in his *Modern English Literature* (1898), knows
only a "classical" poetry during the lifetime of Pope and puts
the term "classical" in quotation marks.[21] In Oliver Elton's

16. *French Revolution,* Centenary ed., *3,* (3 vols. London, 1899),
205.

17. "Armand Carrel," in *Dissertations and Discussions, 1* (2nd ed.,
2 vols. London, 1867), 233.

18. *Lectures and Essays in Criticism,* ed. R. H. Super (Ann Arbor,
1962), p. 122.

19. *Appreciations* (London, 1924), p. 245.

20. "W. S. Landor," in *Studies in Literature 1789–1877* (London,
1878), p. 182.

21. London, 1898, pp. 214, 215.

*Augustan Ages* (1899) the terms "French Classicism" and the English "representatives of classicism" are used,[22] and Herbert Grierson, in a later volume of the same series, *The First Half of the Seventeenth Century* (1906), says casually that "in our period the classicism of the Augustan ages is taking shape."[23] I could not prove it with statistical accuracy, but I believe that only Louis Cazamian's *Histoire de la littérature anglaise* (1925), which calls a whole section "Classicism (1702–1740)," established the academic usage, particularly in the United States, as Legouis-Cazamian was the standard history of English literature when I was a student in the twenties.

Some of the evidence presented here is undoubtedly far from complete. Some of the dates for first occurrences of the terms, though they antedate the examples given in the *NED*, could probably be pushed back further. But in its general outlines the sketch must be correct: the late acceptance of the term "classicism" for English literature of the late seventeenth and early eighteenth centuries shows that English literary thinking for a long time shied away from the abstraction and the shorthand implicit in the use of the term. It shows also that attention was turned elsewhere. When we read what nineteenth-century authors have to say about Pope, Dryden, Swift, and Addison, we get almost exclusively discussions of their lives, personalities, and ethics, and possibly of their religious and political views. If we get criticism, it is usually content with anthologizing or some general reflections still very much in the tradition of the eighteenth-century debates: Was Pope a poet? Were Pope and Dryden classics of our prose? The idea of a period as a unit of style is late and was later in England than on the Continent. But it would be

22. Edinburgh, 1899, pp. 265–66.
23. Edinburgh, 1906, pp. 376–77.

a mistake to ignore the fact that the older terms, "The Augustan Age," "The Age of Queen Anne," "The Age of Pope," etc., did imply some awareness of a definite period in English literature which, during the early nineteenth century, became a target of attack or a banner of defiance against the new taste. In my earlier paper on "The Concept of Romanticism" (1949) I argued that even without the term many English writers "had a clear consciousness that there was a movement which rejected the critical concepts and poetic practice of the 18th century."[24] Jeffrey, who wrote in 1811 that "Pope was much the best of the classical Continental school,"[25] sums up what most of us would think today.

Jeffrey's word "Continental" raises the crucial problem. English classicism was assumed to be an importation from France—the direct result of the Restoration of 1660 when the Stuarts returned from exile. Pope stated this in well-known lines:

> We conquer'd France, but felt our captive's charms;
> Her Arts victorious triumph'd o'er our Arms.[26]

De Quincey in 1851 saw the difficulty of this chronological sequence and perversely interpreted the English conquest of France as referring to the battle of Agincourt in 1415 instead of the victories of Marlborough over the armies of Louis XIV, which Pope must have had in mind. De Quincey, in his contempt for the French, goes so far as to deny that "either Dryden or Pope was even slightly influenced by

24. Reprinted in my *Concepts of Criticism* (New Haven, 1963), p. 152.

25. "The Dramatic Works of John Ford (1811)," in *Contributions to the Edinburgh Review, 2* (3 vols. London, 1844), 292.

26. "The First Epistle of the Second Book of Horace," lines 263–64, in *Imitations of Horace,* ed. J. Butt (London, 1939), p. 217.

French literature" and to assert that "the thing they did they would have done though France had been at the back of China."[27] A little later Hippolyte Taine, in his *Histoire de la littérature anglaise* (1864), devoted some eloquent pages to contrasting the gentle, wise, and polite Molière with the brutal, gross, and vulgar Wycherley, and the refined and elegant Racine with the bombastic and obscene Otway. The characters of English Restoration tragedies, Taine concluded, are as much like Racine's as "the cook of Madame de Sévigné is like Madame de Sévigné."[28] Katherine E. Wheatley, in a recent book, *Racine and English Classicism* (1956), displayed, with some pedantic glee, all the misinterpretations and mistranslations of English translators and adapters of Racine. She argues that there was a deep gulf between the two literatures and suggests that the English lacked a psychological tradition comparable to the French *moralistes* and the Racinian analysis of passion.[29] Henri Peyre, in his *Qu'est-ce que le Classicisme?* (1953), emphasized the distinctness and uniqueness of French classicism and argued that "the relations between French literature of the 17th century and that of antiquity" were much looser than is usually assumed.[30] As for English literature, P. S. Wood had pointed to "Native Elements in English Neo-Classicism" (1926),[31] and since then many scholars have demonstrated the continuity between the Elizabethan Age and the Restoration. As early as

27. *Collected Writings,* ed. D. Masson, *11* (14 vols. London, 1896), 61.

28. Vol. 3 (2nd ed. 5 vols. Paris, 1866), 216: "la cuisinière de Mme de Sévigné à Mme de Sévigné."

29. Austin, Texas, 1956.

30. Quoted from expanded ed., *Le Classicisme français* (New York, 1942), p. 32: "Combien lâches sonts les rapports entre la littérature française du XVIIe siècle et celle de l'antiquité."

31. In *Modern Philology, 24* (1926), 201–08.

1898 Felix Schelling proclaimed Ben Jonson the father of the English "Classical School."[32]

Surely, in an international history of criticism these arguments for the divorce between French and English literature of that time are not convincing. They merely push the matter back into the past, to the common sources of the neoclassical —i.e. Aristotelian and Horatian—theory which was formulated first in Italy early in the sixteenth century and a little later by Scaliger, an Italian active in France, and then again by Dutch scholars such as Vossius and Heinsius. Ben Jonson, as was shown long ago, paraphrased and translated these writers,[33] and the French seventeenth-century critics were clearly influenced by them, at least in dramatic theory.[34] English classicism is, in critical theory, part and parcel of the huge Western European neoclassical tradition. It was in direct contact with France, particularly with Boileau,[35] but drew also on the sources of French classical theory in antiquity and Italian and Dutch humanism. English classicism is rightly so named. Our little history must have shown that it was named on the analogy of French classicism.

But how did the French come to speak of classicism? It will be necessary to go further into the history of the term. Every dictionary tells us that the word "classicus" occurs first in Aulus Gellius, a Roman author of the second century after

32. "Ben Jonson and the Classical School," *PMLA, 13* (1898), 221–49; reprinted in *Shakespeare and 'Demi-Science' "* (Philadelphia, 1927).

33. See J. E. Spingarn, "The Sources of Jonson's *Discoveries,"* *Modern Philology, 2* (1905), 451–60, and the edition of *Timber, or Discoveries,* by M. Castelain (Paris, 1906).

34. See Edith G. Kern, *The Influence of Heinsius and Vossius upon French Dramatic Theory* (Baltimore, 1949).

35. Cf. A. F. B. Clark, *Boileau and the French Classical Critics in England* (Paris, 1925).

Christ, who in his miscellany, *Noctes Atticae,* refers to "classicus scriptor, non proletarius," transferring a term of the Roman taxation classes to the ranking of writers.[36] "Classicus" thus meant originally "first class," "excellent," "superior." The term seems not to have been used in the Middle Ages at all, but reappears during the Renaissance in Latin and soon in the vernaculars. The first recorded occurrence in French, in Sébillet's *L'Art poétique* (1548), refers, surprisingly, to "les bons et classiques poètes françois comme sont entre les vieux Alain Chartier et Jean de Meun."[37] The names of two medieval poets show that the word had no association with classical antiquity and simply meant "standard," "superior," "excellent." I am not aware of any study that traces the process by which the term became identified with the ancients, as in the term "classical antiquity," though the reason for the shift is obvious enough. "Classical" came to mean Roman and Greek and it still implied superiority, authority, and even perfection. Nor am I aware of any study that shows how "classical" came to be associated with the classroom, with the texts taught in schools, though again the reason for the shift in meaning is obvious enough: the ancient classics were the only secular authors studied, and they were studied as models of style and sources of ideas. Ernst Robert Curtius, in *Europäische Literatur und lateinisches Mittelalter* (1948), has raised the question of the formation of a canon of ancient authors and of the great writers in the modern literatures. It would be worthwhile to trace the process in detail for every literature. Pope in 1737 wrote that "who lasts a century can

36. *Noctes* 19, 8, 15: "Vel oratorum aliquis vel poetarum, id est classicus assiduusque aliquis scriptor, non proletarius."

37. Quoted from Edmond Huguet, *Dictionnaire de la langue française du seizième siècle, 2,* 308, or Sébillet, *Art Poétique* (Paris, 1910), chap. 3, p. 26.

have no flaw: I hold that Wit a Classic, good in law,"[38] and George Sewell, in his introduction to Shakespeare's *Poems* (a part of Pope's *Shakespeare, 1725*), had asked for careful editions of English authors, which "we in justice owe to our own great writers, both in Prose, and Poetry. They are in some degree our Classics: on their Foundation we must build, as the Formers and Refiners of our Language."[39] Sewell thinks of Shakespeare as deserving and getting such treatment. We are back to the meaning of "classic" assumed by Sébillet. Shakespeare is a standard author.

The same meaning of the term is recorded also in France, though surprisingly somewhat later than in England. Pierre-Joseph Thoulier D'Olivet, in his *Histoire de l'Académie* (1729), complains that "Italy had classical authors and we as yet have none."[40] In a letter to the same Abbé D'Olivet, Voltaire in 1761 proposed to edit the "classical authors" of the French, reserving Corneille for himself as a special favorite.[41] Certainly Voltaire's own *Siècle de Louis XIV* (1751) puts the age and its writers next to other golden ages: those of Leo X, Augustus, and Alexander. Characteristically, the age of Pericles is still missing from the list.[42] In all these discussions the implication of "classicity" as model and standard is dominant. The remoter model behind the great modern writers in antiquity is assumed as a matter of course, but not

38. See above, n. 26. P. 199, lines 55–56. Pope paraphrases Horace's: "Est vetus atque probus, centum qui perficit annos."

39. Quoted by J. C. Maxwell in *Notes and Queries, 10* (June 1963), 220. From Preface to Pope's *Shakespeare, 7*, vii.

40. Ed. Livet, *2* (2 vols. Paris, 1858), 47: "L'Italie avait des auteurs classiques, et nous n'en avons point encore de tels."

41. Voltaire, *Correspondence*, ed. T. Bestermann *40* (Geneva, 1959), 275. See also letter to C. P. Duclos, p. 274. Both letters were written on April 10, 1761.

42. Ed. René Groos, *2* (Paris, 1947), 129.

more so than when Dante is considered a "classic" in Italy or when Spaniards speak of their Golden Age. The matter of style did not come into it.

The decisive event for the development of the concept of "classicism" was, after all, the great romantic-classical debate begun in Germany by the brothers Schlegel. I have discussed these questions at length in several of my writings, largely with emphasis on the romantic side, and I do not wish to repeat myself.[43] For our immediate purpose the transformation of the meaning of the word "classical" from a term of valuation to a term for a stylistic trend, type, or period in which differences of quality are allowed to exist was the crucial turning-point. The historistic revolution brought about the awareness of the existence, side by side, of at least two literary traditions. The Schlegelian dichotomy was first expounded in France by Madame de Staël in *De l'Allemagne* (1814), but a few months before the delayed publication of her book, August Wilhelm Schlegel's *Vorlesungen über dramatische Kunst und Literatur* appeared in a translation by her cousin, Madame Necker de Saussure.[44] In her Preface (1813) the translator commented perceptively: "In Mr. Schlegel's work, the epithet 'classical' is a simple designation of a genre, independent of the degree of perfection with which the genre is treated."[45] We all know the violent polem-

43. "The Concept of Romanticism," in my *Concepts of Criticism*, pp. 128–98; and *A History of Modern Criticism, 2* (4 vols. New Haven, 1955), esp. pp. 12–14, 57–60, 110–11, 226.

44. Madame de Staël's *De l'Allemagne* was printed in 1810 but suppressed by Napoleon. It appeared in French in London in October 1813, and was reprinted in Paris in May 1814. Schlegel's *Cours* appeared in December 1813 in Paris in French translation.

45. "Dans l'ouvrage de M. Schlegel, l'épithète de classique est une simple désignation de genre, indépendante du degré de perfection avec laquelle le genre est traité."

ics which Madame de Staël's book stirred up. But if we examine the texts of the classical-romantic debate we do not find the term "classicisme." It is not in Eggli-Martino's very full collection, *Le Débat romantique 1813–1830,* though the word "romantisme" occurs twice in 1816.[46]

We must go to Italy to find the first occurrence of "classicismo." A very complete collection by Egidio Bellorini, *Discussioni e polemiche sul romanticismo,* would seem to provide a check on the emergence of the term. In September 1818 Giovanni Berchet speaks, in a note, quite casually of "la pedantesca servilità del classicismo,"[47] and Ermes Visconti in November and December of the same year uses the term frequently and freely in "Idee elementari sulla poesia romantica." He distinguishes, for example, between the "admirable classicism of the ancients" and the "scholastic classicism of the moderns."[48] It is difficult to believe that the term could have emerged so casually and be used as a matter of course. I suspect that it must have existed before in the discussions about the revival of antiquity in the fine arts initiated by Winckelmann and David. But I have failed to find the word in all the obvious texts: Milizia, Cicognara, Ennio Quirino Visconti, or the many writings about Canova.

What matters for our history is that Stendhal picked up the term in Milan—he read and paraphrased Visconti, whom he also knew personally—and then gave, in his *Racine et Shakespeare* (1823), the famous facetious definitions of classicism

46. Ed. Edmond Eggli and Pierre Martino *1813–1816, 1* (Paris, 1933), pp. 445 and 472–73.

47. "Del Criterio ne' discorsi," in Giovanni Berchet, *Opere, 2* (2 vols. Bari, 1912), 65 n. Not in Bellorini.

48. *Discussioni e polemiche sul romanticismo,* ed. Egidio Bellorini, *1* (2 vols. Bari, 1943), 436: "il classicismo degli antichi, originale e ammirabile, il classicismo dei moderni . . . scolastico."

and romanticism. "Romanticism is the art of presenting to different peoples those literary works which, in the existing state of their habits and beliefs, are capable of giving them the greatest possible pleasure. Classicism, on the contrary, presents to them that literature which gave the greatest possible pleasure to their great-grandfathers."[49] But it would be an error to think that classicism became an established term in France soon after Stendhal's use. It occurs only infrequently in the great debate of the next years which led to the Preface to *Cromwell* (1827). In a careful monograph devoted to the debate of the year 1826 I found it only twice in a pamphlet by Cyprien Desmarais, *Le Temps présent*.[50] No doubt the old word "classique" sufficed for most purposes, and "classicisme" was felt as an ugly neologism. It is called a neologism as late as 1863 in Littré's *Dictionary* and it has never gained admittance into the Dictionary of the French Academy. Champfleury, the champion of the new term "realism," perceptively remarked in *Le Réalisme* (1857) that "the power of the word 'classique' prevented in spite of the efforts of some people (Stendhal among others) the adoption of the designation 'classicisme.' "[51] In Italy Niccolò Tommaseo, the great lexicographer, apparently felt the same. In

49. *Racine et Shakespeare* (Paris, 1905), pp. 32–33: "Le *romanticisme* est l'art de présenter aux peuples les œuvres littéraires qui, dans l'état actuel de leurs habitudes et de leurs croyances, sont susceptibles de leur donner le plus de plaisir possible. Le *classicisme,* au contraire, leur présente la littérature qui donnait le plus grand plaisir possible à leurs arrière-grands-pères."

50. Christian A. E. Jensen, *L'Evolution du Romantisme. L'Année 1826* (Geneva, 1959), pp. 50, 120.

51. Champfleury, *Le Réalisme* (Paris, 1857), Préface: "Ce qui fait la force du mot classique c'est que malgré les efforts de quelques-uns (Stendhal entre autres), la désignation de classicisme n'a pu être adoptée."

his *Dictionary of the Italian Language* (1858 ff.) "classicismo" is defined as "the party of those who say they honor the classics by imitating their forms and using them as a whip against their enemies," and he adds with heavy irony: "Parola elegante come la cosa."[52] Other nations apparently did not feel the aesthetic objections to the word so strongly: Goethe uses the term reporting on "Klassiker und Romantiker in Italien" (1820),[53] and Pushkin in 1830 praises a poet, F. N. Glinka, for "not professing either ancient or French classicism and not following either Gothic or modern Romanticism."[54] At the end of Chapter 7 of *Evgeny Onegin* (1828) Pushkin had paid ironic "homage to classicism" by addressing belatedly the Epic Muse and announcing his theme: "I sing of a young friend."[55] In Spain the word seems to occur quite late: the date 1884 is given in Corominas' *Diccionario*.[56]

In France an important development took place, whatever term was used: the exaltation of the French seventeenth century as the classical age in sharp contrast to the eighteenth century, which to us may seem stylistically and in critical theory a direct continuation of the seventeenth. But in the early

52. *Dizionario della lingua italiana, 2* (7 vols. new ed. Torino, 1915), 1465: "Partito di coloro che dicono d'onorare i Classici imitandone le forme, e servendosi di quelli come di scudiscio contro i loro avversarii."

53. *Sämtliche Werke, Jubiläumsausgabe, 37* (40 vols. Stuttgart, 1902–07), 118. Note that the text (uncorrected in the critical edition) speaks of "Romantizismus und Kritizismus" as "zwei unversöhnliche Sekten."

54. Review of *Kareliya,* in *Pushkin o literature,* ed. N. V. Bogoslovsky (Moscow, 1934): "On ne ispoveduet ni drevnego, ni frantsuzkogo klassitsizma, on ne sleduet ni goticheskomu, ni noveishemu romantizmu."

55. *Onegin,* VII, stanza 55, line 13: "Ja klassitsizmu otdal chest."

56. *Diccionario crítico etimológico de la lengua castellana, 1* (Madrid, 1954), 817.

nineteenth century the two periods were contrasted for reasons which are easy to understand: the seventeenth century appealed to the conservative political and religious reaction, while the eighteenth century *philosophes* bore the onus of preparing and even causing the French Revolution. The men who were responsible for the definition of this ideology do not use the term "classicism" or use it rarely. Désiré Nisard's *Histoire de la littérature française* (4 vols., 1844–61) is dominated by a conception of the French spirit which reaches its perfection in the seventeenth century, while everything since appears as decadence. Nisard had actually been the first who accused the romantics of decadence. His *Etudes des mœurs et de critique sur les poètes latins de la décadence* (2 vols., 1834) was a harshly critical discussion of the writers of Silver Latinity which led up to an explicit indictment of the French literature of Nisard's own age. Modern French poetry, he argues, shows all the symptoms of the decadence of late antiquity, while the age of Louis XIV parallels that of the great Augustus. With the triumphs on the stage of Rachel in the seventeenth-century tragedies, the dismal failure of Hugo's *Les Burgraves,* and the great success of Ponsard's "classical" tragedy *Lucrèce* in 1843, something like a comeback of classicism seemed to be accomplished. Ponsard rather coyly pretended hardly to remember that one used to distinguish between "classics and romantics, or people who were called something like that."[57] Ponsard later (1847) asserted that "innovation or reaction, romanticism or classicism are only words which fit formulas" and concluded that

57. *Revue de Vienne, 3* (1840), 490; quoted in Camille Latreille, *La Fin du théâtre romantique et François Ponsard* (Paris, 1899), p. 302n.: "Des classiques et des romantiques, ou des gens qu'on appelait à peu près ainsi."

"in art there is nothing but good or bad,"[58] a sentiment which would have found the approval of Croce. But nothing came of it: the new enthusiasts for classical antiquity spoke rather of the "pagan school" or called their style "néo-grec." It was definitely a new Hellenism which saw itself as very different from the tradition of French classicism. Sainte-Beuve's famous essay "Qu'est-ce qu'un Classique?" (1850) must be seen in this context. While insisting on the Greco-Latin tradition, Sainte-Beuve aims at enlarging the concept. He recognizes the existence of something transcending the tradition: Homer, Dante, and Shakespeare are classics, though they do not conform to the demands of what we would call French classicism. This kind of classicism, with its rules, he knows, is definitely a thing of the past. Still, he pleads, we must preserve the notion and the cult of the classics and at the same time widen it and make it more generous.[59]

Sainte-Beuve and Taine do not use the word "classicism." Sainte-Beuve, however, restated the sense of the classical tradition, while Taine dealt it a severe blow when, in *Origines de la France contemporaine* (1874), he associated the abstract utopianism of the Jacobins with the rationalism of the Cartesian tradition and made the Revolution appear as the logical outcome of the classical spirit.[60] Later in the century the new champion of French classicism, Ferdinand Brunetière, hardly ever used the term. Only in a review of a book

---

58. "A Propos d'Agnès de Méranie," in *Œuvres Complètes* (Paris, 1876), p. 356: "L'innovation ou la réaction, le romanticisme ou le classicisme, sont des mots qui s'appliquent à des formules. L'art ne connaît que le bon et le mauvais."

59. *Causeries du Lundi, 3* (16 vols. Paris, 1945), 38–55.

60. Chap. 2 of Bk. III, in *Ancien Régime, 1* (16 vols. Paris, 1947), 288 ff.

by Emile Deschanel, *Le Romantisme des classiques* (1882), does Brunetière use the term several times, infected as he is by Deschanel's frequent use;[61] while Jules Lemaître, reviewing the same book, got along without it.[62] I cannot, of course, exclude the possibility that the term might be found elsewhere, but I have the impression that it became fully established only about 1890. In 1889 Georges Pellisier's *Le Mouvement littéraire au XIXe siècle* contains an introductory chapter "Le Classicisme." Eugène François Lintilhac published an important article, "J. C. Scaliger, fondateur du classicisme" (1890),[63] and in 1897 Louis Bertrand put the term on the title page of his book *La Fin du classicisme et le retour à l'antique,* a careful study of the late eighteenth-century classical revival. But Gustave Lanson, in his standard *Histoire de la littérature française* (1894), still avoids the term in the text, though the title of a chapter calls Guez de Balzac, Chapelain, and Descartes "Trois Ouvriers du classicisme" and a caption speaks of "a union of Cartesianism and art in classicism."[64]

Louis Bertrand later belonged to a group of conservatives who, after the turn of the century, launched the antiromantic campaign which, contrary to Taine, accused romanticism of all the evils of the French Revolution and the anarchy of our own time. Charles Maurras, the editor of *Action française,* Pierre Lasserre, who praised Maurras in a pamphlet *Charles Maurras et la Renaissance classique* (1902) and then

61. "Classiques et romantiques," in *Etudes critiques sur l'histoire de la littérature française, 3* (8 vols. 2nd ed. Paris, 1890), 293, 299, 315, 319, 320, 321, 325.

62. "Le Romantisme des Classiques," in *Les Contemporains,* 8ème série (Paris, 1918), pp. 159–75.

63. In *La Nouvelle Revue, 64* (1890), 333–46, 528–47.

64. Paris, 1894. 1912 ed. quoted, p. 391: "union du cartésianisme et de l'art dans le classicisme."

wrote the spirited *Le Romantisme français* (1907), and the Baron Ernest Seillière, who wrote a good dozen books on the romantic disease, made "classicism" a new slogan which was also a political and philosophical war-cry. The implication in the Dreyfus affair and in the anti-German campaign before 1914 is obvious: Germans and Nordics in general were equated with romanticism, Latinity and France with classicism. The fierce and exclusive nationalism of this interpretation of the classical spirit would, one might think, have limited its appeal to France. Still, Irving Babbitt's *Rousseau and Romanticism* (1919) draws its basic ideas and attitudes from this French group, even though Babbitt as a good American and republican finally shrank from its political consequences.[65] But T. S. Eliot, during his stay in Paris (1910–11), soaked up these ideas and recognized even later that Maurras' *L'Avenir de l'intelligence* (1905) had exerted a great influence on his intellectual development.[66] In England T. E. Hulme drew heavily on these new French classicists: "Romanticism and Classicism" (published in 1924, but written in 1913) provided the most quoted statement of the new classicism. I cannot help thinking that this is unfortunate: Hulme's essay is confused and contradictory and makes classicism amount to a belief in original sin, the stability of human nature, the impossibility of progress, and the possibility of a new dry, visual verse.[67] French seventeenth-century classicism was universal in its appeal, at least in am-

65. Cf. "Racine and the Anti-Romantics" (originally in *The Nation*, Nov. 18, 1909), reprinted in *The Spanish Character and Other Essays* (Boston, 1940), p. 90; and Marcus Selden Goldman, in F. Manchester and O. Shepard, eds., *Irving Babbitt: Man and Teacher* (New York, 1941), p. 235, reporting on Babbitt's views in 1923.

66. See *Nouvelle Revue française*, 9 (Nov. 1923), 619–25.

67. In *Speculations*, ed. Herbert Read (London, 1924), pp. 113–40.

bition. The new classicism is an arid creed and has, with Maurras, Hulme, and Ezra Pound, definite Fascist overtones. It is no wonder that it has not caught on in spite of T. S. Eliot's defense of a much more generous and inclusive tradition. His essay *What is a Classic?* (1944) restates, even in detail, Sainte-Beuve's conception, though Eliot assures us that he had not read Sainte-Beuve's essay for some thirty-odd years. "The blood-stream of European literature," Eliot formulates, "is Latin and Greek—not as two systems of circulation, but one, for it is through Rome that our parentage to Greece must be traced."[68]

A rejection of this view is precisely the distinguishing feature of German classicism, or rather what Germans call their "Klassik." "Klassik" is the pervasive term in German books on literature. Nobody seems to be aware of the fact that it is a new term, and nobody has traced its history. In such a solid scholarly enterprise as *Grundriss der germanischen Philologie,* in the volume *Deutsche Wortgeschichte* (1942), we are given the false information that "Romantik" is a parallel and analogous formation to the word "Klassik."[69] Actually, "Romantik" was used by Novalis in 1800, but I cannot find "Klassik" before the year 1887. There is, however, one quite isolated instance. Friedrich Schlegel, in notes published only in 1963 but dated 1797, jotted down these somewhat mystifying statements: "Absolute Classik also annihilirt sich selbst"; and "Alle Bildung ist Classik Abstraction."[70] This is at least the provisional result of my search.

68. London, 1945, pp. 8, 31.
69. Friedrich Kainz, "Klassik und Romantik," in F. Maurer and F. Stroh, *Deutsche Wortgeschichte, 2* (2nd ed. Berlin, 1959), 3222.
70. *Philosophische Lehrjahre,* ed. E. Behler, *1* (11 vols. Munich, 1963 [= Vol. 18 of *Sämtliche Werke*]), 23. In *Literary Notebooks,* ed. H. Eichner (Toronto, 1957), p. 76, the term occurs once, also in 1797.

Otto Harnack uses it in his *Goethe in der Epoche seiner Vollendung* (1887), first in quotation marks and then in the phrase about Euphorion as "der geniale Spross der vermählten Klassik und Romantik."[71] Harnack seems to have felt that the word is an innovation, as in a later book, *Der deutsche Klassizismus im Zeitalter Goethes* (1906), he explains in his Preface: "I could not this time avoid the unpleasant expressions 'classicism' and 'classicist,' for which I usually substitute 'Klassik' and 'klassisch,' because usage has given the word 'klassisch' a special narrow meaning in relation to German poetry."[72] Harnack draws a distinction between "Klassizismus," the imitation of antiquity, and "Klassik," a term designating the works of the great German classics, Goethe and Schiller. The term "Klassik" caught on, at first, only slowly. Eugen Wolff and Heinrich Hart use it in manifestoes of naturalism, or what they call "Die Moderne," in 1888 and 1890.[73] Carl Weitbrecht, in his book *Diesseits von Weimar. Auch ein Buch über Goethe* (1895), recommends that "klassisch" and "klassizistisch" should be sharply distinguished, as he argues that "Klassizismus" "derailed" Goethe's genius from its proper path.[74] Otto Harnack used

71. Leipzig, 1887, pp. 133, 152.

72. Berlin, 1906, Vorrede: "Die unschönen Ausdrücke 'Klassizismus' und 'klassizistisch', für die ich sonst 'Klassik' und 'klassisch' zu setzen pflege, habe ich diesmal nicht vermeiden können, weil der Sprachgebrauch dem Worte 'klassisch' in Bezug auf die deutsche Poesie eine besondere enge Bedeutung gegeben hat."

73. Eugen Wolff, "Die jüngste Litteraturströmung und das Prinzip der Moderne," *Literarische Volkshefte* (1888), p. 44; reprinted in Erich Ruprecht, ed., *Literarische Manifeste des Naturalismus* (Stuttgart, 1962), p. 138. Heinrich Hart, "Der Kampf um die Form in der zeitgenössischen Dichtung" in *Kritisches Jahrbuch, 1* (1890), 76; reprinted in Ruprecht, p. 191.

74. Stuttgart, 1895, p. 35: "Aus dem Geleise gebracht." Cf. pp. 33–34.

the term in the title of his *Deutsches Kunstleben im Zeitalter der Klassik* (Weimar, 1896). So teutonizing a literary historian as Adolf Bartels adopted the word in 1906 for a chapter of his *Handbuch zur Geschichte der deutschen Literatur*.[75] Also at the other end of the German cultural spectrum, with Friedrich Gundolf, the disciple of Stefan George, the new term replaces the older "classicism." In *Shakespeare und der deutsche Geist* (1911) the final chapter is called "Klassik und Romantik."[76] In his *Goethe* (1916) we are given a definition of the difference. "Klassizismus ist bewusste und gewollte, nicht naive Klassik";[77] and in 1922 Fritz Strich put the term on the title page of his *Deutsche Klassik und Romantik: oder Vollendung und Unendlichkeit* (Munich, 1922), the most influential German typology, which applies Wölfflin's principles of art history to literature. Since then the term is ubiquitous. There is a thesis by Alexander Heussler, a pupil of Fritz Strich, *Klassik und Klassizismus in der deutschen Literatur* (1952),[78] which elaborates the distinction between the terms without any awareness of its novelty. "Classicism" for Heussler is Gottsched and Johann Elias Schlegel, "Klassik" Goethe and Schiller. The triumph of the new term was, however, not general at first. Oskar Walzel in 1922 consistently speaks of "Klassizismus" when referring to Goethe.[79] Paul Merker, in a report on literary scholarship in the same year, does not know the new term,[80]

75. Leipzig, 1906. He uses also "Nachklassik."
76. Berlin, 1911, pp. 310, 321.
77. Berlin, 1916, p. 428.
78. Bern, 1952.
79. "Zwei Möglichkeiten deutscher Form," in *Vom Geistesleben alter und neuer Zeit* (1922), cf. pp. 117, 119, 122–23, 130, 141.
80. *Neuere deutsche Literaturgeschichte* (Stuttgart, 1922), pp. 74 ff.

and Franz Schultz, in a paper dating from 1928, expressly disavows the use of the neologism. "Recently," he says, "one has got accustomed to separating—apparently under the influence of Fritz Strich—'Klassizismus' and 'Klassik.' 'Klassizismus' is seen as the older strivings for an imitation of antiquity, 'Klassik' as the opposite of 'Romantik' at the turn of the 18th and 19th centuries, i.e., the thought, theory and poetical practice of Goethe and Schiller. I should like to keep to the older concept and call 'Klassizismus' the movement" which began with Winckelmann and ended with Hegel.[81] But Schultz himself succumbed to the new fashion: he later wrote two volumes entitled *Klassik und Romantik der Deutschen* (1935, 1940).[82]

We can account for the success of the new term. "Classicism," in a sense resembling that of French classicism or the classicism in the plastic arts at the end of the eighteenth century, is not a very appropriate term for most of the writings of Goethe and Schiller if one excepts the stages in their careers when they consciously aimed at the imitation of the ancients —i.e. when Schiller wrote "Die Götter Griechenlands" (1788) and speculated on "Classizität" in a letter to Körner

81. "Der Mythus des deutschen Klassizismus," *Zeitschrift für deutsche Bildung, 4* (1928), 3: "Man hat sich neuerdings daran gewöhnt—wohl unter dem Einfluss von Fritz Strich—Klassizismus und Klassik zu sondern, unter Klassizismus die älteren Bestrebungen zur Nachahmung der Alten und unter 'Klassik' das Gegenstück zur 'Romantik' um die Wende des 18. und 19. Jahrhunderts zu erblicken, d.h. die Gedankenwelt, Kunstanschauung und Kunstübung der beiden Weimaraner Goethe und Schiller und ihre Nachwirkungen. Ich möchte bei der älteren Begriffsbildung bleiben und unter dem deutschen Klassizismus jene Bewegung verstehen, die von Winckelmann . . . bis Hegel führte."

82. Stuttgart, 1935, 1940.

about a planned epic on Frederick the Great,[83] and when Goethe wrote *Iphigenie auf Tauris,* went to Italy, and then produced *Römische Elegien,* the fragment *Achilleis,* the idyll *Hermann und Dorothea,* and in the plastic arts advocated a rigid classicism of themes and forms. But classicism is clearly a term which does not fit *Goetz von Berlichingen* and *Werther* or *West-östlicher Divan* and *Faust* and even less *Die Räuber, Wallensteins Lager,* and *Die Jungfrau von Orleans,* subtitled by Schiller himself "eine romantische Tragödie." The term "Klassik" resumes the old meaning of standard or model, while the stylistic association with the ancients almost ceases to be felt. It has become a term such as "Goethezeit" or "Deutsche Bewegung,"[84] which pries the German classics loose from international classicism and yet resists the Western tendency to call Goethe and Schiller romantics.

In German literature we have, as in French literature, a little-explored process: the establishment of the great eighteenth-century writers as "Klassiker" and the Weimar period as the "classical" age. Germans still recognize six "Klassiker": Klopstock, Lessing, Wieland, Herder, Goethe, and Schiller,[85] an extremely heterogeneous group, of which Klopstock today would appear to belong to what might be called preromanticism or sentimentalism; Lessing, in spite of his polemics against the doctrines of French tragedy, would appear as a rationalistic classicist who worshiped Aristotle; Wieland would appear as a man of the Enlightenment whose art strikes

83. Letter to Körner, March 10, 1789, in *Briefe,* ed. F. Jonas, 2 (7 vols. Stuttgart, 1893), 252. Cf. an earlier letter using "Classizität," to Friedrich Schröder, Dec. 18, 1786, ibid., *1,* 320.

84. H. Korff's *Geist der Goethezeit.* "Deutsche Bewegung" is a term invented by Herman Nohl.

85. See, e.g., Wilhelm Münch, "Über den Begriff des Klassikers," in *Zum deutschen Kultur- und Bildungsleben* (Berlin, 1912), p. 248.

us often as rococo; Herder would seem an irrationalistic preromantic. How can a writer be called "klassisch" who exclaimed, as Herder did in 1767, "O the cursed word 'Classisch,' "[86] and who attacked Goethe's and Schiller's turn toward classicism as a betrayal of his teachings?

But Goethe and Schiller did not call themselves "Klassiker" and had an ambiguous and complex attitude toward the whole enterprise of establishing a classical literature. Goethe in 1795, in a remarkable article, "Literarischer Sansculottismus," argues that no German author considers himself "klassisch" and that he would not desire "the revolutions which could prepare classical works in Germany."[87] The paper was written when the French Revolution had not yet run its course: Goethe feared the dangers of centralization and the abolition of the little German states, with one of which he was so closely identified, since "classical" meant to him writing which would express the unity of a nation. Only after the Schlegels had excited the great debate did Goethe use the term more freely, either denying the distinction and clinging to the older meaning of excellence or taking sides against the romantics. A letter in 1804 reports that Goethe rejected the difference between the romantic and the classic because "everything excellent is *eo ipso* classic."[88] But later in 1829 Goethe made his famous pronouncement: "I call the Classic

86. *Sämtliche Werke,* ed. B. Suphan, *1,* (Berlin, 1877 ff.), 412: "O, das verwünschte Wort, Classisch!"

87. *Sämtliche Werke, Jubiläumsausgabe, 36,* 139–44, p. 141: "Wir wollen die Umwälzungen nicht wünschen, die in Deutschland klassische Werke vorbereiten könnten."

88. A letter by Heinrich Voss, Jr., to B. R. Abeken, Jan. 26, 1804, reporting Goethe as saying, "Alles was vortrefflich sei, sei *eo ipso* klassisch." In *Goethes Gespräche. Auswahl,* ed. F. von Biedermann (Wiesbaden, 1949), p. 163.

the healthy, the Romantic the sickly."[89] One should, however, remember the historical context: Goethe was disturbed
by the excesses of such German writers as Zacharias Werner
and E. T. A. Hoffmann, and he disliked the new French
*roman frénétique.* Later he called Hugo's *Notre Dame de
Paris* the "most disgusting book ever written."[90] He had lost
sight of the original, much wider meaning of the contrast,
though in a conversation with Eckermann in 1830 Goethe
claimed wrongly that the Schlegels merely renamed Schiller's
distinction between the naïve and the sentimental.[91] Goethe
himself always professed to stand above the battle: in *Helena*
and specifically in the figure of Euphorion, Goethe aimed at
"reconciliation of the two poetic forms."[92]

While Goethe viewed the debate rather detachedly, he
was, during his lifetime, fast becoming the German "Klassiker" or at least one of the two "Klassiker." It is still not common knowledge that Goethe, after the international success
of *Werther,* fell into comparative oblivion and that only the
success of *Hermann und Dorothea* (1797) and the effect of
the *Xenien,* written in collaboration with Schiller, gave him
a commanding position in German literature. But even in the
late eighteenth century Goethe had many enemies: orthodox
Christians who suspected him of atheism and paganism, utilitarian enthusiasts for the Enlightenment who thought him too
aesthetic, and radical irrationalists who thought him too cold,

89. To Eckermann, April 2, 1829: "Das Classische nenne ich das
Gesunde, und das Romantische das Kranke," in J.P. Eckermann,
*Gespräche mit Goethe,* Houben ed. (Leipzig, 1948), pp. 263–64.

90. Ibid., p. 604, June 27, 1831: " Das abscheulichste Buch das je
geschrieben worden." Cf. letter to Zelter, June 28, 1831.

91. Ibid., March 21, 1830, pp. 322–23.

92. Ibid., Dec. 16, 1829, p. 299: "wo beide Dichtungsformen . . .
eine Art von Ausgleichung finden."

commonsensical, and classicistic.[93] Goethe's towering reputation was secured first by the Schlegels, who played him up against Schiller yet did not consider either Schiller or Goethe classics. Friedrich Schlegel hoped as early as 1800 that Goethe would accomplish the task of "harmonizing the classical and romantic."[94] In August Wilhelm Schlegel's *Dramatic Lectures* (1809–11) Goethe is discussed along with the romantic drama written in the wake of Shakespeare.

We know only in very general terms how Goethe and Schiller became the German "Klassiker." Certainly claims for Goethe's transcendent greatness were made very early: e.g. Friedrich Schlegel in 1798[95] called Goethe, Dante, and Shakespeare "the great trichord" of modern poetry and classed *Wilhelm Meister* with Fichte's philosophy and the French Revolution as the great epoch-making events of the age.[96] And in Ludwig Tieck's *Zerbino* (1799) Goethe, Shakespeare, Cervantes, and Dante appear as "the sacred four" in the Garden of Poetry.[97] In a book by K. A. Schaller, in 1812, I found Goethe called "admittedly the first poet of Germany and at this time certainly without any serious rival among the other nations of Europe."[98] We all know Byron's dedica-

93. Cf. Albert Bettex, *Der Kampf um das klassische Weimar* 1788–98 (Zurich, 1935).

94. "Gespräch über die Poesie" (1800), in *Kritische Schriften,* ed. Wolfdietrich Rasch (Munich, 1956), p. 334: "Die Harmonie des Klassischen und Romantischen."

95. Athenäums-fragment No. 247, ibid., p. 52: "der grosse Drei-klang der modernen Poesie."

96. Athenäums-fragment No. 216, ibid., p. 46.

97. In *Romantische Dichtungen* (Jena, 1799): "die heilige Vier."

98. *Handbuch der klassischen Literatur der Deutschen* (Halle, 1812), p. 21: "Anerkannt der erste Dichter Deutschlands und gewiss gegenwärtig auch ohne gültigen Mitbewerber unter den übrigen europäischen Nationen."

tion of *Sardanapalus* as that of a "literary vassal to his liege-Lord," though Byron—who knew no German—could hardly have had an adequate conception of Goethe's eminence,[99] and we know of the constant stream of admiring visitors in Goethe's later years. They did not only come from Germany, but included Madame de Staël, Benjamin Constant, Jean-Jacques Ampère, Thackeray, Mickiewicz, Oehlenschläger, Kollár, and many others.[1]

Goethe seems to have penetrated very early into German schools.[2] But adoption as reading in schools is only a symptom of the success with the wider public, with audiences in the theater, and most decisively, with the authorities which guided the educational systems of Prussia and the other German states. The role of Wilhelm von Humboldt and the other founders of the German *Gymnasium* must have been most important precisely because of the alliance between the ideal of Greek culture, *paideia,* and Goethe's and Schiller's pedagogical or pedagogically exploited classicism. The twentieth-century tendency to divorce Goethe and Schiller from classicism is a symptom of the decay of the classical *Gymnasium* and the whole ideal of liberal culture as it was, partly with Goethe in mind, formulated also in England by Matthew Arnold. I can only allude to the role of Bettina von Arnim's *Goethes Briefwechsel mit einem Kinde* (1835) and Eckermann's *Gespräche mit Goethe* (1835) in shaping Goethe's image as an Olympian in spite of the political and liberal attacks of the Young Germans or Heine's attempt to relegate

99. Quoted in Fritz Strich, *Goethe und die Weltliteratur* (Bern, 1946), p. 301.

1. See ibid., Eckermann, etc.

2. A chapter, "Goethe im Deutschunterricht," in Wolfgang Leppmann, *Goethe und die Deutschen* (Stuttgart, 1962). This chapter is an addition to the German version of Leppmann's *The German Image of Goethe* (Oxford, 1961).

Goethe to a past "Kunstperiode." Soon after Goethe's death his position as the German Klassiker was secure, though apparently in the forties and fifties there was a temporary decline of his position, at least in relation to Schiller.

Still, in literary histories Goethe and Schiller were not considered "Klassiker" or as representing "classicism" for a long time; e.g. in Franz Horn's *Geschichte und Kritik der deutschen Poesie und Beredsamkeit* (1805), the handbook used by Carlyle, we hear only of a "Klopstock-Lessing-Goethe period."[3] The whole early nineteenth century in Germany, dominated as it was by romantic theory and taste, would not have considered the term "classicism" as flattering. Friedrich Schlegel in 1800 pronounced most contemptuously on "the so-called classical poets of the English: Pope, Dryden and whoever else."[4] August Wilhelm Schlegel's Berlin and Vienna lecture courses treated all forms of classicism—French, English, and German—with polemical harshness. The most influential literary histories avoided the term "classicism" and "classical." Thus Gervinus, in his *Geschichte der poetischen Nationalliteratur der Deutschen* (5 vols., 1835–42), never, I think, refers to Goethe and Schiller as "klassisch" or "Klassiker," though once he describes Schiller's review, *Die Horen,* as having stabilized style and taste so that the "classical period" of the language could begin. But Gervinus also freely refers to the new edition of *Faust* (1808) as putting Goethe "in the vanguard of romantic trends."[5] A. F. C. Vilmar, who wrote an extremely popular *Geschichte der deutschen Nation-*

3. Berlin, 1805, p. 190.

4. "Gespräch über die Poesie" (1800), in *Kritische Schriften,* p. 288: "die sogenannten klassischen Dichter der Engländer . . . den Pope, den Dryden oder wer sonst noch Klassiker sei."

5. *Geschichte der deutschen Dichtung,* 5 (5th ed. Leipzig, 1871–74), 492: "ihre klassische Periode"; 5, 789: "auf die Spitze der romantischen Richtungen."

*alliteratur* (1857), calls Goethe the "greatest genius of our modern times" and refers to his period as the "second period of the flowering of German literature,"[6] but never uses the word "classical" or "classicism." In a now forgotten valuable book which is expressly concerned with the classical tradition, Carl Leo Cholevius' *Geschichte der deutschen Poesie nach antiken Elementen* (2 vols., 1856), Goethe and Schiller are described as "accomplishing a unification of the Romantic and the Antique," though Cholevius speaks also of the *Roman Elegies* as having been written during Goethe's "classical period."[7] As far as I could ascertain, the term "Klassizismus" first becomes common in Hermann Hettner's *Literaturgeschichte des achtzehnten Jahrhunderts* (6 vols., 1856–70). Hettner, however, reserves the term "Klassizismus" for the French, who were supposedly "overthrown" by Goethe and Schiller. In the last volumes of his great history Hettner refers to the "classical age of German literature"—but that was in 1870.[8] Before that Rudolf von Gottschall's popular *Die deutsche Nationalliteratur des 19. Jahrhunderts* (1854) had referred to Goethe and Schiller consistently as "die Klassiker,"[9] and no doubt this had become the accepted convention, which was immensely strengthened when, in 1867, the privileges protecting the reprinting of the works of Goethe and Schiller were abolished and "Klassikerausgaben" began to

6. Vol. 2 (2 vols. Marburg, 1857), 168: "dieser grösste Genius unserer Neuzeit"; p. 226: "Unsere zweite Blüteperiode."

7. Leipzig, 1856: "Schiller und Goethe vollenden die Ineinsbildung des Romantischen und des Antiken" (Inhaltsangabe to p. 118); "Classische Periode" (p. 297).

8. *Literaturgeschichte des achtzehnten Jahrhunderts* (6 vols. Braunschweig, 1856–70). E.g. Vol. 2 (1859), "Lessing, Goethe und Schiller haben den französischen Klassizismus gestürzt"; 5 (1870), 25: "Das klassische Zeitalter der deutschen Literatur."

9. 6th ed. Breslau, 1891, reprints "Vorrede" to 1st ed. (1854), p. viii.

proliferate.[10] The German middle classes acquired sets of the great and not so great writers, and with the founding of the empire the works of Goethe and Schiller more and more assumed the role of a national palladium: a cultural heritage surrounded by almost superstitious awe. The founding of the *Goethe-Gesellschaft* (1885),[11] the long-drawn-out publication of the Weimar edition of Goethe's complete works, and the simultaneous emergence of a whole new profession, *Goethe-Philologie,* are symptoms of this victory. But as for terminology, we still observe the same vacillations as in France and England: A. Kuhn, in *Schillers Geistesgang* (1863), speaks, e.g., of "the time of 'Classizität' in our literature,"[12] a term preferred also by the Danish critic Georg Brandes in his *Hauptströmungen der Literatur des neunzehnten Jahrhunderts.*[13] Others stuck to "classicism": e.g. Julian Schmidt speaks of the break of the Schlegels with "Classizismus,"[14] but in Wilhelm Scherer's standard *Geschichte der deutschen Literatur* (1883) the term "classicism" occurs only in the Table of Contents, while the text speaks of "classische Mode." Only once, I think, does Scherer refer to "our modern classical period."[15] One can see how the dissatisfaction with the term "classicism" came about and why the new term "Klassik" replaced it. In the atmosphere of the last eighty

10. See Peter Frank, "Chancen und Gefahren von Klassikerausgaben," *Merkur, 17* (1963), 1201.

11. A detailed sociological and statistical study in Leppmann.

12. Berlin, 1863, p. 354: "In der Zeit der Classizität unserer Literatur."

13. See G. Brandes, *Die Emigrantenliteratur* (Berlin, 1914), p. 223, or *Die Reaktion in Frankreich* (Charlottenburg, 1900), p. 248. These lectures appeared in 1872 and 1874.

14. *Geschichte der deutschen Literatur, 4* (5 vols. Berlin, 1890): "Der Bruch der Schlegel mit dem Classizismus, 1797."

15. Berlin, 1883, p. 576: "Der Geist unserer modernen classischen Litteraturperiode."

years the German "Klassiker" were more and more teutonized and romanticized as national assets, while the term "classics" clung to them in an almost Pickwickian sense.

In retrospect, it is obvious that the term "classicism" is a
nineteenth-century term. It occurs first in Italy in 1818, in
Germany in 1820, in France in 1822, in Russia in 1830, in
England in 1831. In Germany in 1887 the new term "Klassik" (invented in 1797 by Friedrich Schlegel) expelled "Klassizismus." Clearly the terms have something in common: the
reference to excellence, to authority, and to the relation to
antiquity. But in the countries discussed, "classicism" refers
to three distinct bodies of literature: the French seventeenth-
century, the English late seventeenth- and early eighteenth-
centuries, and the German very late eighteenth-century literature. They differ widely in substance and form, in claim to
authority and greatness, and even in the relation to antiquity.
To characterize these differences would mean writing the literary history of three countries in two centuries. I remark only
briefly that French and German classicism have preserved an
authority which is absent from English classicism in spite of
the attempts to reinstate it in its position and the increased
and, I believe, deserved scholarly interest in the great writers
of the period: Pope and Swift in particular. T. S. Eliot seems
right in saying that "we have no classic age, and no classic
poet, in English," though he reminds us that "unless we are
able to enjoy the work of Pope, we cannot arrive at a full understanding of English poetry."[16] I can only hint that French
and English classicism are far more "Latin" than German
classicism, which is more definitely and self-consciously
"Greek." In a history of European styles of literature based on
an analogy with art history, French seventeenth-century classicism will appear as clearly baroque—a muted, subdued ba-

16. T. S. Eliot, *What is a Classic?* (London, 1945), p. 17.

roque, as Leo Spitzer has shown in a fine essay[17]—while English classicism seems most enlightened, commonsensical, even realistic, though on ocassion it has affinities with what could be called rococo. This seems at least true of Pope's *Rape of the Lock*.[18] German classicism, even in its most self-consciously neoclassical stage, will appear to us as romantic or possibly nostalgic and utopian, as was also the contemporary classicism elsewhere. The elegiac note is prominent in Chénier, and the painters and sculptors of the return to antiquity, David, Canova, and Thorwaldsen, have a sentimental streak. The dream of the golden age is never far away.[19] The Empire style of Napoleon is classicistic, but Napoleon carried *Werther* and *Ossian* about with him.

The ramifications of my subject are endless. I have barely touched the surface and, I am sure, can be corrected on dates and details. But I am not thinking of my topic as only a contribution to lexicography or the history of terminology. I have the model of the late Leo Spitzer in mind. Spitzer is probably best remembered as a student of stylistics and etymology, but he was also a master of what he called "historical semantics." His papers on *Classical and Christian Ideas of World Harmony* and on *"Milieu and Ambiance"*[20] show how he could focus on the learned key-words of our civilization and write word history within a general history of thought, combine lexicography with the history of ideas. This is also the ambition of this sketch, which I should like to see as paralleling

17. "Die klassische Dämpfung in Racines Stil," in *Romanische Stil- und Literaturstudien, 1* (2 vols. Marburg, 1931), 135–268.

18. Cf. Friedrich Brie, *Englische Rokoko-epik* (Munich, 1927).

19. Cf. Rudolf Zeitler, *Klassizismus und Utopie* (Uppsala, 1954).

20. *Classical and Christian Ideas of World Harmony,* ed. Anna G. Hatcher, Foreword by René Wellek (Baltimore, 1963); *"Milieu and Ambiance,"* in *Essays in Historical Semantics* (New York, 1948), pp. 179–316.

and supplementing my older papers on the concepts of the baroque, romanticism, and realism.[21] I am ultimately working toward a history of literary periodization, a key concept of my old project: a history of literary history and literary scholarship within a history of modern criticism.

## Bibliographical Note

The history of the term has hardly been investigated. Some remarks are to be found in Pierre Moreau, *Le Classicisme des romantiques* (Paris, 1932); Henri Peyre, *Le Classicisme français* (New York, 1942; rev. ed. Paris, 1965): chap. 2, "Le Mot Classicisme," deals with the word "classique" and has nothing to say about "classicisme" as a word; Ernst Robert Curtius, *Europäische Literatur und lateinisches Mittelalter* (Bern, 1948), esp. pp. 251 ff.; Harry Levin, "Contexts of the Classical," in his *Contexts of Criticism* (Cambridge, Mass., 1957), pp. 38–54; Georg Luck, "Scriptor Classicus," *Comparative Literature, 10* (1958), 150–58.

Most other discussions of "classicism" are analytical, ideological, or historical. Here is a small selection: P. Van Tieghem, "Classique," *Revue de synthèse historique, 41* (1931), 238–41, purely analytical; Gerhart Rosenwaldt, "Zur Bedeutung des Klassischen in der bildenden Kunst," *Zeitschrift für Aesthetik, 11* (1916), 125, contains a striking definition: "Klassisch ist ein Kunstwerk das vollkommen stilisiert ist, ohne von der Natur abzuweichen, so dass dem Bedürfniss nach Stilisierung und Nachahmung in gleicher Weise Genüge getan ist." Helmut Kuhn, " 'Klassisch' als historischer Begriff," in Werner Jaeger, ed., *Das Problem des Klassischen und die Antike* (Stuttgart, 1933; reprinted 1961), pp. 109–28; *Concinnitas: Beiträge zum Problem des Klassischen. Heinrich Wölfflin zum achtzigsten Geburtstag . . . zugeeignet* (Basel, 1944); Kurt Herbert Halbach, "Zum Begriff und

---

21. Now collected in my *Concepts of Criticism*.

Wesen der Klassik," in *Festschrift Paul Kluckhohn und Hermann Schneider gewidmet* (Tübingen, 1948), pp. 166–94.

Fritz Ernst, *Der Klassizismus in Italien, Frankreich und Deutschland* (Zürich, 1924), is a thin sketch. Sherard Vines, *The Course of English Classicism from the Tudor to the Victorian Age* (London, 1930), is lively but confused. Two books on Goethe's fame are relevant: Reinhard Buchwald, *Goethezeit und Gegenwart,* (Stuttgart, 1949), and Wolfgang Leppmann, *The German Image of Goethe* (Oxford, 1961). German version: *Goethe und die Deutschen* (Stuttgart, 1962).

Three encyclopedia entries merit attention: Antonio Viscardi, "Classicismo," in *Dizionario letterario Bompiani delle opere, 1* (Milan, 1947), 22–43; Henri Peyre, "Le Classicisme," in *Encyclopédie de la Pléiade. Histoire des littératures, 2* (Paris, 1956), 110–39; and W. B. Fleischmann, "Classicism," in *Encyclopedia of Poetry and Poetics,* ed. A. Preminger (Princeton, 1965), pp. 136–41.

# The Term and Concept of Symbolism
## in Literary History

The term and concept of symbolism (and symbol) is so vast a topic that it cannot even be sketched within the limits of this paper. The word goes back to ancient Greece and, there, had a complex history which has not, I suspect, been traced adequately in the only history of the term, Max Schlesinger's *Geschichte des Symbols,* published in 1912.[1]

What I want to discuss is something much more specific: not even symbol and symbolism in literature but the term and concept of symbolism as a period in literary history. It can, I suggest, be conveniently used as a general term for the literature in all Western countries following the decline of nineteenth-century realism and naturalism and preceding the rise of the new avant-garde movements: futurism, expressionism, surrealism, existentialism, or whatever else. How has it come about? Can such a use be justified?

We must distinguish among different problems: the history of the word need not be identical with the history of the concept as we might today formulate it. We must ask, on the one hand, what the contemporaries meant by it, who called himself a "symbolist," or who wanted to be included in a movement called "symbolism," and on the other hand, what modern scholarship might decide about who is to be included and what characteristics of the period seem decisive. In speaking

1. Berlin, 1912.

of "symbolism" as a period-term located in history we must also think of its situation in space. Literary terms most frequently radiate from one center but do so unevenly; they seem to stop at the frontiers of some countries or cross them and languish there or, surprisingly, flourish more vigorously on a new soil. A geography of literary terms is needed which might attempt to account for the spread and distribution of terms by examining rival terms or accidents of biography or simply the total situation of a literature.

There seems to be a widespread agreement that the literary history of the centuries since the end of the Middle Ages can be divided into five successive periods: Renaissance, baroque, classicism, romanticism, and realism. Among these terms baroque is a comparative newcomer which has not been accepted everywhere, though there seems a clear need of a name for the style that reacted against the Renaissance but preceded classicism.[2] There is, however, far less agreement as to what term should be applied to the literature that followed the end of the dominance of realism in the 1880s and 90s. The term "modernism" and its variants, such as the German "Die Moderne,"[3] have been used but have the obvious disadvantage that they can be applied to any contemporary art. Particularly in English, the term "modern" has preserved its early meaning of a contrast to classical antiquity or is used for everything that occurred since the Middle Ages. *The Cambridge Modern History* is an obvious example. The attempts to discriminate between the "modern" period now belonging

2. See my paper "The Concept of Baroque in Literary Scholarship" (1945) and my "Postscript" (1962), in *Concepts of Criticism* (New Haven, 1963), pp. 69–127.

3. Eugen Wolff, *Die jüngste Literaturströmung und das Prinzip der Moderne* (Berlin, 1887), seems the source of this form. In 1884 Arno Holz urges "Modern sei der Poet,/Modern vom Scheitel bis zur Sohle."

to the past and the "contemporaneous" seem forced, at least terminologically. "Modo," after all, means "now." "Modernism" used so broadly as to include all avant-garde art obscures the break between the symbolist period and all post-symbolist movements such as futurism, surrealism, existentialism, etc. In the East it is used as a catchall for everything disapproved as decadent, formalistic, and alienated: it has become a pejorative term set against the glories of socialist realism.

The older terms were appealed to at the turn of the century by many theorists and slogan writers, who either believed that these terms are applicable to all literature or consciously thought of themselves as reviving the style of an older period. Some spoke of a new "classicism," particularly in France, assuming that all good art must be classical. Croce shares this view. Those who felt a kinship with the romantic age, mainly in Germany, spoke of "Neuromantik," appealing to Friedrich Schlegel's dictum that all poetry is romantic. Realism also asserted its claim, mainly in Marxist contexts, in which all art is considered "realistic" or at least "a reflection of reality." I need only allude to Georg Lukács' recent *Aesthetik,* in which this thesis is repeated with obsessive urgency. I have counted the phrase "Widerspiegelung der Wirklichkeit" in the first volume; it appears 1,032 times. I was too lazy or bored to count it in Volume Two. All these monisms endanger meaningful schemes of literary periodization. Nor can one be satisfied with a dichotomy such as Fritz Strich's "Klassik und Romantik," which leads away from period concepts into a universal typology, a simple division of the world into sheep and goats. For many years I have argued the advantage of a multiple scheme of periods, since it allows a variety of criteria. The one criterion "realism" would divide all art into realistic and nonrealistic art and thus would allow only one approving adjective: "real" or some variant such as "true" or "lifelike." A multiple scheme comes much closer to the actual variety of the process of history. Period must be conceived neither as some essence which has to be intuited as a Platonic idea nor as a mere arbitrary linguistic label. It should be understood as a "regulative idea," as a system of norms, conventions, and values which can be traced in its rise, spread, and decline, in competition with preceding and following norms, conventions, and values.[4]

"Symbolism" seems the obvious term for the dominant style which followed nineteenth-century realism. It was propounded in Edmund Wilson's *Axel's Castle* (1931) and is asumed as a matter of course in Maurice Bowra's *Heritage of Symbolism* (1943). We must beware, of course, of confusing this historical form with age-old symbolism or with the view that all art is symbolic, as language is a system of symbols. Symbolism in the sense of a use of symbols in literature is clearly omnipresent in literature of many styles, periods, and civilizations. Symbols are all-pervasive in medieval literature and even the classics of realism—Tolstoy and Flaubert, Balzac and Dickens—use symbols, often prominently. I myself am guilty of arguing for the crucial role of symbol in any definition of romanticism, and I have written at length on the long German debate from Goethe to Friedrich Theodor Vischer about the meaning of the term "symbol" and its contrast to the term "allegory."[5]

For our purposes I want to focus on the fortunes of the

4. See my "Periods and Movements in Literary History," in *English Institute Annual, 1940* (New York, 1941), pp. 73–93, and the chapter "Literary History" in my and Austin Warren's *Theory of Literature* (New York, 1949).

5. See my paper "The Concept of Romanticism in Literary History" (1949), in *Concepts of Criticism* (New Haven, 1963), pp. 128–99, and the passages on symbol and allegory in my *History of Modern Criticism* (4 vols. New Haven, 1955–65), e.g. *1,* 210–11; *2,* 41–42, 76, 174–75; *3,* 221–22.

concept as a term, first for a school, then as a movement, and finally as a period. The term "symbolisme" as the designation for a group of poets was first proposed by Jean Moréas, the French poet of Greek extraction. In 1885 he was disturbed by a journalistic attack on the decadents in which he was named together with Mallarmé. He protested: "the so-called decadents seek the pure Concept and the eternal Symbol in their art, before anything else." With some contempt for the mania of critics for labels, he suggested the term "Symbolistes" to replace the inappropriate "décadents."[6] In 1886 Moréas started a review *Le Symboliste,* which perished after four issues. On September 18, 1886, he published a manifesto of "Symbolisme" in the *Figaro.*[7] Moréas, however, soon deserted his own brainchild and founded another school he called the "école romane." On September 14, 1891, in another number of the *Figaro* Moréas blandly announced that "symbolisme" was dead.[8] Thus "symbolisme" was an ephemeral name for a very small clique of French poets. The only name still remembered besides Moréas' is Gustave Kahn. It is easy to collect pronouncements by the main contemporary poets repudiating the term for themselves. Verlaine, in particular, was vehemently resentful of this "Allemandisme" and even wrote a little poem beginning "À bas le symbolisme mythe/ et termite."[9]

6. Paul Bourde in *Le Temps,* Aug. 6, 1885, was the aggressor. See Moréas in *XIXe Siècle:* "Les prétendus décadents cherchent avant tout dans leur art . . . le pur Concept et l'éternel Symbole"; quoted from Guy Michaud, *Message poétique du symbolisme, 2* (3 vols. Paris, 1947), 331.

7. Reprinted in André Barre, *Le Symbolisme* (Paris, 1911), p. 110.

8. Quoted in M. Décaudin, *La Crise des valeurs symbolistes* (Toulouse, 1960), p. 22.

9. See Barre, pp. 160–61. Verlaine's verse in *Invectives* (1896).

In a way which would need detailed tracing, the term, however, caught on in the later 80s and early 90s as a blanket name for recent developments in French poetry and its anticipations. Before Moréas' manifesto, Anatole Baju, in *Décadent,* April 10, 1886, spoke of Mallarmé as "the master who was the first to formulate the symbolic doctrine."[10] Two critics, Charles Morice, with *La Littérature de tout à l'heure* (1889) and Téodore de Wyzéwa, born in Poland, first in the essay "Le Symbolisme de M. Mallarmé" (1887), seemed to have been the main agents, though Morice spoke rather of "synthèse" than of symbol, and Wyzéwa thought that "symbol" was only a pretext and explained Mallarmé's poetry purely by its analogy to music.[11] As early as 1894 Saint Antoine (pseudonym for Henri Mazel) prophesied that "undoubtedly, symbolism will be the label under which our period will be classed in the history of French literature."[12]

It is still a matter of debate in French literary history when this movement came to an end. It was revived several times expressly—e.g. in 1905 around a review, *Vers et prose.* Its main critic, Robert de Souza, in a series of articles, "Où Nous en sommes" (also published separately, 1906), ridiculed the many attempts to bury symbolism as premature and proudly claimed that Gustave Kahn, Verhaeren, Vielé-Griffin, Mae-

10. Michaud, *2,* 335: "Le maître qui a formulé le premier la doctrine symbolique."

11. See ibid., pp. 355 ff.; cf. pp. 427 ff. See also Téodor de Wyzéwa, *Nos Maîtres* (Paris, 1895), pp. 115–29. On Morice see Paul Delsemme, *Un Théoricien du symbolisme: Charles Morice* (Paris, 1958). On Wyzéwa see Elga L. Duval, *Téodor de Wyzéwa: Critic without a Country* (Geneva, 1961).

12. Quoted by Décaudin, p. 15, from *L'Ermitage* (June 1894): "Telle est sans doute l'étiquette sous laquelle notre période sera classée dans l'histoire de la littérature française."

terlinck, and Régnier were then as active as ever.[13] Valéry
professed so complete an allegiance to the ideals of Mallarmé
that it is difficult not to think of him as a continuator of symbolism, though in 1938, on the occasion of the fiftieth anni-
versary of the symbolist manifesto, Valéry doubted the existence of symbolism and denied that there is a symbolist aesthetic.[14] Marcel Proust, in the posthumously published last
volume of his great series *Le Temps retrouvé* (1926), formulated an explicitly symbolist aesthetics. But his own attitude
to symbolist contemporaries was often ambiguous or negative.
In 1896 Proust had written an essay condemning obscurity in
poetry.[15] Proust admired Maeterlinck but disliked Péguy and
Claudel. He even wrote a pastiche of Régnier, a mock-solemn
description of a head cold.[16] When *Le Temps retrouvé* (1926)
was published and when a few years later (1933) Valery
Larbaud proclaimed Proust a symbolist, symbolism had, at
least in French poetry, definitely been replaced by surrealism.[17]

André Barre's book on symbolism (1911) and particularly
Guy Michaud's *Message poétique du symbolisme* (1947), as
well as many other books of French literary scholarship, have,
with the hindsight of literary historians, traced the different
phases of a vast French symbolist movement: the first phase,

13. In *Vers et prose, 1* (mars–avril–mai 1905), 79: "Il me semble
d'abord que l'enterrement du Symbolisme était un peu prématuré.
Craignons les inhumations hâtives."

14. "Existance du symbolisme" (1938), in *Oeuvres, 1,* Pléiade ed.
(Paris, 1957), 686–706.

15. "Contre l'Obscurité," *Revue blanche* (July 15, 1896); reprinted
in *Chroniques*.

16. For details see Walter A. Strauss, *Proust and Literature* (Cambridge, Mass., 1957), pp. 191–93, 204.

17. Preface to Emeric Fiser, *L'Esthétique de Marcel Proust* (Paris,
1933).

with Baudelaire (who died in 1867) as the precursor; the second, when Verlaine and Mallarmé were at the height of their powers, before the 1886 group; the third, when the name became established; and then, in the twentieth century, what Michaud calls "Néo-symbolisme," represented by "La Jeune Parque" of Valéry and *L'Annonce faite à Marie* of Claudel, both dating from 1915.[18] It seems a coherent and convincing conception which needs to be extended to prose writers and dramatists: to Huysmans after *A Rebours* (1884), to the early Gide, to Proust in part, and among dramatists, at least to Maeterlinck, who, with his plays *L'Intruse* and *Les Aveugles* (1890) and *Pelléas et Mélisande* (1892), assured a limited penetration of symbolism on the stage.

Knowledge of the French movement and admiration for it soon spread to the other European countries. We must, however, distinguish between reporting on French events and even admiration shown by translations, and a genuine transfer and assimilation of the French movement in another literature. This process varies considerably from country to country; and the variation needs to be explained by the different traditions which the French importation confronted.

In English, George Moore's *Confessions of a Young Man* (1888) and his *Impressions and Opinions* (1891) gave sketchy and often poorly informed accounts of Verlaine, Mallarmé, Rimbaud, and Laforgue. Mallarmé's poetry is dismissed as "aberrations of a refined mind," and symbolism is oddly defined as "saying the opposite of what you mean." The three essays on Mallarmé by Edmund Gosse, all dating from 1893, are hardly more perceptive. After the poet's death Gosse turned sharply against him. "Now that he is no longer here the truth must be said about Mallarmé. He was hardly a poet."

18. See also Michaud's paper "Symbolique et symbolisme," *Cahiers de l'Association Internationale des Etudes Françaises*, 6 (1954), 75 ff.

Even Arthur Symons, whose book *The Symbolist Movement in Literature* (1899) made the decisive breakthrough for England and Ireland, was very lukewarm at first. While praising Verlaine (in *Academy,* 1891) he referred to the "brain-sick little school of *Symbolistes*" and "the noisy little school of *Décadents,*" and even in later articles on Mallarmé he complained of "jargon and meaningless riddles."[19] But then he turned around and produced the entirely favorable *Symbolist Movement.* It should not, however, be overrated as literary criticism or history. It is a rather lame impressionistic account of Nerval, Villiers de l'Isle-Adam, Rimbaud, Verlaine, Laforgue, Mallarmé, Huysmans, and Maeterlinck, with emphasis on Verlaine. There is no chapter on Baudelaire.[20] But most importantly, the book was dedicated to W. B. Yeats, proclaiming him "the chief representative of that movement in our country." Symons had made his first trip to Paris in 1889; he had visited Mallarmé, met Huysmans and Maeterlinck, and a year later met Verlaine, who in 1893 became his guest on his ill-fated visit to London. Symons knew Yeats vaguely since 1891, but they became close friends in 1895 only after Yeats had completed his study of Blake and had elaborated his own system of symbols from other sources: occultism, Blake, and Irish folklore. The edition of Blake Yeats had prepared with Edwin Ellis in 1893 was introduced by an essay on "The Necessity of Symbolism." In 1894 Yeats visited Paris in the company of Symons and there saw a performance of Villiers de l'Isle-Adam's *Axël.*[21] The essay "The

19. For references see Bruce Morrissette, "Early English and American Critics of French Symbolism," in *Studies in Honor of Frederick W. Shipley* (St. Louis, 1942), pp. 159–80.

20. A chapter on Baudelaire was added to the expanded edition in 1919.

21. See Richard Ellmann's Introduction to the 1958 New York reprint of *The Symbolist Movement.* On Symons see Roger Lhom-

Symbolism of Poetry" (1900) is then Yeats' first full statement of his symbolist creed.[22] Symons' dedication to Yeats shows an awareness of symbolism as an international movement. "In Germany," he says, exaggerating greatly, "it seems to be permeating the whole of literature, its spirit is that which is deepest in Ibsen, it has absorbed the one new force in Italy, Gabriele D'Annunzio. I am told of a group of symbolists in Russian literature, there is another in Dutch literature, in Portugal it has a little school of its own under Eugenio de Castro. I even saw some faint stirrings that way in Spain."

Symons should have added the United States. Or could he in 1899? There were intelligent and sympathetic reports of the French movement very early. T. S. Perry wrote on "The Latest Literary Fashion in France" in *The Cosmopolitan* (1892), T. Child on "Literary Paris—The New Poetry" in *Harper's* (1896), and Aline Gorren on "The French Symbolists" in *Scribner's* (1893). The almost forgotten Vance Thompson, who, fresh from Paris, edited the oddly named review *M'lle New York,* wrote several perceptive essays, mainly on Mallarmé in 1895 (reprinted in *French Portraits,* 1900) which convey some accurate information on his theories and even attempt an explication of his poetry with some success.[23] But only James Huneker became the main importer of recent French literature into the United States. In 1896 he defended the French symbolists against the slurs in Max Nordau's silly *Entartung* and began to write a long series of articles on Maeterlinck, Laforgue, and many others, not

---

breaud, *Arthur Symons, A Critical Biography* (London, 1963), and Ruth Zabriskie Temple, *The Critic's Alchemy: A Study of the Introduction of French Symbolism into England* (New Haven, 1953).

22. Reprinted in *Ideas of Good and Evil* (1903); then in *Essays and Introductions* (New York, 1961), pp. 153–64.

23. Cf. Morrissette's paper quoted above, n. 19.

bothering to conceal his dependence on his French master, Remy de Gourmont, to whom he dedicated his book of essays *Visionaries* (1905).[24] But the actual impact of French symbolist poetry on American writing was greatly delayed. René Taupin, in his *L'Influence du symbolisme français sur la poésie américaine* (1929), traced some echoes in forgotten American versifiers of the turn of the century, but only two Americans living then in England, Ezra Pound around 1908 and T. S. Eliot around 1914, reflect the French influence in significant poetry.

More recently and in retrospect one hears of a symbolist period in American literature: Hart Crane and Wallace Stevens are its main poets; Henry James, Faulkner, and O'Neill, in very different ways and in different stages of their career, show marked affinities with its techniques and outlook. Edmund Wilson's *Axel's Castle* (1931) was apparently the very first book which definitely conceived of symbolism as an international movement and singled out Yeats, Joyce, Eliot, Gertrude Stein, Valéry, Proust, and Thomas Mann as examples of a movement which, he believed, had come to an end at the time of his writing. Here we find the conception formulated which, very generally, is the thesis of this paper and the assumption of many historians since Wilson's sketch. Wilson's sources were the writings of Huneker, whom he admired greatly, and the instruction in French literature he received in Princeton from Christian Gauss.[25] But the insight into the unity and continuity of the international movement and the selection of the great names was his own. We might

24. See Arnold T. Schwab, *J. G. Huneker, Critic of the Seven Arts* (Stanford, 1963).

25. On Huneker see Edmund Wilson, *Classics and Commercials* (New York, 1950), p. 114, and his *The Shores of Light* (New York, 1952), p. 73. On Gauss see the essay introducing that volume.

only deplore the inclusion of Gertrude Stein. But I find it difficult to believe that Wilson's book could have had any influence outside the English-speaking world.

In the United States Wilson's reasonable and moderate plea for an international movement was soon displaced by attempts to make the whole of the American literary tradition symbolist. F. O. Matthiessen's *The American Renaissance* (1941) is based on a distinction between symbol and allegory very much in the terms of the distinction introduced by Goethe. Allegory appears as inferior to symbol: Hawthorne inferior to Melville. But in Charles Feidelson's *Symbolism and American Literature* (1956) the distinction between modern symbolism and the use of symbols by romantic authors is completely obliterated. Emerson, Hawthorne, Poe, Melville, and Whitman appear as pure symbolists *avant la lettre,* and their ancestry is traced back to the Puritans, who paradoxically appear as incomplete, frustrated symbolists. It can be rightly objected that the old Puritans were sharply inimical to images and symbols and that there is a gulf between the religious conception of signs of God's Providence and the aesthetic use of symbols in the novels of Hawthorne and Melville and even in the Platonizing aesthetics of Emerson.[26]

The symbolist conception of American literature is still prevalent today. It owes its dominance to the attempt to exalt the great American writers to myth-makers and providers of a substitute religion. James Baird, in *Ishmael* (1956), puts it unabashedly. Melville is "the supreme example of the artistic creator engaged in the act of making new symbols to replace the 'lost' symbols of Protestant Christianity."[27] A very active trend in American criticism expanded symbolist interpreta-

26. Cf. Ursula Brumm, *Die religiöse Typologie im amerikanischen Denken* (Leiden, 1963), e.g. pp. 81 ff.

27. Baltimore, 1956, p. xv.

tion to all types and periods of literature, imposing it on writings which have no such meaning or have to be twisted to assume it. Harry Levin rightly complained in an address, "Symbolism and Fiction" (1956), that "every hero may seem to have a thousand faces; every heroine may be a white goddess *incognita;* and every fishing trip turns out to be another quest for the Holy Grail."[28] The impact of ideas from the Cambridge anthropologists and from Carl Jung is obvious. In the study of medieval texts a renewed interest in the fourfold levels of meaning in Dante's letter to Can Grande has persuaded a whole group of American scholars, mainly under the influence of D. W. Robertson, to interpret or misinterpret Chaucer, the *Pearl* poet, and Langland in these terms.[29] They should bear in mind that Thomas Aquinas recognized only a literal sense in a work invented by human industry and that he reserved the other three senses for Scripture.[30] The symbolist interpretation reaches heights of ingenuity in the writing of Northrop Frye, who began with a book on Blake and, in *The Anatomy of Criticism* (1957), conceived of the whole of literature as a self-enclosed system of symbols and myths, "existing in its own universe, no longer a commentary on life or reality, but containing life and reality in a system of verbal relationships." In this grandiose conception all distinctions between periods and styles are abolished: "the literary

28. *Contexts of Criticism* (Cambridge, Mass., 1957), p. 207.

29. I allude particularly to D. W. Robertson, *A Preface to Chaucer* (Princeton, 1963), and D. W. Robertson and B. F. Huppé, *Piers Plowman and Scriptural Tradition* (Princeton, 1951).

30. Cf. Morton W. Bloomfield, "Symbolism in Medieval Literature," *Modern Philology, 56* (1958), 73–81. He quotes Thomas Aquinas, *Questiones quodlibetales,* VII.a.16: "Unde in nulla scientia, humana industria inventa, proprio loquendo, potest inveniri nisi litteralis sensus; sed solum in ista Scriptura, cujus Spiritus sanctus est auctor, homo verum instrumentum."

universe is a universe in which everything is potentially identical with everything else."[31] Hence the old distinctions between myth, symbol, and allegory disappear. One of Frye's followers, Angus Fletcher, in his book on *Allegory* (1964), exalts allegory as the central procedure of art, while Frye still holds fast to symbolism, recognizing that "the critics are often prejudiced against allegory without knowing the real reason, which is that continuous allegory prescribes the direction of his commentary, and so restricts his freedom."[32]

The story of the spread of symbolism is very different in other countries. The effect in Italy was ostensibly rather small. Soffici's pamphlet on Rimbaud in 1911 is usually considered the beginning of the French symbolist influence, but there was an early propagandist for Mallarmé, Vittorio Pica, who was heavily dependent on French sources, particularly Téodor de Wyzéwa. His articles, in the *Gazetta letteraria* (1885–86), on the French poets do not use the term; but in 1896 he replaced "decadent" and "Byzantine" by "symbolist."[33] D'Annunzio, who knew and used some French symbolists, would be classed as "decadent" today, and the poets around Ungaretti and Montale as "hermetic." In a recent book by Mario Luzi, *L'Idea simbolista* (1959), Pascoli, Dino Campana, and Arturo Onofri are called symbolist poets, but Luzi uses the term so widely that he begins his anthology of symbolism with Hölderlin and Novalis, Coleridge and Wordsworth, and can include Poe, Browning,

31. Princeton, 1957, pp. 122, 124.
32. Ibid., p. 90.
33. See Olga Ragusa, "Vittorio Pica: First Champion of French Symbolism in Italy," *Italica, 35* (1958), 255–61, and Luigi de Nardis, "Prospettive critiche per uno studio su Vittorio Pica e il decadentismo francese," *Rivista di letterature moderne e comparate, 19* (1966) 202–09.

Patmore, Swinburne, Hopkins, and Francis Thompson among its precursors. Still, his list of symbolist poets, French, Russian, English, German, Spanish, and Greek, is, on the whole, reasonable.[34] Onofri was certainly strongly influenced by Mallarmé and later by Rudolf Steiner; Pascoli, however, seems to me no symbolist in his poetry, though he gave extremely symbolist interpretations of Dante.[35] It might be wiser to think of "ermetismo" as the Italian name for symbolism: Montale and possibly Dino Campana are genuine symbolists.

While symbolism, at least as a definite school or movement, was absent in Italy, it is central in the history of Spanish poetry. The Nicaraguan poet Rubén Darío initiated it after his short stay in Paris in 1892. He wrote poems under the symbolist influence and addressed, for instance, a fervent hymn to Verlaine.[36] The influence of French symbolist poetry changed completely the oratorical or popular style of Spanish lyrical poetry. The closeness of Guillén to Mallarmé and Valéry seems too obvious to deny, and the Uruguayan poet Julio Herrera y Reissig (1873–1909) is clearly in the symbolist tradition, often of the obscurest manner.[37] Still, the Spanish critics favor the term "Modernismo," which is used sometimes so inclusively that it covers all modern Spanish poetry and even the so-called "generation of 1898," the

34. Milano, 1959. Luzi lists, besides the French, Bryusov, Balmont, Ivanov, Blok; Yeats, Eliot; George, Hofmannsthal, Rilke, Benn; Pascoli, D'Annunzio, Onofri, Campana; Darío, Antonio Machado, Jiménez; and the Greek Chantzopulos.

35. Pascoli, *Minerva oscura* (1898), in *Conferenze e studi dantesche* (1921), etc.

36. "Verlaine: Responso," beginning "Padre y maestro mágico, liríforo celeste." On Darío see E. K. Mapes, *L'Influence française dans l'œuvre de Rubén Darío* (Paris, 1925).

37. Cf. Bernard Gicovate, *Julio Herrera y Reissig* (Berkeley, 1957).

prose writers Azorín, Baroja, and Unamuno, whose associations with symbolism were quite tenuous.[38] "Symbolism" can apply only to one trend in modern Spanish literature, as the romantic popular tradition was stronger there than elsewhere. García Lorca's poetry can serve as the best known example of the peculiar Spanish synthesis of the folksy and the symbolical, the gypsy song and the myth. Still, the continuity from Darío to Jiménez, Antonio Machado, Alberti, and then to Guillén seems to me evident. Jorge Guillén in his Harvard lectures, *Language and Poetry* (1961), finds "no label convincing." "A period look," he argues, does not signify a "group style." In Spain there were, he thinks, fewer "isms" than elsewhere and the break with the past was far less abrupt. He reflects that "any name seeking to give unity to a historical period is the invention of posterity." But while eschewing the term "symbolism," he characterizes himself and his contemporaries well enough by expounding their common creed: their belief in the marriage of Idea and music —in short, their belief in the ideal of Mallarmé.[39] Following a vague suggestion made by Remy de Gourmont, the rediscovery of Góngora by Ortega y Gasset, Gerardo Diego, Dámaso Alonso, and Alfonso Reyes around 1927 fits into the picture: they couple Góngora and Mallarmé as the two poets who in the history of all poetry have gone furthest in the search for absolute poetry, for the quintessence of the poetic.[40]

38. See Gustav Siebenmann, *Die moderne Lyrik in Spanien* (Stuttgart, 1965), esp. pp. 43 ff., and Guillermo Díaz-Plaja, *Modernismo frente a Noventa y Ocho* (Madrid, 1961).

39. Cambridge, Mass., 1961, p. 214.

40. Remy de Gourmont, *Promenades littéraires*, IVe série (Paris, 1912). Dámaso Alonso, *Góngora y la literatura contemporánea* (Santander, 1932); also in *Estudios y ensayos gongorinos* (Madrid, 1955).

In Germany the spread of symbolism was far less complete than Symons assumed in 1899. Stefan George had come to Paris in 1889, had visited Mallarmé and met many poets, but after his return to Germany he avoided, I assume deliberately, the term "symbolism" for himself and his circle. He translated a selection from Baudelaire (1891) and smaller samples from Mallarmé, Verlaine, and Régnier (in *Zeitgenössische Dichter,* 1905), but his own poetry does not, I think, show very close parallels to the French masters. Oddly enough, the poems of Vielé-Griffin seem to have left the most clearly discernible traces on George's own writings.[41] As early as 1892 one of George's adherents, Carl August Klein, protested in George's periodical, *Blätter für die Kunst,* against the view of George's dependence on the French. Wagner, Nietzsche, Böcklin, and Klinger, he says, show that there is an indigenous opposition to naturalism in Germany as everywhere in the West.[42] George himself spoke later of the French poets as his "former allies," and in Gundolf's authoritative book on George the French influence is minimized, if not completely denied.[43] Among the theorists of the George circle Friedrich Gundolf had the strongest symbolist leanings: *Shakespeare und der deutsche Geist* (1911) and

41. See B. Böschenstein, "Wirkungen des französischen Symbolismus auf die deutsche Lyrik der Jahrhundertwende," *Euphorion, 58* (1964), 375–95. Werner Vordtriede, in "Direct Echoes of French Poetry in Stefan George's Works," *Modern Language Notes, 60* (1945), 461–68, lists trivial parallels to Baudelaire and Mallarmé. More in Claude David, *Stefan George. Son Oeuvre poétique* (Paris, 1952).

42. *Blätter für die Kunst, 1,* No. 2, "Über Stefan George, eine neue Kunst"; reprinted in *Die Sendung Stefan Georges* (Berlin, 1935), pp. 69–70.

43. "Stern des Bundes," quoted in David, p. 285, Friedrich Gundolf, *George* (Berlin, 1920), pp. 50–51.

*Goethe* (1916) are based on the distinction of symbol-allegory, with symbol always the higher term.[44] Still, the term symbolism did not catch on in Germany as a name for any specific group, though Hofmannsthal—e.g. in "Das Gespräch über Gedichte" of 1903—proclaimed the symbol the one element necessary in poetry.[45] Later, the influence of Rimbaud—apparently largely in German translation—on Georg Trakl has been demonstrated with certainty.[46] But if we examine German books on twentieth-century literature, symbolism seems rarely used. I found a section so called in Willi Duwe's *Die Dichtung des 20. Jahrhunderts* (1936) which includes Hofmannsthal, Dauthendey, Calé, Rilke, and George, while E. H. Lüth's *Literatur als Geschichte (Deutsche Dichtung von 1885 bis 1947)*, published in 1947, treats the same poets under the label "Neuromantik und Impressionismus." Later, however, we find a section, "Parasymbolismus," which deals with Musil and Broch. Hugo Friedrich, in his *Struktur der modernen Lyrik* (1956), avoids the terms and argues that the quick succession of modernist styles—dadaism, surrealism, futurism, expressionism, unanimism, hermetism, and so on—creates an optical illusion which hides the fact of a direct continuity through Mallarmé, Valéry, Guillén, Ungaretti, and Eliot.[47] The little anthology in the back of the book adds St. John Perse, Jiménez, García Lorca, Alberti, and Montale to these names. Friedrich's list seems to

44. See *Shakespeare und der deutsche Geist* (Berlin, 1914), pp. 1–2, for the distinction of symbol-allegory; and *Goethe* (Berlin, 1916), pp. 16, 28, for classification of Goethe's works.

45. *Prosa II*, 104.

46. See Böschenstein, above, n. 41, and Herbert Lindenberger, "Georg Trakl and Rimbaud," *Comparative Literature, 10* (1958), 21–35. Trakl read the translation by K. L. Ammer (pseudonym of Karl Klammer) published in 1907.

47. Hamburg, 1956, p. 108.

me the list of the main symbolist poets, even though Friedrich objects to the name. Clearly, German literary scholarship has not been converted to the term, though Wolfgang Kayser's article "Der europäische Symbolismus" (1953) had pleaded for a wide concept in which he included, in addition to the French poets, D'Annunzio, Yeats, Valéry, Proust, Virginia Woolf, and Faulkner.[48]

In Russia we find the strongest symbolist group of poets who called themselves that. The close links with Paris at that time may help to explain this, or possibly also the strong consciousness of a tradition of symbolism in the Russian Church and in some of the Orthodox thinkers of the immediate past. Vladimir Solovëv was regarded as a precursor. In 1892 Zinaida Vengerova wrote a sympathetic account of the French symbolists for *Vestnik Evropy*,[49] while in the following year Max Nordau's *Entartung* caused a sensation by its satirical account of recent French poetry which had repercussions on Tolstoy's *What is Art?*, as late as 1898. Bryusov emerged as the leading symbolist poet: he translated Maeterlinck's *L'Intruse* and wrote a poem "Iz Rimbaud" as early as 1892.[50] In 1894 he published two little volumes under the title *Russkie simvolisty*. That year Bryusov wrote poems with titles such as "In the Spirit of the French Symbolists" and "In the Manner of Stéphane Mallarmé" (though these were not published till 1935) and brought out a translation of Verlaine's *Romances sans paroles*.[51] Bryusov had later contacts with René Ghil, Mallarmé's pupil, and derived

48. In *Die Vortragsreise*, Bern, 1958, pp. 287–304.

49. Vol. 9 (1882), 115–43; reprinted in *Literaturnye Kharakteristiki* (St. Petersburg, 1897).

50. Cf. G. Donchin, *The Influence of French Symbolism on Russian Poetry* (The Hague, 1958), p. 23.

51. In *Neizdannye stikhotvoreniya* (Moscow, 1935), pp. 426, 428.

from him the idea of "instrumentation" in poetry which was to play such a great role in the theories of the Russian Formalists.[52] In the meantime Dimitri Merezhkovsky had, in 1893, published a manifesto: *On the Causes of the Decline and the New Trends of Contemporary Russian Literature,* which recommended symbolism, though Merezhkovsky appealed to the Germans: to Goethe and the romantics rather than to the French.[53] Merezhkovsky's pamphlet foreshadows the split in the Russian symbolist movement. The younger men, Blok and Vyacheslav Ivanov as well as Bely, distanced themselves from Bryusov and Balmont. Blok, in an early diary (1901–02), condemned Bryusov as decadent and opposed to his Parisian symbolism his own, Russian, rooted in the poetry of Tyutchev, Fet, Polonsky, and Solovëv.[54] Vyacheslav Ivanov in 1910 shared Blok's view. The French influence seemed to him "adolescently unreasonable and, in fact, not very fertile," while his own symbolism appealed to Russian nationalism and to the general mystical tradition.[55] Later Bely was to add occultism and Rudolf Steiner and his "anthroposophy." The group of poets who called themselves "Acmeists" (Gumilëv, Anna Akhmatova, Osip Mandelshtam) was a direct outgrowth of symbolism.[56] The mere

52. See *Lettres de René Ghil* (Paris, 1935), pp. 13–16, 18–20, and Ghil's *Traité du verbe* (Paris, 1886).

53. *O prichinakh upadka i o novykh techenyakh sovremennoy russkoy literatury* (St. Petersburg, 1893).

54. "Yunocheski dnevnik Aleksandra Bloka" (1901–02), *Literaturnoe Nasledstvo, 27–28* (1937), 302.

55. "Zavety simvolizma," *Apollon, 8* (1901), 13, and in *Borozdy i mezhi* (Moscow, 1916), p. 133.

56. For a good discussion see Jurij Striedter, "Transparenz und Verfremdung: Zur Theorie des poetischen Bildes in der russischen Moderne," in *Immanente Aesthetik: Aesthetische Reflexion,* ed. Wolfgang Iser (Munich, 1966), pp. 263–89.

fact that they appealed to the early symbolist Innokenty Annensky shows the continuity with symbolism in spite of their distaste for the occult and their emphasis on what they thought of as classical clarity. Symbolism dominates Russian poetry between about 1892 and 1914, when Futurism emerged as a slogan and the Russian Formalists attacked the whole concept of poetry as imagery.

If we glance at the other Slavic countries we are struck by the diversity of their reactions. Poland was informed early on about the French movement, and Polish poetry was influenced by the French symbolist movement, but the term "Młoda Polska" was preferred. In Wilhelm Feldmann's *Współczesna literatura polska* (1905) contemporary poetry is discussed as "decadentism," but Wyspiański (a symbolist if ever there was one) appears under the chapter heading: "On the Heights of Romanticism."[57] All the histories of Polish literature I have seen speak of "Modernism," "Decadentism," "Idealism," "Neo-romanticism," and occasionally call a poet such as Miriam (Zenon Przesmycki) a symbolist, but they never seem to use the term as a general name for a period in Polish literature.[58]

In Czech literature the situation was more like that in Russia: Březina, Sova, and Hlaváček were called symbolists, and the idea of a school or at least a group of Czech symbolist poets is firmly established. The term "Moderna" (possibly

57. In vol. 3: "Na wyżynach romantyzmu."
58. Zenon Przesmycki had written an essay on Maeterlinck in 1891 (in *Świat*). More in Henryk Markiewicz, "Młoda Polska i 'izmy,' " in *Z Problemów literatury polskiej XX wieku, 1* (Warsaw, 1965), pp. 7–51, esp. 15; Teofil Wojeński, *Historia literatury polskiej* (Warsaw, 1946), has chapters "Symbolizm" and "Neoromantyzm w Polsce"; Julian Krzyżanowski, *Neoromantyzm Polski, 1890–1918* (Wrocław-Warsaw, 1963), has a chapter "Drama naturalistyczno-symboliczny" (pp. 182 ff.).

because of the periodical *Moderní Revue,* founded in 1894) is definitely associated with decadentism, *fin de siècle,* a group represented by Arnošt Procházka. A hymnical, optimistic, even chiliastic poet such as Březina cannot and could not be classed with them. The great critic F. X. Šalda wrote of the "school of symbolists" as early as 1891, calling Verlaine, Villiers, and Mallarmé its masters but denied that there is a school of symbolists with dogmas, codices, and mani- festoes.[59] His very first important article, "Synthetism in the New Art" (1892), expounded the aesthetics of Morice and Hennequin for the benefit of the Czechs, then still mainly de- pendent on German models.[60]

The unevenness of the penetration of both the influence of the French movement and very strikingly of the acceptance of the term raises the question whether we can account for these differences in causal terms. It sounds heretical or ob- scurantist in this age of scientific explanation to ascribe much to chance, to casual contacts, and to personal predilections. Why was the term so immensely successful in France, in the United States, and in Russia, less so in England and Spain, and hardly at all in Italy and Germany? In Germany there was even the tradition of the continuous debate about sym- bol since Goethe and Schelling; before the French movement Friedrich Theodor Vischer discussed the symbol elaborately and still the term did not catch on.[61] One can think of all

59. In "O škole symbolistů," in *Kritické projevy, 1* (Prague, 1947), 185–86; originally as "Zasláno," *Literární listy, 13* (1891), 46–48, 65–66, 85–86. See J. Pistorius, *Bibliografie díla F. X. Šaldy* (Prague, 1948), p. 79.

60. "Syntetism v novém unmění," originally in *Literární listy* (1891–92). See a brief discussion in my "Modern Czech Criticism and Literary Scholarship," in *Essays on Czech Literature* (The Hague, 1963), pp. 179–80.

61. "Das Symbol" (1887), *Altes und Neues. Neue Folge* (1889).

kinds of explanations: a deliberate decision by the poets to distance themselves from the French developments; or the success of the terms "Die Moderne" and "Neuromantik." Still, the very number of such explanations suggests that the variables are so great that we cannot account for these divergencies in any systematic manner.

If we, at long last, turn to the central question of what the exact content of the term is, we must obviously distinguish among the four concentric circles defining its scope. At its narrowest, "symbolism" refers to the French group which called itself "symbolist" in 1886. Its theory was rather rudimentary. These poets mainly wanted poetry to be non-rhetorical—i.e. they asked for a break with the tradition of Hugo and the *Parnassiens*. They wanted words not merely to state but to suggest; they wanted to use metaphors, allegories, and symbols not only as decorations but as organizing principles of their poems; they wanted their verse to be "musical," in practice to stop using the oratorical cadences of the French alexandrines, and in some cases to break completely with rhyme. Free verse—whose invention is usually ascribed to Gustave Kahn—was possibly the most enduring achievement which has survived all vicissitudes of style. Kahn himself in 1894 summed up the doctrine simply as "antinaturalism, antiprosaism in poetry, a search for freedom in the efforts in art, in reaction against the regimentation of the *Parnasse* and the naturalists."[62] This sounds very meager today: freedom from restrictions has been, after all, the slogan of a great many movements in art.

It is better to think of "symbolism" in a wider sense: as

62. Quoted by Décaudin, *La Crise*, p. 15, from *La Société nouvelle* (avril 1894). "Anti-naturalisme, anti-prosaïsme de la poésie, recherche de la liberté dans les efforts dans l'art, en réaction contre l'enrégimentation parnassienne ou naturaliste."

the broad movement in France from Nerval and Baudelaire to Claudel and Valéry. We can restate the theories propounded and will be confronted by an enormous variety. We can characterize it more concretely and say, for example, that in symbolist poetry the image becomes "thing." The relation of tenor and vehicle in the metaphor is reversed. The utterance is divorced, we may add, from the situation: time and place, history and society, are played down. The inner world, the *durée,* in the Bergsonian sense, is represented or often merely hinted at as "it," the thing or the person hidden. One could say that the grammatical predicate has become the subject. Clearly such poetry can easily be justified by an occult view of the world. But this is not necessary: it might imply a feeling for analogy, for a web of correspondences, a rhetoric of metamorphoses in which everything reflects everything else. Hence the great role of synesthesia, which, though rooted in physiological facts and found all over the history of poetry, became at that time merely a stylistic device, a mannerism easily imitated and transmitted.[63] This characterization could be elaborated considerably if we bear in mind that style and world view go together and only together can define the character of a period or even of a single poet.

Let me try to show, at least, how diverse and even incompatible were the theories of two such related poets as Baudelaire and Mallarmé. Baudelaire's aesthetic is mainly "romantic," not in the sense of emotionalism, nature worship, and exaltation of the ego, central in French romanticism, but rather in the English and German tradition of a glorification

63. See the many articles by Albert Wellek, e.g. "Das Doppelempfinden in der Geistesgeschichte," *Zeitschrift für Aesthetik, 23* (1929), 14–32; "Das Doppelempfinden im 18. Jahrhundert," *Deutsche Vierteljahrschrift für Literaturwissenschaft und Geistesgeschichte, 14* (1936), 75–102.

of creative imagination, a rhetoric of metamorphoses and universal analogy. Though there are subsidiary strands in Baudelaire's aesthetics, at his finest he grasps the role of imagination, "constructive imagination," as he calls it in a term ultimately derived from Coleridge.[64] It gives a metaphysical meaning, "a positive relation with the infinite."[65] Art is another cosmos which transforms and hence humanizes nature. By his creation the artist abolishes the gulf between subject and object, man and nature. Art is "to create a suggestive magic containing at one and the same time the object and the subject, the external world and the artist himself."[66]

Mallarmé says almost the opposite in spite of some superficial resemblances and the common attachment to Poe and Wagner. Mallarmé was the first poet radically discontent with the ordinary language of communication; he attempted to construe an entirely separate language of poetry far more consistently than older cultivators of "poetic diction" such as the practitioners of *trobar clus,* or Góngora, or Mallarmé's contemporary, Gerard Manley Hopkins. His aim of transforming language was, no doubt, in part negative: to exclude society, nature, and the person of the poet himself. But it was also positive: language was again to become "real," language was to be magic, words were to become things. But this is not, I think, sufficient reason to call Mallarmé a mystic. Even the depersonalization he requires is not mystical. Impersonality is rather objectivity, Truth. Art reaches for the

64. "Constructive imagination," quoted in English from Catherine Crowe, *The Night Side of Nature,* in *Curiosités esthétiques,* Conard ed. (Paris, 1923), p. 279.

65. Ibid., p. 275: "Elle est positivement apparentée avec l'infini."

66. *L'Art romantique,* Conard ed. (Paris, 1925), p. 119: "C'est créer une magie suggestive contenant à la fois l'objet et le subjet, le monde extérieur à l'artiste et l'artiste lui-même."

Idea, which is ultimately inexpressible, because so abstract and general as to be devoid of any concrete traits. The term "flower" seems to him poetic because it suggests the "one, absent from all bouquets."[67] Art thus can only hint and suggest, not transform as it should in Baudelaire. The "symbol" is only one device to achieve this effect. The so-called "negative" aesthetics of Mallarmé is thus nothing obscure. It had its psychological basis in a feeling of sterility, impotence, and final silence. He was a perfectionist who proposed something impossible of fulfillment: the book to end all books. "Everything on earth exists to be contained in a book."[68] Like many poets before him, Mallarmé wants to express the mystery of the universe but feels that this mystery is not only insoluble and immensely dark but also hollow, empty, silent, Nothingness itself. There seems no need to appeal to Buddhism, Hegel, Schopenhauer, or Wagner to account for this.[69] The atmosphere of nineteenth-century pessimism and the general Neoplatonic tradition in aesthetics suffice. Art searches for the Absolute but despairs of ever reaching it. The essence of the world is Nothingness, and the poet can only speak of this Nothingness. Art alone survives in the

67. *Oeuvres complètes,* Pléiade ed. (Paris, 1949), p. 368: "une fleur . . . l'absente de tous bouquets."

68. Ibid., p. 378: "Tout, au monde, existe pour aboutir à un livre."

69. Jacques Scherer, in *L'Expression littéraire dans l'œuvre de Mallarmé* (Paris, 1947), pp. 155 ff., collects evidence for Mallarmé's contacts with Platonism and occultism. Mallarmé denied knowledge of Buddhism in *Propos sur la poésie,* ed. H. Mondor (Monaco, 1946), p. 59. Hasye Cooperman, in *The Aesthetic of Stéphane Mallarmé* (New York, 1933), makes much of the influence of Wagner. The only evidence of concern for Hegel is a letter of Villiers de l'Isle-Adam to Mallarmé, quoted in Henri Mondor, *Vie de Mallarmé* (Paris, 1941), p. 222: "Quant à Hegel, je suis vraiment bien heureux que vous ayez accordé quelque attention à ce miraculeux génie."

universe. Man's main vocation is to be an artist, a poet, who can save something from the general wreckage of time. The work or, in Mallarmé's terms, the Book is suspended over the Void, the silent godless Nothingness. Poetry is resolutely cut off from concrete reality, from the expression of the personality of the poet, from any rhetoric or emotion, and becomes only a Sign, signifying Nothing.[70] In Baudelaire, on the other hand, poetry transforms nature, extracts flowers from evil, creates a new myth, reconciles man and nature.

But if we examine the actual verse of the symbolists of this period, we cannot be content with formulas either of creative imagination, of suggestion, or of pure or absolute poetry.

On the third wider circle of abstraction we can apply the term to the whole period on an international scale. Every such term is arbitrary, but symbolism can be defended as rooted in the concepts of the period, as distinct in meaning, and as clearly setting off the period from that preceding it: realism or naturalism. The difference from romanticism may be less certainly implied. Obviously there is a continuity with romanticism, and particularly German romanticism, also in France, as has been recently argued again by Werner Vordtriede in his *Novalis und die französischen Symbolisten* (1963).[71] The direct contact of the French with the German romantics came late and should not be overrated. Jean Thorel, in "Les Romantiques allemandes et les symbolistes français," seems to have been the first to point out the relation.[72] Maeterlinck's article on Novalis (1894) and his little anthol-

70. See Guy Defel, *L'Esthétique de Stéphane Mallarmé* (Paris, 1951).
71. Stuttgart, 1963.
72. In *Entretiens politiques et littéraires* (Sept. 1891).

ogy (1896) came late in the movement.[73] But Wagner of course mediated between the symbolists and German mythology, though Mallarmé's attitude, admiring toward the music, was tinged with irony for Wagner's subject matter.[74] Early in the century Heine, a *romantique défroqué* as he called himself, played the role of an intermediary which, to my mind, has been exaggerated in Kurt Weinberg's study, *Henri Heine: Héraut du symbolisme français* (1954).[75] E. T. A. Hoffmann, we should not forget, was widely translated into French and could supply occult motifs, a transcendental view of music, and the theory and practice of synesthesia.

Possibly even more important were the indirect contacts through English writers: through Carlyle's chapter on symbolism in *Sartor Resartus* and his essay on Novalis; through Coleridge, from whom, through another intermediary, Mrs. Crowe, Baudelaire drew his definition of creative imagination; and through Emerson, who was translated by Edgar Quinet.[76]

Also, French thinkers of the early nineteenth century knew the theory of symbolism at least, from the wide application to all the religions of the world made by Creuzer, whose *Symbolik* was translated into French in 1825.[77] Pierre Le-

73. In *La Nouvelle Revue* (1894) and *Les Disciples à Saïs, suivi de fragments* (Bruxelles, 1895). The article on Novalis is included in *Le Trésor des humbles* (1896).

74. Cf. his "Richard Wagner: Rêverie d'un poète français" (1885), *Oeuvres*, pp. 541–45.

75. New Haven, 1954.

76. A. G. Lehmann, in *The Symbolist Aesthetic in France, 1885–1895* (Oxford, 1950), makes good suggestions.

77. Friedrich Creuzer, *Symbolik und Mythologie der alten Völker* (1810), appeared as *Religions de l'antiquité considerées dans leurs formes symbolistes,* translated by J. D. Guigniaut in 1825.

roux used the idea of "symbolic poetry" prominently in the early thirties.[78] There was Edgar Allan Poe, who drew on Coleridge and A. W. Schlegel and seemed so closely to anticipate Baudelaire's views that Baudelaire quoted him as if he were Poe himself, sometimes dropping all quotations marks.[79]

The enormous influence of Poe on the French demonstrates, however, most clearly the difference between romanticism and symbolism. Poe is far from being a representative of the romantic world-view or of the romantic aesthetic, in which the imagination is conceived as transforming nature. Poe has been aptly described as an "angel in a machine": he combines a faith in technique and even technology, a distrust of inspiration, a rationalistic eighteenth-century mind with a vague occult belief in "supernal" beauty.[80] The distrust of inspiration, an enmity to nature, is the crucial point which sets off symbolism from romanticism. Baudelaire, Mallarmé, and Valéry all share it; while Rilke, a symbolist in many of his procedures and views, appears as highly romantic in his reliance on moments of inspiration. This is why Hugo Friedrich excludes him from his book on the modern lyric and even disparages him in a harsh passage.[81] This is why the attempt to make Mallarmé a spiritual descendant of Novalis, as Vordtriede tried, must fail. Mallarmé, one might grant, aims at transcendence, but it is an empty transcendence, while Novalis rapturously adores the unity of the

78. See his "Du Style symbolique," *Le Globe* (March 29 and April 8, 1829), and a series of articles in *La Revue Encyclopédique* (1831). See my *History of Modern Criticism, 3*, 27–28.

79. In the essay on Gautier Baudelaire reproduces "The Poetic Principle." See also Marcel Françon, "Poe et Baudelaire," *PMLA, 60* (1945), 841–59.

80. See my chapter in *History of Modern Criticism, 3*, 152–63.

81. *Struktur der modernen Lyrik*, p. 116; in rev. ed. (1962), pp. 161–62.

mysterious universe. In short, the romantics were Rousseau-
ists; the symbolists, beginning with Baudelaire, believe in the
fall of man or, if they do not use the religious phraseology,
know that man is limited and is not, as Novalis believed, the
Messiah of nature. The end of the romantic period is clearly
marked by the victory of positivism and scientism, which
soon led to disillusionment and pessimism. Most symbolists
were non-Christians and even atheists, even if they tried to
find a new religion in occultism or flirted with Oriental religions. They were pessimists who need not have read Schopenhauer and Eduard von Hartmann, as Laforgue did, to
succumb to the mood of decadence, *fin de siècle, Götter-
dämmerung,* or the death of God prophesied by Nietzsche.[82]

Symbolism is also clearly set off from the new avant-garde
movements after 1914: futurism, cubism, surrealism, expressionism, and so on. There the faith in language has
crumbled completely, while in Mallarmé and Valéry language preserves its cognitive and even magic power: Valéry's
collection of poems is rightly called *Charmes.* Orpheus is the
mythological hero of the poet, charming the animals, trees,
and even stones. With more recent art the view of analogy
disappears: Kafka has nothing of it. Postsymbolist art is abstract and allegorical rather than symbolic. The image, in
surrealism, has no beyond: it wells, at most, from the subconscious of the individual.

Finally, there is the highest abstraction, the wide largest
circle: the use of "symbolism" in all literature, of all ages.
But then the term, broken loose from its historical moorings,
lacks concrete content and remains merely the name for a
phenomenon almost universal in all art.

These reflections must lead to what only can be a recom-

82. See the review of Vordtriede's *Novalis* by Hans Robert Jauss
in *Romanische Forschungen, 77* (1965), 174–83.

mendation, to use the third sense of our term, to call the period of European literature roughly between 1885 and 1914 "symbolism," to see it as an international movement which radiated originally from France but produced great writers and great poetry also elsewhere. In Ireland and England: Yeats and Eliot; in the United States: Wallace Stevens and Hart Crane; in Germany: George, Rilke, and Hofmannsthal; in Russia: Blok, Ivanov, and Bely; in Spain and South America: Darío, Machado, and Guillén. If we, as we should, extend the meaning of symbolism to prose, we can see it clearly in the late Henry James, in Joyce, in the later Thomas Mann, in Proust, in the early Gide and Faulkner, in D. H. Lawrence; and if we add the drama, we recognize it in the later stages of Ibsen, Strindberg, and Hauptmann, and in O'Neill. There is symbolist criticism of distinction: an aesthetics in Mallarmé and Valéry, a looser creed in Remy de Gourmont, in Eliot, and in Yeats, and a flourishing school of symbolist interpretation, particularly in the United States. Much of the French "new criticism" is frankly symbolist. Roland Barthes' new pamphlet, *Critique et vérité* (1966), pleads for a complete liberty of symbolist interpretation.

Still, we must not forget our initial reminder. A period concept can never exhaust its meaning. It is not a class concept of which the individual works are cases. It is a regulative idea: it struggles with preceding and following ideals of art. In the time under consideration the strength of the survivals was particularly great: Hauptmann's *Die Weber* was performed in the same year (1892) as *Blätter für die Kunst* began to appear; Blok's *Poems on the Beautiful Lady* were written in the same year (1901) as Gorky's *Lower Depths*. Within the same author and even within the same work of art the struggle was waged at times. Edmond Jaloux called

Joyce "at the same time a realist and a symbolist."[83] The same is true of Proust and Mann. *Ulysses* combines symbolism and naturalism, as no other book of the time, into a synthesis of grand proportion and strong tension. In Trieste Joyce lectured on two English writers and on two English writers alone: they were characteristically Defoe and Blake.[84]

As agreement on the main periods of European literature grows, so agreement to add the period term "symbolism" to the five periods now accepted should increase. But even were a different term to be victorious (though none I can think of seems to me even remotely preferable), we should always recognize that such a term has fulfilled its function as a tool of historiography if it has made us think not only about individual works and authors but about schools, trends, and movements and their international expansion. Symbolism is at least a literary term which will help us to counteract the dependence of much literary history on periodization derived from political and social history (such as the term "Imperialism" used in Marxist literary histories, which is perfectly meaningless applied to poetry at that time). Symbolism is a term (and I am quoting the words I applied to baroque in 1945) "which prepares for synthesis, draws our minds away from the mere accumulation of observations and facts, and paves the way for a future history of literature as a fine art."[85]

83. Quoted by Harry Levin in *James Joyce* (Norfolk, Conn., 1941), p. 19: "À la fois réaliste et symboliste."

84. See Richard Ellmann, *James Joyce* (New York, 1959), pp. 329–30. The lectures in 1912 were called "Verismo ed idealismo nella letteratura inglese."

85. See my *Concepts of Criticism,* p. 114.

# Immanuel Kant's
# Aesthetics and Criticism

Thomas De Quincey, the author of *Confessions of an English Opium Eater,* wrote in one of his essays that Kant was "something of a brute." "It is very evident," he says, "that Kant's original determination was a coarse, masculine pursuit of science and that literature in its finer departments . . . was to him, at all parts of his life, an object of secret contempt." Kant, he tells us, "in all probability never read a book in his life," no book of poetry or fiction, only voyages and travels and scientific treatises.[1] This image of Kant as the uncouth German pedant still lingers on and has not been completely eradicated, though a mass of evidence has been accumulated to show that it is very far from the truth. Kant's writings, lecture notes, conversations, and letters show that he had a considerable knowledge of imaginative literature, especially poetry; that he composed some occasional verses himself as a young man; and that, in his social life, he was a man of exquisite courtesy and fine manners who had great interest in the pleasures of the table and in good conversation. His taste in literature was, no doubt, old-fashioned in the Germany of the last decades of the eighteenth century, when his fame and influence were at their height. We must remember that Kant was born in 1724 and thus formed his taste in the 1740s, before the great age of German literature, before the rise of

1. *Collected Writings,* ed. David Masson, 8 (14 vols. Edinburgh, 1896), 90, 91, 93.

Lessing, Goethe, and Schiller. Kant knew his Latin poets: even when old and feeble, he could recite long passages from Virgil and his favorite Persius.[2] He had a definite taste especially for two kinds of literature: satire and didactic philosophical poetry. He quoted Horace and Lucretius, admired Erasmus of Rotterdam, Samuel Butler's *Hudibras,* Swift, and especially Pope's *Essay on Man.* He knew Cervantes, Montaigne, and Milton, and was swept off his feet, temporarily at least, by Rousseau. But as he grew older, he became hostile to the new literature springing up around him; he disapproved of the extravagant cult of genius in the German *Sturm und Drang* and disliked all sentimentalism; he thought the man unhappy who had a novel-reading wife. "In her imagination she was married to Sir Charles Grandison and she is now his widow. She won't have much inclination to look after things in the kitchen."[3] Kant, we must conclude, was a cultivated gentleman, well-read in the literature of the Romans and of his youth, with a taste for poetry which we should call neoclassical. He could not change or enlarge his taste, as time went on, just as most of us cling to the artistic experiences of our youth. His knowledge of the other arts was more limited: he had never traveled beyond the confines of East Prussia and thus had no firsthand view of great architecture or painting; it seems not surprising to hear that he liked the engravings of Hogarth best. But one can have real access to the experience of art even if only in a narrow range, and surely the fact of that experience is the only thing that mattered to Kant, or

2. Reported by two of Kant's earliest biographers, L. E. Borowski and E. A. C. Wasianski, in *Immanuel Kant: Sein Leben in Darstellungen von Zeitgenossen,* ed. Felix Gross (Berlin, 1912), pp. 78, 232 ff.

3. Quoted from a lecture note by Erich Adickes in "Kant als Aesthetiker," *Jahrbuch des Freien Deutschen Hochstifts* (1904), p. 322.

should matter to any philosopher thinking about the nature of art.

Kant was not a practical critic of the arts. In the *Critique of Judgment* he mentions only two poets, Homer and Wieland, in the same sentence, and only once does he appeal to specific poetic texts to illustrate a point: to lines from a French poem by Frederick the Great and to a metaphor in an obscure contemporary, Withof.[4] Kant was not even a philosopher of art. He says very little about the individual arts as such, and nothing about their historical development or forms. Rather, he was preoccupied with two problems: aesthetics, in the narrow sense of the word as it was understood in his time to mean our response to the beautiful, and the theory of criticism—or rather, with one central question: whether the judgment of taste is subjective or objective, relative or absolute. On both these problems, aesthetics and theory of criticism, Kant has things to say which seem relevant and substantially true even today.

Kant must be considered the first philosopher who clearly and definitely established the peculiarity and autonomy of the aesthetic realm. Croce claimed that Vico was the founder of aesthetics, but Vico was unable to distinguish between poetry and myth, and assigned poetry to the early stages of mankind, as a sort of prelogical thinking. Baumgarten, who invented the term aesthetics and wrote the first book called *Aesthetica,* published in 1750, conceived his science rather as a kind of inductive logic, a science of perception, in which, for instance, telescopes, thermometers, and barometers are treated as important instruments. Only in Kant do we find an elaborate argument that the aesthetic realm differs from the realm of morality, utility, and science because the aes-

4. *Kritik der Urteilskraft,* in his *Sämtliche Werke,* ed. E. Cassirer, 5 (11 vols. Berlin, 1912–22), 384, 391.

thetic state of mind differs profoundly from our perception of the pleasurable, the moving, the useful, the true, and the good. Kant invented the famous thesis that the aesthetic response consists in "disinterested satisfaction." "Disinterested" in this formula refers to a lack of interference from desire, a directness in our access to the work of art. Our access is undisturbed, uninterfered with by immediate utilitarian ends.

The idea of the autonomy of art was not, of course, totally new with Kant: it was being prepared throughout the century, and anticipations can be found in thinkers such as the Scotsman Francis Hutcheson and the German-Jewish philosopher Moses Mendelssohn. But in Kant the argument was stated for the first time systematically in a defense of the aesthetic realm against all sides: against sensualism and its reduction of art to pleasure, against emotionalism and its view of art as stimulus or emotion, against the age-old moralism, which reduces art to a form of the useful, and against intellectualism, which sees in art only an inferior, more popular way of knowing, a kind of second-rate (because less systematic) philosophy. Many attempts have been made to refute Kant's conclusions. Whatever the difficulties of Kant's solution, he has put his finger on the central issue of aesthetics. No science is possible which does not have its distinct object. If art is simply pleasure, or communication of emotion or experience, or moral teaching, or inferior reasoning, it ceases to be art and becomes a substitute for something else.

Art or the beautiful is not pleasure, because pleasure is something purely subjective, not referable to an object: pleasure can never err or be false. Pleasure is momentary, it is consumed, it ceases after being satisfied. But aesthetic contemplation is, as if arrested in time, repeatable, though free from desire. Pleasure or pain accompanies all our actions, but pleasure does not set off the realm of the aesthetic. The tragic or the grotesque or the ugly depicted in art may even be painful in the ordinary sense of the word.

Art is not good or useful either. It does not serve an immediate purpose, it does not arouse a desire to consume or use it. Kant's view does not, as we shall see, preclude the moral significance of art. What mattered to him was the special nature of art, the way we would say aesthetic experience is "framed," is distanced, is set off from the feelings of desire and willing. He wanted to distinguish the whole world of illusion which is created by art and demands another attitude than that of immediate use or consumption.

Nor is the aesthetic state of mind an inferior way to abstract knowledge. Kant does not always carefully enough guard against an intellectualistic misinterpretation. On the whole, he understands the danger clearly, but one of the key terms which he introduces, his "aesthetic Idea," raises many difficulties. This "Idea," he knows, is not identical with general idea or concept. An aesthetic Idea is a representation of the imagination which has the semblance of reality. The term "Idea" is near to the term "symbol," which was introduced in its modern meaning to aesthetics by Goethe and Schiller. "Idea" points to a pervasive problem of Kant's *Critique,* the union of the general and the particular, the abstract and the sensuous, achieved by art.

The aesthetic realm is thus that of imagination, not of thought or goodness or utility but of imagination represented, objectified, symbolized, distanced, contemplated. However we rephrase it, it seems to me that Kant has clearly grasped the nature of the aesthetic and the realm of art.

He has stated with equal clarity and has answered the central question concerning a theory of criticism. Kant speaks of the judgment of "taste." The term "taste" was first applied to things of the mind in the seventeenth century but elicited a considerable debate only in the eighteenth century, when Montesquieu, Voltaire, Hume, and Burke took a prominent part. There were two conceptions of "taste" with which Kant was confronted and which, in different forms, are still debated today. One group of thinkers answered that taste is simply another sense, a sixth sense, completely irrational, something, as we should say, purely subjective. As the old saying runs, *de gustibus non est disputandum.*

But another group argued that taste is the discovery of objective principles, or rules, or laws, and that it differs from the process of reasoning only by being quicker and surer, a kind of shortcut possible because of training and exercise. We recognize things better if we have seen them before and know what others found in them: taste is merely a knowledge of principles and rules, an acceptance of the wisdom and verdict of the ages.

Kant begins with this dilemma; he is quite familiar with this dispute. He holds firm to the subjective side of the argument, recognizing that judgments of taste, our pleasure or boredom, can neither be refuted nor enforced. He rejects any view of criticism by a priori principles, by laws or rules. Kant argues elaborately that it is quite true that taste is subjective; yet aesthetic judgments differ from a taste, say, in olives or oysters, by claiming universality. If it were like a taste in olives, nobody could or would argue about works of art. On the other hand, if aesthetic judgment were an appeal to laws or eternal principles, all argument would stop, too. It would be merely a question of application. We should not need to collect examples, any more than we need to collect examples of the law of gravity: *all* things fall. The aesthetic judgment is rather something in between. It is subjective, but there is an objectivity in the subjective; in the aesthetic judgment egoism is overcome: we appeal to a general judgment, to a common sense of mankind, but this is achieved by inner experience, not by accepting the opinions of others or consulting them or counting their opinions. It is not an appeal to men, but an appeal to humanity, to an ideal totality of judges. I cannot know whether I have actually, in my judgment, hit on the sentiment of this hidden ideal totality, yet my aesthetic judgment is a pointing to this higher unity, a call to myself and others to discover it. It is thus hypothetical, problematical. To rephrase this in modern terms, aesthetic judgment is neither relative nor absolute: it is neither completely individual, as this would mean an anarchy and a complete frustration of criticism, nor is it absolute in the sense that we can apply established, eternal norms. Criticism is personal but it aims to discover a structure of determination in the object itself: it assumes some standard of correctness in the judgment, even though we may not be able to draw the exact line between the subjective and the objective in each given instance. Kant, it seems to me, succeeds in avoiding both of two extremes which have at different times paralyzed criticism: anarchic subjectivity and frozen absolutism. While Kant recognizes the role of personal feeling in art, he sees that there is paradoxically something like an aesthetic duty. Nobody ought to like olives, but all of us *should* respond to great art and distinguish between the good and the bad if we are to be fully human. Still, the aesthetic "ought" is by no means the same as the ethical "ought," Kant's categorical imperative, which demands action from every man without distinction, at any time and in any place. The aesthetic duty, paradoxically, is only subjective and contemplative.

In Kant there cannot be any rules or laws of art which are given a priori. Thus Kant quite logically (though one may be surprised at this) makes much of original genius. We must not, of course, think that Kant's genius is the egotistical superman he became in the hands of certain romantics, or the savage, inspired creature he had become during Kant's own lifetime among the geniuses of *Sturm und Drang*. Kant's concept of genius is exactly parallel to his concept of judgment. He recognizes in genius a basic irrationality: the source of genius is in the unconscious. Genius is innate, a gift of nature. It cannot invent general prescriptions for works of art, as this would make art the application of precepts and concepts; it is always original genius. But there can be, of course, original nonsense (just as there can be nonsensical, false judgments of taste). Hence the products of genius must be "exemplary," normative, prescriptive, as true taste is prescriptive. Genius is the "talent by which nature prescribes rules to art."[5] Works of art claim recognition, and the critic has the duty to give it to them.

But how precisely can criticism proceed? For Kant there cannot be anything like a doctrine or principles which can be taught. Criticism is always judging by examples, from the concrete. Criticism thus is historical, in the sense of being individual, while science (and Kant thinks of physical science) is general, abstract, aiming at a systematic doctrine. The method of criticism is thus the comparative method. The capacity to choose with universal validity, another definition of taste, is nothing but the capacity of comparing oneself with others; and that process is, of course, not just a juxtaposition with others but a self-criticism, an introspection, an examination of one's feelings.

I personally think that Kant leaves us too much in the realm of the subjective: I recognize, of course, that this agrees with his general position on the theory of knowledge. Kant rarely comes to grips with the concrete realm of art. Poetry as such is hardly treated in the *Critique* except in the classifi-

5. Ibid., p. 382.

cation of the arts, where it is listed as an "art of speech" with rhetoric and put first among the arts, because it liberates the imagination and rises to "ideas."[6] But Kant did suggest or rather revive a very important criterion for the judgment of art: the analogy of the organism. The similarity of a work of art to an organism was, I believe, first suggested in a famous passage of Aristotle's *Poetics,* but there it is simply a principle of wholeness, a recognition of the implication of the parts in a whole, a totality or unity: the organistic analogy had been only a variety of the old insight that a work of art is a unity in diversity. But in Kant we are confronted with a different idea: art and nature are conceived as much stricter analogies. The work of art is parallel to a living organism because art and organic nature must both be conceived under the head of what Kant calls paradoxically "purposeless purposiveness." The *Critique of Judgment* has two parts: the "Critique of Aesthetic Judgment" and the "Critique of Teleological Judgment"; one is concerned with what we call aesthetics and art, the other with what we should call biology, or rather the theory of biology. This is not, as some people have thought, an odd scholastic scheme which brings incompatibles under one artificial heading: it is a central insight of Kant's philosophy. Art and organic nature point to an ultimate overcoming of the deep dualism which is basic to Kant's system of thought. The world, according to Kant, is divided into two realms: that of appearance (hence of necessity, of physical causality), accessible to our senses and the categories of our understanding, and that of moral freedom, accessible only in action. Kant glimpses in art a possibility of bridging the gulf between necessity and freedom, between the world of deterministic nature and the world of moral action. Art accomplishes a union of the general and the particular, of in-

6. Ibid., p. 402.

tuition and thought, of imagination and reason. Organic nature, life, does exactly the same. They together guarantee the
existence of what Kant calls the "supersensuous," for only in
art and life, through "intellectual intuition," do we have access to what Kant calls the "intellectual archetype."[7] To put
this in more modern terms: art and life point to some realm
of values, or ends, or purposes, discernible in the activity of
genius, in our response to beauty, and in the purposeful structures of living beings. But Kant hesitates to come to this conclusion: the "supersensuous substratum of nature," the union
of the realm of necessity and freedom, escapes, he would insist, any *theoretical* knowledge. Hegel, who boldly proclaimed
the reality of the spirit, was to complain about Kant: "It is the
character of Kant's philosophy to have a consciousness of the
highest idea, but always to eradicate it again."[8] But while
Kant hesitates to assign to art the role of mediatress between
man and nature, he discovers and correctly emphasizes a most
important criterion of aesthetic judgment: the analogy between art and organism. The term "purposeless purposiveness" as applied to organism becomes clear if we understand
that by "purpose" Kant does not mean conscious intention
and aim, but harmony of parts, unity, totality, with every
member having its own proper function in the system. This
purposiveness, this unity, is at the same time purposeless in
Kant's sense, as it is disinterested, not directed to any immediate outside aim. Such coherence in itself, such beautiful
unity, is also a standard of aesthetic judgment: the more complex the work of art, the more composed, the greater the totality, the greater the beauty. Thus Kant, while envisaging the
analogy between nature and art as of great philosophical importance, does not go all the way in identifying art with orga-

7. Ibid, p. 487.
8. *Sämtliche Werke, 16* (18 vols. Berlin, 1832–44), 127.

nism. He knew the difference and always insisted that creatures are subject to the laws of causality and physics, while works of art are not, because they are illusion, semblance, make-believe.

One other motif of Kant's aesthetics proved of great historical importance. Kant inherited from the eighteenth century the division of the aesthetic realm into the beautiful and the sublime. The distinction seems to me untenable in its rigidity, but Kant's theory of the sublime, though applied by him exclusively to nature, could easily be and soon was transferred to tragedy. The sublime is frightening, upsetting, even horrifying, but at the same time attractive. Man in the experience of the sublime in nature confronts either magnitude or power, both of which transcend the capabilities of his imagination. While beauty induces sensibility and understanding to collaborate harmoniously, sublimity causes a conflict between imagination and reason. Our imagination fails to grasp the infinity of the universe or the omnipotence of nature displayed in storms, earthquakes, and other natural catastrophes. But while we experience our impotence before nature, we still assert our humanity, a sense of our freedom, of our supersensuous destiny. Thus the sublime proves to be another road to the supersensuous, not, of course, grasped by reason, but glimpsed merely by imagination. If we apply the sublime to art (as Kant did not explicitly), we have found another way to give metaphysical and moral meaning to art. Kant himself hesitates, for he sees in sublimity a hint of man's freedom from the natural order of the universe. A theory which starts with a sharp delimitation of the aesthetic, if stretched so as to unite the beautiful and the sublime, will end with a justification for the greatest metaphysical and moral claims for art. In Kant these claims are put forward hesitatingly, gropingly, cautiously, as suits his temperament and critical method.

One may look upon the whole history of general aesthetics after Kant as a series of discussions, repudiations, and developments of Kant's thought. I have purposely ignored or minimized the systematic exposition, the scholastic divisions and subdivisions, the whole elaborate argumentation of Kant's *Critique*. I have ignored, for instance, the awkward distinction between free and adherent beauty. Hardly anybody has preserved the exact architecture of Kant's thought. But all the main motifs and solutions propounded by Kant have proved extremely influential and fruitful.

The idea of the autonomy of art was almost immediately taken up by Kant's first distinguished pupil in aesthetics, the poet Schiller. Schiller resolutely embraces Kant's doctrine of the distinctness and apartness of the aesthetic realm. In some of his formulations he seems to come near to that idea of art for art's sake of which he has been claimed one of the main progenitors. But to see him in this way is a gross misunderstanding of Schiller's actual point of view and of the unfortunate and misleading term "play," which he borrows from Kant in describing the free aesthetic activity. Play has, for Schiller, nothing to do with the lack of consequence, the frivolity and unreality of a child's game. It is a term which designates the artist's freedom from immediate practical purposes, from utilitarian and moral considerations: his creativity, his self-activity. More resolutely than Kant, Schiller conceives the artist as a mediator between man and nature, between intellect and sense. Art, in Schiller, assumes an enormous civilizing role, described in his *Letters on the Aesthetic Education of Man* (1795). It heals the wounds of civilization, the split between man and nature, and between man's intellect and his senses. Art makes man whole again, reconciles him with the world and with himself. But the world of art is a world of illusion, of semblance, of *Schein,* a term with Neoplatonic overtones of light and luminosity as well as illusion. It was used by Kant only casually twice, I believe, in the *Critique.*[9]

While Schiller held fast to the principle of the autonomy of art, the German romantics again blurred all distinctions. Schelling, the most important aesthetician in the succession of Kant, Fichte, Schelling, and Hegel, makes art or poetry really an all-embracing, all-conquering term in which all distinctions disappear. In the program of his philosophy, which Schelling drew up in 1796, at the age of twenty-one, the philosopher is said to have as much aesthetic power as the poet. "There is no philosophy or history any more; poetry alone will outlive all other sciences and arts."[10] This claim for the preeminence of art must not, of course, be confused with later nineteenth-century aestheticism; it is rather an attempt to abolish all distinctions between art, religion, philosophy, and myth. While Kant was at great pains to distinguish between the good, the true, and the beautiful, Schelling exalts beauty as the highest value, and his beauty is actually truth and goodness in disguise. The same identification of art with religion and philosophy is even more explicit in Novalis and in the later stages of Friedrich Schlegel's speculations. Among the German romantics only the sober mind of August Wilhelm

9. *Kritik der Urteilskraft, 5,* 402–03, 411.

10. "Das älteste Systemprogramm des deutschen Idealismus," in Friedrich Hölderlin, *Sämtliche Werke,* ed. L. von Pigenot (3rd ed. 4 vols. Munich, 1943), *3,* 623–25. I accept the view that this manuscript was composed by Schelling and not by Hölderlin. Cf. Ludwig Strauss, "Hölderlins Anteil an Schellings frühem Systemprogramm," *Deutsche Vierteljahrschrift für Literaturwissenschaft und Geistesgeschichte, 5* (1927), 679–747.

Schlegel, though he criticized Kant severely for his hesitations and cautions,[11] holds fast, for the most part, to the principle of aesthetic autonomy. Hegel knows the peculiar nature of art but is unable to hold to it steadily: he often identifies it with myth or sees it as a mere stepping-stone to religion and philosophy. Among the German philosophers, Schopenhauer seems to have most clearly kept to the Kantian distinction of the aesthetic realm, but with him it often becomes intellectualized. The disinterested will-less contemplation of ideas becomes only a version of the philosopher's contemplation of the universe. On the whole, the great movement of German thought after Kant's *Critiques* rather tended to weaken the distinctness of the realm of aesthetics and more and more made art a short cut to the absolute, a popular version of philosophy. Art was exalted but at the price of being lost in the Platonic triad of the beautiful, the good, and the true.

The principle of the autonomy of art was picked up by Victor Cousin and other popularizers of German philosophical thought in what is known as the "art-for-art's-sake" movement in France. This term was used, apparently for the first time, by Benjamin Constant with reference to Kant's aesthetics in his *Intimate Diary* in 1804.[12] It became a prominent slogan, particularly with Gautier and Flaubert. Gautier, for instance, praised Baudelaire because he had "defended the absolute autonomy of art and would not allow poetry to have any other purpose than itself, or any task other than that of arousing in the reader's heart a sense of the beautiful in the absolute meaning of the word."[13] But in Gautier and his pupil

11. *Vorlesungen über schöne Literatur und Kunst,* ed. J. Minor, *1* (2 vols. Heilbronn, 1884), 64–89.

12. *Journaux intimes,* ed. A. Roulin and C. Roth (Paris, 1952), p. 58.

13. *Portraits et souvenirs littéraires* (Paris, 1892), p. 182.

Wilde, of course, "art for art's sake" is not so much an expression asserting the autonomy of art as a polemical weapon against the social and didactic demands of the middle-class society surrounding them: autonomy of art becomes something Kant would never have dreamed of, an assertion of the superiority of the artist to the Philistine, a proclamation of his hostility to the society in which he lives and which he has long ago given up the hope of reforming or changing in his own image. The ivory tower—a term we owe, I believe, to Vigny—or the symbolist theories about absolute or pure poetry, whether of Mallarmé or Valéry, have little to do with Kant's concept of the autonomy of art.

The Kantian point of view still is an issue in the philosophical literature of aesthetics and was restated most persuasively by Croce in his *Estetica* (1902). Croce, like Kant, sharply distinguishes art from pleasure, utility, and conceptual knowledge, but, unlike Kant, extends its realm to the whole of language and to any intuitive activity of man. Croce criticizes Kant rather severely for what he considers his intellectualism, his final surrender to the view that the aesthetic "Idea" is really only a sensuous concept, but he holds firm to Kant's concept of the autonomy of art. Many modern aestheticians have restated the same concept in different terms. Others, such as Santayana, Richards, and Dewey, have attacked it and have again tried to identify art with pleasure, with emotion, or with experience in general. Kant's delimitation of the aesthetic realm has proved the leading motif of modern aesthetics, the central issue which will again and again divide and unite minds of the most diverse tastes and persuasions.

It is different with Kant's answer to the problem of criticism: if one looks at the history of aesthetics, there can be little doubt that subjectivism and relativism have been victorious, at least since the general dissolution of German idealism after the death of Hegel. The victory of relativism has been due not only to philosophical motives but to the enormous spread of the historical point of view and even simply to our growing knowledge of the inexhaustible variety of the world's kinds of art both in space and time. Today we seem to like and admire everything: Negro sculpture and Bach, cavemen's paintings and T. S. Eliot. On the other side of the iron curtain Marxist dialectical materialism has erected relativism and historicism into a scientific system which, by a dialectical reversal, amounts in practice to a new dogmatism. In the Western world, in recent decades, there are more and more assertions of a new faith in objective critical principles, but most of them seem to come from outside aesthetics: from T. S. Eliot's religious assumptions or from Thomism. Attempts to found a new theory of the arts based on objective universal principles are rare or, if they are made, usually amount only to the assertion of a specific individual taste or the taste of a particular group which is defending itself and erecting its demands into laws. They have to be classified as dogmatism in Kant's sense: his peculiar in-between solution which recognizes the subjectivity of taste and still demands a world of norms which we approach from different radii—a kind of "perspectivism," as I have tried to name this view—has hardly been formulated with theoretical clarity.

Kant's analogy between art and nature was also extremely influential in his time. Goethe, Schelling, and the Schlegels threw Kant's caution to the winds and spoke boldly of a work of art as if it were a plant or an animal grown and not made— procreated, begottten, not planned and constructed. Goethe admired the *Critique of Judgment* greatly, studied it diligently, and asserted that he owed to it "a most joyful epoch" in his life.[14] He was pleased to see that poetry and comparative natural science were so closely related. But Kant, of course, would not have drawn Goethe's conclusion that "a work of art must be treated as a work of nature and a work of nature as a work of art."[15] In Schelling art also appears as an analogue of nature and of nature's creative powers. Art constitutes an active link between the soul and nature. Art does not imitate nature but has to compete with the creative power of nature, "the spirit of nature which speaks to us only in symbols." A work of art expresses the essence of nature and is excellent in the degree to which it shows us "this original power of nature's creation and activity."[16] The poet is, as it were, the liberator of nature and, as Novalis said of man in general, the Messiah of nature.

We have, I think, ceased to understand these ideas: we do not believe in such a humanization of nature and naturalization of art. During the nineteenth and twentieth centuries the gulf between man and nature has grown in theory, and the particular use of "nature" as the ideal general state of man, which in Kant is still central, has disappeared. Kant's grouping of biology and art under one cover has long since been felt to be an artificial requirement of his systematic thought.

At the same time, the more special idea of art as organism, partly Kantian in origin, has had a great success in the modern world. The German romantics are full of it. August Wilhelm Schlegel formulated the difference between the organic

14. "Einwirkung der neueren Philosophie" (1820), in *Sämtliche Werke,* ed. E. von der Hellen, *39* (40 vols. Stuttgart, 1902–07), 31.

15. "Kampagne in Frankreich" (1792), ibid., *27,* 122.

16. "Über das Verhältnis der bildenden Künste zu der Natur" (1807), in *Sämtliche Werke,* ed. K. F. A. Schelling, *7* (14 vols. Stuttgart and Augsburg, 1856–61), 300 ff.

and the mechanical with special skill, and his formulas were taken over by Coleridge. Today in the English-speaking world the term "organism" as applied to art is associated with Coleridge and has been widely revived in recent decades. Not only the American "New Critics" but also Croce and many Germans can be described as propounders of this parallelism which, I feel, should not be pressed too far and certainly leads only to misleading analogies if taken too literally.

Almost as successful was Kant's definition of the aesthetic Idea, of the peculiar union of the individual and the general, the concrete and the universal. Shortly after the *Critique* Goethe discovered the word "symbol" for this union, and after him many German aestheticians—Schelling, the Schlegels, Hegel, and others—elaborated, sometimes with a different terminology, the distinction between allegory and symbol, between aesthetic idea and concept. Art is the "sensuous shining of the Idea," according to Hegel. But in Hegelianism, Idea soon assumed merely the meaning of general concept, and much German and other nineteenth-century criticism became a hunt for central ideas, for capsule formulas, for abstract philosophical or moral messages. At the same time, the concrete universal, more clearly described in Hegel than in Kant, and the concept of symbol penetrated almost everywhere: Coleridge picked it up from Goethe, the Schlegels, and Schelling; so did Carlyle; and their version of symbolism or idealism became most important for Emerson and Poe. From all kinds of sources, from the German romantics, especially Hoffmann and Heine, from Poe and Carlyle, the concept of the artistic symbol arrived in France and led there to an aesthetic theory, that of the French symbolists, expressly centered around this concept. The French, of course, like some of their precursors, had moved far away from the Kantian source: symbol becomes with them often nothing but a mystical cipher, a dim shadow or suggestion of the supernatural world. But whatever the fortunes of the term "symbol" or "idea," the union of the particular and the general, the "concrete universal" has been recognized increasingly as the central structure of all art. After the vague mystical use of the symbolists, "symbol" has become again the object of philosophical and aesthetic speculations—in Cassirer's *Philosophy of Symbolic Forms,* for instance, or in Susanne K. Langer's *Feeling and Form,* to name two authors who recognize an explicit debt to Kant and his immediate pupil, Schiller.

There is, I suppose, least to be said in favor of Kant's concept of the sublime. Most aestheticians have given up the concept and have rejected its implied division of the realm of art. Kant can rightly be criticized for defining the beautiful far too narrowly, in terms of an abstract neoclassicism. In some of his reflections Kant is surely in danger of falling into an extreme Formalism. He emphasizes, for instance, design in the fine arts and would apparently dispense with color as a mere sensual stimulus. He thinks of music as only a play of sounds. In the concept of the sublime Kant found a way out of such Formalism but surely found it only at the expense of consistency and coherence. Kant's view of the sublime was, however, immediately important, as it suggested the theory of tragedy formulated by Schiller and August Wilhelm Schlegel. They were paraphrasing Kant's theory of the sublime when they said that tragedy shows man's revolt against the necessity of nature, in which he perishes physically, though he triumphs spiritually. We may feel that Schiller and Schlegel have described only one kind of tragedy, but it seems an important central kind. To me this formula is more illuminating than Aristotle's obscure view of purgation and more convincing than the Hegelian concept of tragedy as that of a reconciliation of two equal moral forces. In English, A. C. Bradley's exposition of Hegel's view seems to have carried the day, but the Kantian view should appeal to those who are not content with a justification of the ways of God to man.

Whatever our judgment about special points of Kant's aesthetics may be, enough has been said to prove its enormous fertility and influence. Yet I should not want to stake out a claim for attention to Kant merely on historical grounds, merely in terms of his widespread influence and his role of initiator. The specific solutions given by Kant to aesthetic problems are alive and important even today. The autonomy of art is a vital issue today, and I would argue that Kant has seen it rightly: with his grasp of the distinctness of the realm of art and of the truth that it must not be confused with pleasure or utility or knowledge or even with intuition and experience in general. I am not so sure that Kant's solution of the problem of criticism does not suffer from his general emphasis on the subjective and the phenomenological. Personally, I would launch out more boldly into a realm of objective structures, into the world of existing art objects. Kant cautiously stays with the indubitable fact of the subjective judgment and only hesitatingly and provisionally appeals to some final common sense of man. Today we probably do not know what to do with the idea of the reconciliation between man and nature by art. We must put the civilizing function of art in different terms. But we must acknowledge the significance of conceiving some parallelism between a work of art and an organism. Surely one of the criteria of all art is some kind of unity in diversity, some kind of coherence, wholeness, or whatever else one may wish to call it. Kant's view of the relation between particularity and universality seems also right even today. The emphasis on the particular during the last hundred years or so has gone too far: it has cut off art from a universal meaning and driven it into the minutiae of local-color descriptions, naturalistic detail, or the private, introspective worlds of the psychological novel. We are not likely to return to the abstract neoclassicism against which the emphasis on the particular was an overviolent reaction. The recognition of both the individuality of a work of art and its universal significance, in terms such as "concrete universal" or "symbol," has become more and more prevalent.

Kant, we may conclude, is the founder of modern aesthetics. He has put clearly some of the central problems to which aesthetic thinking will have to return: the question of the autonomy of art, the problem of criticism, its subjectivity or objectivity, the relation of nature and art, the organicity of the work of art, the relation between the particular and the general in art, reconciled by Kant in what he calls "Idea" and what we would prefer to call "symbol," and finally the character of the sublime, which has been applied to the theory of tragedy. In aesthetics and criticism Kant decidedly has something to say to this age, 180 years after the publication of his *Critique of Judgment*.

# English Literary Historiography
## during the Nineteenth Century

In *The Rise of English Literary History* (1941) I attempted to tell the history of the growth of English literary historiography from its beginnings in the sixteenth century to its first achievements in the eighteenth, culminating in Thomas Warton's *History of English Poetry* (1774–81). A second volume bringing the history of literary history down to the present age was planned, but my interests shifted and broadened, and eventually only some marginal attention was given to the topic in the four volumes of my *History of Modern Criticism* (1955–65). Still, it might be of some interest to sketch, in schematic fashion, the development of English literary historiography since Warton up to the publication of J. W. Courthope's *History of English Poetry* (1895–1910).

We must find some scheme of principles which will allow us to group the literary histories of the time and to discern the changes and fluctuations in historiographical concepts. The central concept of literary historiography (as distinct from literary scholarship or criticism) is the concept of literary development. Thus we shall ask questions such as these: Did literary historians recognize the development of literature, its continuity and evolution, or did they conceive of it merely as a static series of isolated works? If they chose the dynamic conception of change, how was it conceived? Was literature thought of as completely determined by the social, political, and ideological changes of its background and thus reduced to a reflex of social changes? Or was it conceived of as an evolutionary process on the analogy of biological evolution? If these fundamentally naturalistic conceptions were rejected, was literature thought of as the expression of some spiritual substratum such as the national mind, or was it described as a self-evolving dialectical process? As we answer these questions, men and books begin to group themselves, revealing their philosophical affiliations and relationships. An outline of the development of literary historiography emerges.

We must distinguish between two main stages: the romantic age and the period vaguely called Victorian. I can only allude to the enormous impact during the romantic age of the vast accumulation of new texts from medieval and Elizabethan literature,[1] and I can only refer to my *History* for a discussion of the revaluation of the past by literary critics. But in the actual writing of literary history surprisingly little was achieved during the first decades of the century, especially if we think of the success of narrative history on the Continent, with the writings of the Brothers Schlegel and Bouterwek in Germany or Sismondi, Villemain, and Ampère in France. No complete history of English literature was produced until Robert Chambers' modest little *History of English Language and Literature* (1836). This was a textbook for "those lectures on English literature, which are given in so many institutions for mechanics and others,"[2] and it is the first book to cover,

1. A brief account of "Interest in Foreign Literature and Earlier English Literature" may be found in Ian Jack, *English Literature 1815–1832* (Oxford, 1963), esp. pp. 399–405. Arthur Johnston's *Enchanted Ground: The Study of Medieval Romance in the Eighteenth Century* (London, 1964) provides more details, some on the last decades of the 18th century, supplementary to my *Rise of English Literary History*.

2. Edinburgh, 1836, p. 1.

however inadequately, all periods and genres of English literature. Warton's *History of English Poetry* was not replaced but was republished twice with notes, corrections, and new introductory matter.[3] His scheme of literary evolution in three stages, from imagination to a synthesis of imagination and reason during the Elizabethan age and hence to reason, was therefore constantly before the eyes of the age and proved most important for other attempts to write fragments of English literary history.

Thus Robert Alves' *Sketches of the History of Literature* (1794) adopts Warton's triad of periods adding a fourth, his own time, characterized by the prevalence of criticism. George Ellis' "Historical Sketch of the Rise and Progress of the English Language and Literature" (1801), preceding his *Specimens of the Early English Poets* as well as Thomas Campbell's *Essay on English Poetry* (1819), are dependent on Warton's scheme and terminology, even where they go beyond the times treated by him in detail. Echoes of Warton's view of the Elizabethan age as an age of equilibrium between imagination and reason determine the main conceptions of a book such as Nathan Drake's *Shakespeare and His Times* (1817) and can be found also in Hazlitt and elsewhere. Hazlitt, in his *Lectures on the English Poets* (1818), attempts to construe a somewhat different scheme of evolution from the imagination of the Elizabethans to the fancy of the metaphysicals and hence to the wit of the Restoration period and the commonplaces of the eighteenth century.[4]

However, much literary-history writing of the time exemplifies, rather, a type even preceding the psychological concept of evolution implicit in Warton. The concept of a uniform progress toward one ideal standard of style or meter or

3. By Richard Price in 1824 and Richard Taylor in 1840.
4. In *Complete Works,* ed. P. P. Howe, 6 (London, 1930), 83.

simply "enlightenment" was by no means dead during the romantic period. Nathan Drake, in tracing the history of English prose style in his *Essays, Biographical and Historical, Illustrative of the Tatler, Spectator and Guardian* (1805), sees it only as a series of approximations toward the ideal style of Addison and Steele. Elizabethan prose is, for instance, disparaged as "quaint, uncouth and tedious, insufferably prolix," and exhibiting "barbarous and pedantic stiffness."[5] As late as 1835 William Gray, in a *Historical Sketch of the Origin of English Prose Literature,* looks back constantly from the "lofty vantage ground of knowledge and refinement on the undefined and clouded obscurity of barbarism and ignorance"[6] exhibited in older English prose. Even Sharon Turner's extensive history of Anglo-Saxon and Middle English Literature contained in his *History of England* (1799–1815) sees literature purely in terms of uniform progress toward the glories of his own enlightened age. "Poetry and literature have never ceased to advance and are still in their progress. It would be violence in our nature to make them retrograde."[7] Turner condemns Anglo-Saxon poetry as barbarous, savage, and written in a bloated style, and finds even in Chaucer little beyond historical interest. Also George F. Nott, in a "Dissertation on the State of English Poetry before the Sixteenth Century," prefixed to his elaborate edition of Surrey (1815), traces the history of English versification merely in terms of the standard supposedly fixed by Surrey. "All poets," he argues, "before him, must be read in reference to the particular age in which they lived . . . But of this allowance Sur-

5. Pp. 3–4 of Vol. *21,* containing "Of the Progress and Merits of English Style, and on the Style of Addison in Particular."

6. Oxford, 1835, p. 1.

7. *History of England,* Vol. *2: From the Accession of Edward I to the Death of Henry I* (London, 1815), p. 554.

rey never stands in need." Nott obviously realizes the historical "conditionedness" of older literature but considers it as something purely negative. He praises Surrey because there is "hardly anything in all his writings to remind us that he lived three hundred years ago."[8] Examples of this unhistorical belief in uniform progress could be multiplied indefinitely but would only show what we have long known: that the historical sense was slow in awakening in England, and rationalist eighteenth-century conceptions remained alive all through the romantic age.

More skeptical minds turned toward the alternative theory of cyclical progress, which had been known already to Sir William Temple. Progress in literature, though genuine, is accomplished only in leaps and jerks or in an undulatory way, with relapses and retrogressions. This is the view which permeates Joseph Berington's *Literary History of the Middle Ages* (1814) and is also implicit in Henry Hallam's *Introduction to the Literature of Europe* (1837–39). Berington, though a Catholic priest, was an eighteenth-century rationalist who saw medieval literature as a painful progress toward the light of humanism. Even Chaucer appears to him "overrated," and he was "with difficulty prevailed to peruse him."[9] Henry Hallam was essentially a skeptic, with humanistic tastes, critical of progress, especially in literature. He gives us a catalogue of isolated books rather than a history, and great writers appear in it as lucky accidents rather than as links in the context of the process of literature.[10]

8. *The Works of Henry Howard Earl of Surrey,* ed. G. F. Nott, *1* (London, 1815), ccliii.

9. London, 1814, p. 451.

10. There is a review of Hallam in the *Edinburgh Review, 72* (Oct. 1840), 194 ff., which makes most of these same criticisms. The author was Herman Merivale (1806–74). I owe this information to Walter E. Houghton.

The cyclical conception easily led to the idea that literary evolution represents the struggle of two elements, a sequence of actions and reactions, a seesaw between creative and reflective, original and imitative, natural and artificial, or romantic and classical ages. Through Coleridge the contrast between two types of literature—romantic and classical—imported from Germany, had become familiar. But Coleridge's own work, though he planned to write a large-scale history of English literature, is rarely historical in its scale or method. Thus Shakespeare is repeatedly described as "never coloured by the spirit or customs of his age," and we are assured that "there is nothing common to Shakespeare and to other writers of his day—not even the language they employed."[11] The lecture courses which sometimes cover wider fields of literary history make comparatively little use of even the dualism of classical and romantic, and are important in our context largely because they expound the critical revaluation of the past carried out by romantic critics. Thus, in contrast to Drake, the prose writers of the seventeenth century become in Coleridge the "patterns and integers of English style."[12]

The terms "romantic" and "classical" were still largely thought of as psychological types not only by Coleridge but also by the many contemporary writers who adopted the distinction. Variations like the dualism of artificial and natural seem to have lent themselves better to inclusion in a dynamic scheme of development. Robert Southey, in "Sketches of the Progress of English Poetry from Chaucer to Cowper," which introduce his *Life of Cowper* (1836), conceives of English

11. The plan of a history of English literature in a letter to Southey, July 1803, in *Collected Letters,* ed. E. L. Griggs, *2*, 955–56. The quotations are from *Shakespearean Criticism,* ed. T. M. Raysor (1930), *1*, 245; *2*, 125.

12. *Miscellaneous Criticism,* ed. T. M. Raysor (1936), 218.

literature as a "succession of heresies" against the gospel of nature, with intervals of orthodoxy in the Elizabethan age and his own. Southey speaks of "fashions in literature which supply a real or supposed defect; and in both cases the spirit of antagonism has generally given rise to the opposite error." This sounds like a scheme similar to that in Lowes' *Convention and Revolt* or in Cazamian's *Histoire de la littérature anglaise,* which assumes an oscillation of the rhythm of the English national mind. But Southey carries it out with little historical sense or tolerance: the age of Dryden and Pope is to him the "dark" age or the "pinchbeck" age of English poetry.[13] A similar scheme stressing the alternation of original and imitative ages permeates Robert Chambers' much more judicious but also rather colorless *History of the English Language and Literature* (1836). "In the progress of literature," says Chambers, "it would almost seem a fixed law that an age of vigorous original writing and an age of imitation and repetition, should regularly follow each other." In an attempt to account for the changes of taste, Chambers observes that, "Not until men begin to tire of a constant reproduction of the same imagery and the same modes of composition" is a "fresh class of inventive minds allowed to come into operation."[14] Similarly, De Quincey contrasted creative and reflective ages in his essay on *Style* (1840),[15] referring to his classical source, Velleius Paterculus. He, more impartially than Southey, saw the accumulations of English creative energy during the Elizabethan age, the age of Queen Anne, and in his own lifetime, while both the seventeenth century and the

13. *Works of Cowper, 21* (London, 1836), 114, 123, 129, 138, 141.

14. *English Language and Literature,* p. 190.

15. *Collected Writings,* ed. David Masson, *10* (Edinburgh, 1889–90), 186 ff., 202.

latter part of the eighteenth appeared to him as ages of reflection and incubation.

All these schemes imply a necessary, internal evolution of literature—some self-propelling dialectics in the process of literature. But few attempts were made at that time to trace the history of a genre concretely in terms of its evolution. John Payne Collier's *History of English Dramatic Poetry up to the Time of Shakespeare* (1831) is the one ambitious attempt to trace the history of a genre as a developing form. Taking hints from Percy and Malone, Collier elaborates the view that English drama was not created by one man or in one age. He shows first how the mystery plays almost imperceptibly "deviated into the morality, by the gradual intermixture of allegory with sacred history." The morality plays, in turn, "gave way to tragedy and comedy by the introduction, from time to time, of characters of actual life, or supposed to be drawn from it."[16] In practice, Collier's book is less satisfying than his program, as he was starting too many hares at a time: he gives us a long list of plays and performances and much information on the theatres, and loses sight of his ideal of a history of genre as an art form.

Besides these new methods in the study of the evolution of literature, new concepts deriving from a social view of literature became more and more important for the writing of literary history. The eighteenth century had already studied literature as a source for the history of manners and society, but little, except in general and vague terms, was done to show the specific dependence of literature on social changes. Among literary biographies Scott's lives of Dryden and Swift were particularly important for their deliberate attempt to set the authors into the context of their times.[17] But among liter-

16. Vol. 1 (London, 1831), xi–xiii.
17. See a good discussion of Scott's *Life of Dryden* in J. M. Osborn, *Dryden: Facts and Problems* (New York, 1940), pp. 72 ff.

ary histories proper only John Dunlop's *History of Fiction* (1814) is planned definitely in close relationship with the history of society. Dunlop was no mere reteller of tales nor was he a proper historian of the novel who would pay attention to the evolving craft of fiction. To him fiction serves first and foremost as "a successive delineation of a people's prevalent modes of thinking, a picture of their feelings and tastes and habits." The social explanations for these changes are surprisingly numerous and concrete for the time. For instance, the creation of marvelous fictions is described as facilitated by a small society of scanty means of communication, where the "limits of probability were not precisely ascertained." Or he sees the mercantile spirit opposed to the extravagant courage and refined gallantry of the feudal classes in the rise of the Italian *novella*. Or, again, he tries to explain the failure of the French heroic romance in England by the contrast between the Court of Louis XIV and that of Charles II, and he concludes that "from the very nature of domestic fiction, it must vary with the forms and habits and customs of society, which it must picture as they occur successively."[18]

The view that literature is the expression of a specific society and age is preparatory to the idea that literature is the expression of a national spirit and, in some vague way, the creation of a national mind. Partly under the influence of German ideas, with the growing strength of an "organic" view of society and the increased taste for popular literature, this idea gradually assumed a central position in the programs for the writing of literary history. Coleridge used the term "Gothic mind" and disparaged the Latin civilizations from a vague Nordic point of view.[19] Southey objected strongly to Pope's and Thomas Gray's schemes for the history of English

18. 2nd ed. Edinburgh, 1816, *1*, xxx–xxxi, 119–20, 156–57; *2*, 150–51, 157–58.

19. *Miscellaneous Criticism*, pp. 12–15, 32.

literature as ignoring the fact that the English have a "costume and character of [their] own." Southey speaks of the "home-growth" of English verse and of English literature as "colored by the national character, as wine of different soils has its raciness."[20] The nearer the soil and nature, the better and the more national the poetry. Thomas Carlyle, who, like Coleridge and Southey, planned a new history of English literature,[21] formulated the new conception most clearly in his scathing review of William Taylor of Norwich's *Historic Survey of German Poetry* (1831).

> The history of a nation's poetry is the essence of its history, political, scientific, religious. With all these the complete Historian of Poetry will be familiar: the national physiognomy, in its finest traits, and through its successive stages of growth, will be clear to him; he will discern the grand spiritual tendency of every period, which was the highest Aim and Enthusiasm of mankind in each, and how one epoch evolved itself from the other. He has to record the highest aim of a nation, in its successive directions and developments; for by this the Poetry of the nation modulates itself; this *is* the Poetry of the nation. Such were the primary essence of a true history of poetry.[22]

Here all the key terms of historicism are assembled: individuality, nationality, development, the spirit of a nation and an age, continuity. Carlyle's conception was to dominate at

20. *Works of Cowper,* p. 126.

21. Carlyle's plan (1827) in *Two Notebooks,* ed. C. E. Norton (New York, 1898), p. 120. For Coleridge's plan, see above, n. 11. Southey's plan is in *Life and Correspondence,* ed. C. C. Southey, *5* (1850), 245; from a letter to Grosvenor C. Bedford, Feb. 18, 1826.

22. *Essays* in Centenary Ed. *2* (London, 1896–99), 341–42; originally in *Edinburgh Review, 53,* No. 105 (1831).

least one important strand of historiography during the remainder of the century.

Still, the intellectual atmosphere changed considerably during the Victorian age. The literary historiography of the time can be best discussed in terms of two oppositions: first, the age-old disagreement between those who think of literature as a series of isolated works and those who find at the very center of literary history the problem of its continuity and development; and second, the conflict, specifically characteristic of the Victorian Age, between those who want to assimilate literary history to the methods and results of the natural sciences and those who use inherited concepts of the idealistic philosophical tradition. As these contraries overlap, we arrive at four broad types of literary histories: the scientific and static, the scientific and dynamic, the idealistic and static, and the idealistic and dynamic. So formulated, this is, of course, merely a convenient classification. It can be made useful and convincing only in its application to the concrete variety of history.

In first discussing the attempts to make literary history a science, we must distinguish between the mere general adoption of the attitude of modern science and the actual transfer of scientific concepts to the study of literature. I think it is a common mistake to consider all regard for meticulous accuracy, completeness of evidence, and disinterested objectivity as due to the prestige of the natural sciences. The humanists of the Renaissance or the Jesuit and Benedictine scholars of the seventeenth century frequently cultivated these scholarly virtues without much attention to physical science. Unquestionably, in the nineteenth century the successes of the natural sciences enhanced the regard for these virtues. But if a scholar like F. J. Furnivall proclaimed himself a "scientific botanist," he was merely trying to justify the validity of objective metrical tests for the determination of a chronology of Shakespeare's plays. In his violent controversy with Swinburne he rudely ridiculed the poet's reliance on his "long hairy, thick and dull ear," because Swinburne had dared to doubt some of his findings.[23] In practice, scholarly research meant an avoidance of all wider questions, a suspension of all critical judgment, a resigned attitude to the accumulation of isolated external facts, and a vague hope that some day these "bricks" may be used in building the great pyramid of learning. The influence of academic German scholarship, which was well organized and well trained, worked in the same direction: attempts at synthesis were being discouraged or postponed to a distant future. In England A. W. Ward, who himself had written a *History of English Dramatic Literature* (1875),[24] became the main exponent of this view, which he called *Realpolitik*.[25] The success and limitations of this attitude can be seen in the growing flood of dictionaries, monographs, contributions, notes, and queries. They almost always imply an atomistic, static conception of literature and are hence inimical to the writing of literary history. The use of contemporary psychological conceptions was also of little importance for literary history proper. For instance, William Minto, in his books on *English Prose* (1872) and the *Characteristics of English Poets* (1874), could analyze only isolated

23. *The "Co." of Pigsbrook and Co.* (London, 1881), p. 4; *Mr. Swinburne's "Flat Burglary" on Shakespeare* (London, 1879), p. 4.

24. In the first chapter some general theories about the English national character, drawn from Ten Brink and Henry Morley, are used (*1* [London, 1899], 48, 64, etc.), but the body of the book is rather annals of the stage than a proper history.

25. *Collected Papers: Historical, Literary, Travel and Miscellaneous,* 5 (5 vols. Cambridge, 1921), 300. From a review of Creizenach, originally in *Modern Language Review* (July 1909).

details of literary form, because he had adopted the purely
atomistic psychology of Mill and Bain.[26]

We move beyond these static conceptions when we turn to
the writers who thought of literature as completely determined by its social background. In his later years Leslie
Stephen held this view in an extreme form: literature appeared
to him only a by-product of the social development, the "noise
of the wheels of history."[27] Most of the positivists in the Com-
tian sense, studied not so much literary history as intellectual
history reflecting social evolution. John Morley thus recommends, especially for the study of literature, "an ordered and
connected survey . . . of the manifold variations that time
and circumstances are incessantly making in human society."[28] Morley, in practice, in his biographies and essays,
aimed at "tracing the relations of the poet's ideas . . . through
the central currents of thought, to the visible tendencies of an
existing age."[29] In an attenuated form we find echoes of this
point of view in many academic historians—for example, in
Sir Sidney Lee, who defined the study of literature expressly
as the study of the "external circumstances—political, social,

26. *A Manual of English Prose Literature* (Edinburgh, 1881), pp.
3, 5, 7, 10, 11, 23, 27, etc. Minto clearly realizes the opposition of
his analytical method to the grandiose generalizations of Taine. Cf.
*Characteristics of English Poets* (2nd ed. Edinburgh, 1881), pp. 1,
276.

27. Frederick William Maitland, *The Life and Letters of Leslie
Stephen* (London, 1906), pp. 283–84. Cf. "Literature is a particular
function of the whole social organism," in "The Study of English
Literature," *Cornhill Magazine, 8* (May 1886), 492. The same phrase
is in *English Literature and Society in the Eighteenth Century* (London, 1904), p. 14.

28. "On the Study of Literature" (1887), in *Studies in Literature*
(London, 1891), pp. 219–20.

29. "Byron," in *Critical Miscellanies, 1* (London, 1886), 209–10.

economic—in which literature is produced."[30] However, in Lee and in many others of his type we get, in practice, little more than isolated attempts to trace specific literary phenomena to their supposed social antecedents or causes, which are understood to constitute a principle of explanation.

Much more fruitful for literary history was the attempt to transfer the concept of biological evolutionism to the history of literature. On a small scale, in literary biography, we find Spencerian ideas of integration in as well-known a book as Edward Dowden's *Shakespeare: His Mind and Art* (1875). Shakespeare's development is conceived of as a moral self-integration, an illustration of a general human pattern. Using the terminology of Spencer's *Biology,* Dowden attempts to show how "the structural arrangement of Shakespeare's whole nature became more complex and involved" until his work became "the expression of a complete personality."[31] The Spencerian thesis of progress from communal to individual life also permeates H. M. Posnett's *Comparative Literature* (1886).[32] But only in John Addington Symonds do we find a literary historian who clearly conceived of literary evolution in terms of Darwinian biology. His book in *Shakspere's Predecessors in the English Drama* (1884)[33] and a paper on the "Application of Evolutionary Principles to Art and Literature" (1890)[34] propound the theory that a genre runs a well-defined course of germination, expansion, efflorescence, and

30. "The Place of English Literature in the Modern University" (1913), in *Elizabethan and other Essays* (London, 1929), p. 7.

31. Eleventh ed. London, 1897, pp. 44, 46, 107, 224, 328.

32. London, 1886, p. 20.

33. *Shakspere's Predecessors* was written largely in 1866, though published only in 1884. See *Letters and Papers,* ed. Horatio F. Brown (London, 1923), p. 147.

34. In *Essays, Speculative and Suggestive, 1* (London, 1890), 42–84.

decay. This development he describes as an e-volution, an unfolding of the embryonic elements to which nothing can be added and which run their course with iron necessity to their predestined exhaustion. Thus the initiative of the individual is completely suppressed and even the individuality of the different chains of evolution disappears. English drama and Italian painting evolve in exactly the same manner. Literary history becomes a sort of biology, in which individual cases are only documents for the illustration of a general scientific law. In practice, Symonds is saved from some of the worst consequences of his scientific scheme only by an innate aestheticism which contrasts rather oddly with his rigid theory. Symonds at least saw the problem of evolution in literature: he recognized its continuity, its change, its direction toward specific aims. But he sacrificed the individual and thus could not achieve a basis for successful literary history.

In Symonds we see naturalism rampant: literary history as a branch of biology. However, there was considerable opposition to naturalism in the Victorian age, a hostility from two directions: from the aesthetic movement and from the new idealism which we associate with Oxford Hegelianism. Besides, a third distinct type of opposition can be described as a survival: the romantic concept of literature as the expression of the national mind. The aesthetes objected to the lack of critical judgments in literary history and stressed the importance of the individual's enjoyment and appreciation. As this was dependent on the artist's unfettered sensibility, aestheticism worked also for a static conception of literature. Certainly, no grasp of the continuity of literature can be ascribed to the erratic writings of Swinburne. Edmund Gosse, in his *Short History of Modern English Literature* (1897), professed to show the "movement of English literature" and, "above all else," to "give a feeling of the evolution of English literature," but in practice, his books are a series of critical remarks on authors and some of their works. He was only paying lip service to an ideal which began to spread from France. Later, Gosse quite rightly disclaimed any interest in Taine and stressed his indebtedness to Sainte-Beuve.[35]

Also in this group is George Saintsbury. On the whole, he endorses the creed of "appreciation"[36] and asks the critic to be passive as a photographer's plate. Saintsbury does have, however, great merits as a literary historian. His stress on the art of literature and on the comparative method, and his idea of a map of literature, go beyond mere critical impressionism. But Saintsbury disliked and distrusted philosophy, aesthetics, and linguistics so much that his most ambitious books, such as the *History of Criticism* (1900–04), the *History of English Prosody* (1906), and the *History of English Prose Rhythm* (1912), are vitiated by confused assumptions or strange exclusions. Much in his many surveys of English and French literature is superficial, and his writings on things German and Russian are almost comic exhibitions of ignorance and prejudice.[37] Still, Saintsbury had a considerable flair for ques-

35. Evan Charteris, *The Life and Letters of Sir Edmund Gosse* (London, 1931), p. 477; from a letter to F. C. Roe, March 19, 1924.

36. "The enthusiastic appreciation of letters [is] really the highest function of criticism," in *History of English Criticism, 3* (Edinburgh, 1911), 375. Cf. endorsement of Pater, ibid., pp. 498–504. Photographer's plate, ibid., pp. 499, 521. Cf., for "map of literature," *Inaugural Address* (Edinburgh, 1895), p. 24, and the whole essay "The Kinds of Criticism," in *Essays in English Literature, 1780–1860* (London, 1890).

37. Heine is called "as deep as Dante"! Gottfried Keller is considered a "scholar in the older forms of modern languages," apparently in confusion with Heinrich Adalbert Keller, the editor of the publications of the *Stuttgarter Litterarische Verein*. Tolstoy's novels are "hardly works of art at all," pronounces Saintsbury, without

tions of form and knew what is meant by problems of wider and widest scope—by literary movements, ages, and the total development of Western literature—even though his criteria were impressionistic and personal. He did good work in stressing the art of literature as against the excessive intellectualism of the age. The dangers of irresponsible subjectivism become far more apparent in the work of Sir Walter Raleigh, who completely disapproved the conception of literary scholarship as organized knowledge. His constant refuge is the position that he can do no more than enjoy or cry over a given work of literature.[38] This negative, even profoundly skeptical, attitude toward scholarship became fashionable in England early in the twentieth century and paralyzed all work except technical antiquarianism or rambling, allusive, and whimsical essays in the "art of praise."

A second distinct intellectual movement of the Victorian age was philosophical idealism, as it was most clearly formulated by the Oxford Hegelians. But the British Hegelians rejected precisely the most fruitful idea of Hegelianism: the dialectics. The brother of F. H. Bradley, A. C. Bradley, analyzed Shakespearean tragedy from the point of view of Hegel's theory of tragedy, but his interests were not in literary history as such. W. P. Ker also advocated an unhistorical static idealism. In his essay on the "Philosophy of Art," published in the Hegelian manifesto *Essays in Philosophical Criticism* (1883), he contends that a work of art is not a chain in a series, that it cannot be explained causally, and that it is above the world of

---

even mentioning *War and Peace,* and in discussing Dostoevsky, ignores the *Brothers Karamazov* and *The Idiot.* See *The Later Nineteenth Century* (London, 1907), pp. 199, 206, 339–40, 344.

38. Sir Walter Raleigh, *Letters,* ed. Lady Raleigh, *1* (London, 1926), 164, 268–69. Cf. *The Study of English Literature* (Glasgow, 1900).

movement.[39] In a lecture on Thomas Warton (1910) he elaborated the contrast between literary history dealing with an ever-present matter which it can merely point to, as a guide in a gallery points to the pictures, and political history which reconstructs a vanished past.[40] As one would expect, in most of his books—such as *Epic and Romance* (1897) or *English Literature: Medieval* (1912)—conceptions of static literary types prevail. Not until his lectures given in 1912 did Ker see that "if the history of literature is to be properly a history and not merely a series of biographies—lives of the poets and essays on their works—then there must be a study of what is continuous and common, of the tendencies which different authors share, the forms and fashions which they inherit, the origins of their art."[41] Though Ker is still rightly skeptical about the evolution of genres as understood by Symonds and Brunetière, he sees the problem of literary development clearly.

But conceptions of dialectical evolution were by no means limited to scholars associated with Hegelianism. Leslie Stephen's early book *The History of English Thought in the Eighteenth Century* (1876) conceives of the development of eighteenth-century thought as a continuous debate leading to the conclusion of agnosticism, worked out in a rich scheme of contraries which is inclusive enough to take account of social influences and of the relationship of ideological movements to the life of the imagination. Even Walter Pater, who is usually considered to have been a mere impressionist, recognized dynamic evolution as the "essence of the historic, the really critical method,"[42] though actually he did little which

39. Reprinted in *Collected Essays, 2* (London, 1925), 231–68.
40. Ibid., *1*, 100.
41. *Form and Style in Poetry,* ed. R. W. Chambers (London, 1928), p. 50.
42. *Plato and Platonism* (London, 1893), pp. 9–11.

could be described as literary history proper. The ideas of a dialectical process remained, on the whole, confined to intellectual historians and are, for example, most clearly used by Mark Pattison, who considered the laws of dialectic "the thread that must be taken up to follow through the mazes of history."[43]

But there survived most persistently in the Victorian age another concept of literary development: that of the history of literature conceived as the history of the national mind as formulated by Carlyle. Literary history thus became the history of national ideals, and literature the mouthpiece of the nation. These ideas are obviously derived from German romanticism and are labeled "organological" by German scholarship. We find them often curiously confused with other concepts in the most popular handbooks of the time, in the writings of David Masson, and especially in the many books of Henry Morley. Masson can use phrenological jargon about the "national brain of Britain which had suffered a sudden contraction in the frontal organs of ideality, wonder and comparison." He can, as early as 1859, speak about "self-contained evolution," a "natural law" by which genres detach themselves or are "thrown off" from a nondescript original form. He can ask his students to study "that vital and essential something—a clear transparency—which we call the mind or spirit of the time."[44] Morley thinks of English literature as the "national biography," "the story of the English mind," "the continuous expression of one national character." In Morley these conceptions were, in practice, overshadowed by consid-

43. "Theology in Germany" (1857), in *Essays*, ed. H. Nettelship, 2 (London, 1889), 232.

44. *British Novelists and their Styles* (Cambridge, 1859), pp. 35, 76. "How Literature May Illustrate History" (1871), in *The Three Devils: Luther's, Milton's, and Goethe's, and other Essays* (London, 1874).

erations of a purely pedagogical nature. Literature becomes almost a system of national ethics, "an embodiment of the religious life of England," a collection of uplifting passages and inspiring lives.[45]

At the end of our period W. J. Courthope wrote his *History of English Poetry* (1895–1910), which, it seems to me, combines in a skillful way some of the leading concepts of the time: "national imagination" is at the center, but its history mirrors the development of society and politics, which are conceived as growing like a biological organism. Politics and literature are thought of as springing from one common source: the evolution of national character and mentality. But the evolution itself is seen as a long dialectical process, as a conflict between individualism and collectivism which goes right through English history. Their perfect synthesis and harmony is Courthope's own political and poetical ideal. In the Middle Ages there was an unhealthy preponderance of collectivism. During the Renaissance a harmony was established, while in modern times, mainly through romanticism, individualism tends to prevail both in poetry and in politics. The English constitution, with its harmony of freedom and authority, is to Courthope a model for the ideal harmony between the individuality of the poet and the national tradition. Courthope is a master in evoking long vistas into intellectual history. The flexibility of his general conception and the boldness with which it is carried out put Courthope's five volumes in the very front rank of English literary histories. But his critical power is frequently cramped by rigid moralism and academic classicism. His main defects emerge in his analyses of individual writers: his sense of poetic form is rather

45. *English Writers: The Writers before Chaucer* (London, 1864), Preface; Henry S. Solly, *The Life of Henry Morley* (London, 1898), pp. 288–89, 330.

weak, and a final impression prevails that the history of English poetry is an abstract play of massive intellectual movements and tendencies, in which the art of literature seems almost completely lost.[46] We must therefore conclude that none of the many Victorian histories of English literature can satisfy the ideal of purely *literary* history. They are either histories of civilization as mirrored in literature, or collections of critical essays in chronological order. The first type is not a history of *art,* the other not a *history* of art.

But the Victorian age worked out at least the possibility of literary history with a central concept of continuous dynamic evolution. Biological evolutionism, which came in about 1860, denied individuality but for the first time conceived clearly the problem of an internal evolution of art. About 1880 aestheticism restored the balance by reasserting the individuality of the work of art, but it was apt to dissolve literature again into a series of unconnected works. The actual synthesis was never achieved except in the possible approximation of Courthope's rather eclectic scheme. To write a really satisfactory history of English literature, which would not be the history of something else but the history of the *art* of literature, is still a problem and a task for the future.

46. Some of these criticisms are in Oliver Elton, "The Meaning of Literary History," in *Modern Studies* (London, 1907), pp. 138–48.

# Vernon Lee, Bernard Berenson, and Aesthetics

In *La Casa della Vita* Mario Praz recalls an English woman writer then living in Florence, Violet Paget, who used the pseudonym Vernon Lee (1856–1935). In 1920 she put him in touch with the *London Mercury* and thus smoothed his way into the English literary world. When he was in England in 1925, she wrote him a letter which Praz quotes with approval. His special talent, it seemed to her, is the personal essay which "you do better than mere literary criticism."[1] Mario Praz has increasingly followed this bent of his mind: his travel books, his essays collected as *Fiori freschi (1943)*, *Motivi e figure (1945)*, *Lettrice notturna (1952)*, *La Casa della fama (1952)*, *Bellezza e bizzarria (1960)*, could be called testimonies to her foresight. It is no chance that Vernon Lee gave him a copy of Lamb's *Specimens of English Dramatic Poets* before he left for England in 1923 and that his first publication in book form was a translation of Lamb's *Essays of Elia* (1924).

After her death on February 13, 1935, Mario Praz wrote an essay which gives an impression of her personality and discusses some of her many books: the collection of stories *Vanitas* (1892), through which "echoes a note of reproach and regret for frivolous existences," her sketches of Italian towns, landscapes, and gardens, her studies of Italian eighteenth-century literature and music and of Italian Re-

1. *La Casa della Vita* (Milano, 1958), p. 262.

naissance art and poetry, and her discussions of the style of English writers. "All the flavor" of her essays, Praz comments, "is based on an exceptional response to vivid experience, on some poet's verse she has contemplated so long it has become emblematic. This makes the originality and strength of her essays but also their weakness." The essays are not nourished by a critical erudition; she is rather an imaginative personal writer who must not be judged for her contribution to scholarship. A beautiful thing is for her an "aid to devotion," it serves as "a tuning-fork to make her vibrate with the rhythm of universal life."[2] Vernon Lee is a sensitive appreciator, an aesthete, though Praz knows that she was ashamed of her leisure and became passionately absorbed in political and civic causes.

Recently the book by Peter Gunn has given us glimpses of her tortured emotional life and an outline of her manifold activities.[3] It could draw on the collection of her letters printed in a limited private edition[4] and on several articles on her relations with Henry James, Carlo Placci, and others.[5] But her writings have not been reprinted and are little read

2. *Studi e svaghi inglesi* (Florence, 1937). The essay uses earlier articles in *La Stampa*, 1930 and 1935, and in *Pègaso*, 1932. See p. viiin. Quotations on pp. 328, 330–31, 335. Oddly enough it is not listed in the bibliography of writings on Vernon Lee in Peter Gunn's *Vernon Lee* (London, 1964).

3. See above, n. 2.

4. *Vernon Lee's Letters*, Preface by her Executor (privately printed for Irene Cooper Willis, London, 1937). Limited to 50 copies.

5. Carl J. Weber, "Henry James and His Tiger-Cat," *PMLA, 68* (1953), 672–87; Burdett Gardner, "An Apology for Henry James's 'Tiger-Cat,' " ibid., pp. 688–95; Leon Edel, "Henry James and Vernon Lee," ibid., *69* (1954), 677–78; Sybille Pantazzi, "Enrico Nencioni, William Westmore Story and Vernon Lee," *English Miscellany, 10* (1959), 249–60, and her "Carlo Placci and Vernon Lee," ibid., *12* (1961), 97–122.

today for reasons gently hinted at in Praz's essay: her erudition is obsolete, her minute studies of feelings in relation to town and landscape are superseded by the subtler pages of Proust, and her long-winded, earnest moralizing about dead public issues stamps her as a Victorian. Still, something can be done to rescue her from oblivion by paying attention to what was, after all, the central concern of her intellectual life: aesthetics. We must attempt to locate her in a history of thought and to confront her with Bernard Berenson, who, in matters of theory, is nearest to her.

Vernon Lee's early writings can be described as generally in the tradition of Walter Pater. Hardly out of her teens, she developed an "entirely unabstract, unsystematic, essentially personal" aesthetics, a clearly articulated "formalism" which sees that "the only perfection of art is perfection of form." The work of art is an "existing, definite form," quite different from the "association, recollection, fancy" it may attract, from the whole literary content of visual art, which leads her to the conclusion that "we have caught ourselves almost regretting that pictures have any subjects." At this stage Vernon Lee decisively rejects identification of the beautiful and the good, the whole Ruskinian morality of art, as false and argues that artistic and private personality need not be the same. Vasari's account of Perugino serves as a test case: the "unique painter of archangels and seraphs appears a base commercial speculator, a cynic, an atheist." She concludes that "Beauty is pure, complete, egotistic: it has no other value than it being beautiful." This is to her a "bitter confession" for which she has, at that time, only the consolation that art still has "a moral value; it is happiness, and to bestow happiness is to create good."[6] The two volumes of *Euphorion* (1884) dedi-

6. *Belcaro* (London, 1881), pp. 9, 48, 182–83, 66, 205–06, 172, 210–11, 229.

cated to Walter Pater sustain basically the same point of view. One of the essays, "The Italy of the Elizabethan Dramatists," relies far too heavily on the divorce between art and morality, on a simple contrast between the "nation chaste and true," which wrote "tales of incest and treachery," and "the foul and false nation," which wrote "poetry of shepherds and knights-errant."[7] Mario Praz was to discuss Machiavelli in England with far greater erudition and much better sense. But in the same year *Euphorion* was published, Vernon Lee's novel *Miss Brown,* dedicated to a reluctant Henry James, showed her acute disappointment with aesthetes and aestheticism. It is an acid satire on the circles she had frequented in England. Henry James, after a long delay in commenting on her book remonstrated with her: "You are really too savage with your painters and poets and dilettanti: life is less criminal, less obnoxious, less objectionable, less crude, more *bon enfant,* more mixed and casual, and even in its most offensive manifestations, more *pardonable,* than the unholy circle with which you have surrounded your heroine."[8] In the introduction dedicated to Carlo Placci, of a new collection of essays, *Juvenilia* (1887), Vernon Lee discards her aesthetic concerns as *juvenilia.* The realm of art appears to her now as an Elysium which "was never a reality, but only a phantom place of our fantastic building." She worries now over industrialization and poverty symbolized by a glimpse of Newcastle on Tyne and warns that the "convenient division of property and class cannot be kept up for good."[9] She became absorbed in

7. *Euphorion, 1* (2 vols. London, 1884), 87.

8. *Selected Letters of Henry James,* ed. L. Edel (New York, 1955), p. 206, dated May 10, 1885. In the story "Lady Tal" *(Vanitas: Polite Stories* [London, 1892]) the hero, Jervase Marion, was taken to be a caricature of Henry James. For the repercussions see Leon Edel, *Henry James, The Middle Years* (Philadelphia, 1962), pp. 332–35.

9. *Juvenilia, 1* (2 vols. London, 1887), 6, 11.

socialism, feminism, and pacifism: she argued about Tolstoy and much later with H. G. Wells. But surprisingly and possibly illogically, just at the time she was going through a crisis in which all that she had loved before seemed stale or unimportant, she discovered a new theory of art which allowed her to preserve her old love with a new justification.

The process of this discovery and its exact chronology and sources remain somewhat obscure, as her own account is, I suspect, too highly colored by her piety for her friend Clementina Anstruther-Thomson (1857–1921), whom she met in 1887 in England and who came to stay with her in Florence in 1888.[10] Miss Anstruther-Thomson had some training as a painter at the Slade School of Art but, apparently out of her own self-observation, developed an interest in describing her reactions to works of art. Vernon Lee ascribes to her influence the recognition that "much as I had written and even much as I had read about works of art, I did not really know them when they were in front of me." "Until then I really knew of works of art only that much which can be translated into literature." At first Vernon Lee imagined that this deficiency was due to a lack of training in drawing, or knowledge of perspective and anatomy, but she soon saw that it was nothing technical or intellectual. It had never occurred to her that "such high philosophical topics could be dealt with as a part of the science of Mind and Mind's relations with Body."[11] With the help of her friend she was made aware that works of art do something to us: induce us to make hidden motor adjustments to the forms we contemplate, to imitate them inwardly and to project our inner bodily movements on to the objects so that we move with the lines of a painting, lift our-

10. See *Vernon Lee's Letters,* pp. 271, 315.

11. Clementina Anstruther-Thomson, *Art and Man,* ed. with an Introduction by Vernon Lee (London, 1924), pp. 29, 46.

selves with the swing of an arch or feel a flat surface as deep or bulky. In an entirely empirical way the two women discovered the general principle of an aesthetics of *empathy*. Vernon Lee began to study the psychological literature. In 1894 she bought William James' *Principles of Psychology* (1890), she read an Italian book by Giuseppe Serpi, *Dolore e Piacere* (1894), and soon she must have studied German technical literature: she refers to Theodor Lipps and to Karl Groos,[12] and she read Adolf Hildebrand's little pamphlet *Das Problem der Form in der bildenden Kunst* (1893). Hildebrand, the German sculptor, who had lived in Florence since 1872, was an old acquaintance, and Mrs. Jessie Hillebrand, the widow of the German essayist Karl Hillebrand, another old friend, was then translating the essay into English.[13] Vernon Lee knew German from girlhood and threw herself into the study of the German psychologists with astonishing zeal.

The lectures she gave in London in 1895 to a miscellaneous audience, published in the *Contemporary Review* (1896) and later reprinted as *Laurus nobilis* (1909), seem still untouched by technically psychological interests. They imply, rather, an earlier prescientific stage of the aesthetics of *Einfühlung,* the idea of projection, of "lending" to the object, of identification which has its modern source in Herder but was mostly clearly expounded by F. T. Vischer and by Hermann Lotze.[14] It is

12. *Letters,* p. 384 on William James. She refers to Hildebrand's essay (p. 671n.), and to Groos and Lipps in "Beauty and Ugliness," *Contemporary Review 72* (Oct. 1897), 544–69, 669–88.

13. See Bernhard Sattler, *Adolf von Hildebrand und seine Welt* (Munich, 1962). On Jessie Hillebrand's translation (never finished) see letter of Sept. 17, 1893, in *Letters,* p. 415. Vernon Lee had dedicated her story *Ottilie* (1883) to Karl Hillebrand (1829–84).

14. For antecedents of *Einfühlung* see Paul Stern, *Einfühlung und Association in der neueren Ästhetik* (Hamburg, 1898). A recent ac-

combined with what could be called "vitalism," a variation of hedonism which at that time was formulated by Guyau in France and of course by Nietzsche, of whom she also might have heard from Karl Hillebrand, one of his earliest admirers.[15] One passage alludes to the German term:

> Beauty is a power in our life, because, however intermittent its action and however momentary, it makes us live, by a kind of sympathy with itself a life fuller, more vivid, and at the same time more peaceful. But as the word sympathy, with-feeling—*(einfühlen,* "feeling into," the Germans happily put it)—as the word *sympathy* is intended to suggest, this enlivening and pacifying power of beautiful form over our feelings is exercised only when our feelings enter, and are absorbed into, the form we perceive; so that (very much as in the case of sympathy with human vicissitudes) we participate in the supposed life of the form while in reality lending our life to it.

She speaks also of "following the life of the visible and audible forms, and living yourself into their pattern and rhythm."[16] The heightening of our vitality is considered the aesthetic phenomenon par excellence.

In 1896 Vernon Lee must have felt securely advanced in her understanding of the theory of *Einfühlung* to write a re-

---

count with bibliographies is in Guido Morpurgo-Tagliabue, *L'Esthétique contemporaine* (Milan, 1960). Compare also the comments in Edgar Wind's *Art and Anarchy* (London, 1963), esp. pp. 50, 150–51.

15. Hillebrand had reviewed Nietzsche's *Unzeitgemässe Betrachtungen* favorably and corresponded with him.

16. *Laurus Nobilis* (London, 1909), pp. 239–40, 242. Originally in *Contemporary Review* (1896).

view of Bernard Berenson's *Florentine Painters of the Renaissance* (1896) for the philosophical review *Mind*. She recommends the book for its interest to psychologists, though "Mr. Berenson himself is not a student of mental sciences . . . and his book shows no traces of psychological training."[17] Vernon Lee endorses his vitalism and then explains Berenson's theory of tactile values. "We watch," she quotes, "those tautnesses of muscles and those stretchings and relaxings and ripplings of skin which, translated into similar strains in our own persons, make us fully realize movement."[18] Vernon Lee objects only to what she considers the complication, in Berenson, with the notion of a self-conscious "Wille zur Macht" and his deliberate neglect of mere "Beauty." Still, she welcomes the tactile value theory and recommends it, somewhat condescendingly, to a professional audience.

Vernon Lee had met Berenson possibly as early as 1891. To judge from the few published letters, all dating from 1892, of Berenson to Mary Costelloe (the later Mrs. Berenson), Berenson's impressions were far from favorable. He complains that she "monologized. I never heard such *spropositi* as she aired for an hour. I was scarcely polite in my stern dissent." He repeats on another occasion that she "talks like a steam engine" and he suspects her of wanting to get information from him. "There is a man she thinks who has done all the dirty work, all the unskilled labor. Let me use my real intelligence in exploiting him. You may imagine I don't feel too much like being exploited. But she is stimulating in a way." Miss Anstruther-Thomson, however, seems to him "stupid."[19] Vernon Lee saw him in London in July 1893;

17. *Mind,* n.s., 2 (1896), 270–72.
18. *Florentine Painters* (New York, 1896), p. 86.
19. *The Selected Letters of Bernard Berenson,* ed. A. K. McComb (Boston, 1964), pp. 11, 14, 15, 24. All early 1892.

she reports to her mother that Miss Anstruther-Thomson took her and Berenson, "that little art critic who appears destined to become famous," to see the Velazquezes at Apsley House.[20]

We must understand the relation of the two at that time. Vernon Lee, nine years older than Berenson, was then a famous or near-famous authoress, a well-to-do woman prominent in Florentine English society. Berenson had not published a single book (except an anonymous guide), though he might have told her that among his articles he contributed as an undergraduate to the *Harvard Monthly* (1886) was a review of her collection of essays, *Baldwin*.[21] There Berenson praised *Studies in the 18th Century in Italy* as her best book and described *Belcaro* and *Euphorion* sympathetically. But *Miss Brown* seem to him "not quite a work of art," and he complained of "fog-banks of metaphysics, theology and economics" in *Baldwin*. He was then working on his first book, *The Venetian Painters of the Renaissance* (1894), which still shows no interest in a theory of empathy or any psychological aesthetics. The book is full of generalizations about the spirit of the Renaissance and, with an Arnoldian term, its "adequacy" to life, and the rise and decline of Venetian painting. The point of view is art for art's sake. Venetian painting "serves no obvious purpose either of decoration or suggestion, but giving pleasure by the skillful management of light and shadow." In two passages vague Pateresque parallels to music are drawn. The "colouring" of the Venetians "not only gives direct pleasure to the eye, but acts like music upon the moods." The angels in Titian's "Assumption" are "embodied joys, acting on our nerves like the rapturous outburst of the orchestra at the end of *Parsifal*." The story of the decline of Venetian painting concludes oddly

20. *Vernon Lee's Letters*, p. 353, July 21, 1893.
21. *Harvard Monthly, 2* (July 1886), 207–09.

with a profession of faith "in a great future for humanity." "Nothing has yet happened to check our delight in discovery or our faith in life."[22]

Some time in 1894 or 1895 an illumination came over Berenson: he discovered "tactile values," *Einfühlung,* "volume" as a criterion of painting. Even in the book on *Lorenzo Lotto* (1895) there is no trace yet of the new creed. The printed sources are deficient, but a letter to Mary Costelloe, dated July 31, 1895, tells her as something of a novelty that "even if our primary sensations of space be three-dimensional (which I would not deny) the third dimension in precise form must largely be the result of tactile and loco-motor sensation."[23] He is writing from Berlin. That summer he saw and admired the Wittelsbach fountain of Adolf Hildebrand in Munich.[24] He must have read Hildebrand's pamphlet, which says exactly what Berenson was to say in *The Florentine Painters:* "Seeing is really touching." "The task of art is the conversion of depth images into plane impressions, in order to create spatial values." Empathy is an "inward acting with and our lending this inner action to the outer phenomena as cause." In a note Hildebrand, who was primarily concerned with sculpture and particularly a defense of the relief, refers to pictures of the early Renaissance as illustrating the process of learning to make the picture appear as receding in space.[25] The background of the theory of tactile values is thus clear enough. Form in Hildebrand's

22. *The Venetian Painters of the Renaissance* (2nd ed. New York, 1895), pp. 67, 2, 40, 78.

23. *The Bernard Berenson Treasury,* ed. Hanna Kiel (New York, 1962), pp. 83–84.

24. *Selected Letters,* p. 30, Aug. 21, 1895.

25. *Das Problem der Form in der bildenden Kunst* (3rd ed. Strassburg, 1901), pp. 19, 32, 95, 65n.

sense, volume, bulk, becomes the standard of art. Color is subordinated. In looking at Masaccio's frescoes in the Brancacci Chapel Berenson experiences "the strongest stimulation of his tactile consciousness." "I feel that I could touch every figure, that it would yield a definite resistance to touch, that I should have to spend thus much effort to displace it, that I could walk around it." By Botticelli's "Venus Rising out of the Sea," we are told, "the tactile imagination is roused to a keen activity, by itself almost as life heightening as music." Berenson, however, nowhere attempts to go beyond this type of observation in which form is replaced by tactile value, bulk, and volume. Once, however, he attempts to illustrate the increase of intensity with which we are supposed to realize a given object. It is assumed to double our mental activity and hence our pleasure. Form in painting "lends a higher coefficient of reality to the object represented, with the consequent enjoyment of accelerated psychical processes, and the exhilarating sense of increased capacity in the observer." The problem of art and illusion, of optical illusion is posed, but one can hardly say that it is approached scientifically or even systematically. "Tactile values" remain an evocative metaphor. It is difficult to see how we are made "to feel better provided for life," as Berenson claims.[26] In practice, an exclusive standard of art is set up which depreciates color and two-dimensional geometric art.

In the meantime Vernon Lee and her friend had assembled their observations and published a long article, "Beauty and Ugliness," in the *Contemporary Review* (1897). There a special note refers to Berenson's new book as "having the great merit, not only of drawing attention to muscular sensations (according to him in the limbs) accompanying the sight of works of art, but also of claiming the power of vitalizing

26. *Florentine Painters,* pp. 29, 71, 10–11.

or as he calls it, enhancing life. Mr. Berenson offers a different and more intellectual reason for this fact than is contained in the present notes."[27] The two authors assembled a mass of observations on physical changes in observing works of art: changes in breathing, shiftings from one foot to another to achieve equilibrium, stretching of muscles, etc. They are still quite modest in their somewhat bewildered claims and clearly are not able to distinguish between very different questions: so-called "inner mimicry," the projection of our emotions on an object, and such purely physiological processes as increased breathing.

Berenson was sent the proofs of the article to St. Moritz, where he was for the summer, and from there he wrote Vernon Lee a letter (August 24, 1897) accusing Miss Anstruther-Thomson of being "a recording angel, I must add, a benevolent recording angel, one who stores up nothing against one, but takes the whole burden upon his own shoulders." Berenson rejects the main thesis of the article (probably the emphasis on the physiological reactions induced by works of art) but complains that "your instances, examples and *obiter dicta* are such familiar cherished friends." He ironically congratulates Vernon Lee for her "gift of putting things freshly," for her "divine gift of utterance," which he sees, however, accompanied by "unconsciousness and, under its ethical aspect [lack of] conscience." He speaks of his friends in St. Moritz discussing art with him at length, "so that they will be well prepared to appreciate the originality of your method and results in aesthetics."[28]

Vernon Lee understood the ironical letter perfectly and wrote Berenson indignantly: "The plain English of all this equivocating sarcasm is that Miss Anstruther-Thomson and

27. *Contemporary Review* (1897), p. 681.
28. *Selected Letters,* pp. 55–56.

I have stolen the larger part of our essay from our conversations." She rejects the accusation as "ludicrous," "detestable," "untenable," and "slanderous." She appeals to her article in *Mind* to show that she wanted to state "how much of your views we then knew and how little we agreed with them." She had, besides, she reminds him, read to him elaborate notes she had made on the proof sheets of his *Florentine Painters,* a reading which she says "was the end of our conversation on aesthetics." Vernon Lee still professes the greatest admiration for his talents, reminding him that she had shown it in writing twice about him and in helping him in his tongue-tied days (presumably with his English style), but she wants to shield her friend, who was ill, from the accusation and wants him to keep silent about it. If he should persist she would insist on a "specified account of at least some of the alleged plagiarisms."[29]

It is not clear what followed, as the further exchange of letters has not been published or has not been preserved. The accusation could not of course be kept from Miss Anstruther-Thomson. According to Vernon Lee's later account, the ladies "demanded chapter and verse; and when such allegations were tardily produced, they had to be refuted and confuted by endless quotations, references to notes and diaries, elaborate legal disproof over what my poor ill friend, still quite unfit for the easiest reading and writing, pored for weeks, disproving accusations which took shape only when insisted on, and which at last melted into the nothingness out of which our own insistence had helped to evoke them."[30] Clearly, social relations with Berenson were broken. In later years Vernon Lee saw the matter with some detachment. In a

29. Ibid., pp. 57–60, Sept. 2, 1897.

30. In Introduction to Anstruther-Thomson, *Art and Man,* pp. 56–57.

letter to Carlo Placci (May 28, 1913) she calls Berenson "an ill-tempered and egotistic *ass* to mistake us for plagiarists," but admits that "we were not very intelligent in mistaking him for a slanderer and a villain. The whole incident was merely a comedy in which the usual (indeed perhaps more than usual!) human incapacity for understanding other people's ideas and the naïve human demand that other people should *exactly* understand *one's* own, played the chief and not at all amusing parts."[31] Even more mildly, in her introduction to Miss Anstruther-Thomson's posthumous volume *Art and Man* (1924), she comments: "I have often thought in later years that what we treated, and perhaps made into, such may have been originally meant merely as a half humorous, half ill-humoured *boutade* on the part of the rather inexperienced young writer from whom it came; and that, whether or not seriously intended, it was not to be seriously taken."[32] Apparently in 1922 (after the death of Miss Anstruther-Thomson) visiting relations between Vernon Lee and the Berensons were reestablished. In the spring of 1923, we learn from Miss Nicky Mariano, Vernon Lee wrote a letter to Berenson in which "she admitted that looking through Miss Anstruther-Thomson's annotations during Berenson's talks with them she had realized that his accusation of plagiarisms was not wholly unjustified."[33] As this letter has not been published, it is impossible to see how it could be reconciled with the presumably contemporary statement that "of the charge of plagiarism nothing indeed remained."[34]

So far as I am aware, Berenson never referred to the matter in his published writings and hardly ever mentioned Vernon

31. *Selected Letters*, p. 61.
32. *Art and Man*, p. 56.
33. Nicky Mariano's Postscript to *Selected Letters*, p. 298.
34. *Art and Man*, p. 57.

Lee except in passing. He speaks, for instance, of meeting
Carlo Placci first at Vernon Lee's, or mentions that he had
read *Belcaro* when still at Harvard. Once he complains of
the myth that he "could infallibly tell the authorship of an
Italian picture. A famous writer on the Renaissance, Vernon
Lee, thought it was close and even mean of me not to let her
share the secret."[35] Still, Berenson's silence about the quarrel
is deceptive. It must have been constantly on his mind and
it did, I think, give a decisive turn to his intellectual ambitions.
He insistently denies having read the German psychologists
and art historians interested in aesthetics. In 1942 the diary
discusses Johannes Volkelt's *Aesthetik des Tragischen*
(1896). He had never read anything of his before, but "if he
had he would have had to acknowledge that he had anticipated him." "I did not read Lipps, of whose writings I heard.
I went so far as to buy one or more of the earliest but I did
not read beyond a few pages. I disliked his vocabulary and
his way of developing his theory of *Einfühlung*."[36] In 1947
Berenson saw Wölfflin's *Prolegomena zu einer Psychologie
der Architektur* (1886) and recognized that it "contains in
essence and more than in essence my entire philosophy of
art." He envies him for having had Burckhardt and Volkelt
as teachers while he had read only Pater. "Charles Eliot
Norton's interest in art was only historical and illustrative."[37]
Berenson increasingly asserted his boredom with aesthetics
and abstract speculation in general, and confesses his inability
to comprehend it. Though he knew William James, Santayana, and Bertrand Russell personally, one has the im-

35. *Rumor and Reflection* (New York, 1952), p. 11; *Sunset and
Twilight* (New York, 1963), p. 73; *Sketch for a Self-Portrait* (New
York, 1949), p. 43.

36. *Rumor and Reflection*, pp. 73–74, Jan. 23, 1942.

37. *Sunset and Twilight*, p. 22.

pression that he had little contact with their abstract thought. He professed a strong distaste for Croce, whom he even calls "very stupid or at least one-tracked in a Wilsonian fashion," though he recognized on meeting him that he is "the most candid, innocent and goodest of Italians." Berenson is simply unable to understand "his general theory, or rather sheer axiom." Croce is a "narrow conceptualist and anti-psychologist and anti-empiricist."[38] The antagonism of the two types of mind could not be put more strongly.

But the paradox of Berenson's intellectual development is that—to judge from his later autobiographical writings and his diaries—Berenson was profoundly dissatisfied with the turn his work had taken around 1895 and constantly cherished the ambition of his youth to become a philosopher of art. He regretted the years he devoted to *expertise* (though this alone could have given him the wealth and public position he acquired), considered himself "a failure" in his own eyes, and recurred to the crucial summer of 1895, when he had visions, "clear, detailed visions." "Remember," he reflects, "you mapped out one book on ideated sensations, and another on life-enhancement, and a third on the portrait." One may query what "mapping out" may have meant or whether one can speak of "books," but whatever the distortions of memory may have been, we must recognize that Berenson in his later years felt strongly that he had been

38. *Selected Letters*, p. 99, June 2, 1926; *One Year's Reading for Fun*, ed. John Walker (New York, 1960), p. 22; *Sunset and Twilight*, p. 284. Accounts of two visits in *Sunset and Twilight*, pp. 146, 267. Other remarks in *One Year's Reading*, pp. 16, 22, 28, 37. Croce translated and reprinted an essay by Howard Hannay criticizing Berenson in *Conversazioni critiche* (Bari, 1932), *3*, 115–18, and took exception to some of his distinctions in *Nuovi saggi di estetica* (Bari, 1948), pp. 230, 274, 282. He condemns all theories of *Einfühlung* as hedonism (see essay in *Ultimi Saggi* [Bari, 1948], pp. 180–87).

diverted from his original path. "You should not have competed with the learned nor let yourself become that equivocal thing, an 'expert.' "[39] He ascribes much to accident, to a constellation of circumstances, and in an excessively self-deprecatory mood, he even says that he is not a scholar. "I am not an archeologist, nor an antiquarian, nor even an art historian or art critic. If anything definable, I am only a picture-taster, the way others are wine or tea-tasters."[40] In looking at some of the finest pictures of Manet, he deplores his own inarticulateness. "If I was worth the name of 'critic' I should be able to say of what this quality consists, and thereby be able to communicate it to others. Not at all! I remain dumbmouthed before it, like a 'savage' who first saw a steam engine."[41]

Here in negative terms of the dumbmouthed or the ineffable, Berenson states what is actually the central concern of his aesthetics and his experience, not only of art: a final sense of ecstasy, a mystical rapture which he sometimes calls It-ness, for which works of art serve only as instruments.[42] Berenson recognizes one obvious source of inspiration: Walter Pater. *Marius the Epicurean* seemed to him his "own spiritual autobiography." Pater "was the genius who revealed to me what from childhood I had been instinctively tending toward."[43] But behind Pater there was also New England

39. *Sketch for a Self-Portrait,* pp. 4, 7, 39, 38.

40. *Sunset and Twilight,* p. 229.

41. Ibid., p. 178.

42. *Aesthetics and History* (New York, 1948), p. 72, and *Sketch for a Self-Portrait,* pp. 161 ff.

43. *One Year's Reading for Fun,* p. 105; *Sketch for a Self-Portrait,* p. 163. Berenson was disappointed in meeting Pater *(Sunset and Twilight,* p. 526) and made other criticisms *(Sunset,* pp. 348, 452; *One Year's Reading for Fun,* p. 124).

transcendentalism and particularly Emerson. "As I attempt to look back on life and try to recall what influenced me in my formative years of boyhood and youth, I recall at the very start Emerson's insistence on becoming, on being, rather than doing."[44] But also more specifically in aesthetics, that Boston education left its deep traces on Berenson's mind. The whole notion of ecstasy leads to the view that art is only a means to an end. Berenson "emancipated himself from the need of art." "He had become his own artist, as it were, and saw in terms of art." In a revealing passage he tells of visiting the Freer Collection in Detroit and looking for hours at Chinese pictures of trees in snowy landscapes. "The light of day was failing, and as no lamps or candles were permitted, there was nothing to do but to start going away. As I was getting up from the table I turned around, and without realizing that I was looking through a window at the out of doors, at natural objects and not artifacts, I cried out, 'Look, look, these trees are the finest yet!' So they were, for how can man compete with 'nature'?"[45] Nature supersedes art. Berenson, like Emerson, must doubt the use of art. Like Emerson, he could have asked: "Why should a man spend years upon carving an Apollo who looked Apollos into the landscape with every glance he threw?"[46] The old puzzle about a "Raphael without hands" seems solved: we can look Apollos or Chinese trees into the landscape. Berenson saw them everywhere. He was, as the diaries show, a fervent devotee of the picturesque, of topographical landscape as an art-experience. A final confusion of art and nature, a Neoplatonism similar to Emerson's is implied.

44. *Sunset and Twilight*, p. 496.
45. *Aesthetics and History*, p. 73.
46. *Journals*, 5 (10 vols. Boston, 1909), 129–30, 1838.

Still, we must recognize that this ultimate position, It-ness, the ecstasy, was a kind of personal inner sanctum and that in practice Berenson held standards of judgment which were not purely appeals to this state of illumination. The "tactile values," the idea of three-dimensional illusionist painting, were central to a definition of his taste. But even these terms were far too general to allow him to make the distinctions necessary for the student of attributions, the great arbiter of identifications. In a paper, "Rudiments of Connoisseurship" (1902), Berenson gave some practical advice: we should look at the treatment of the ears, the hair, the hands, the drapery, etc., as he assumes that just the details which are least expressive will be most stereotyped for each painter and thus give away his "signature" or what he calls his "penmanship." But finally he has to admit that, at the last resort, the expert has to depend on his "sense of quality"[47]—i.e. his intuition for physiognomy, character, individuality. There is nothing mystical about this, but still he appeals to something immediate, intuitive, while the scientific apparatus is set aside as irrelevant. Berenson neatly illustrates the basic conflict in much nineteenth-century criticism: the preoccupation with science, optics, perspective, the illusion of volume, which links him also with the painters he admired and studied most: Giotto, Masaccio, Botticelli, the whole movement away from the "primitives" to the glories of classical art. But luckily Berenson's sensibility far exceeded his scientific preoccupation. While he preserved his general preference for Italian art of the fifteenth and sixteenth century and was very hostile to Picasso, cubism, abstract art, and the avant-garde in general, he developed a wide sympathy for all kinds of art forms: Egyptian, Chinese, Indian, Byzantine. He protests against a comparison with Malraux's wider interests,

47. In *The Study and Criticism of Italian Art* (2nd series, London, 1902), esp. pp. 111–48.

yet can say that "I have always written with a sense and feeling for the whole world's art in the back of my mind."[48]

Still, there remains the cleavage between intuition and even mystical ecstasy and the scientific armory which may be psychological (though only vaguely so) or purely technical or, of course, historical. Berenson wavered all his life between the two. His ambition to develop a psychology of art faltered, possibly under the impact of the controversy with Vernon Lee and her friend, when he realized how far afield such research would lead him. His immensely successful study of attributions and authenticity, which required technical knowledge and wide erudition in art history, disillusioned him, as it seemed a distraction from both the essential experience of art and the ambition to formulate an aesthetics. In later years Berenson became very critical of *Geistesgeschichte* (particularly Strzygowski) and in general of academic art history. He wanted to be assured that the Harvard Art Department would not become "Teutonized" before leaving I Tatti to his alma mater.[49] Even when he expounded his theoretical conceptions and his views of history at some length, as in *Aesthetics and History,* he always came back to the *unum necessarium:* "I can be uplifted, transported and enraptured, I can sing and dance within myself."[50]

Vernon Lee and "Kit" Anstruther-Thomson were concerned precisely with this inner singing and dancing. They tried very hard to analyze their raptures and transports, using questionnaires, experimenting with patterns, posing in front of pictures and churches. Like Berenson, they wanted to find some scientific explanation for their subjective reactions and

48. *Sunset and Twilight,* p. 494. The allusion to T. S. Eliot's "Tradition and the Individual Talent" is curious.

49. *Selected Letters,* pp. 212, 223; *Sunset and Twilight,* p. 358.

50. *Aesthetics and History,* p. 97.

ended like him in something purely personal and incommunicable. They struggled for years to extricate themselves and clear up matters in their mind. In a paper, "The Central Problem of Aesthetics," first published in German in the *Zeitschrift für Aesthetik* (1910),[51] Vernon Lee lucidly sorted out the different problems and came to the reasonable conclusion that the highly physiological effects described by the strenuous Miss Anstruther-Thomson were idiosyncratic and irrelevant to the problem of aesthetics. Later she again expounded her theory of empathy in a little book, *The Beautiful* (1913), and late in life she published the results of her painstaking years-long inquiries into the effect of music. *Music and its Lovers* (1932) is a neglected book mainly because it is overburdened with the testimonies of her "subjects" in experimentation, but her distinction between "listeners" attending to the music as such and "hearers" stimulated by music to emotions, associations, and imaginings seems convincing even today. Much detail contributes to an empirical description of music enjoyment.

Vernon Lee started as a historian and an aesthete; she then wanted to become a scientist, an empirical psychologist, but never could make a great impact, as her work was not original and not systematic enough to impress the German specialists and was too isolated within the English tradition. Her long absorption in moral, civic, and political questions had little effect, since she could not command a voice of authority or political influence. A lesson on the ephemerality of politics in the widest sense could be drawn from her. What remains of

51. "Weiteres über Einfühlung und ästhetisches Miterleben," *Zeitschrift für Aesthetik,* 5 (1901), 145–90. The English original in *Beauty and Ugliness* (London, 1912), as "The Central Problem of Aesthetics," pp. 77–152. Lipps reviewed the original *Contemporary Review* article severely in *Archiv für systematische Philosophie,* n.F., 6 (1900), 385–90.

her work is, after all, as Mario Praz saw in his essay, the writings which give her a niche in the English aesthetic movement: the study of Italy in the eighteenth century, the many essays on topics from the Renaissance, the sketches of Italian landscapes and towns she loved. Her studies of stylistics and the technique of the novel, though published late in her life,[52] belong to her early work: they seem often elementary but are full of shrewd observations unusual for the time (the 1890s) in which they were written. A mind untrammeled by authority, often groping in expressing its meaning but always directly in contact with the phenomena before her, constitutes her attraction for a sympathetic reader. He has to discount her Victorian prolixity and obstinacy: the final appeal to the ego, the most personal experience, the rapture which seems not too different from Berenson's. Pater and Emerson also loom in her background.[53] The scientific work in which she wanted to break out of the egocentric predicament seems superseded, the great moral effort spent.

Berenson, on the other hand, has gained in stature since his death. His early work on the Italian Renaissance painters may also appear today as only a minor contribution to the aesthetic movement. The theory of tactile values seems undeveloped, though the problem raised is still being discussed, e.g., most elaborately by E. H. Gombrich in *Art and Illusion*. A judgment of the technical work of ascriptions and identifications of pictures made by Berenson must be left to the special-

52. *The Handling of Words* (London, 1923); reprinted, with an Introduction by Royal A. Gettmann (Lincoln, Nebraska, 1968); e.g. the chapter "On Literary Construction" appeared in *The Contemporary Review, 68* (1895), 404–19.

53. "As regards Emerson, I am aware of his exceptional influence on maturing my thought" (a critical essay in *Gospels of Anarchy* [London, 1908], p. 44). Originally published as "Emerson Transcendentalist and Utilitarian," *Contemporary Review, 67* (1895), 345–60.

ists: his decisions have been and will be challenged, rectified, and incorporated in an almost anonymous growing body of knowledge. He himself changed his mind continuously about them. But in old age Berenson achieved something a mere scholar and historian cannot achieve: he became a diarist, a portraitist of himself, "a preacher to himself." In the frequently informal and casual entries of the published diaries and in the finely composed pages of the *Sketch for a Self-Portrait* Berenson emerges as a person: Eastern Jew, Harvard graduate, a man of cosmopolitan culture, self-critical, contrite and modest, erudite and mystical, skeptical and hopeful. He has perpetuated his image, succeeded in describing his House of Life, which may preserve his memory even longer than his villa and garden at Settignano.

# Leo Spitzer (1887–1960)

Leo Spitzer died suddenly of a heart attack on September 16, 1960, at Forte dei Marmi, north of Viareggio. At the Congress of the International Federation of Modern Languages and Literatures at Liège, early in the same month, he had read a paper on the study of style and received a prolonged ovation which moved and cheered but also slightly puzzled him. It need not have done so.

With Spitzer the last of the quartet of great German literary scholars in Romance philology—the peer of Vossler, Curtius, and Auerbach—is gone. Spitzer was born in Vienna on February 7, 1887. He studied Romance philology with the great master W. Meyer-Lübke, received his Dr. Phil. in 1910, and became *Privatdozent* at the University of his native city in 1913. His career was interrupted by the First World War, which he spent in part in the Austrian Censorship Office, where he collected materials for his studies of Italian circumlocutions for hunger and the letters of Italian prisoners of war (A8 and 11).[1] He moved to Bonn in 1920, then as *Professor ordinarius* to the University of Marburg in 1925, and from there to Cologne in 1930.

With the accession of Hitler to power in 1933, Spitzer had to leave Germany and accept a position at Istanbul, where he was put in charge of a large program of modern languages. There was a magnificent palace with a view of the blue Sea of

1. References to the bibliography, below, pp. 216–24.

Marmara, and beadles at every door, but almost no books. The dean explained, as Spitzer recalled, "We don't bother with books. Books burn." Fires were part of the tradition at Istanbul. Unlike Auerbach, who had also come to Istanbul but stayed there throughout the war, Spitzer was able to join the Johns Hopkins faculty in 1936, where he remained for the rest of his life.

At first he was isolated and had only a few devoted students. Even in 1947, I remember vividly, he complained of being "echolos" in this country. But then his English publications in book form established contact with an American audience and his scattered papers on topics from English and even American literature attracted wide attention. Recognition came increasingly from Europe, particularly from Italy. In 1955 he received the Premio Internazionale Fetrinelli from the Accademia dei Lincei in Rome, and two collections of his studies in Italian (A24, 27) all but founded a Spitzer cult in Italy. For his seventieth birthday a distinguished group of scholars from many nations collected a testimonial volume of papers *(Studia philologica et litteraria in honorem L. Spitzer,* ed. A. G. Hatcher and K. L. Selig [Bern, 1958]); and in 1959 Niemeyer in Tübingen brought out a huge tome of 994 pages collecting 49 papers in the five languages Spitzer wrote with ease (German, French, Italian, Spanish, and English) on topics from every Romance literature, including medieval and Renaissance Latin, Provençal, and Rumanian (A26). After Spitzer's death, *Stilstudien* (1928), which had been very hard to find, were reissued in Germany (A15). His *Essays on English and American Literature,* interpretations of texts from Yeats, Whitman, Tennyson, Poe, Keats, Marvell, Milton, Herrick, Donne, Spenser, and of three Middle English poems were collected by Anna Hatcher in 1962 (A29). In the following year *Classical and Christian Ideas of World Harmony,* originally published in the review *Traditio* in 1944 and 1945, appeared, in book form, in a greatly expanded version, also edited by Anna Hatcher (A32). The book on World Harmony also appeared in Italian translation (A34), as did a new selection of his essays (A33) as well as five essays on Spanish topics (A31). Spitzer's contributions to the study of old Spanish poetry were collected in Spanish translation in Buenos Aires (A30). All his books together, however, do not exhaust the range and scope of Spitzer's writings scattered lavishly over the learned periodicals of the world. A complete bibliography, amounting to about 800 items even without the innumerable and often very important reviews, is a prime desideratum which apparently cannot be supplied from his own incomplete records.

This is hardly the time to make a considered assessment of Spitzer's total work. It will be difficult to find a person adequate to the task. He would have to be a linguist, particularly in Romance languages, in order to judge Spitzer's numerous contributions to etymology, word formation, and syntax, the original preoccupations which he never quite abandoned even in his last years. He would have to be a literary historian of awe-inspiring breadth, since Spitzer discussed, in concrete detail, a multitude of texts from all Romance literatures—from the earliest Provençal lyrics to quite recent French writers, from the great classics to many ephemeral authors. He would have to have an immense knowledge of relevant literary scholarship, since Spitzer reviewed and criticized all the prominent scholars in his fields of interest. He would have to be a general historian of ideas, since Spitzer in several papers, which he classed as "historical semantics," practiced something like an intellectual history of the whole Western tradition clustered around some key concepts. And finally, he would have to be a critic and theorist of literature, since Spitzer constantly discussed method and defined his position with self-conscious determination.

I shall attempt here a discussion of only this last aspect of his work. I shall try to give a coherent account of Spitzer's position in aesthetics, poetics, and the theory of criticism, with some regard to his development. The very multitude and diversity of his studies precludes a decision on their individual merits and the often highly specialized and controversial issues raised in them. Spitzer's favorite method of exposition often obscures a proper grasp of his general position. He is likely to start an article by quoting or referring to a text, or by questioning the opinion of another scholar. He has obviously no patience with human weaknesses; we must trust him that it is worthwhile examining the text under his guidance. He quotes all the main Western languages in the most diverse historical forms and he is not afraid of accumulating examples for pages, listing many instances of the same stylistic device. In the new volume, *Romanische Literaturstudien* (1959), some articles in German have a postscript in Italian and some in Spanish a postscript in German. Spitzer tucks away important materials and ideas in long footnotes, and there are often footnotes to footnotes. The scope and competence of his writing and the casual assumption that the reader is also a learned specialist do not make things easy. Though a critic with great sensitivity to poetry and poetic form, Spitzer had little interest in composing his own papers and did not write a single unified book. This is no doubt a German academic habit—the professor in the seminar commenting on the texts selected for his "exercises"—but there is also a theory behind the method. Philology is to Spitzer the love of the word, "die Andacht zum Kleinen," as Jakob Grimm called it. We must start with close attentive reading of the text, and criticism is often necessarily criticism of criticism, rectification or refutation of previous opinions. Spitzer was convinced that his own position can be best defined by relating it to that of others, by distinguishing, defining, and redefining. But the impact of Spitzer's work has been lessened by this immersion in detail and by the polemics, which seem necessary to his mind and are part and parcel of his method.

On occasion Spitzer has formally reflected on his method. Three papers in particular, from different years, have been taken as the sum of Spitzer's theoretical wisdom. I myself, in *Theory of Literature,*[2] based my comments on the two early German papers then known to me, which writers on stylistics have debated again and again.[3] But it seems a mistake to single out these statements. They do not define his literary theory very fully, especially as it developed in his later years; they emphasize only one question and that somewhat excessively. Two self-descriptive papers (B80, 85)[4] dating from the last year of his life were published shortly after his death and should do something to rectify the perspective. If we collect his scattered pronouncements, however, a unified point of view can be arrived at even now.

In his early pronouncements Spitzer was mainly concerned with justifying a method of psychological stylistics. In the 1925 paper, "Wortkunst und Sprachwissenschaft," he appeals to the precedent of the French *explication de texte,* to Thibaudet's studies of Mallarmé and Flaubert, to some pages on Goethe's early style in Gundolf's *Goethe,* and to Vossler, even calling his own attempts "a realization of Vossler's theo-

2. New York, 1949, pp. 187–88. Spitzer's comment in A29, pp. 194–95. *Theory of Literature* was written in 1944–47, before Spitzer's *Linguistics and Literary History* was available.

3. "Wortkunst und Sprachwissenschaft," *Germanisch-romanische Monatsschrift, 13* (1925), 169–86; reprinted in A15, *2,* 494–536; "Zur sprachlichen Interpretation von Wortkunstwerken," *Neue Jahrbücher für Wissenschaft und Jugendbildung, 6* (1930), 632–51; reprinted in A17, *1,* 4–54.

4. I want to thank Miss Anna G. Hatcher, Professor Spitzer's literary executrix, for the loan of these two manuscript lectures in 1960.

retical endeavor." The linguistic surface is a biologically necessary effect of the poet's soul; the observation of a stylistic
trait allows the critic to infer the biography of a soul. He need
only transfer himself into the soul of the great speaker, the
poet, in order to witness the act of language creation. Even
this early article describes what Spitzer later came to call the
"philological circle." "One either starts with the word and
infers the personality behind it or *vice versa.*" In a final note
Spitzer describes the feeling of evidence he has when the two
ways coincide by quoting Erich Rothacker's "I have it."
Spitzer called it "heureka"—the same sensation which he later
named "the click."

The second programmatic piece, "Zur sprachlichen Interpretation," published in 1930, repeats the appeal to Vossler
as a model and formulates more sharply the "postulate" that
"a linguistic deviation from normal speech usage as utterance
corresponds to a psychic excitement which deviates from the
normal habitus of our psychic life and that one can thus infer
a psychic center of emotions from a linguistic deviation from
the normal." We must assume that "the peculiar linguistic expression is a mirror-image of something peculiarly psychic."
Spitzer emphasizes now that "the most certain way of hitting
at the psychic centers of excitement in a writer or poet (they
after all speak inwardly before they write) is just reading
ahead until something linguistic strikes one. If one puts together several linguistic observations, they certainly allow
themselves to be reduced to a common denominator, and one
can link it with the psychic, and even bring it into correspondence with the composition, with the structure and its parts, as
well as with the ideological content of the work of art." While
the emphasis on "Draufloslesen" is new, the philological
circle is again implied. In this article, however, Spitzer abandons the ideal of "stylistics," with which he has been wrongly
identified. He disapproves—as early as 1930—of the attempt

to make stylistics a special "science" and he even vows to work toward its disappearance in literary scholarship. He recognizes that the work of literary art is not merely a linguistic phenomenon and that a total analysis leads to a study of compositional technique, of characterization, and even of the implicit world view. The interlocking of the different aspects is demonstrated by a sketchy analysis of *Quinze Joyes de mariage*. A series of metaphors in the fifteenth-century text about confinement and lack of freedom in marriage allows him to "throw a bridge" to the compositional technique of a medieval work (its closed-in pictures with a didactic-monotonous frame) and from there to its point of view and technique of characterization (typicality, etc.). All the traits can be reduced to a common denominator—the medieval feeling of stuffiness and enclosure of life on earth.

The third programmatic statement,[5] dating from 1948, puts the method into an autobiographical frame and relates it to the tracing of etymologies. There is a new shift of emphasis. Spitzer now speaks of "the common spiritual *etymon*," "the psychological root," "the *radix* of the soul," and the "psychogram" of a writer, and he now defends the method by identifying it with the "circle of understanding" described by Dilthey and Schleiermacher in their theories of hermeneutics. Spitzer insists that this is not a vicious circle but rather a to-and-fro movement or a "pendulum movement."[6] One of the new features of the paper is Spitzer's strongly defensive attitude toward behaviorism. "Without belief in a human soul, there is no science," he asserts. In the second part of the essay, evidently written somewhat later, he quotes a letter from an ex-student that expresses some doubts whether Spitzer has a technique which can be described as a step-by-step procedure. (The student, I hear, is Miss Anna G. Hatcher.) In his com-

5. "Linguistics and Literary History," in A22, pp. 1–39.
6. A phrase used in B4 as early as 1926.

ment Spitzer agrees and propounds the view that his method is rather the result of "talent, experience, and faith." He appeals again to the sense of inner evidence, calling it now "the click" (A22, pp. 26, 29).

Spitzer came back to this idea of the "circle" as the basis of his method, repeating the image and the scheme—from the detail to the whole and then back to the detail—in many different contexts. He used it also to set off his own method against that of comparable scholars. Thus he sees a contrast between Auerbach's approach to the *Divine Comedy* and his own: he starts with the analysis of a detail, assuming that the whole of the work is still unknown to him, whereas Auerbach supposedly starts with an unrivaled knowledge of the whole of the poem (A26, p. 59n.). In criticizing Dámaso Alonso, Spitzer complains of the lack of the "philological circle" in Alonso's method and rejects Alonso's assumption of a divorce between the outer and the inner in poetic creation. Alonso, Spitzer argues, stops with an "either-or," "outer-inner," or "inner-outer," whereas Spitzer has presumably reached the unity of soul and word (B56). In an interview Spitzer explained the circle in the simplest terms as "an extension of our usual manner of forming judgments." "A young man walks into my office. The first thing that strikes me is some inconsequential detail, such as a flashy tie." (Surely Spitzer knew why he wears a highly figured tie on his photograph above the text!) "I proceed to a tentative psychological hypothesis. I decide that this man is given to asserting his personality at the expense of good taste. The next step consists in verifying whether the same characteristic extends to other areas of his personality. . . . The circular procedure consists in passing from observed detail to hypothesis and back to other details" (In *The Johns Hopkins Magazine,* April 1952, p. 20).

I have expounded these pronouncements so carefully because Spitzer himself placed so much stress on the philological circle. But it seems to me that the circle is no panacea and that it does not define Spitzer's own method. As far as the procedure of the circle is true, it is trite and valid universally, as Spitzer himself recognizes in the example of the tie or of a doctor's diagnosis or when he describes the way "a scientist may observe a physical phenomenon, develop a principle to explain it, then test to see whether or not the principle applies to other parallel phenomena" (ibid.). The image of the circle seems to me false and misleading if it is taken literally as a step-by-step procedure, if it assumes that anyone (and Spitzer of all people!) could start with a *tabula rasa,* "read ahead," and then from chance observations deduce a psychological *radix,* the truth of which will finally be verified by further observations, reading in other critics, etc. Spitzer himself gave the argument away in his comments on Miss Hatcher's letter. He recognized that "even the 'first step' is preconditioned. We see, indeed, that to read is to have read, to understand is equivalent to having understood" (A22, p. 27). How, we may ask, can anyone read an author without a mind full of memories, anticipations, nets of questions, and, if he is Spitzer, without a mind full of linguistic categories, literary information, psychological concepts, and many other "presences" and even evaluations? How can he keep the three steps apart, and how can he stop the process of observation and reflection? The advice to get into a circle amounts only to a recommendation of careful observation of details, of submission to a text, of what Spitzer calls the "cleansing of the mind from distraction by the inconsequential" (A22, p. 29)—a sensible though hardly novel admonition. The second step, the inference of a "psychological etymon" or "psychogram," and the search for a psychological explanation for every stylistic trait, reflects only one phase of Spitzer's practice, the phase which he himself repudiated and which is most open to criticism. And the third step, verification, can hardly be limited or considered necessarily final.

The usual Croce-Vossler-Spitzer pedigree seems to me mistaken. Spitzer started rather with a combination of philology and psychology. He did not know Croce at first and only later came to admire him as a great figure and to agree with his rejection of nineteenth-century positivism. One cannot describe Spitzer as a follower of Croce; he rejects and must reject the basis of Crocean aesthetics, the identification of intuition and expression, of aesthetics and linguistics. "To found linguistics on expression which itself is identified with impression, that is, to found it on poetic intuition, means destroying the life of language while pretending to put poetry in its place," said Spitzer in his last lecture. Croce's own critical practice leads to "paralysis," since we cannot do anything but admire. "In asking the critic to distinguish between the poetic and the non-poetic parts of the *Divine Comedy,* in abandoning the inviolable organicity of the work of art, in splintering its structure, how can one consider the style of a work as conforming with its content?" (B85; also A26, p. 564). In his paper on "The Transitions in La Fontaine" Spitzer remarks that he wanted to "distance himself" from both Croce and Vossler, since La Fontaine cannot be understood by means of their categories (A26, p. 205). Spitzer's attitude toward Vossler is ambivalent. He without doubt admired Vossler and agreed with his general aims, but criticized as premature his attempt to write a history of French culture in the mirror of language. He speaks of Vossler's "psychological improvisations," of "something autodidactic" in his work, and calls him even a "dilettante" in linguistics (B85; B4; B73, p. 599n.).

Spitzer strongly emphasized the influence of Freud. Freud "taught the idea of a constancy of certain motifs in the psyche of poets and their constant external manifestations" (B66). But surely the use of Freud even by the early Spitzer is far from orthodox. Freud is rather used as a justification of a search for "latency," for a hidden key, a recurrent motif, a basic *Erlebnis*, and even the world view of an author. Only a few papers in Spitzer's extensive work infer sexual or pathological motivation. The study of Barbusse's obsession with sadistic images of blood and wounds (A7) is early; the brilliant essay on "The Style of Diderot" (1948), which sees his cumulative gradated sentence structure as an imitation of the rhythm of the sexual act, Spitzer himself called the "last in the Freudian vein" (in A22; cf. B70, p. 371). But the bulk of the psychological papers attempts to establish connections between style and world view—e.g. between the repetitive style of Charles Péguy and his Bergsonism, or between Charles-Louis Philippe's mannerism of loosely using the construction "à cause de" and his belief in a melancholy, somewhat provisional fatalism (all in A15). Spitzer's earliest publication, his dissertation on Rabelais (A1), tries to show how Rabelais' word formations (e.g. his fantastic suffixes added to Sorbonne in order to create repulsive nicknames) suggest that in Rabelais there was a tension between the real and the unreal, between comedy and horror, between utopia and naturalism. Similarly, analyzing the word myths of Christian Morgenstern, Spitzer interprets his view of language as "swathing further veils over an impenetrably dark world" (A4).

However ingenious Spitzer's observations and interpretations of stylistic traits may be, it seems to me impossible to prove that the *etymon,* the *radix,* or simply the *Weltanschauung* of the writer was inferred purely on the basis of linguistic observation. It would be impossible to show that the stylistic traits were all deduced from a knowledge of the author's temperament or world view. A linguistic surface cannot be observed without recourse to meaning nor can meaning be known without language. To establish the precise order in which Spitzer arrived at his insights seems to me both futile and impossible. A dialectics of the mind must assume the relatedness of everything with everything and will reject a diagrammatic scheme, whether of a circle or a pendulum movement, as inadequate to the complexities of the actual processes of thought.

Still, the critics who reject the circle and simply grant that Spitzer has "talent," "intuition," or even "genius" are mistaken if they try to dismiss his results as arbitrary, subjective, or lucky guesses.[7] Some of Spitzer's own pronouncements lend support to this comfortable view, and at one period of his life he formulated religious convictions which allowed his opponents to label him an irrationalistic mystic.[8] In some contexts Spitzer asserts that a faith in God is a needed justification for causal explanation and the reduction to one principle or root. "The weakening of the idea of God" seemed to him "a signal for the weakening of causal thinking" (B42, p. 249), and the explanation of a poem appeared to him "strongly akin to the practice *omnia in majorem Dei gloriam.* In both one refers all observable details and facts to one central force resuming the whole and by a 'to-and-fro' (or 'tautological') movement between the whole and the parts, one hopes to grasp the ultimately ungraspable (*individuum ineffabile)"* (B35, p. 603). But this monotheistic faith is surely no defense of mysticism or denial of science. It is merely cited as a parallel between the enterprise of philology and the religious insight into cosmic unity and order and its postulate of

7. Particularly Charles Bruneau, "La Stylistique," *RP,* 6 (1951), pp. 1 ff.; cf. B54.

8. L. Bloomfield, *Language, 20* (1944), 45; cf. B42.

a First Cause. Later Spitzer himself confessed that he changed "from an intellectual who half deplored the loss of faith and the Renaissance" to a "decided friend of light and clear form" (A26, p. 6). The charge of mysticism is thoroughly false. The choice between a step-by-step rationalistic procedure by circle or pendulum and some irrational intuition poses an unreal dilemma. One can describe Spitzer's theories and methods without recourse to either of these extremes of rationalism and irrationalism. Significantly, Spitzer later accepted the criticism directed against the psychological method. He saw the danger of valuing art by *Erlebnis* and recognized that the search for *Erlebnis* is only a revised version of the biographical fallacy. The assumption of a necessary relationship between certain stylistic devices and specific states of mind is often fallacious and always without proof. Spitzer repudiated the psychological approach and turned rather to a total literary scholarship which would not be psychologistic or stylistic but simply and centrally literary.

At times he seems to advocate a double standard. Psychological stylistics, he tells us, is "applicable only to writers who think in terms of the 'individual genius,' of an individual manner of writing, that is, to writers of the eighteenth and later centuries: in previous periods the writer (even Dante) sought to express objective things in an objective style. Precisely the insight that 'psychological stylistics' is not valid for earlier writers (Montaigne being one glaring exception) has reinforced in me another tendency which was present in my work from the beginning, that of applying to works of literary art a structural method that seeks to define their unity without recourse to the personality of the author" (B70, p. 371). But oddly enough, in the discussion of Dámaso Alonso, Spitzer seems to congratulate himself for having started with modern authors who lend themselves to the psychological approach, while Alonso is faced with the impersonal authors of the Spanish Golden Age whose lyrical "I's" remain didactic and not empirical like Rousseau's and his followers'. If Spitzer had stayed with Rabelais, he could probably, he suggests, have arrived only at the general *radix* Renaissance (B56). Clearly Spitzer's own attitude toward the psychological method remained somewhat ambiguous, though he saw its dangers and particularly the difficulties of applying it to writers from the remote past. He cites the example of a student of his who worked on Agrippa d'Aubigné's *Les Tragiques* and came up with "emotional clusters" (a term of Kenneth Burke's) such as "milk" and "poison," "mother" and "serpent," "wolf" and "lamb"—antithetic doubles that were simply suggested by the tradition of the Bible (A22, p. 32; B80, p. 31, repeated in B85). Spitzer also came to recognize that the psychological approach does not promote criticism as evaluation. He admits that he once overrated authors for whom style was "an *hors d'œuvre* or a cheaply come-by recipe" which can be easily imitated. Spitzer mentions Jules Romains (B80, p. 30), but he could have added, at least, Barbusse and Charles-Louis Philippe.

By far the bulk of Spitzer's writings and all his later work can be interpreted and understood without recourse to the philological circle, mystical intuition, or depth psychology. The impressive success of Spitzer's work may be attributed to unmysterious though rare qualities: to his unsurpassed knowledge not only of facts but of the use of grammatical, stylistic, and historical categories, which he combined with an insight into the nature of art and the nature of criticism. This combination seems to me crucial; there have been many very learned scholars who, after a lifetime of incessant labor, left only a heap of unrelated findings and opinions; there are many critics of sensitivity but of little knowledge, range, and theoretical awareness. Spitzer has both knowledge and theoretical insight and he has the urge to define and describe his insight. He has been criticized for his indulgence in fierce polemics, but one should recognize that they are part of his process of self-definition, and that he was convinced that "critical discussion is the best way toward that *consensus omnium* which is the ultimate goal in philology as well as any of the sciences" (A29, p. 37; cf. also B76, p. 56).

Spitzer had arrived at something that no amount of learning and diligence can compensate for: a firm grasp of the aesthetic fact, its distinction from life, and its peculiar self-contained nature. He grasped the logical consequences of an aesthetic conviction: the need of practicing literary scholarship concerned with this aesthetic fact and combating the manifold distractions which, with a Crocean term, he called *allotria*. He saw that "art and outward reality should, at least while the work of art is being studied, be kept separate." He felt that "our enjoyment of any work of art comes from the deeply grounded feeling we have that art is not life, but a new architecture, built of fancy and the poetic will, apart from life and beyond life" (B35, pp. 595–96). He constantly speaks of works of art as "artistic and autarkic organisms," of their "integrity and unity," their "interior aesthetic cohesion and construction," the unity of form and content, of *Gestalt* and *Gehalt* (e.g. A26, pp. 113–14, 250, 467, 529, 747).

Spitzer insistently defends organistic aesthetics against its usual misinterpretation as mere Formalism. The common adage that "content is inseparable from form" does not, he argues, mean that "content no longer exists or must be dissolved into style—for otherwise Genesis and the *Celestina* would only differ in 'style,' or to say it bluntly, the term 'style' would have become entirely meaningless" (B65, pp. 146–47). At least in his later years, Spitzer rejected the imperialism of modern stylistics, the view voiced, e.g., by Dámaso Alonso, that there cannot be any other literary study than stylistics.[9] In a lecture, a few months before his death, Spitzer stated emphatically that "aesthetic criticism cannot be exhausted by a consideration of style; there is aesthetics also in the plot, the fable of the poetic work." "The structural element, the architecture of thought reflected in poems," he proclaims, "has more and more absorbed my attention. Stylistics, because it is good gymnastics for attentive reading, can be only one of the aids to artistic perception" (B80, p. 33). Structural study as practiced by Spitzer thus means neither pure Formalism, in the sense of exclusive attention to the aesthetic surface, nor an ivory-tower aestheticism.

Against this misinterpretation, Spitzer states that the phrase "a self-contained work of art" means only "aesthetic self-containedness (without other than aesthetic relevance) and not an uncommunicative resting of the work of art in itself, readerless." Precisely the "need of a poem for a reader" is for Spitzer an argument against relativistic historicism. "Aesthetically, the work of art acts by itself, and may do so because its aesthetic content is self-contained in it and in him" (B35, p. 602). Over and over again he asserted the "eternal character of a work of art" and argued against historical relativists such as George Boas that the "indispensability of a [previous] knowledge of the 'cultural background' for the understanding of a work of art is usually greatly overrated." Though he himself was steeped in historical lore and highly aware of the historical setting, Spitzer always saw that there is a point at which historicism must fail. "There is one inconsistency in nineteenth century historicism, that wholly given up to historical relativism, it has not yet learned to see the

9. Dámaso Alonso, *Poesía española* (Madrid, 1950), p. 429. "La Estilística será la única Ciencia de la Literatura."

relativity of its procedure conditioned by certain definite events of modern history; and that it has not learned to take itself as a historical fact, subject to change. Before itself, it ceases to think historically." Thus Spitzer must reject the many attempts to absorb literary study into cultural history or history of ideas. They should not be "substituted for a poised and self-contained aesthetic meditation before a particular work of art that is unique and unrepeatable by nature" (B35, pp. 598, 602, 604).

"Aesthetic meditation," "the eternal meaning of art," "an immanent organic criticism" are the key terms of the later Spitzer. From them necessarily follow his reservations against the biographical approach, his rejection of the methods which break up a work of art into a mosaic of sources and influences, his resistance to the reduction of a work of art to intellectual terms, to its use as a document in the history of ideas or the history of feelings about time or space. He surely seems right in protesting against the constant confusion of the "poetic I" with the "empirical and pragmatic I" (A26, p. 104). "It is a quite illegitimate procedure, one most detrimental to any *explication de texte* (although widely current with our academic positivism) to 'utilize' indiscriminately 'what we know of the poet's biography,' because this may destroy the artistic framework carefully devised by the poet: the boundary between art and life which he perhaps may have wished to erect" (A29, p. 128). Spitzer constantly argues against the methodological error of the "invasion of practical biography into the orbit of a poem" (A26, p. 485). Discussing Milton's sonnet "Methought I saw my late espoused saint," he protests against the "brusque introduction" by another interpreter, George Boas, of "the mater-of-fact, opaque name Katherine Woodcock into the transparent and transcendent atmosphere of our poem . . . as shocking as the whole proposition of making the

poem more empirically concrete than it has been conceived"
(A29, pp. 128–29). The clumsy guesses of E. V. Lucas as to
the exact friends who may be referred to in Lamb's "The Old
Familiar Faces" seem a demonstration how "the indiscreet
intervention of the biographical at the wrong time prevents
the appreciation of the tone-contents of the poem (in this case
even of the 'idea' of the poem) from materializing" (B35, p.
588). Spitzer shows how the damage done by the biographical
approach is particularly severe in the case of medieval literature; he demonstrates, convincingly to my mind, that Mrs.
Grace Frank misinterprets the poems of Jaufré Rudel because
she assumes the necessity of exploiting the biographical information about his participation in a Crusade (A19, also in 26).
Similarly, Spitzer shows how unwarranted are the biographical readings of such texts as the *Libro de buen amor* of the
Archpriest of Hita (B11). He cites many examples of medieval
writers appropriating material from other sources—not even
concealing them—and presenting them as personal experience (A26, pp. 100–12). The confusion between the "I" of a
speaker and the empirical life of the author has done much to
prevent a correct interpretation and aesthetic evaluation of
literature of all ages.

Similarly, Spitzer sees that most "source-study" is "utterly
destructive of aesthetic apperception." "To delve into the
'source' of a poem (by which is meant not the real source:
the mind of the poet—but always the previous work of someone else) means to undo the work of the poet: one looks for
another aggregation of new materials than that which the
poet chose (and others failed to choose)" (B35, pp. 591, 593).
He gives many concrete instances of the falsity of the positivistic conception of "the direct influence of a source-work on
its derivative." Analogously, the totally material procreation
of one poetic genre by another poetic genre "is quite incon-

ceivable as an explanation of spiritual realities" (A26, p. 406n). The paper which Spitzer considered his first attempt at a structural interpretation, "Ehrenrettung von Malherbes 'Consolation à Monsieur du Périer,' "[10] starts by refuting an attempt to disparage the poem because of its sources in Ronsard and Montchrestien. Even then Spitzer could not "go along with a judgment that somehow assumes the possibility of transferring individual parts of one work of art into another and of a creation groping ahead along the verses of predecessors." He of course continued to study sources, though always with a great awareness of their merely contributory relevance for an illumination of a work of art. When in a paper on Valéry's "La Fileuse" he actually dwells on the sources at length, he apologizes somewhat wryly: "I did it against my habits and possibly in order to prove my lack of all one-sided fanaticism" (A26, pp. 343–52, esp. p. 352). The rejection of extrinsic methods in Spitzer is always relative; he knows the damage they have done to an aesthetic study of literature but recognizes their peripheral validity. Thus he reflects that comparative literature arose in the romantic period—"the age when there was felt the need for a *Weltliteratur*, a *cosmopolitisme littéraire*. This, too, incidentally, has since degenerated into a subtler means of diversion, distraction and evasion; the direction is always away from the extant concrete work of art" (B35, p. 601).

Along similar lines of argument Spitzer criticizes any attempt to reduce the work of art to a mere vehicle of ideas, whether it is done by the devices of Lovejoy's history of ideas or in the service of existential philosophies. He objects to the atomistic presuppositions of Lovejoy, the very conception of "unit-idea." When Lovejoy tried to trace some of Hitler's

10. In *Die Neueren Sprachen, 34* (1926), 191–96, reprinted in A15, 2, 18–29.

ideology to its antecedents in German romantic writers, Spitzer, in the midst of the war, came to the rescue of the Germans, arguing that Lovejoy's "analytical procedure destroys the organic entity and makes the understanding of the whole no longer possible." "It is not the letter of any idea, or any set of ideas, but the spirit in which the ideas are carried out and allowed to associate with each other—it is the total system of ideas charged with emotion that explains an historical movement." Thus in Spitzer's view there cannot be a real continuity between the Schlegels and Hitler, even though individual concepts and slogans may seem similar or identical. "Via its immediate French models (Lanson's history of the idea of progress)" Lovejoy's method comes from "the analytical philosophy of history of the French Encyclopedists, more specifically from Voltaire's *Dictionnaire philosophique* which obviously rests on the assumption that, just as words may be listed in a dictionary detached from the whole of the linguistic system in question (and, supposedly, may exist as detached items), so ideas are detachable from their 'climate' " (B40, pp. 192, 201). But "climate," "harmony," *Stimmung,* a feeling for the *Zeitgeist* are Spitzer's preoccupations. Consistent thinking in global terms requires such concepts. Spitzer is therefore not impressed by Lovejoy's plea to discard the term "romanticism." "Because the term cannot be straightforwardly defined he proceeds as though the phenomenon did not exist. Since the whole is ungraspable he clings to individual facts of thought." It seems to Spitzer a "bias to believe that understanding must always wait on definition" (B40, p. 190).

His own contributions to a history of ideas, the paper on "Classical and Christian Ideas of World Harmony (Prolegomena to an Interpretation of the Word *'Stimmung')"* (A32) and the related piece on *"Milieu* and *ambiance"* (A21, pp. 179–

316), concern precisely the concepts and words suggesting atmosphere, harmony, and totality. Spitzer always keeps in mind the principle that "the boundaries between words are never fixed: and it is impossible to trace the history of a single word without taking into account the whole conceptual field *(Begriffsfeld)*" (B40, p. 202). Lovejoy's rejoinder shows that Spitzer underrated his awareness of these issues; and one must grant that Lovejoy's own practice, particularly in *The Great Chain of Being,* is much nearer to Spitzer's own than some of Lovejoy's theoretical formulations would seem to recognize. But Spitzer makes his point against the intellectualism of Lovejoy's method. At the same time, stoutly battling on his middle ground, he objects to the anti-intellectualism of the existentialist position.

Especially in the last decade of his life, Spitzer conceived a strong aversion to irrationalistic philosophizing. He often refers disparagingly to Heidegger: to the "high-sounding metaphysical solemnity" of his definition of poetry as "Stiftung des Daseins," to his metaphysical puns and "precious verbal pomp," and to his abuse of German etymology (B65, p. 147; B52, pp. 143, 145). Of Mörike's poem "Auf eine Lampe," which had become the topic of a debate between Heidegger and Staiger, Spitzer surely gives the most balanced and finely felt interpretation. In the famous line, "Was aber schön ist, selig scheint es in ihm selbst," he rejects both Heidegger's attempt to make the word "scheint" signify "lucet" and Staiger's forced reading of a feeling of exclusion on the poet's part. He does this by emphasizing the shape of the lamp and its symbolic value for the poem (B52, pp. 136–38). The text and the precise limitations imposed by the text on its reading are standards held so strenuously that Spitzer resents all speculative interpretations. In criticizing some rather farfetched readings by Stephen Gilman of passages in *La*

*Celestina,* Spitzer declares that he wants "to establish once and forever a 'negative reading list' (that is a list of books *not* to be read) for our younger scholars who deal with older literature." Buber, Bergson, Dilthey, Freud, Heidegger, Ortega, Sartre, Scheler, Spengler, Unamuno (B68, p. 19n) make up this black list—pedagogical advice that Spitzer happily did not himself follow as a young man. What would he have become without, at least, three names on the list: Freud, Dilthey, and Bergson?

The rejection of existential criticism by Spitzer includes, in particular, the studies on human time by Georges Poulet. In an elaborately courteous open letter to this colleague, Spitzer shows that the method of studying the time feeling of different French authors practiced by Poulet leads to a destruction of the work of art, to a deformation of the "literary concrete," and imposes the "systématisme" of the philosopher on what should be the "caméléonisme" of the philologist (A26, pp. 248, 276). Spitzer takes Poulet's analysis of Marivaux's *La Vie de Marianne* and shows that he misreads the text completely. Instead of the disintegration of rational order and moral nihilism which Poulet reads into the book by tearing passages out of context, Marivaux actually proclaims the optimism of the eighteenth century, its cult of genius, nature, and originality. Marianne is a glorification of feminine intuition, of the stability of a woman's heart, and not a creature of the moment, of discontinuity and confusion, as Poulet interprets her (A26, pp. 252, 261–62, 270). Spitzer has picked the weakest chapter in Poulet's books and he has borne down too hard on a few passages in Gilman's book on the *Celestina;* but one should acknowledge how consistently he keeps his methodological "stance"—the concentration on the structural and aesthetic interpretation of the single work of art.

Spitzer thus stands very near to the aims and methods of the American New Criticism, and in the Liège lecture he treats the movement with some sympathy as parallel to the efforts of German stylistics and Russian Formalism. In other contexts he expressed approval of specific interpretations made by Cleanth Brooks (A29, pp. 41, 88). But on the whole, Spitzer treats the American movement with a certain amount of condescension and with many reservations. The condescension comes from his emphasis, excessive to my mind, on the purely pedagogical origins of the American movement. Its source, Spitzer believes, is exclusively in the undergraduate college (B85). He obviously cannot agree with any rejection of learning and literary history. The reservations follow from his strong insistence on the singleness of meaning and the possibility of our attaining it. Spitzer argues both against skeptical relativists, such as Boas, who see only the "whirligig of taste," and against interpreters, such as Empson, who search for the most inclusive meaning, for the greatest number of ambiguities (A29, pp. 116, 129–30, and B85). He believes that "philology rests on the assumption that all men on earth are basically alike and that the modern commentator is enabled, by his training and studiousness, to approximate and, perhaps, restore, the original 'meaning' of a work of art composed at another time and place" (A29, p. 116). For Spitzer there is "only one meaning which must be isolated with an energy bent on discrimination" (B85).

Other less central issues divide Spitzer from the American New Criticism. He objects to what he calls "imagistic positivism," "the exaggerated reliance of contemporary critics on imagery to the detriment of other elements of poetry . . . structure, thought, psychology [which] must play parts at least equal to imagery" in any proper interpretation. Spitzer sees this tendency as an antihumanistic technicality. "We have in-

deed come to the point where the quiet de-humanized professional of literary criticism considers it his duty to deal with
'imagery' and similar specialized, technical, or philological
questions, to the exclusion of the human element which is at
the bottom of all poetry and consequently should inform philology, the humanistic science" (A29, pp. 99, 101n.). He is
shocked by dissertations which classify "images," on the model of Caroline Spurgeon's work, according to their sources in
nature or books, and is bewildered and disturbed by the
tortuous imagistic "metagrammar" of Earl Wasserman's
interpretation of Keats's "Ode on a Grecian Urn" (A29,
pp. 67–97).

While the isolation and exaggeration of imagery seems to
Spitzer to lead to a distortion of works of art, he is equally
suspicious of the attempts to allegorize, to seek a hidden
meaning, to find a religious significance in every text. "The
four distinct meanings of Dante in the *Convivio* have destroyed the common sense of many contemporary critics,
particularly in America, as they, undoubtedly under religious
or semi-religious influences, allegorize *à tort et à travers*"
(A26, p. 491; cf. p. 731). Spitzer's most striking example,
concerning a medieval Spanish text, *Razón de amor,* elicits
the comment that "such aberrations are possible in our time
because non-philological tendencies have invaded the soul
of the critic: he believes to do a pious deed by offering a so-
called religious interpretation" (A26, p. 682). On this point
of allegory Spitzer, to my mind, has somehow missed his
mark; his examples are never central to American criticism.
They are rather drawn from learned medievalists, both
American and European, who exercise their scholarly ingenuity quite untouched by the New Criticism. The real new
trend of American criticism, myth criticism, is never discussed
by Spitzer, though one can imagine that it would be open
to the objections he raised against Empson—the uncontrol-

lable caprice of finding meaning, any meaning, in any text. Spitzer, as far as I am aware, did not comment on the other new group in recent American Criticism, the Chicago Aristotelians. In discussing a piece by Hoyt Trowbridge on Yeats' "Leda and the Swan," he indirectly expressed his suspicion of the overemphasis on genre which is central to their doctrine. Trowbridge "dwells on those features of the poem" which make it "representative of a genus" instead of approaching the poem as "an incomparable, unique poetic entity in itself," instead of looking for its "inner dynamics . . . the *flüssige Band* (to use the Goethean expression) that holds the artistic unity together" (A29, pp. 4–5).

This overriding concern for the particular poem, for "the most individual, the least cataloguable features" (A29, p. 4), seems to me sufficient explanation for Spitzer's predilection for monographic and even micrological treatments of specific poems. He shunned discussions of the total works of an author and never wrote literary history as narrative. He knows himself that the "depiction of a personality in its totality" is difficult for him; he is struck rather by its "outstanding features, its edges and protuberances." He feels that one can get at a ball of thread only by pulling out single strands and winding them up one by one (A26, p. 204). He attempted synthesis, a total literary portrait, as in the essays on Calderón and Rabelais, only when he was prompted by some outward occasion—an inaugural lecture or a popular series of lectures (A17, *2*, 189–210; B59, *1*, 126–47).

The reason for Spitzer's reluctance to go beyond an individual work of art is not only the theory of uniqueness and the concern for individual traits. It follows also from his demand that the critic take an empathic and even submissive attitude toward the individual work of art. Spitzer really knows only a "criticism of beauties" (A26, p. 413). He describes his general method when he asks that "the critic must be an *advocatus dei,*" though in this context he speaks only of medieval poets. He would like to "leave judicial criticism to others," aware of the dangers of evaluation, preferring description, phenomenology, even the preparation of materials for observation to a real estimate.[11] Actually, Spitzer is too modest when he seems to disavow the task of evaluative criticism. He does have critical standards and one can discover them. His main criterion is that of coherence. He believes that "if the parts of a work of art cannot be integrated into a harmonious whole, the aesthetic value of such a work is automatically made doubtful" (A26, p. 467). He must demonstrate aesthetic cohesion and construction in order to value a work. Thus an Italian medieval treatise, *Mare amoroso,* is elaborately defended for its unity, though Spitzer is compelled to admit its "schematic architecture, pedantry and virtuosity" (A26, p. 413).

Only very rarely did Spitzer move beyond the criterion of internal coherence. It was, I believe, only a passing phase of his development when he suggested a function and value of poetry that might be called religious. "Poetry," he once surprisingly says, "is the form best fitted to convince man emotionally of supernal verities. Apperception of poetry may be, then, to a certain extent, religious service." Poetry is "characterized by the vision it opens before us of a world radically different from our everyday and workaday world of ratiocination and practicality and by the relief it offers us from the daily burden of our environment" (A29, p. 218). But this escape into another higher world is invoked only in a paper on three medieval English poems (1951) and does not reflect the general tendencies of his far more inclusive and usually quite secular taste.

11. See *Germanisch-romanische Monatsschrift, 13* (1925), 123; reprinted in A15, Vol. 2.

Spitzer more frequently invokes the standard of historical representativeness. A certain poem is great in that "it offers an overly rich condensation of the whole wealth of medieval thought and feeling about one of the basic forces of mankind" (A29, p. 216). In practice, when Spitzer moves out of the realm of the single object, he appeals to the concept of representativeness, to national representativeness, period representativeness, and finally to something which must be described as general *Geistesgeschichte*. Unlike most German scholars, he is extraordinarily wary of these concepts, because he knows the abuses to which they lend themselves and how they have been exploited by nationalistic ideologies or fanciful philosophers of history. He often protests against glib generalizations about national characteristics and the whole use of literary scholarship for the purposes of patriotism; for instance, he chides Dámaso Alonso for engaging in "national tautology," "a way of thinking to which German and French literary critics succumb most readily while Italian and English critics are least prone to it; but which unfortunately occurs with almost all Spanish scholars." By "national tautology" Spitzer means "the implicit assertion that a Spanish work of art is great because it is genuinely Spanish and that it is genuinely Spanish if it is great" (B56, p. 251). While Spitzer, at home in six cultures, can hardly be suspected of any specific nationalism, he still operates frequently with such entities as "esprit français" and "âme française" (A26, pp. 258–367, 373, 384, 388n.), or allows himself to generalize about "Italianità," Italian "histrionism and autopersiflage" (A26, pp. 358n., 505n.). He speaks of the "innate necessity of the German soul" to see historical development as a brute unalterable fact (A26, p. 792) and speculates rashly about the Romans who "felt less well protected in the universe, less at home with the infinite than did the Greeks"

(A21, p. 192). He is often severe at the expense of Klemperer's *Dauerfranzose* or of Américo Castro's "phantasmagoria" of the Spanish national character (B5, p. 244; B55, p. 12n.); but Spitzer himself seems unable to escape these habits of mind.

Similarly, Spitzer is quite aware of the dangers of reckless speculations about the nature of the specific historical periods, the Middle Ages, the Renaissance, the baroque, or the romantic. But again he is willing to pronounce truths about the Middle Ages *in toto,* and to declare confidently this or that trait Renaissance or rococo (e.g. A26, pp. 380, 382, 249). In a lecture on the Spanish baroque (1943) he speculates quite in the style of German *Geistesgeschichte* about the baroque as "a re-elaboration of two ideas, one mediaeval, the other Renaissance, in a third idea which shows us the polarity between the feelings and nothingness, beauty and death, the temporal and the eternal." Commenting on the paper in the reprint, Spitzer himself deplores a certain confusion between a religious and an aesthetic creed (A26, pp. 798–802; see p. 802n.). He was one of the first scholars to use the term "baroque" for French classicism, an idea which has since caught on even in France.[12] A note in his earlier study, "Die klassische Dämpfung in Racines Stil" (1928), endorses the view that French classicism is a form of the baroque but a mild, tamed, or muted form. The text of the long paper consists of an elaborate analysis of Racine's classical "muffling," a term which Spitzer derived from Oskar Walzel's description of German classicism.[13] Only Spitzer's much later paper,

12. See the history of the term in my "The Concept of Baroque in Literary Scholarship," *Journal of Aesthetics and Art Criticism, 5* (1946), 77–109; reprinted in my *Concepts of Criticism* (New Haven, 1963), pp. 69–127.

13. In *Archivum romanicum, 12* (1968), 361–472, reprinted in A17, *1*, 135–268; on baroque, A17, *1*, 255–56n.; on Walzel, p. 267 and B80, p. 27.

"The Récit de Théramène" (1948), interprets Racine's *Phèdre* as a baroque tragedy of *desengaño* and calls Racine's *Weltanschauung* baroque. Spitzer does this because he wants to defend the famous speech of Théramène by shifting the emphasis of the play away from Phèdre to Thésée. He is animated by the basic principle that a "great masterpiece is perfect in all its parts" and that philology is apologia, an "attempt to justify the *So-sein*," "the being so and not otherwise of exemplary texts" (A22, pp. 87–134, especially pp. 89, 105, 128).

Above all these national and period concepts rise two others: the folk and the spirit, *das Volk* and *der Geist*. Especially in recent years Spitzer has emphasized the basic truth of the romantic concept of popular creativity. He has expounded the discussions of Theodor Frings of the minnesingers and troubadours and buttressed them by describing the newly discovered Mozarabic lyrics (B55); and he has criticized Joseph Bédier and Lucien Foulet for turning away from historical tradition and the "supporting mother-soil of the people" (A26, p. 93). To his mind "the now fashionable anti-popular trend reflects the sociological situation of the 20th century scholar, his resentful estrangement from the common people, and his jealous defense of a social position which he feels to be already jeopardized" (B55, p. 3n.). Similarly, Spitzer accepts the other key term of German romantic philology, *Geist,* which, he hastens to reassure us, is "nothing ominously mystical or mythological but simply the totality of the features of a given period or movement which the historian tries to see as a unity" (B40, p. 202). Thus Spitzer reveals himself, in his advocacy of *Volksgeist* and *Zeitgeist* and in his strong avowal of organistic aesthetics, as a true descendant of the German founders of Romance philology, though he has, of course, refined their methods by a far greater analytical skill in stylistic observations and a far more sophisticated insight into the complexities of the human psyche.

Spitzer's great mental urge is that toward unity, of reduction to the one, which was also the great motivating power of the romantics. On occasion he bolsters his desire for unity by allusions to Judaic monotheism, but we can account for it more plausibly by the model of the great romantic tradition and even more simply by the logical necessities of the human mind. The continuities in Spitzer's thought are not, one must admit, always clearly visible. There is a gap between his mastery of minute details and his lofty generalizations on nations and spirits. He does not provide the concrete theory of literature which might fill it. Often Spitzer's way of presenting materials resembles the stylistic device he has studied in modern poets, "chaotic enumeration" (A20, reprinted in A25). But such catalogues as those of Walt Whitman and Paul Claudel—two poets Spitzer greatly admired—are inspired rather by a desire for simplicity and unity. Like these poets, Spitzer emerges as a monist in method and conviction. The impression of bewildering variety is deceptive. There is a unity not only of temperament but also of theory and practice in all his work.

### A Selected Bibliography of Leo Spitzer

#### A. Books and Pamphlets (A Complete List)

1. *Die Wortbildung als stilistisches Mittel exemplifiziert an Rabelais,* Nebst einem Anhang über die Wortbildung bei Balzac in seinen "Contes drolatiques," Beihefte zur Zeitschrift für romanische Philologie, No. 19, Halle, 1910.
2. *Über einige Wörter der Liebessprache,* 4 Aufsätze, Leipzig, 1918.

3. *Aufsätze zur romanischen Syntax und Stilistik,* Halle, 1918.

4. *Motiv und Wort. Studien zur Literatur- und Sprachpsychologie* (Hans Sperber, Motiv und Wort bei Gustav Meyrink; Leo Spitzer, Die groteske Gestaltungs- und Sprachkunst Christian Morgensterns), Leipzig, 1918.

5. *Betrachtungen eines Linguisten über Houston Stewart Chamberlains Kriegsaufsätze und die Sprachbewertung im allgemeinen,* Leipzig, 1918.

6. *Fremdwörterhatz und Fremdvölkerhass, Eine Streitschrift gegen Sprachreinigung,* Vienna, 1918.

7. *Studien zu Henri Barbusse,* Bonn, 1920.

8. *Die Umschreibungen des Begriffes "Hunger" im Italienischen,* Beihefte zur Zeitschrift für romanische Philologie, No. 68, Halle, 1921.

9. *Lexikalisches aus dem Katalanischen und den übrigen iberoromanischen Sprachen,* Biblioteca dell'Archivum Romanicum, Series II, No. 1, Geneva, 1921.

10. *Beiträge zur romanischen Wortbildungslehre* (with E. Gamillscheg), Biblioteca dell'Archivum Romanicum, Series II, 2, Geneva, 1921.

11. *Italienische Kriegsgefangenenbriefe,* Bonn, 1921.

12. *Italienische Umgangssprache,* Bonn and Leipzig, 1922.

13. *Hugo Schuchardt-Brevier. Ein Vademecum der allgemeinen Sprachwissenschaft,* Zusammengestellt und eingeleitet von Leo Spitzer, Halle, 1922.

14. *Puxi, eine kleine Studie zur Sprache einer Mutter,* Munich, 1927.

15. *Stilstudien,* 2 vols. Munich, 1928, reprinted Darmstadt, 1961.

16. *Meisterwerke der romanischen Sprachwissenschaft,* 2 vols. Munich, 1929–30.

17. *Romanische Stil- und Literaturstudien,* 2 vols. Marburg, 1931.

18. *Die Literarisierung des Lebens in Lopes "Dorotea,"* Bonn and Cologne, 1932.

19. *L'Amour lointain de Jaufré Rudel et le sens de la poésie des troubadours,* University of North Carolina Studies in the Romance Languages and Literature, No. 5, Chapel Hill, 1944. (Included in 26).

20. *La Enumeración caótica en la poesía moderna,* Colección de estudios estilísticos, Anejo 1, Buenos Aires, 1945. (Included in 25.)

21. *Essays in Historical Semantics,* Testimonial Volume in Honor of Leo Spitzer on the Occasion of his Sixtieth Birthday, New York, 1948.

22. *Linguistics and Literary History: Essays in Stylistics,* Princeton, 1948.

23. *A Method of Interpreting Literature,* Northampton, Mass., 1949.

24. *Critica stilistica e storia del linguaggio,* Saggi raccolti a cura e con presentazione di Alfredo Schiaffini, Bari, 1954.

25. *Lingüística e historia literaria,* Madrid, 1955.

26. *Romanische Literaturstudien, 1936–56,* Tübingen, 1959.

27. *Marcel Proust e altri saggi di letteratura francese moderna,* Con un saggio introduttivo di Pietro Citati, Turin, 1959.

28. *Interpretationen zur Geschichte der französischen Lyrik,* Herausgegeben von Dr. Helga Jauss-Meyer und Dr. Peter Schunck, Heidelberg, 1961.

29. *Essays on English and American Literature,* ed. Anna Hatcher, foreword by Henri Peyre, Princeton, 1962.

30. *Sobre antigua poesía española,* Buenos Aires, 1962.

31. *Cinque saggi di Ispanistica.* Presentazione e contributo bibliografico a cura di Giovanni Maria Bertini, Turin, 1962.

32. *Classical and Christian Ideas of World Harmony. Prolegomena to an Interpretation of the Word "Stimmung,"* ed. Anna Granville Hatcher, preface by René Wellek, Baltimore, 1963.

33. *Critica stilistica e semantica storica,* Bari, 1966.

34. *L'armonia del mondo. Storia semantica di un' idea.* Traduzione di Valentina Poggi, Bologna, 1967.

B. Selected Papers and Reviews, Mainly Concerned with Literature, not Included in the Books

1. "Stilistisch-Syntaktisches aus den spanisch-portugiesischen Romanzen," *Zeitschrift für romanische Philologie, 35* (1911), 192–230, 257–308.

2. "Matilde Serao (Eine Charakteristik)," *Germanisch-romanische Monatsschrift, 6* (1914), 573–84.

3. "Zur stilistischen Bedeutung des Imperfekts der Rede," *Germanisch-romanische Monatsschrift, 9* (1921), 58–60.

4. Review of E. Winkler, *Die neuen Wege und Aufgaben der Stilistik*, in *Literaturblatt für germ. und rom. Philologie, 47* (1926), 89–95.

5. "Der Romanist an der deutschen Hochschule," *Die Neueren Sprachen, 35* (1927), 241–60.

6. "Pícaro," *Revista de filología española, 17* (1930), 258–94.

7. "Zu den Gebeten im 'Couronnement Louis' und im 'Cantar de mio Cid,' " *Zeitschrift für französische Sprache und Literatur, 56* (1932), 196–209.

8. "Erhellung des 'Polyeucte' durch das Alexiuslied," *Archivum Romanicum, 16* (1932), 473–500.

9. "Zur Nachwirkung von Burchiellos Priameldichtung," *Zeitschrift für romanische Philologie, 52* (1932), 484–89.

10. "Racine et Goethe," *Revue d'histoire de la philosophie et d'histoire générale de la civilisation, 1* (1933), 58–75.

11. "Zur Auffassung der Kunst des Arcipreste de Hita," *Zeitschrift für romanische Philologie, 54* (1934), 237–70.

12. "Die 'Estrella de Sevilla' und Claramente," *Zeitschrift für romanische Philologie, 54* (1934), 533–88.

13. "Zur 'Passion' und zur syntaktischen Interpretation," *Zeitschrift für französische Sprache und Literatur, 58* (1934), 437–447.

14. "En Lisant le *Burlador de Sevilla*," *Neuphilologische Mitteilungen, 36* (1935), 282–89.

15. "Une Habitude de style—le rappel—chez Céline," *Le Français moderne, 3* (1935), 193–208.

16. "Notas sobre romances españoles," *Revista de filología española, 22* (1935), 153–74. (See also Adiciones, ibid., pp. 290–91).

17. "Explication linguistique et littéraire de deux textes français," *Le Français moderne, 3* (1935), 315–23; *4* (1936), 37–48.

18. "Zum Text und Kommentar der Flamenca," *Neuphilologische Mitteilungen, 37* (1936), 85–98.

19. "Kenning und Calderóns Begriffspielerei," *Zeitschrift für romanische Philologie, 56* (1936), 100–02.

20. "Remarques sur la différence entre 'poesía popular' et 'poesía de arte,' " *Revista di filología española, 23* (1936), 68–71.

21. "Die Frage der Heuchelei des Cervantes," *Zeitschrift für romanische Philologie, 56* (1936), 138–78.

22. "A mis soledades voy," *Revista de filología española, 23* (1936), 397–400.

23. "Au sujet de la répétition distinctive," *Le Français moderne, 4* (1936), 129–35.

24. "Bemerkungen zu Dantes *Vita Nuova*," *Travaux du Séminaire de philologie romance, 1*, Istanbul, 1937, 162–208.

25. "Pour le Commentaire de Villon *(Testament* v. 447)," *Romania 64* (1938), 522–23.

26. "Le Lion arbitre moral de l'homme," *Romania, 64* (1938), 525–30.

27. "Eine Stelle in Calderón's Traktat über die Malerei," *Neuphilologische Mitteilungen, 39* (1938), 361–70.

28. "Mes Souvenirs de Meyer-Lübke," *Le Français moderne, 6* (1938), 213–24.

29. "Verlebendigende direkte Rede als Mittel der Charakterisierung," *Vox romanica, 4* (1939), 65–86.

30. "Le prénom possessif devant un hypocoristique," *Revue des Études indoeuropéennes, 1* (1939), 2–4, 5–17.

31. "Reseñas" [Review of Félix Lecoy's *Recherches sur le Libro de Buen Amor de Juan Ruiz, archiprêtre de Hita,* Paris, 1938], *Revista de Filología Hispánica, 1* (1939), 266–74.

32. "La Soledad primera de Góngora, notas críticas y explicativas

a la nueva edición de Dámaso Alonso," *Revista de filología hispánica, 2* (1940), 151–81.

33. "Le Prétendu Réalisme de Rabelais," *MP, 37* (1940), 139–50.

34. "Le 'Bel aubépin' de Ronsard, nouvel essai d'explication," *Le Français moderne, 8* (1940), 223–36.

35. "History of Ideas versus Reading of Poetry," *SR, 6* (1941), 584–609.

36. "El Conceptismo interior de Pedro Salinas," *Revista hispánica moderna, 7* (1941), 33–69.

37. "A Linguistic and Literary Interpretation of Claudel's *Ballade*," *French Review, 16* (1942), 134–43.

38. "Notas sintáctico-estilísticas a propósito del español 'que,' " *Revista de filología hispánica, 4* (1942), 105–26, 253–65.

39. "Why Does Language Change?" *MLQ, 4* (1943), 413–31.

40. "Geistesgeschichte vs. History of Ideas Applied to Hitlerism," *Journal of the History of Ideas, 5* (1944), 191–203.

41. "Le Vers 830 du *Roland*," *Romania, 68* (1944–45), 471–77.

42. "Answer to Mr. Bloomfield *(Language* 20, 45)," *Language, 20* (1944), 245–51.

43. Correspondence on Robert Hall, "State of Linguistics: Crisis or Reaction?" *Modern Language Notes, 61* (1946), 497–502.

44. "The Style of *Don Quixote*," in *Cervantes Across the Centuries*, ed. Angel Flores and M. J. Benardete, New York, 1947, pp. 94–100.

45. Review of Américo Castro, *España en Su Historia, Nueva Revista de filología hispánica, 3* (1949), 141–49.

46. "German Words, German Personality and Protestantism Again," *Psychiatry, 12* (1949), 185–87. (With Arno Schirokauer.)

47. "Sobre las Ideas de Américo Castro a propósito de *El villano del Danubio* de Antonio de Guevara," *Boletín del Instituto Caro y Cuervo, 6* (1950), 1–14.

48. "Dos Observaciones, sintáctico-estilísticas a las coplas de Manrique," *Nueva Revista de filología hispánica, 4* (1950), 1–24.

49. "Analyse d'une chanson de Noël anglaise du 14ème siècle, 'I sing of a maiden,' " *Archivum linguisticum, 2* (1950), 74–76.

50. "The Formation of the American Humanist," *PMLA, 46* (1951), 39–48.

51. "Ronsard's 'Sur la mort de Marie,' " *The Explicator, 10,* No. 1 (1951), 1–4.

52. "Wiederum Mörikes Gedicht 'Auf eine Lampe,' " *Trivium, 9* (1951), 133–47.

53. "La Danse macabre," *Mélanges de linguïstique offerts à Albert Dauzat,* Paris, 1951, pp. 307–21.

54. "Les Théories de la stylistique," *Le Français moderne, 20* (1952), 160–68.

55. "The Mozarabic Lyric and Theodor Fring's Theories," *CL, 4* (1952), 1–22.

56. Review of Dámaso Alonso, *Poesía española,* in *Romanische Forschungen, 64* (1952), 213–40.

57. "Language—the Basis of Science, Philosophy and Poetry," in *Studies in Intellectual History,* ed. G. Boas, Baltimore, 1953, pp. 67–93.

58. "Balzac and Flaubert Again," *MLN, 68* (1953), 583–90.

59. "The Works of Rabelais," in *Literary Masterpieces of the Western World,* ed. Francis H. Horn, Baltimore, 1953, pp. 126–47.

60. "La Mia Stilistica," *La Cultura moderna* (Bari), No. 17 (Dec. 1954), pp. 17–19.

61. "The Ideal Typology in Dante's *De Vulgari Eloquentia,*" *Italica, 32* (1955), 75–94.

62. "Stylistique et critique littéraire," *Critique, 11* (1955), 597–609.

63. "Le Due Stilistiche di Giacomo Devoto," *Lo Spettatore italiano, 8* (1955), 356–63.

64. "The Individual Factor in Linguistic Innovations," *Cultura Neolatina, 16* (1956), 71–89.

65. Review of Herbert Seidler, *Allgemeine Stilistik, CL, 8* (1956), 146–49.

66. "Risposta a una critica," *Convivium,* n.s., *5* (1957), 597–603.
67. "Situation as a Term in Literary Criticism Again," *MLN, 72* (1957), 224–28.
68. "A New Book on the Art of the *Celestina," Hispanic Review, 25* (1957), 1–25.
69. "A New Synthetic Treatment of Contemporary Western Lyricism," *MLN, 72* (1957), 523–37.
70. Review of Stephen Ullmann, *Style in the French Novel, CL, 10* (1958), 368–71.
71. "Una Questione di punteggiature in un sonetto di Giacomo da Lentino," *Cultura Neolatina, 18* (1958), 61–70.
72. Review of Wolfgang Kayser, *Das Groteske,* in *Göttinger Gelehrte Anzeigen, 212* (1958), 95–110.
73. Review of M. Riffaterre, *Le Style des Pléiades de Gobineau,* in *MLN, 73* (1958), 68–74.
74. "Zu einer Landschaft Eichendorffs," *Euphorion, 52* (1958), 142–52.
75. "La Bellezza artistica dell'antichissima elegia giudeo-italiana," *Studi in onore di Angelo Monteverdi,* Modena, 1959, pp. 788–806.
76. "The Artistic Unity of Gil Vicente's *Auto da Sibila Casandra," Hispanic Review, 27* (1959), 56–77.
77. "Die Figur der Fénix in Calderón's *Standhaftem Prinzen,"* *Romanistisches Jahrbuch, 10* (1959), 305–35.
78. "La particella 'si' davanti all'aggettivo nel romanzo stend-haliano *Armance," Studi francesi, 8* (1959), 199–213.
79. Review of Ludwig Schrader, *Panurge und Hermes, zum Ursprung eines Charakters bei Rabelais, CL, 12* (1960), 263–65.
80. "Lo Sviluppo di un metodo," *Ulisse, 13* (1960), 26–33. A fuller version in *Cultura neolatina, 20* (1960), 109–28.
81. "Rabelais et les 'rabelaisants,' " *Studi francesi, 4* (1960), 401–23.
82. "For de la bella cayba," *Lettere Italiane, 12* (1960), 133–40. Not identical with piece of same title in A 24.

83. "Mathias Claudius' *Abendlied,*" *Euphorion, 56* (1960), 70–82.

84. "Adiciones a Camino del poema *(Confianza* de Pedro Salinas)," *Nueva revista de filología hispánica, 14* (1960), 33–40.

85. "Les Etudes de style et les différents pays," in *Langue et littérature, Actes du VIIIe Congrès de la Fédération Internationale des Langues et Littératures modernes,* Paris, 1961, pp. 23–38.

86. "Quelques aspects de la technique des romans de Michel Butor," *Archivum linguisticum, 13* (1961), 171–95.

87. "The Influence of Hebrew and Vernacular Poetry on the Judeo-Italian Elegy," in *Twelfth-Century Europe and the Foundations of Modern Society,* ed. M. Clagett, G. Post, and R. Reynolds, Madison, Wis., 1961, pp. 115–30.

88. "On the Significance of Don Quijote," *Modern Language Notes, 77* (1962), 113–29.

# Genre Theory, the Lyric, and *Erlebnis*

The theory of genres has not been at the center of literary study and reflection in this century. Clearly this is due to the fact that in the practice of almost all writers of our time genre distinctions matter little: boundaries are being constantly transgressed, genres combined or fused, old genres discarded or transformed, new genres created, to such an extent that the very concept has been called in doubt. Benedetto Croce, in his *Estetica* (1902), launched an attack on the concept from which it has not recovered in spite of many attempts to defend it or to restate it in different terms. In my and Austin Warren's *Theory of Literature* (1949), in a chapter on "Literary Genres" written by Mr. Warren, some of these attempts at renovation of the concept are surveyed and endorsed. Genre exists as an institution exists. "One can work through, express oneself through, existing institutions, create new ones . . . one can also join, but then reshape, institutions." Genres are aesthetic (stylistic and thematic) conventions which have molded individual works of art importantly. Genres can be observed even in the apparently anarchic welter of twentieth-century literary activity. Yet Mr. Warren was frankly dubious whether the division of poetry into three basic kinds, the epic, the drama, and the lyric, can be upheld and whether these three kinds can have "ultimate status."[1]

Since our book was written (in 1944–46), Emil Staiger's *Grundbegriffe der Poetik* (1946) and Käte Hamburger's

1. New York, 1949, pp. 235, 238.

*Logik der Dichtung* (1957) have presented theories which make impressive efforts to arrive at basic distinctions of poetry with new arguments in different philosophical contexts. Miss Hamburger appeals to phenomenology, Emil Staiger to Heideggerian existentialism. Miss Hamburger defends a dichotomy, Staiger a threefold division. In both theories the lyric or the lyrical presents the crux of the matter and thus will be the focus of our discussion.

Miss Hamburger draws the main distinction between two kinds of poetry: fictional or mimetic and lyrical or existential. Lyrical poetry is a "real utterance" *(Wirklichkeitsaussage)* of the same status as a letter or a historical narrative, while epic and drama are "fiction," the invention of actions and characters. The dividing criterion is the speaker: in the lyric the poet himself speaks, in the epic and drama he makes others speak. The novel in the first person *(Ich-Roman)* is resolutely grouped with lyrical poetry, as the author speaks there himself. Miss Hamburger's observations on the novel and the narrator in a novel have attracted much attention. Her thesis that the past tense in the novel loses its temporal function and becomes a present tense is stated persuasively. She buttresses this view by the observation that adverbs of time can be used in fictional contexts in disregard of the past meaning of the verbs. Without denying her thesis that, in some narrative contexts, the past verb loses its pastness, one may, however, object that combinations such as "he was coming to her party to-night," which she quotes from Virginia Woolf's *Mrs. Dalloway,*[2] can only occur in narrated monologue *(Erlebte Rede)* and do not set off all fiction. Still, her reflections on the narrator and the narrative function are ingenious and stimulating.

2. *Die Logik der Dichtung* (Stuttgart, 1957), pp. 9, 35. See also her defense: "Noch einmal: Vom Erzählen," *Euphorion, 59* (1965), 46–71.

Miss Hamburger's other side of the bifurcation has, however, not aroused much discussion. Her attempt to prove the lyric to be "real utterance," undistinguishable from a passage in a letter if we dissolve a poem into prose, has gone unchallenged. In many variations she asserts the thesis that a lyrical poem is a real utterance with its origin in an "I" *(Ich-Origo)* in which the object must be understood to be experienced *(erlebt)* by the speaker. She rejects the idea of a "fictive I," a "persona" or mask, propounded in our *Theory of Literature* as "falser and more misleading than the older naïve conception that a lyrical poem betrays much of the experience of the poet."[3] Still, she constantly appeals to a criterion of "subjektive Erlebnisechtheit," even though she may not believe in a literal transcription of actual events in the poet's life. But the criterion of "genuineness," "sincerity," "intensity," etc., is a psychological criterion which puts the onus on a completely unprovable and elusive past experience of the poet. It is of course also not in any way peculiar to lyrical poetry. Miss Hamburger, in her psychologism, even arrives at a formula which divorces the inner act from the outward expression. A lyrical poem, she says, is a "secondary phenomenon" since it is only "the expression, and proclamation of the will of the subject." She argues that "the lyrical intensity of the lyrical I may be stronger than the expression, the form." Thus any bad love poem by a schoolboy is "constituted by the lyrical I."[4] She does not see that the very same problem raised by the sincere rhyming schoolboy occurs also in fiction. We can imagine a charming yarn-spinning "raconteur" inventing conversations and characters in a real life situation. The boundary between art and nonart, art and life, disappears in Miss Hamburger's scheme, because she believes in the possibility of

3. *Logik,* pp. 183 (referring to *Theory of Literature,* p. 15), 186 (for quotation).

4. Ibid., pp. 202 ff.

a purely phenomenological description of art apart from value judgment, from criticism.[5] But it is a contradiction to speak of art as nonvalue or even disvalue. It is value-charged by definition.

Miss Hamburger not only considers "lived experience," intensity, *Erlebnis* the criterion of lyrical poetry, she also endorses the view that a lyrical poem can have a function in reality. She quotes a hysterical passage from a letter by Rahel Varnhagen commenting on a charming gallant poem by Goethe, "Mit einem gemalten Band," addressed to Friederike Brion: "Es musste sie vergiften. Dem hätte sie nicht glauben sollen? . . . Und zum ersten Male war Goethe feindlich für mich da."[6] Moreover, Miss Hamburger endorses Staiger's in its sexual metaphor, embarrassing characterization of the contemporary "Mailied" addressed to the same woman. "Friederike ist zugegen. Goethe ist durchdrungen von ihr, wie ihn seinerseits das Gefühl beglückt, dass sie von ihm durchdrungen sei."[7] But soberly examined, all these high-flown phrases mean little more than that Goethe expressed his feelings of love and happiness successfully in fine poetry and that he addressed his poems, as other poets before and after him, to real persons in a concrete situation, a fact which has never been doubted. But the purpose, the aim of persuasion to love, can not constitute value and will not set the poem off from any other utterance, a letter, a speech, a treatise, even a fable or a fiction invented to serve a practical purpose. The poem remains the same even if we should discover that the poet changed the addressee, as Ronsard and Lamartine did with some of their love poems, or that we were mistaken in identifying the woman addressed as Minna Herzlieb or Marianne von Willemer.

5. Ibid., p. 5.
6. Ibid., p. 183.
7. *Goethe, 1* (3 vols. Zürich, 1952), 56.

But Miss Hamburger is too sophisticated and subtle not to notice the difficulties raised with her insistence on "real utterance." She has to account for lyrical poetry, which is simply a descriptive statement about some natural object. She quotes some German verses of this kind and then draws from Hermann Amman's *Die menschliche Rede* the view that in such poetry we encounter sentences "which have no proper place in human intercourse"—e.g. "Der Bach rauscht, der Wind weht." She endorses Amman's view that such a statement is "ein Stück Leben . . . es sind die Dinge selbst, die hier zu Worte kommen," "the utterance about the things has no function in a reality nexus: they are seized, animated and hence transformed." But why could a statement such as "der Bach rauscht" not be made about a rushing brook outside a poetic context? How could one distinguish such a pronouncement, which she calls "meaningless in isolation," or "aufeinander zugeordnet," from any speech-situation comprehensible only in a context? The phrase about "the things speaking for themselves," "the piece of life," seem to me only farfetched metaphors for romantic animism. The conclusion that a lyrical poem is a "real utterance which still has no function in a reality nexus"[8] is not only a flat contradiction to the discussion about the Friederike poems but is simply an attempt to describe aesthetic distance, *Schein,* illusion—what I would call fiction—in such a way that the thesis of "real utterance" and "nonfiction" is preserved, at least verbally.

Usually, however, Miss Hamburger argues that we "must use external, even biographical investigations" for the explanation of a lyrical poem, considering this a "categorical distinction" between the lyric and fiction. It is, however, hard to see why biographical evidence is not as relevant to the study of Tolstoy, Dante, Proust, or Gide as to a lyrical poet like Mallarmé or Valéry, or what can be the justification for her

8. *Logik,* pp. 176 ff., 180.

view—exactly inverting the contrast between the "loose baggy monsters" of Tolstoy and the tight-closed realm of a poem by Hopkins—in asserting that drama and novel are "closed structures" while "every lyrical poem is an open structure." She argues that every lyrical poem eludes complete explanation while even the most obscure surrealistic symbolic novel is explainable in principle. All fiction, in her view, is through and through rational and hence knowable: a lyrical poem is open to the experience of the uttering "I," "toward the irrational life of the poet."[9] She thinks it an argument for her view that biographical research has been most intense on the lives of poets, as if Napoleon, Tolstoy, Voltaire, or Dr. Johnson had not as much or more attention than Hölderlin or Keats. She admits that "how far the lyrical I is the poet-I can never be settled and the poet himself would hardly be able to do so,"[10] a concession she should have extended to fictional characters such as Pierre Bezukhov or Konstantin Levin, to give examples from an author particularly dear to Miss Hamburger.

One difficulty of her theory worries her: the use of lyrical poems in the novel. Are the poems fiction, utterances of the characters, or are they "real utterances"? She draws a justifiable distinction between Goethe's use in *Wilhelm Meister* and that of Eichendorff in his novels and stories. The Mignon and Harper songs are clearly more closely related to the fictional speakers than those of Eichendorff's shadowy and often interchangeable characters. But the conclusion drawn by Miss Hamburger that Eichendorff's poems remain "Wirklichkeits-aussage," while Goethe's are part of his fiction construes an untenable contrast.[11] Goethe, after all, reprinted these poems

9. Ibid., p. 187.
10. Ibid., pp. 190, 186.
11. Ibid., pp. 204 ff.

among his collections of lyrical poetry, and they have been
read and sung by many who have never read *Wilhelm Meister;*
and Eichendorff's poems have also a characterizing function:
the singing makes these men the carefree, melancholy, nature-
loving, wandering, musical fellows that they are. The distinction simply does not hold. It seems impossible to exclude
from the lyric cycles such as Petrarch's Canzoniere, Shakespeare's Sonnets, or Donne's Songs and Sonnets, which imply
some thread of a story or progression or vary their speakers,
and to assign them to "fiction" in Miss Hamburger's scheme.

This is the same difficulty raised by the "Rollenlyrik,"
which Miss Hamburger quite wrongly dismisses as "eine an
sich unbedeutende Erscheinung."[12] Half the world's lyrical
poetry could be described as such. It is ubiquitous in folk
poetry: the oldest Romance lyrics recently discovered, the
eleventh-century Mozarabic poems, put into the mouths of
women, and certainly much of English poetry, often mis-
named "dramatic monologue" or even "poetry of experience"
(Robert Langbaum), from Donne to Browning and Eliot
would have to be classed here. Its history is completely distorted when Miss Hamburger explains the "Rollengedicht" as
derived from the ancient picture inscription and considers it
"as the germ for the formation of the ballad form."[13] Neither
the popular women's poem nor the medieval ballad has anything to do with the Alexandrian *ekphrasis.* Nor can she convince by dismissing the ballad as "a museum piece," if we
think, for instance, of recent American and Russian examples. Finally she seems to admit some ambiguity and complains "of a betrayal of the lyric" to fiction in the ballad,[14] a
telltale phrase for her annoyance with the breakdown of her

12. Ibid., p. 220.
13. Ibid., p. 214.
14. Ibid., p. 217.

scheme. In order to save it, she has recourse to an obscure distinction between "fictiv" and "fingiert." Mörike's poem "Früh, wann die Hähne krähn," put into the mouth of a girl, is "fingiert," while "Nur wer die Sehnsucht kennt," spoken by Mignon, is apparently "fiktiv." Miss Hamburger knows that a man, Eduard Mörike, wrote the first poem and that Mignon, a fictional figure, sings the second poem in a novel, but as texts the two poems do not differ in their status: they are both spoken by a "persona," a fictive speaker, a young girl. As a matter of fact, "Das verlassene Mägdlein" occurs also first in Mörike's novel, *Maler Nolten*. Miss Hamburger can thus complain that the ballad (and she includes the "Rollenlyrik" as a subdivision) is "ein struktureller Fremdling im lyrischen Raum."[15]

She has to treat the first person narrative as an analogous stranger in the epic-fictional space. She still insists that the first person narrative is nonfiction, a form of real utterance, though she admits that in an "Ich-Roman" the fixed teller who makes persons in the past engage in dialogue comes very near the epic "I," the narrative function.[16] But she has again recourse to her concept of "Fingiertsein," which she once admits would require further analysis,[17] to account for the obvious fact that the "I" of a first person narrative may be very different from the poet's. She speaks of this difference as containing a "factor of uncertainty," though there seems no doubt, for instance, in what specific way Felix Krull is not Thomas Mann, or the judge in *La Chute* not Albert Camus. She parallels this uncertainty with the uncertainty about the lyrical speaker, though the speaker in a lyric may be clearly identified and distinguished from the poet (as in Browning's "Cavalier

15. Ibid., p. 220.
16. Ibid., p. 231.
17. Ibid., p. 233.

Tunes"), and though a third-person narrative may raise the same doubts about the relationship of the teller to the writer as a first-person story.

Miss Hamburger also does not properly face the question of the ease and frequency of the switch from first person to third person and the other way round. Joyce, in some sections of *Ulysses,* shifts in almost every other sentence. Dostoevsky transcribed the original first person confession of Raskolnikov into the third person, often changing only the inflectional endings. Miss Hamburger herself refers to the two versions of Gottfried Keller's *Grüner Heinrich,* the later with a part rewritten from the original third person into the first. What would she say to a novel like Michel Butor's *La Modification,* written throughout in the second person? What can she do with Caesar's *Commentaries* or *The Education of Henry Adams,* both told by their authors in the third person? At one point she seems to admit that the "form does not guarantee the reality content," but she insists that a third-person narrative, however close to empirical reality, will always be fiction, while a first-person narrative, however fantastically unreal, will still be nonfiction, *Wirklichkeitsaussage.* "It is the form of the I utterance which preserves the character of a reality utterance even for the most extreme unreality utterance."[18] One must quote such an awkward sentence to see that Miss Hamburger throughout the book simply reiterates one undoubted fact: many poems and novels use "I" as the speaker, while other novels and some poems use "he" and have characters speak for themselves. All the talk about the "logic of poetry," all the ingenuity spent in relating her observations to a theory of knowledge lead only to a meager result: a gram-

18. Ibid., p. 235: "Es ist die Form der Ichaussage, die auch der extremsten Unwirklichkeitsaussage noch den Charakter der Wirklichkeitsaussage belässt."

mar of poetry, the description of stylistic devices, a restate-
ment of the ancient division of poetry by speaker.

Miss Hamburger herself appeals to historical precedence:
she recognizes that she revives Aristotle's concept of *mimesis,*
which she oddly enough thinks was first "restored to honor"
by Erich Auerbach. As if the Neo-Thomists, the Marxists,
and the Chicago Aristotelians had not honored it long before
1946! Actually, her division descends from Plato's *Republic*[19]
and was codified by the fourth-century grammarian Dio-
medes. Plato distinguishes three kinds of imitation: pure narrative, in which the poet speaks in his own person; narrative
by means of imitation, in which the poet speaks in the person
of his characters; and mixed narrative, in which he speaks
now in his own person and now by means of imitation. The
epic would be the mixed kind; what we call lyric would appear under first-person narrative. The theory has been restated many times since: in Germany, for instance, in Johann
Joachim Eschenburg's *Entwurf einer Theorie und Litteratur
der schönen Wissenschaften* (1783), where the lyric, ode,
elegy, and even satire, allegory, and epigram consistently appear under epic. Also, the well-known common scheme
drawn up by Goethe and Schiller, "Über epische und dramatische Dichtung" (1797), distinguishes the two kinds in terms
of the speaker: "the rhapsode who as a higher being ought
not to appear in the poem, so that we may separate everything
personal from his work, and may believe that we are hearing
only the voice of the Muses in general," while "the *mime,* the
actor, constitutes the opposite. He presents himself as a distinct individuality."[20] The lyric is completely ignored, but
Goethe's later scheme, "Die Naturformen der Dichtung"

19. III 392 D–394 C.
20. Cf. Goethe, *Sämtliche Werke, Jubiläumsausgabe, 36* (40 vols.
Stuttgart, 1962–07), 149–52.

(1819), finds a place for the lyric distinguished from the "clearly telling epic" and the "personally acting drama" by being "enthusiastically excited."[21] Goethe, one sees, introduced the totally different criterion of tone, excitement, enthusiasm, in order to accommodate the third kind.

The division was restated most strikingly in Jean Paul's *Vorschule der Ästhetik* (1804), in a discussion of the lyric added in the second edition (1813). Jean Paul apologizes for having ignored the lyric in the first edition and then restates Eschenburg's dichotomy: one can look at the poet like philosophers arguing about God's relation to the world, as either "extramundane" or "intramundane." But Jean Paul asks then:

> could there be a more fluid division right in the middle of the poetic sea? For neither the intrusion nor the concealment of the poet decides what form a poem may take . . . How easy it would be—if the trivialities of speaking und letting speak made the division—to fuse forms with forms. The same dithyramb e.g. would become quickly epical if the poet were to say or chant at the outset that he is going to chant about another poet; or it would be quickly lyrical with a few words saying that he is to sing himself; or quickly dramatic if he were to insert him, without himself saying a word, in a dramatic soliloquy. But mere formalities, at least in poetry, are not forms.[22]

21. Ibid., *5,* 223.

22. *Sämtliche Werke,* ed. E. Berend, I, *11* (Weimar, 1935), 254: "Gibt es dann aber eine flüssigere Abtheilung und Abscheidung mitten im poetischen Meere? Denn weder die Einmengung, noch die Versteckung des Dichters entscheidet zwischen zwei Formen des Gedichts . . . Wie leicht wären, falls nur die Kleinigkeiten des Sprechens und des Sprechenlassens abtheilten, Formen in Formen einzuschmelzen, und derselbe Dithyrambus würde, z. B. bald episch, wenn der Dichter

Here, 144 years before Miss Hamburger's *Logik der Dichtung,* her theory is cogently refuted.

Miss Hamburger arrives at a dichotomy splitting the realm of poetry: telling versus saying, fiction versus real utterance, "he" versus "I". Many other genre theories arrive at a triad, in defense of the three established kinds: lyric, epic, tragedy. Emil Staiger's *Grundbegriffe der Poetik* (1946) is the most influential attempt to reformulate the triad on new grounds: to replace the kinds by categories which he calls "the lyrical," "the epical," "the dramatic." Every piece of poetry is conceived as located somewhere between these three extremes, since only very few works embody or fulfill the idea of the lyrical, the epical, or the dramatic. Staiger's examples, which he analyzes sensitively—Brentano for the lyrical, Homer for the epical, Kleist for the dramatic—are not meant to be normative. The three attitudes (not kinds) are coordinated mainly with the three dimensions of time: the past with the lyrical, the present with the epical, the future with the dramatic, and these time dimensions are interpreted in terms of Heidegger's conception: the past implies recollection ("Er-innerung," in Heidegger's punning term); the present "Vorstellung," presentation; the future, "Spannung," tension. "Stimmung" for the lyrical, "Verfallen" for the epical, "Verstehen" for the dramatic mode is another series of coordinates drawn from Heidegger; it corresponds to the three ages of man: the lyrical to childhood, the epical to youth, the dramatic to maturity. The triad of man's faculties is introduced by calling the lyrical "emotional" or "sinnlich," the epical "bildlich" or "anschau-

---

vorher sagte und sänge, er wolle einen fremden singen, bald lyrisch durch die Worte, er wolle seinen eignen singen, bald dramatisch, wenn er ihn ohne ein Wort von sich in ein tragisches Selbstgespräch einschöbe. Aber blosse Förmlichkeiten sind—in der Poesie wenigstens— keine Formen."

end," the dramatic "logical" or "begrifflich," and the activities of "fühlen, zeigen, beweisen" correspond closely. Finally, we are told the three modes are correlated with the series: syllable, word, and sentence. Cassirer's theories provided the terminology here.

The crux of the scheme lies in the coordination of the "lyrical" with the "past," which seems to contradict all the usual analyses of lyrical presence or immediacy. But the Heideggerian use of "Erinnerung" allows the term to mean a lack of distance between subject and object: "Gegenwärtiges, Vergangenes, ja sogar Zukünftiges kann in lyrischer Dichtung erinnert werden."[23] The time scheme is abolished for the lyrical mode, permitting gestures toward the mystical and ineffable. We are told that "lyrisches Dichten ist jenes an sich unmögliche Sprechen der Seele." A contradiction between the lyrical and the nature of language is asserted.[24] Lyrical poetry somehow happens: "der lyrische Dichter leistet nichts," and even the relation of man and nature is reversed. I do not understand what is meant by saying "die Natur erinnert den Dichter"[25] or what the meaning of the last sentence of the chapter could be: "Ein ungeheuerliches Dasein, das die Beseligungen der Gnade mit einer erschütternden Hilflosigkeit in allem, was Verdienst ist, erkauft, das Glück der Übereinstimmung mit einer im Alltag blutenden Wunde, für die auf Erden kein Heilkraut blüht."[26] One need not be a rationalist to doubt whether anybody could coincide with a wound bleeding on a sober day. Quite seriously Staiger calls the lyrical "the liquid element," or speaks of the soul as being "the fluidity [*die Flüssigkeit*] of a landscape in recollection," an at-

23. *Grundbegriffe* (Zürich, 1946), p. 67.
24. Ibid., pp. 83, 82.
25. Ibid., p. 67.
26. Ibid., p. 88.

tempt to use distinctions from Franz Baader's theosophic
speculations to which Staiger alludes with apparent approval.[27]

The trouble with the scheme is primarily its lack of relation
to actual poetry. It could be arrived at without any literary
evidence, as Staiger admits when he says that the "ideal meaning" of the lyrical can be experienced in front of a landscape,
of the epical, in front of a stream of refugees (an example
suggested by *Hermann und Dorothea*), the dramatic from a
quarrel.[28] The terms which are, after all, derived from and
devised for poetics become names for human attitudes in an
existential "anthropology." Nor can one imagine a poem
made out of syllables and not of words or sentences, as even
Dada poetry uses words (and of course syllables are often
words, particularly in monosyllabic languages). The examples
on which Staiger demonstrates his concept of the "lyrical" are
all German romantic "Stimmungsgedichte," private moody
musings for which even the admired "Über allen Gipfeln" is
too rational, too pointed. "Warte nur, balde Ruhest du auch"
is not completely lyrical in Staiger's sense. The poem, after all,
was written with an eye to the point: it was conceived because of that point. Staiger asserts "im Augenblick des
Verstehens aber hört das lyrische Dasein auf."[29] In practice,
we are sent off to the grossest irrationalism, to an "inwardness" which cannot be expressed in words and hence cannot
be art or poetry. Staiger had disclaimed that his scheme has
anything to do with valuation and he even makes the admis-
sion which, one would think, questions the validity of the
whole enterprise when he says that "in English or the Romance languages everything looks different." "The Italian

27. Ibid., pp. 223, 227 ff., 231.
28. Ibid., p. 9.
29. Ibid., p. 79.

when he speaks of *lirica* thinks of Petrarch's 'Canzoniere.'
For us Petrarch's work is no prototype of the lyrical style."[30]
But these differences are dismissed as merely "annoying"
*(ärgerlich),* and in the postscript to the second edition (1952)
the claim to practical application to concrete literature is asserted much more clearly. Staiger recognizes somewhat cautiously that his scheme has to do with traditional kinds,
though he should like to interpret them freely, with a "Spiel-
raum" around them. He even allows the possibility of a "Mu-
sterpoetik" of the ode, the elegy, the novel, and the comedy,
though he disclaims any intention of furnishing it. But he does
make value judgments according to his assumed genre scheme
on Klopstock's *Messias* and on Keller's lyrical poetry. He
recognizes, however, that his "Fundamentalpoetik" is not an
appropriate instrument to grasp the type of poetry represented
by Horace, in which the echo, the artistic game, share in the
nature and value of the verse.[31]

Fortunately, Staiger's practice of interpretation always
eludes his theory. The three volumes on Goethe successfully
combine narrative and interpretation as well as judgment and
use only occasionally the scheme of the *Grundbegriffe.* Staiger
introduces the more general concept of a "rhythm" of Goethe's life and work which he constantly tries to characterize
as the achievement of a moment, "Augenblick," a metaphor
for harmony, "erfüllte Gegenwart," suggested by Faust and
interpreted in Heideggerian terms. But "rhythm" remains a
hieroglyph, a gesture toward something felt, even though
Staiger appeals to Gustav Becking's completely fanciful idea
of "Schlagfiguren." He wisely decided at last that he will not
demonstrate Goethe's "Schlagfigur" (he could not anyhow)

30. Ibid., pp. 246, 245.
31. *Grundbegriffe* (5th ed. Zürich, 1961), pp. 248, 246.

and is content to speak vaguely of the structure of his imagination or the rhythm of his life.[32]

The peculiarity of Staiger's genre theory is the adaptation of the Heideggerian time scheme, with the paradoxical result of assigning the lyric (or rather in Staiger "the lyrical") to the past, the epic to the present, the drama to the future. In contrast to other theories, Staiger's does not appeal to the speaker as a criterion. With his Heideggerian assumptions, the subjective-objective dichotomy is abolished: the lyrical poem is described in terms of such a mystical fusion.[33] The account of Goethe's Strassburg lyrics, in the Goethe book, plays another variation on the theme of the subject-object identity often phrased pantheistically or sentimentally. Goethe's feeling that "his heart is the heart of creation and the heart of creation his heart" is proclaimed the main accomplishment of the whole German literary revival![34]

In the history of genre theories the triadic division is a leading theme. In a well documented thesis, *Die Lehre von der Einteilung der Dichtkunst* (1940), Miss Irene Behrens tried to show that the triad is only the result of eighteenth-century theorizing. She considers Charles Batteux's *Les Beaux Arts réduits à un même principe* (1746) the crucial document and traces its codification and general acceptance to the later German critics. Her own book contains many examples of the triads used in earlier centuries often quite casually. Many Italian examples could also be given from other sources.[35] Two of the greatest English poets, Milton

32. *Goethe, 3* (3 vols. Zürich, 1959), 474, 478 ff.
33. *Grundbegriffe* (1946), p. 64.
34. *Goethe, 1,* 59.
35. See, e.g., Antonio Possevino (1593), cited in Bernard Weinberg, *A History of Literary Criticism in the Italian Renaissance* (Chicago, 1961), p. 336, or Gregorio Leti (1667), cited in Ciro Trabalza, *La Critica letteraria* (Milano, 1915), p. 239.

and Dryden, use the distinction casually. Milton speaks of the "laws of a true Epic poem, of a Dramatic and a Lyric,"[36] and Dryden, in the Preface to the *Essay of Dramatic Poetry,* speaks of "the English poets who have written either in this, the epic, or the lyric way."[37] The lyric is here used not, as often in earlier times, as some minor genre but as the alternative to epic and drama exhausting all possibilities. One can find other examples: for instance, in Muratori, who includes even satire under lyric.[38]

But the mere number three means little. All depends on the principle of division. The rediscovery of dialectics with Kant and Fichte is obviously the crucial event. Genre theory was resolutely connected with a theory of knowledge in Schiller's *Über naive und sentimentalische Dichtung* (1795), which arrives at a scheme of the relationship between man and nature which is at the same time a historical scheme and a genre theory. But Schiller discarded the traditional kinds and devised, within "sentimental" poetry, a triad of genres: satire, elegy, and idyll, which he himself emphasizes have nothing to do with the original names: they are determined by "Empfindungsweisen."[39]

The innovator was Friedrich Schlegel, whose originality and speculative boldness is becoming more widely appreciated since the publication of his early notebooks and manuscripts. In a note dated 1797 Schlegel makes the coordination with subjective-objective still very much within the scheme of the voice categories. "Lyrical [form] is merely subjective; dramatic merely objective. As form the epic has apparently precedence. It is subjective-objective." Two years later he

36. *Treatise of Education* (1644).
37. *Essay of Dramatic Poetry* (1668), Preface to the Reader.
38. *Della Perfetta Poesia italiana, 3* (4 vols. Modena, 1706), 3 ff.
39. See note at beginning of section: "Idylle."

changed the coordination: "epic is objective poetry; lyric, subjective; drama, objective-subjective." But he reverts again to the older coordination in 1800: "the epic is subjective-objective, the drama objective, the lyric subjective." Later notes, "Zur Poesie und Literatur" (1808), reassert that "the epic is the root of the whole and the exact middle between the wholly interior lyrical and the wholly external dramatic poetry."[40] But curiously enough, in Friedrich Schlegel's published writings such a genre theory plays no role. In his histories of Greek literature a sequence, epic (Homer), lyric (Sappho, etc.), drama (Aeschylus, etc.) is traced, and in the Preface to *Über das Studium der griechischen Poesie* (1797) a historical typology is worked out in which "objective" is associated with Greek poetry, while modern poetry is "interesting" or "characteristic." Goethe is considered the hope for a revival of objective poetry in the very same manner Schiller considered Goethe the naïve poet surviving in the modern sentimental age.[41] In the sketch of the phases of Goethe's evolution in *Gespräch über die Poesie* (1800) Goethe's early manner is considered mixed subjective-objective, while the second epoch is "objective to the highest degree."[42] "Objectivity" is here not a genre distinction, as Goethe wrote in all genres, but an attitude, implying aesthetic distance, detachment, classicism.

August Wilhelm Schlegel probably picked up the idea of relating the genres to the dialectics from his younger brother. In notes preserved for the continuation of the Berlin lectures (1803), he remarks: "Episch, lyrisch, dramatisch als These,

40. *Literary Notebooks 1797–1801*, ed. H. Eichner (Toronto, 1957), pp. 48, 175, 204, 238.

41. *Kritische Schriften*, ed. W. Rasch (München, 1956), pp. 105–12.

42. Ibid., p. 334.

Antithese, Synthese. Das Epische das rein objektive im men-
schlichen Geiste. Das lyrische das rein subjektive. Das Drama
die Durchdringung der beiden."[43] At about the same time
Schelling, in his lectures on *Philosophie der Kunst* (1803), for
which he had access to Schlegel's manuscript lectures, uses
the dialectics again: the lyric is characterized by the predominance of the subject of the poet; it is the most individualized,
particular genre. In the epic the poet rises to objectivity, the
drama represents the union of the lyric and the epic, of the
subjective and objective, as in tragedy necessity is objective
(i.e. in the order of the universe) and freedom subjective (i.e.
in the moral revolt of the hero). In comedy the relation is
reversed.[44] Schelling, if I understand him correctly, means
that comic characters are somehow fixed and fated, while the
world and its order is treated with freedom and irony. A puz-
zling question of the history of genre theories is raised, however, by the circumstance that neither August Wilhelm
Schlegel's nor Schelling's lectures were published in their
time.[45] One would have to examine the numerous German
books on poetics during the first decades of the century to
make sure who formulated the dialectical scheme for the first
time in print.

One new motif emerges: the coordination of the main
kinds with the dimensions of time. I find it in Wilhelm von
Humboldt's *Über Goethes Hermann und Dorothea* (1799),
which does not propound a triadic scheme but rather develops
Schiller's theories. Humboldt divides all poetry into "plastic"
and "lyrical," and plastic poetry, in its turn, into epical and

43. *Die Kunstlehre,* ed. E. Lohner (Stuttgart, 1963), p. 306.
44. *Werke,* ed. O. Weiss, *3* (3 vols. Leipzig, 1907), 287, 296, 335,
341; cf. also p. 19.
45. Schlegel's lectures in 1884 by J. Minor, Schelling's in 1859 in
*Sämtliche Werke.*

dramatic. Humboldt then makes the suggestion that the simplest distinction between epic and tragedy is "indisputably" *(unstreitig)* that between past and present time.[46]

Here apparently a coordination between the genres and time is asserted for the first time, but the specific coordination was and is far from "indisputable." Humboldt makes no effort to relate the future to a genre, and the lyric would, presumably, belong to the present. In Schelling's *Philosophie der Kunst* the epic is referred to the past, the lyrical poem to the present, but later Schelling speaks of the epic as indifferent to time, as "beyond time" or timeless.[47] The coordination with all three times is carried out expressly in Jean Paul's *Vorschule der Ästhetik,* in the second edition of 1813. The epic represents the event which develops from the past, the drama the action which extends toward the future, the lyric the emotion confined to the present.[48]

All these motifs meet in Hegel's *Vorlesungen über Ästhetik,* which were given in the twenties but published in 1835. There the genres are worked into a dialectical scheme which is also historical. The objective epic, the thesis, is contradicted by the subjective lyric and synthetized by the drama. Hegel also speaks of the relation to time: "the lyrical effusion has a much nearer relation to time than epical narration, which places real phenomena into the past, and puts them or combines them next to each other in a more spatial unfolding, while the lyric represents the momentary emergence of feelings and images in the temporal succession of their genesis and formation and thus has to shape artistically the diverse temporal motion itself."[49] The Hegelian scheme is developed

46. *Werke,* ed. A. Flitner and K. Giel, *2* (4 vols. Stuttgart, 1961), 272; corresponds to *2, 246,* of the Prussian Academy edition.

47. *Werke, 3,* 291, 298.

48. *Werke, 11,* 254.

49. *Sämtliche Werke,* ed. H. Glockner, *14* (Stuttgart, 1928), 451.

and, in the theory of the lyric, refined in Friedrich Theodor Vischer's *Ästhetik*. The fifth volume on poetry (1857) repeats the subjective-objective scheme and relates the genres to time: "the epic considers the object from the point of view of the past, in lyrical poetry everything becomes present in feeling, in drama the present tends toward the future as the action develops." In developing a theory of the lyric which distinguishes many subgenres, Vischer makes much of the immediacy, the momentariness of the lyric in relation to time. He speaks of its character of "Punktualität: sie ist ein punktuelles Zünden der Welt im Subjecte." Though the detailed discussion brings in much historical knowledge and thus modifies the initial statements, Vischer radically limits the lyric to the overflow of feeling, even passive feeling, suffering. "Erleben, erfahren, heisst durch Leiden gehn."[50]

These theories had some echo also among English and American critics. They could not leave the coordination between the genres and the tenses alone. In Eneas Sweetland Dallas' *Poetics* (1852), for instance, the play is coordinated with the present, the tale with the past, and the song, mysteriously, with the future.[51] John Erskine, in *The Kinds of Poetry* (1920), finds the lyric expresses present time, the drama past, and the epic future. This odd reversal is defended by interpreting tragedy in Ibsen's words as a judgment day on the hero's past, while the epic predicts and projects the destiny of a nation or of the race.[52]

One need not argue any specific influence to see how Staiger's and Miss Hamburger's schemes grow out of a long tradition with roots in the great period of German aesthetic speculation. Their theories of the lyric all have one common

50. *Ästhetik, 5* (5 vols. Stuttgart, 1857), 1260, 1331.

51. London, 1852, pp. 81, 91, 105.

52. New York, 1920, p. 12. The essay was originally published in 1912.

feature: the lyric is subjective; it is the expression of feeling, of experience, *Erlebnis*. This in itself is not new at all. It is an error to consider the idea of personal poetry, of poetry as autobiography, an innovation of romanticism or more particularly of the German *Sturm und Drang*. No doubt, the reaction against formal neoclassicism was then particularly vocal. It is easy to collect passages from Bürger, Stolberg, and others to prove that they thought of poetry as emotional overflow. It is sufficient to quote Franz in *Götz von Berlichingen* (1771): " 'So fühl' ich denn in dem Augenblick, was den Dichter macht, ein volles, ganz von Einer Empfindung volles Herz!"[53] But such pronouncements could be paralleled all over Europe at that time. They are common in the earlier English accounts of original poetry: in 1763 John Brown calls it "a kind of rapturous exclamations, of joy, grief, triumph, or exultation."[54] Robert Burns speaks of his poetry as "the spontaneous language of my heart."[55] Much of this is simply good classical doctrine. It can appeal to Horace: "Si vis me flere, dolendum est/ Primum ipsi tibi" *(De art. poet.,* vv. 102 ff.), which, in the context, applies to the actor but was constantly quoted as a precept for all rhetoric. It is the demand for sincerity which has been discussed throughout history, not only in the context of lyrical poetry. The troubadour Bernart de Ventadour knows that "the song must come from the heart,"[56] and Sir Philip Sidney says: "Look into thy heart and write."[57] Much poetry even in older times was definitely and concretely

53. Goethe, *Werke, 10,* 39; cf. p. 161. Cf., e.g. *Sturm und Drang. Kritische Schriften,* ed. E. Löwenthal (Heidelberg, 1949), pp. 805–11, 798.

54. *Dissertation on the Rise, Union and Power, the Progressions, Separations and Corruptions of Poetry and Music* (London, 1763).

55. *Scrapbook,* No. 434.

56. *Anthology of Provençal Troubadours,* ed. Hill-Bergin (New Haven 1941), No. 26.

57. *Astrophel and Stella* (published 1591), the first sonnet.

autobiographical. It is hard to imagine that a poem like Sir Thomas Wyatt's "They Flee from Me That Sometimes Did Me Seek" (before 1542) does not refer to an intimate personal experience. Such a surmise cannot be refuted in spite of all arguments about the conventionality of many devices, the universalizing of feelings in much older poetry, and the general weight of traditional "topoi" and motifs. But what matters in criticism is the claim that sincerity, emotion, *Erlebnis* is a guarantee of good art. As I have said before, "the volumes of agonizingly felt love poetry by adolescents and the dreary (however fervently felt) religious verse which fills libraries, are sufficient proof" that it is not.[58] Yeats has said this memorably, referring to men in general:

> The best lack all conviction, while the worst
> Are full of passionate intensity.[59]

But lived experience, intense, private experience, became precisely the central value criterion in German lyrical (and not only lyrical) theories. *Erlebnis* became the term around which they crystallize. It makes one reflect that the term cannot be readily matched in other languages and that it is a neologism of the early nineteenth century. Hans Georg Gadamer, in *Wahrheit und Methode* (1960), is, so far as I know, the only writer who has tried to trace the history of the term. He has had information from the German Academy in Berlin which supplied him with the earliest example from a casual letter of Hegel's in 1827 and with isolated occurrences of the word in the thirties and forties, in Tieck, Alexis, and Gutzkow.[60] My own very limited research confirms these findings.

---

58. *Theory of Literature* (2nd ed. New York, 1956), p. 56.

59. "The Second Coming." Yeats, *The Variorum Edition of the Poems,* ed. P. Allt and R. K. Alspach (New York, 1957), p. 402.

60. Tübingen, 1960, pp. 56–60.

The word does not occur in Herder and Goethe, Novalis and Schleiermacher, who would seem to be the natural antecedents for Dilthey. Gervinus, in his discussion of what today would be called "Erlebnislyrik," never uses the term.[61] Nor do Jean Paul and Schopenhauer. The novelty of the word is indicated also by the fact that Hegel makes *Erlebnis* feminine, saying: "Das ist meine ganze Erlebnis,"[62] the kind of vacillation which later afflicted another literary term in German: Baroque.[63]

Gadamer notes that Goethe comes near the term in his very late advice to young poets: "Fragt euch nur bei jedem Gedicht, ob es ein Erlebtes enthalte, und ob dieses Erlebte euch gefördert habe."[64] Thus it seems appropriate that *Erlebnis* occurs in one of Heinrich Laube's *Reisenovellen* (2nd ed. 1847), where it is put in the mouth of Goethe discussing *Die Wahlverwandtschaften:* "Das Benutzen des Erlebnisses ist mir alles gewesen; das Erfinden aus der Luft war nie meine Sache."[65] Laube, however, has no independent source for this pronouncement. He rephrases what Goethe had said to Eckermann about the novel: "Darin ist kein Strich enthalten, der nicht erlebt, aber kein Strich wie er erlebt worden,"[66] and he might have remembered similar pronouncements and known even the advice to the young poets.

---

61. *Geschichte der poetischen Nationalliteratur der Deutschen, 4* (5 vols. Leipzig 1835–42; 2nd ed. 1843), 126, 130, 133, 504.

62. *Briefe von und an Hegel,* ed. J. Hoffmeister *3,* (3 vols. Hamburg, 1954), 179. To his wife from Kassel, Aug. 19, 1827.

63. Johann Willibald Nagel and Jakob Zeidler, in *Deutsch-österreichische Literaturgeschichte* (Wien, 1899), use "die Barocke." "Der Barock" seems to have won out over "das Barock."

64. *Werke, 38,* 326. First published in 1833.

65. 2nd ed. Mannheim, 1847, p. 36.

66. *Gespräche mit Goethe,* ed. H. H. Houben (23rd ed. Leipzig, 1948), p. 315, Feb. 17, 1830. Cf. pp. 498, 583.

*Erlebnis* occurs in early statements by Theodor Storm which bring the meaning nearer to recent usage, though these passages could hardly have been noticed widely. In 1854, in a review of one M. A. Niendorf's *Lieder der Liebe,* Storm asserts that "bei einem lyrischen Gedicht muss nicht allein . . . das Leben, nein da muss geradezu das Erlebnis das Fundament desselben bilden"; and he complains in a review of Julius von Rodenberg's *Lieder:* "Es fehlt überall der Hintergrund des inneren Erlebnisses." In a later preface to his anthology *Deutsche Liebeslieder* (1859) he criticizes J. G. Jacobi for not having written "aus dem Drange ein inneres Erlebnis zu fixieren."[67] Hermann Lotze, in his *Geschichte der Ästhetik in Deutschland* (1868), uses the term in the standard context: "so grossen Werth Göthe und Schiller darauf legen, dass das lyrische Gedicht einem innern Erlebnisse entspringe, die blosse Darestellung der subjectiven Erschütterung galt ihnen doch nicht für genügend."[68]

This passage is about contemporaneous with Dilthey's earliest specific uses. In his *Leben Schleiermachers* (1870), on the very first page of the Introduction *Erlebnis* is used three times most emphatically. Dilthey defines Schleiermacher's importance in the development of European religiosity. "In ihm vollzog sich das grosse Erlebnis einer aus den Tiefen unseres Verhältnisses zum Universum entspringenden Religion," and on the same page he speaks of "dieses Erlebnis seiner Jugend" and again of "dieses Erlebnis." But in the whole long book we hear only once about his "religiös-sittliche Erlebnisse."[69] Surprisingly, in the articles which Dilthey wrote in the sixties and which he eventually used, in a revised and expanded form, in *Das Erlebnis und die Dichtung* (1905),

67. *Werke,* ed. F. Böhme, *8* (9 vols. Leipzig, 1936), 63, 69, 112.
68. München, 1868, p. 643.
69. H. Mulert, ed. (2nd ed. Berlin, 1922), p. XXIII; cf. p. 333.

the word does not occur at all. It is never used in the Novalis essay (1865) and not until the 1905 revision was it introduced into the essays on Lessing (1867) and Hölderlin (1867).[70] Only in the article "Goethe und die dichterische Phantasie" (1877) does the term become central to Dilthey's poetics. There *Erlebnis* reveals a quality of life: it may come from the world of ideas or may be suggested by trivial circumstances, a chance meeting, the reading of a book, etc. One cannot thus accuse Dilthey of simple "biographism," of a reduction of experience to private events or feelings, but the concept, with him, remains psychological. It means an experience, of whatever origin, intense enough to become the stimulus to creation. In one passage, however, the dualism of life and poetry is denied. Dilthey speaks of a "Strukturzusammenhang zwischen dem Erleben und dem Ausdruck des Erlebten; das Erlebte geht hier voll und ganz in den Ausdruck ein."[71] An identification is made which seems the same as Croce's between intuition and expression: an equation which was anticipated also by Dilthey's own revered Schleiermacher. But in general, *Erlebnis* in Dilthey remained another term for intense personal experience, for involvement, or for what in different contexts has been called sincerity, "engagement," and even "belief."[72] Later in his life, in notes which Dilthey wrote for a revision of his *Poetik* (1907–08), he recognized the failure of his psychologistic conception: he speaks of the detachment of the imaginative process from the personal and admits that the "subject with which literary history and poetics have to

70. Novalis, in *Preussische Jahrbücher, 15* (1865), 650–81. Lessing, ibid. *19* (1867), 117–61, 271–94. Hölderlin, in *Westermanns Monatshefte, 20* (1867), 156–65.

71. *Das Erlebnis und die Dichtung* (9th ed. Leipzig 1924), p. 236.

72. Cf. e.g., Hofmannsthal's use in "Der Dichter und diese Zeit" (1906) in *Gesammelte Werke in Einzelausgaben*, ed. H. Steiner, *Prosa* II (Frankfurt/M., 1951), pp. 294, 296.

deal primarily is totally distinct from psychic events in the poet or his hearers."[73] But these notes were not published then and the damage was done: *Erlebnis* became the shibboleth of German poetic theory.

Most often it was used simply as a new term for the old biographical fallacy which found here a less literal-minded formula for the study of the life, its incidents, the models in life, the emotional states preceding a work of art, without having to commit the student to a one-to-one relationship. In Gundolf's distinction between "Urerlebnis" and "Bildungserlebnis" (suggested first by Herman Nohl[74] in 1908) a terminology is established which allows the grading of experiences according to their presumed immediacy, and in Ermatinger's *Das dichterische Kunstwerk* (1921) *Erlebnis* becomes the overriding term, which is then subdivided into "Gedankenerlebnis," "Stofferlebnis," and "Formerlebnis." Everything in poetry is *Erlebnis:* with Ermatinger the term loses its original relation to something given in life. It is simply a term for the artist's activity. It is so broad as to be meaningless.[75]

Certainly the relationship to the lyric or even to biography has been completely lost sight of. Lyrical theory—at least with the terms which we have discussed, *Erlebnis,* subjective, presence, *Stimmung*—seems to have arrived at a complete impasse. These terms cannot take care of the enormous variety, in history and in the different literatures, of lyrical forms and constantly lead into an insoluble psychological cul-de-sac: the

73. *Gesammelte Schriften, 7* (12 vols. Stuttgart, 1913–58), 85. Cf. my discussion in *A History of Modern Criticism, 4* (4 vols. New Haven, 1965), 323.

74. *Die Weltanschauungen der Malerei* (Jena, 1908).

75. Cf. Charlotte Bühler, "Der Erlebnisbegriff in der modernen Kunstwissenschaft," in *Vom Geiste neuerer Literaturforschung, Festschrift für Oskar Walzel,* ed. J. Wahle and V. Klemperer (Wildpark-Potsdam, 1924), pp. 195–209, for more examples.

supposed intensity, inwardness, immediacy of an experience which can never be demonstrated as certain and can never be shown to be relevant to the quality of art. Miss Hamburger, Staiger, Ermatinger, Dilthey and their predecessors, in their different ways, lead all to this central mystery, which remains a mystery to them and possibly to all of us.

The way out is obvious. One must abandon attempts to define the general nature of the lyric or the lyrical. Nothing beyond generalities of the tritest kind can result from it. It seems much more profitable to turn to a study of the variety of poetry and to the history and thus the description of genres which can be grasped in their concrete conventions and traditions. Several German books have shown the way, though some have suffered from confusion with general "Geistesgeschichte." I think of Karl Viëtor's *Geschichte der deutschen Ode* (1923), Günther Müller's *Geschichte des deutschen Liedes* (1925), Friedrich Beissner's *Geschichte der deutschen Elegie* (1941), or of Kurt Schlüter's *Die englische Ode* (1964) all of which show an awareness of the paradoxical task: How can we arrive at a genre description from history without knowing beforehand what the genre is like, and how can we know a genre without its history, without a knowledge of its particular instances?[76] This is obviously a case of the logical circle which Schleiermacher, Dilthey, and Leo Spitzer have taught us not to consider "vicious." It can be solved in the concrete dialectics of past and present, fact and idea, history and aesthetics. Psychological and existential categories such as *Erlebnis,* subjectivity, and *Stimmung* accomplish nothing for poetics.

76. A good discussion in Karl Viëtor's "Probleme der literarischen Gattungsgeschichte," in *Deutsche Vierteljahrschrift für Literaturwissenschaft und Geistesgeschichte,* 9 (1931) 425–47; reprinted in his *Geist und Form* (Bern, 1952), pp. 292–309.

# The Poet as Critic,
# the Critic as Poet,
# the Poet-Critic

We might ask whether the poet *qua* poet can be a critic? Can he be, or has he been, in history, a good critic? Has his being a critic been good for criticism? Or to reverse the direction of our questioning: Has criticism been good for the poet? Has the union of the poet-critic or critic-poet been successful? Has he been a "house divided against himself" or has he been or can he be the integrated man of both sensibility and intellect?

T. S. Eliot, in his "Brief Treatise on the Criticism of Poetry,"[1] distinguishes three types of criticism: the first is the so-called "creative criticism," which is really "etiolated creation,"of which Pater serves as a horrible example. (Incidentally this is quite unjust, as Pater, with the exception of the notorious Mona Lisa passage, hardly ever wrote such "creative criticism.")[2] The second type, historical and moralistic criticism, is represented by Sainte-Beuve. The third type, criticism proper, the only genuine criticism, is that of the poet-critic who is "criticising poetry in order to create poetry."[3] Eliot forgets or ignores the philosophers and theorists who actually determined the history of criticism and who were neither frustrated poets nor historians nor moralists nor poets,

1. *Chapbook*, No. 2 (1920).
2. See the chapter on Pater in my *History of Modern Criticism, 4* (4 vols. New Haven, 1965), 382 ff.
3. "The Perfect Critic," *The Sacred Wood* (London, 1920), p. 14.

although Eliot allows on occasion a single exception, Aristotle.[4] But his success, which was surely greater than that of any other critic in the history of criticism, is quite inexplicable in Eliot's scheme.

Eliot at a later period recognized the limitations of the poet as critic; the poet, he then acknowledged, always tries "to defend the kind of poetry he is writing."[5] In a lecture, "To Criticize the Critic," given at Yale (and elsewhere at about the same time) in November, 1961, and recently published for the first time, he disparaged his own criticism as a mere by-product of his creative activity, as written strictly within the context of the literature of the time. Eliot professes irritation with having his "words, perhaps written thirty or forty years ago, quoted as if I had uttered them yesterday." His criticism is not a "design for a massive critical structure." He is puzzled by the vogue of such terms as "dissociation of sensibility" or "objective correlative." He is always at a loss for what to say when "earnest scholars, or schoolchildren, write to ask [him] for an explanation."[6] Eliot's so-called recantation of his criticism of Milton appeals to the practical situation. In 1936 Milton would have been a bad influence on the writing of poetry; in 1947 we are allowed to admire him, as his example has ceased to be dangerous to young poets.[7] Eliot consistently judges his criticism as strictly occasional, written for his own use and that of other poets; and he hardly ever recognizes that criticism has been written mainly for people other than poets.

Similarly, W. H. Auden admits that the critical opinions of a writer "are for the most part, manifestations of his debate

4. Ibid., pp. 9–10.
5. "The Music of Poetry," *On Poetry and Poets* (London, 1957), p. 26.
6. *To Criticize the Critic* (London, 1965), pp. 14, 19.
7. See *On Poetry and Poets,* pp. 138 ff.

with himself as to what he should do next and what he should avoid." The poet is "a critic who is only interested in one author and only concerned with works that do not yet exist." Auden even says "in unkind moments one is almost tempted to think that all [the poets] are really saying is: 'Read me! Don't read the other fellows!' " "The poet's judgments as he reads are of this kind: 'My God! My Great-Grandfather! My Uncle! My Enemy! My Brother! My imbecile Brother!' "[8]

It would be easy to buttress this recognition of the inevitable egocentricity and narrowness of a poet's criticism by examples drawn from history. To limit myself to the criticism of great English poets, think how Dryden advocates blank verse or rhyme with contradictory arguments at different moments of his career as a dramatist; or think how unjust Wordsworth was to poets like Thomas Gray or Keats, who did not conform to his theory of plain diction. Think how mistaken Coleridge was in preferring Schiller to Goethe or how capricious Yeats' selections in the introduction to *The Oxford Book of Modern Verse* appear even to the most sympathetic reader. But we should reflect that nonpoets as critics have committed as many and as egregious critical errors as poets, and that nonpoet critics are just as inevitably provided with their own sets of blinkers—ideological or aesthetic or just personal—which might narrow their vision even more drastically.

We must come, however, to the conclusion that a poet is creating a concrete work of art and that he does not necessarily either know or care about the nature of his activity and certainly may not be able to formulate it in intellectual terms. Moreover, the poet is not necessarily able to fulfill the critic's main judicial function: the evaluation of the poetry of other poets. Oscar Wilde put this lesson in his witty way: "Indeed,

8. *The Dyer's Hand and Other Essays* (New York, 1962), pp. 5, 9–10, 33, 52.

so far from its being that the artist is the best judge of art, a really great artist can never judge of other people's work at all, and can hardly, in fact, judge of his own. That very concentration of vision which makes a man an artist, limits by its sheer intensity his faculty of fine appreciation. . . . Creation employs all its critical faculty within its own sphere. It may not use it in the sphere that belongs to others. It is exactly because a man cannot do a thing that he is the proper judge of it."[9]

Still, we cannot be satisfied with this conclusion. Oscar Wilde himself was not and did actually recommend "creative criticism," criticism as a work of art, the invasion of criticism by poetry. Criticism, he argued, is itself an art. It treats the work of art simply as a starting point for new creation, as a suggestion for new work of the critic's own that need not necessarily bear any obvious resemblance to the thing he criticizes. Wilde here accepts Anatole France's famous proposal that the critic record "the adventures of his soul among masterpieces," that he speak of himself "on the occasion of Shakespeare or Racine, Pascal or Goethe."[10] Self-expression, even autobiography, is the aim, which, at least in the theoretical formulations, would be entirely divorced from the object "as it really is," and thus criticism, we may conclude, need not be concerned with works of art, but could have its starting point in almost everything under the sun. If we are concerned with criticism as organized knowledge, as interpretation and judgment of publicly verifiable objects, we must dismiss poetic criticism as an irrelevancy. Today the Mona Lisa passage in Pater, the ostentatious fireworks of Swinburne's eloquence, and even the charming reflections of Anatole France have lost their appeal and are no present danger.

9. *Intentions* (New York, 1894), pp. 200–02.
10. *La Vie littéraire, 1* (Paris, 1888), Preface.

But fictional criticism is by no means a thing of the past. It is with us in a new guise: that of the myth critic like Northrop Frye, who spins his fancies in total disregard of the text and even builds fictional universes which he calls, oddly enough, *Anatomy of Criticism*. Frye wants his system to "reforge the broken links between creation and knowledge, art and science, myth and concept";[11] but actually his criticism is an elaborate fiction which loses all relation to knowledge, science, and concept. All manner of substitutions, condensations, and identifications are allowed in this dream universe. As Frye admits: "The literary universe is a universe in which everything is potentially identical with everything else."[12] Criticism, like literature and like mythology, becomes, in his own words, "largely an art of misleading analogies and mistaken identities."[13] A fanciful structure is erected which has as much contact with actual literary history as Blake's *Jerusalem* or Yeats' *A Vision* has with recorded history. It can hardly surprise us that the weird, whimsical, and utterly fantastic interpretations of Greek myths propounded by Ruskin later in his life in *The Cestus of Aglaia* (1865) and *The Queen of the Air* (1869) have been hailed as forerunners of Frye's and Yeats' archetypal criticism.[14] One might recognize the ingenuity and imaginative inventiveness of these writers and might come to think of this criticism as a new literary genre. But it must be distinguished from criticism, which upholds ideals of correctness of interpretation, observes the laws of evidence, and must aim, ultimately, at a body of knowledge which we

11. *Anatomy of Criticism* (Princeton, 1956), p. 354.
12. Ibid., p. 124.
13. *Fables of Identity: Studies in Poetic Mythology* (New York, 1963), p. 35.
14. Harold Bloom, ed., *The Literary Criticism of John Ruskin* (Garden City, N.Y., 1965), Introduction, p. xvi.

hesitate to call "science" only because the natural scientists have preempted the term in English.

The invasion and even subjugation of criticism by poetic or purely imaginative methods, whether in the style of Pater or of Northrop Frye, has not furthered the cause of criticism. The opposite imperialism, the invasion of poetry by criticism, also has damaging effects for poetry. We hear much of the share of criticism in the actual process of poetic composition. Eliot, for instance, said that "the labour of sifting, combining, constructing, expunging, correcting, testing," is a "frightful toil as much critical as creative. I maintain even that the criticism employed by a trained and skilled writer on his own work is the most vital, the highest kind of criticism."[15] But one wonders whether this self-criticism is criticism in the usual sense or merely a metaphor for the labor of composing. The poet, Croce remarks in this context, "cannot complete his work without self-government, without an inner check, without accepting and rejecting, without trial and error." But calling this criticism is like using the term "obstetric criticism" for "the spasms and pauses and new starts of a woman in the labor of childbirth."[16] We need not go so far as Croce in denying even a similarity between the process of composition and criticism proper to see that we are dealing here with a separate problem: the share of intellect in the creative process. It has been debated endlessly, in older times as a conflict between inspiration and craft, and more recently as a conflict between the subconscious and technical manipulation. Coleridge's fib about writing "Kubla Khan" after awaking from a profound sleep in a trance interrupted by the "person on business from

15. "The Function of Criticism," in *Selected Essays* (London, 1932), p. 30.
16. *La Poesia* (4th ed. Bari, 1946), pp. 13–14.

Porlock"[17] contrasts with Poe's stunt or hoax in "The Philosophy of Composition," of describing how the work on "The Raven" proceeded, "step by step, to its completion with the precision and rigid consequence of a mathematical problem."[18]

But these conflicting accounts of the poets have not, to my mind, contributed much either to an elucidation of the poetic process or even to a psychology of writing. T. S. Eliot thought that "the penetration of the poetic by the introspective critical activity is carried to the limit" by Valéry in several essays.[19] But Valéry actually cannot say more than that a poem might arise from the most diverse stimuli: "an empty piece of paper; a little free time; a slip of the tongue; a misreading; a pen which fits the hand agreeably."[20] He tells us only about empirical occasions, suggestions, and sequences. We can observe the same thing in ourselves even as we write private letters or learned papers: they start somewhere, somehow. A Censor (as Auden calls him with a better term than critic)[21] is at work in us as in the poet. Surprisingly, most modern poets support the inspiration version of the poetic process, although they might not like the term. For what else is being described even by the highly rational Valéry when he tells us that "the poetic start is perfectly irregular, inconstant, involuntary, and fragile. . . . We lose it just as we find it by accident"?[22] I need only

17. For a full discussion see Elisabeth Schneider, *Coleridge, Opium and Kubla Khan* (Chicago, 1953), esp. pp. 22 ff.

18. See comment in my *History of Modern Criticism, 3,* 159 ff., and the opinion of Baudelaire quoted on p. 323.

19. *To Criticize the Critic* (London, 1965), p. 41.

20. *L'Invention* (Paris, 1938), p. 150. A different translation in *Aesthetics,* trans. Ralph Manheim (New York, 1964), p. 69.

21. *The Dyer's Hand,* p. 33.

22. *Variété 5* (Paris, 1945), p. 138; also in *The Art of Poetry,* trans. Denis Folliot (New York, 1956), p. 60.

allude to Rilke's description of the ecstasy in which he composed the *Duino Elegies* or to Yeats' well-known lines:

> God guard me from those thoughts men think
> In the mind alone,
> He that sings a lasting song
> Thinks in a marrow bone.[23]

The poet, it seems to me, has told us little about the creative
process, whether he is Valéry (M. Teste, that is, "Head") or
the surrealist relying on his subconscious and on automatic
writing. We owe more to scholars who have studied sources,
like John Livingston Lowes in *The Road to Xanadu,* or to the
students of drafts and revisions, if they are more than just
textual critics, and even to the psychologists and psychoana-
lysts, or to such amateur philosophers as Arthur Koestler.[24]

But the oldest incursion of criticism into poetry, or, if you
prefer, the oldest alliance between criticism and poetry, is
versified criticism: Horace's *De Arte poetica* and, since the
Renaissance, Vida's *Poetica,* Boileau's *Art poétique,* and,
of course, Pope's *Essay on Criticism.* The genre which is
simply a version of the didactic genre of versified philosophy,
astronomy, or history seems to have died out in the eighteenth
century, possibly with Akenside's *The Pleasures of the Imagination,* but actually it reappears, in new forms, even in the
twentieth century. Verlaine's antirhetorical pamphlet, "L'Art
poétique," is in rhyme, and rather recently Karl Shapiro has
written an unrhymed *Essay on Rime.* In general, one can dismiss these poems, if we judge them as poetry, but one should

23. "A Prayer for Old Age," *Variorum Edition of the Poems of
W. B. Yeats,* ed. P. Allt and R. K. Alspach (New York, 1957), p. 553.
24. Arthur Koestler, *The Act of Creation* (London, 1964).

recognize that some of them, particularly Pope's *Essay on Criticism,* display some aesthetic qualities: design, metrical skill, and verbal wit. With the increasing understanding of the nature of poetry, such rhymed or blank verse expositions of abstract ideas have come to be felt as unpoetic and have fallen into desuetude. Still, some poets have tried in their poetry to speak of poetry and the poet: to create something which has been called "meta-poetry" as we speak of "meta-language." This "meta-poetry" is largely concerned with the self-definition of the poet and with his mission or function. It must be associated with the modern questioning of his status as a seer, priest, or sage. In Germany particularly, Hölderlin reasserted in poetry the sacred mission of the poet, and more recently Rilke has, in the seventh Duino Elegy, asked the poet to transform the whole visible world into an "inner space." In France Mallarmé composed his "Toast funèbre" for Théophile Gautier, in which the eternalizing function of art "by a solemn agitation in the air of words" is asserted with desperate defiance. In recent American poetry I might refer to Wallace Stevens' "Notes toward a Supreme Fiction" or to "The Idea of Order at Key West," which addresses a French critic, Ramon Fernandez, to praise the "blessed rage for order . . . the maker's rage to order words." Or we might think of Archibald MacLeish's "Ars Poetica" with its often misunderstood concluding lines:

> A poem should not mean
> But be.

We might even think of meta-poetry as the evocation of other poets in verse: Ben Jonson's eulogy of Shakespeare or Arnold's sonnet on Shakespeare might qualify; or Swinburne's premature elegy on Baudelaire; or even Shelley's *Adonais;* or, in the second part of Goethe's *Faust,* Euphorion, who is meant to represent Byron.[25] In the wide sense of poetry about poets and poetry, meta-poetry would have to include Virgil in the *Divine Comedy* and Goethe's play on Torquato Tasso and all the many dramas and poems about artists in its wake. The ramifications of such a topic are endless, its limitations hard to define. The poet has, throughout history, built up his image, described his mission, put forward his claims, defended his activity, and spoken well or ill of his fellow poets—in verse, as a poet, and inevitably also in prose, as a critic or simply as a man who as any other man has literary opinions.

In the last decades in England and the United States the apology for poetry by poets has assumed new forms: it has become a counterattack against criticism, science, and the intellect in general, a campaign which is, of course, waged with weapons of the intellect and in works of criticism. Some of it is simply anticriticism, anti-intellectualism, like Karl Shapiro's onslaught in his collection of essays, *In Defense of Ignorance*. Shapiro repeats the old argument that "criticism flourishes when literature has failed," but he does not recognize that criticism really flourishes today. If it does, it is the kind of criticism he detests. He simply shies away from "criticism as a branch of philosophy." "The poet and the poet-in-us-all have no business hanging around philosophy." He recommends, as the only genuine criticism, "creative criticism," a "work of art about another work of art," but he continues to write criticism of a type which could not possibly claim to be artistic, while saying, "poet and critic must draw apart, and beyond this I have no message."[26] Similarly, the late Randall Jarrell in an article, "The Age of Criticism," voices

25. See the interesting collection *Poems on Poetry: The Mirror's Garland,* ed. Robert Wallace and James G. Taaffe (New York, 1965).
26. *In Defense of Ignorance* (New York, 1965), pp. 6, 18, 31–32.

the understandable dismay of a poet at the sheer proliferation of criticism in our time. But the remedy he proposes is merely the old personal, impressionist criticism. " 'Principles' or 'standards' of excellence are either specifically harmful or generally useless; the critic has nothing to go by except his experience as a human being and a reader, and is the personification of empiricism." Criticism is seen as strictly subordinated to works of art. "Critics exist simply to help us with works of art." Criticism exists merely "for the sake of the plays and stories and poems it criticizes." Jarrell seems not to be aware of the possibility of theory or history which might not be dependent on the enhancement of the reader's enjoyment. He uses the oldest and most unconvincing argument that the poet alone knows what poetry is. He ridicules some critics discussing Wordsworth: *"they* knew how poems and novels are put together, and Wordsworth . . . did not, but had just put them together. In the same way, if a pig wandered up to you during a bacon-judging contest, you would say impatiently, 'Go away, pig! What do you know about bacon?' "[27] But this is literally true of the pig. It does not know anything about bacon, its flavor or price, and could not appraise bacon in so many words. When a famous poet was proposed for a professorship at Harvard, his appointment was rejected when a witty opponent argued that one would not make an elephant Professor of Zoology.

Shapiro and Jarrell belong to a venerable tradition: that of empiricism, particularly Anglo-Saxon empiricism, suspicious of all theory. John Stuart Mill in 1831, in his *Spirit of the Age,* complained of this aversion. "He is a *theorist:* and the word which expresses the highest and noblest effort of human intelligence is turned into a byword of derision."[28]

27. *Poetry and the Age* (New York, 1955), pp. 81, 84, 65, 66–67.
28. Frederick von Hayek, ed. (Chicago, 1942), p. 21.

Such a position amounts to a retreat or the wish for a retreat into a world untouched by science, the intellect, and reason. It is obscurantist in its consequences.

The poet's attack on criticism is more formidable when it comes from convictions inherent in a different philosophy. The most interesting case is that of T. S. Eliot. I alluded to his lecture "To Criticize the Critic," which indulges in an almost embarrassing self-depreciation. "Humility" was its last word, and it was the last word I ever heard him pronounce. But this self-disparagement is not a chance event in Eliot's intellectual biography. It grows out of his concept of criticism, held since his youth, and was prepared for by similar statements. In the Minnesota lecture, "The Frontiers of Criticism" (1956)— which was, I hear, attended by five thousand persons—Eliot paid no attention to new trends in criticism, but commented on the criticism of sources exemplified in Lowes' *The Road to Xanadu* (1926) and on biographical criticism of Wordsworth by Herbert Read and F. W. Bateson, concluding, rightly I think, that neither source-study nor biography can define the nature of poetry. "When the poem has been made, something new has happened, something that cannot be wholly explained by *anything that went before.*" But then Eliot turns against what in this country is called "explication" or "close reading"; he criticizes a book, *Interpretations,* edited by John Wain, which contains twelve essays by English critics, each analyzing a well-known poem, from Shakespeare's "The Phoenix and the Turtle" to Yeats' "Among School Children." Eliot describes the method: take a poem "without reference to the author or to his other work, analyse it stanza by stanza and line by line, and extract, squeeze, tease, press every drop of meaning out of it that one can. It might be called the lemon-squeezer school of criticism." Eliot complains mildly that this is "a very tiring way of passing the time" and that in reading the interpretation of his own "The

Love Song of J. Alfred Prufrock" he had "one or two minor surprises." But he also makes the more serious general objection that the analyses damaged the appreciation of these familiar poems. "I found I was slow to recover my previous feeling about the poems. It was as if someone had taken a machine to pieces and left one with the task of reassembling the parts." The argument is the old one: analysis spoils enjoyment, and criticism must serve enjoyment. Eliot warns of "the danger of pursuing criticism as if it was a science" and professes not to recall even "a single book or essay, or the name of a single critic, as representative of the kind of impressionistic criticism which aroused my ire thirty-three years ago."[29] (Thirty-three years because Eliot is referring to the essay "The Function of Criticism," which dates from 1923.) But he might have looked into *The Sacred Wood* (1920) and found there expressions of his ire against Swinburne, John Addington Symonds, and Arthur Symons. In effect, Eliot in these last lectures has become another defender of appreciation and has abandoned his older ambition for criticism generally and his own criticism as "the common pursuit of true judgment."[30]

The later surrender to subjectivism and appreciation is, however, clearly prepared for in his early unsatisfactory theory of criticism. Eliot dismissed interpretation as a necessary evil, a makeshift for our imperfections as readers. "If we lived [a work] completely we should need no interpretation" is Eliot's singularly unhelpful conclusion in recommending G. Wilson Knight's *The Wheel of Fire*.[31] It is like saying "If I were God, I would need no theology." While interpretation is tolerated as a necessary evil, judgment is

29. *On Poetry and Poets,* pp. 103, 112, 113, 114, 117.
30. "The Function of Criticism," *Selected Essays,* p. 25.
31. *The Wheel of Fire* (London, 1930), Introduction, p. xix.

surprisingly forbidden to the critic. "The critic must not coerce, and must not make judgments of worse and better." Judgment arises somehow from "elucidation," which seems to differ from interpretation, although I am not sure in what way it could. "The critic," Eliot declares "must simply elucidate: the reader will form the correct judgment for himself."[32] But it is hard to believe that the early Eliot could have meant the rejection of both interpretation and judgment literally; he wanted rather to protest against arbitrary interpretations and against dogmatic rankings of authors. Actually, he constantly recommended interpreters, such as G. Wilson Knight, S. L. Bethell, and even the dreary Leone Vivante. He himself made judgments about "better and worse" in almost every sentence of his criticism. Ranking, judging, is the secret of his success as a critic. One wanted to hear that Crashaw, "was a finished master, and Keats and Shelley were apprentices with immense possibilities before them,"[33] that Campion was a greater poet than Herrick, or Dryden than Pope.

But in theory, Eliot even then upheld the view that there is no objective meaning to a work of art. "A poem may appear to mean very different things to different readers, and all these meanings may be different from what the author thought he meant," seems a reasonable observation from which Eliot draws the conclusion that "the reader's interpretation may differ from the author's and be equally valid—it may even be better. There may be much more in a poem than the author was aware of."[34] This is still acceptable as a defense of the accrual of meaning which occurs in the course of history: *Hamlet* cannot be reduced to the interpretation which Shakespeare might have given to it. But Eliot is on dangerous

32. "The Perfect Critic," *The Sacred Wood*, p. 10.
33. *For Lancelot Andrewes* (London, 1928), p. 120.
34. "The Music of Poetry," *On Poetry and Poets,* p. 30.

ground when, in a conversation reported by Nevill Coghill, he denied that there is a correct interpretation of his *Sweeney Agonistes*. When he saw a production in Oxford, he was "astonished" by it and felt that it ran completely counter to his own interpretation. To the question, "But if the two meanings are contradictory, is not one right and the other wrong? Must not the author be right?" Eliot answered, "Not necessarily, do you think? Why is either wrong?"[35] Eliot, like Valéry, who spoke of "creative misunderstanding" and went so far as to say that there is "no true meaning to a text," does not see that the divorce between work and reader cannot be complete and that there remains the problem of the "correctness" of interpretation. We may debate the theories of Coleridge, Bradley, Stoll, Ernest Jones, and even Eliot about *Hamlet,* but we must reject the view propounded in a full-length book that Hamlet was a woman in disguise in love with Horatio. "The meaning is what the poem means to different sensitive readers"[36] is Eliot's conclusion, which is saved from mere anarchical relativism only by the question-begging adjective "sensitive." The whole theory of criticism propounded by Eliot is in total contradiction to his objectivistic philosophy, which aims at a definition of the tradition and must assume its truth. As I have argued before,[37] Eliot's criticism suffers from the conflict between his emotionalist concept of poetry, his denial that poetry is knowledge or even any kind of knowledge, and the dogmatic ideological superstructure of classicism and later of orthodoxy. With the growing emphasis on appreciation and enjoyment and the

35. *T. S. Eliot: A Symposium,* ed. R. March and Tambimutti (London, 1948), p. 86.

36. "The Frontiers of Criticism," *On Poetry and Poets,* p. 113.

37. See "The Criticism of T. S. Eliot," *Sewanee Review, 64* (1956), 398–443.

growing distaste for analysis, "close reading," or what he considered science, Eliot has widened the gulf between the two sides of his critical practice, his sensibility, and his orthodoxy, and has committed himself to a double standard in criticism: appreciation and "supervision of the tradition by orthodoxy,"[38] which again dissolves the unity of the work of art. Eliot has abandoned aesthetic criticism to the appreciators, to the subjective relativists, in order to uphold what in practice is didactic, ideological criticism ruled by his idea of right religion.

The two eminent American poets who are also eminent literary critics, John Crowe Ransom and Allen Tate, did not turn against criticism as Eliot did, but they were pushed by their theories into views of literary criticism which deny intellectual coherence and historical growth to the enterprise. Ransom—contrary to a common view which considers him peculiarly provincial and "native"—had been a student of philosophy at Oxford. His poetic theories obviously developed from his study of Bergson, Collingwood, and the English expounder of Bergson, T. E. Hulme. Ransom's criticism of abstraction, his distinction between logical structure and irrelevant texture in a poem, his attack on the poetry of ideas, and his advocacy of a poetry of things fit into the whole Bergsonian irrationalistic trend of the time. Imagism, Rilke and his *Dinggedicht,* and Francis Ponge had similar aims. Ransom holds a view of history as a continuous widening of the dualism between science and art by reason of the aggressions of science. "As science more and more completely reduces the world to its types and forms, art, replying, must invest it again with body."[39] Ransom, with his article "Criticism, Inc." and his book *The New Criticism,* did much to

38. *After Strange Gods* (New York, 1934), p. 67.
39. *The World's Body* (New York, 1938), p. 198.

define the movement named by him and to give it academic status. But in his theory of criticism, expounded in the chapter "Wanted: An Ontological Critic," he limits the vocation of criticism drastically to distinguishing between the range of words as meaning and the range of words as sound, and especially between determinate and indeterminate meaning. Since "the indeterminate thing creeps in by the back door of metrical necessity,"[40] much of what Ransom considers criticism par excellence is a study of meter or of the relation between sound and meaning, or a study of metaphors and diction. Ransom, in his later writings, experimented restlessly with his terminology: the dualism of structure and texture appears under new guises as the contrast between the Freudian ego and id. Or he replaces the pair, structure and texture, by a triad of metaphor, logic, and meter; or he adopts the term "icon" for "image" from Charles Morris, or the "Concrete Universal" from Hegel via Bradley. Poetry, however, remains always concrete and he thus rejects as extrapoetic the Chicago Aristotelians' concern for plot, or that of Yvor Winters for morality. But ultimately Ransom embraces a version of the "imitation" theory himself. The little world of objects "sets up a small version of our natural world in its original dignity, not the laborious world of affairs. Indeed, the little world is the imitation of our ancient Paradise, when we inhabited it in innocence."[41] Criticism thus becomes "substantial," referential, and a double standard is introduced or at least permitted: aesthetic and ideological criticism. Ransom defends "the rights of the intellectuals (the moralists or religionists) to isolate the ideas and discuss them on their intellectual merits; inasmuch as the ideas are surely in the poetry." "This is a poetry that can be taken apart. And yet if it is really a poetry it

40. *The New Criticism* (Norfolk, Conn., 1941), pp. 301, 303.
41. *Poems and Essays* (New York, 1955), p. 100.

cannot be hurt; and Kantians [and here Ransom seems to proclaim himself a Kantian] can come back to the whole poetry and see what is poetical about it." The dualistic theory of poetry, with its logical structure and indeterminate, contingent texture, has taken its toll. Ransom leaves criticism with two themes—both outside of art: "natural beauty" and "morals." No wonder that in an article on Cleanth Brooks called "Why Critics Don't Go Mad?" he speaks of the critic's "bad sense of lostness."[42]

Allen Tate's views of criticism have changed considerably in his development. He used to be extremely effective in his attacks on academic literary scholarship. The lecture "Miss Emily and the Bibliographer" (1940) made a fervent plea for the moral obligation of judging and made trenchant criticisms of the academic teaching of literature. Like Ransom, Tate was driven by his disapproval of science—which in him can be called contempt and even hatred—into an anti-intellectualistic position which affected also his theory of criticism. He differs, however, from Ransom not only in tone—his is passionate and sometimes turgid, while Ransom's is urbane and often whimsical—but in philosophical allegiance. Although Ransom wrote his first book, *God Without Thunder*, in defense of a fundamentalist religion, and although he shared the Southern Agrarianism of his Nashville friends and pupils, his view of poetry always remained secular and even basically hedonistic. Poetry is a celebration of the world and of the poet's love of the world, which is being spoiled by the ugly industrial civilization of the North and by Science robbing it of its enchantment and dense particularity. Tate, even very early, is much more concerned with a historical view of the decay of our civilization through science and liberalism, seen as a disintegration of man and his support, religion.

42. Ibid., pp. 185, 147.

Poetry, with Tate, particularly after his conversion to Roman Catholicism, becomes an analogue of religion, a human paradigm of the Word, a parallel to the Incarnation. The role of criticism dwindles, or rather the critic becomes absorbed in the guardian of revealed truth. However, there is an apocalyptic, priestly tone to the speech "The Man of Letters in the Modern World," which rejects the task of communication between men for that of a true communion through love assigned to the "man of letters," while the critic is reduced to the job of "preserving the integrity, the purity, and the reality of language" against the corruptions of the mass media.[43] While the poet and the man of letters are still given exalted functions as masters of the symbolic imagination and re-creators of the image of man, critics and criticism are relegated to a nook and cranny of the intellectual universe. For himself, Tate, like Eliot, disavows system and describes himself as a "casual essayist of whom little consistency can be expected," writing from "a mere point of view," which, however, must not be called relative.[44]

In a late essay, "Is Literary Criticism Possible?" Tate denies that we will ever know this, and discusses first the question of teaching criticism in a university. He hands literary history and sociology to the social sciences and leaves criticism in the university with only one task: the rhetorical study of language. He decides that one cannot teach students to "evaluate" works of literature, though this may be "not less absurd than to try to evaluate them oneself." Even the other possible task of criticism, the communication of insights, is declared to be impossible of being taught to others. Insights "can be only exhibited" is Tate's odd conclusion, though it is

43. *The Man of Letters in the Modern World: Selected Essays: 1928–1955* (New York, 1955), p. 20.
44. Ibid., Preface, pp. 6–7.

difficult to see why the "exhibition" of insights does not communicate them and thus teach them to the right students. In the second part of the paper Tate ignores the quite separate question of pedagogy in an American university and confronts the aims of literary criticism in the abstract. In a scrappy and dense list of problems he says mainly negative things about criticism. Criticism is always inferior to creation. "It is always *about* something else." It is thus parasitic and "perpetually obsolescent and replaceable"—a view which can be upheld only if we confine ourselves to day-by-day reviewers, to the necessary middlemen between author and audience, but which is obviously false if we think of theory, poetics, and history. Tate, of course, recognizes that there is the more systematic and methodical, the purer, criticism which "tends more and more to *sound* like philosophical discourse." He distinguishes three methods: aesthetics, which he dismisses curtly, as "from its point of view it is difficult to say anything about literature that is not merely pretentious." Then Tate allows "stylistics," within its narrow limits, and historical reconstruction, which is not criticism proper. In a next congested paragraph Tate objects to philosophical criticism: criticism which appeals to a philosophical authority in which the critic does not believe. No evidence is presented for why the critic could not believe in a philosopher and use him. We are simply warned, "The language of criticism had better not, then, try to be univocal." There is, however, one type of criticism which finds favor in Tate's eyes, though he asks only tentatively: "What is the primary office of criticism? Is it to expound and to elucidate, with as little distortion as possible, the knowledge of life contained by the novel or the poem or the play? What critic has ever done this?" One would think that all moral and social critics were doing nothing else for centuries, but possibly Tate means something very different from what is usually called knowledge of life. Finally he asks, "It literary criticism possible without a criterion of absolute truth? Would a criterion of absolute truth make literary criticism as we know it unnecessary?" Knowing Tate's convictions from other texts, an affirmative answer is required. In the light of the truth of Revelation, criticism is unnecessary, although immediately afterward Tate declares it "perpetually necessary and, in the very nature of its middle position between imagination and philosophy, perpetually impossible."[45] At risk of being called a rationalist, I consider such exalted eloquence a surrender to unreason, an evasion of the task in front of us. The man of faith has destroyed the critic in Tate.

I have demonstrated the anticriticism of five recent poet-critics at some length in order to show that the union of poet and critic is not always a happy one. No doubt, the poet-critic will not only stay with us but will multiply as a type, since the poet can no longer be a seer, a magician, a popular philosopher and moralist, or even a popular entertainer without self-consciousness. But the union of poet and critic is not necessarily good for either poetry or criticism. It seems to me an illusion that it restores the original whole man, the *uomo universale* of the Renaissance. Our time is obsessed by the fear of "alienation," which is often ascribed to specialization and, in Marx (but not in Hegel), serves as a criticism of the modern division of labor. But the Marxist solution, which would abolish the artist's profession in the classless utopia where, says Marx, there "will not be any painters, but at the most men, who among other things, also paint,"[46] is an absurdly idyllic dream. It would give us Churchills and Eisenhowers exercising their Sunday hobby, while the whole history

45. Ibid., pp. 162–74.
46. Karl Marx and Friedrich Engels, *Über Kunst und Literatur,* ed. Michael Lipschitz (Berlin, 1948), p. 90.

of painting demonstrates the success of the full-time professional and specialist: Titian, Rembrandt, Velázquez, Rubens,
and Cézanne. The same is true of poetry: the great poet is absorbed and even possessed by his task. It is a mistake to glorify
his distractions or to minimize the obstacles in his way. There
were a few shining examples of great poet-critics in history
—Dante, Goethe, Coleridge come most readily to mind—but
I am not sure that it is right to describe them as successful
cases of a union of the two; rather they managed somehow to
alternate poetry and criticism. Dante wrote *De Vulgari Eloquentia* and then the *Divine Comedy;* Goethe, *Faust,* and in
between the two parts, the treatise on "Simple Imitation,
Manner and Style"; Coleridge, "The Rime of the Ancient
Mariner," and years later, *Biographia Literaria.* They were
not torn by inner conflicts between instinct and intellect, but
rather were poets at one moment and critics at another. Our
time has reacted sharply against the "pure" art, the "pure"
scholarship, and the "pure" criticism of the early twentieth
century. We don't want to be specialists; we want to be whole
men; we want to reconcile the conscious and the unconscious,
the life of the senses and the intellect. We want to have poet-
critics. We can hope for them, but as the Devil's advocate, I
can recommend beatification only in very rare cases, with
veritable saints who have accomplished the miracle of reconciliation.

# The Literary Theory and Aesthetics
# of the Prague School

"The Prague School" is an established term in modern linguistics for the work and the teachings of a group of scholars organized as the Prague Linguistic Circle since 1926. The doctrines of the school have been widely debated since the group drew up its theses on the methods of studying language for the First International Congress of Linguists held in the Hague in 1928 and the following year began to publish a series of volumes in French, German, and English, *Travaux du Cercle Linguistique de Prague*. In English there are a recent anthology of their writings and several informative studies.[1]

It is, however, less well-known that the Prague Linguistic Circle included several literary scholars and that they made an ambitious attempt to develop a coherent theory of literature and aesthetics which they called "structuralism," at least as early as 1934.[2] Long before the present fashion for the term,

---

1. Josef Vachek, *A Prague School Reader in Linguistics* (Bloomington, 1964), and *The Linguistic School of Prague: An Introduction to Its Theory and Practice* (Bloomington, 1966). Cf. Henry Kučera, "The Czech Contribution to Modern Linguistics," in *The Czechoslovak Contribution to World Culture,* ed. Miloslav Rechcígl, Jr. (The Hague, 1964), pp. 93–104.

2. The term "structure," which in Czech is a technical term, a foreign word which has none of the associations with building that it has in English, occurs in Mukařovský's *Máj* in 1928 *(Kapitoly z*

a doctrine was evolved in the Prague Circle and applied concretely. This doctrine anticipates many of the newest speculations in literary theory and aesthetics or, at least, parallels some of the most active and promising movements in the West: the American New Criticism, the semantics of Charles Morris, "the style as meaning" view of William K. Wimsatt, and so on, even though there were no direct contacts among them.

Information on the Czech group is scant in English. There are brief accounts scattered throughout my papers, and my *Theory of Literature* (1949), written in collaboration with Austin Warren, is, at least in part, a deliberate attempt to bring together the insights I had acquired as a junior member of the Circle with my new knowledge of American criticism. In Victor Erlich's *Russian Formalism* (1954) some attention is given to the Prague school among the repercussions of the Russian Formalist teachings in Poland and Czechoslovakia. Finally, Paul L. Garvin published in mimeograph form a *Prague School Reader in Esthetics, Literary Structure and Style* (1955) which, however, contains mostly unrepresentative or peripheral specimens of the work of the Circle.[3] Thus a fuller account of the Prague School might be welcome.

It seems to me disingenuous to pretend that the literary theory of the Prague Circle is a collective achievement, as apparently the basic doctrines of the linguists were. For our limited purposes we must concentrate on the writings of Jan Mukařovský (born in 1891), who was undoubtedly the most productive of the Czech participants. The growth, expansion,

---

*české poetiky, 3* [3 vols. Prague, 1948], 12, 89; hereafter cited as *KP*). The term "structuralism," describing his own position, seems not to be used before 1934 (*KP, 1*, 349).

3. See my review in *Language, 31* (1955), 584–87.

and directions of his thought are also a faithful reflection of the trends of the time in literature, in the arts, in scholarship, and, in general, in history. Mukařovský thus becomes a peculiarly representative figure for the intellectual life of Czechoslovakia during those fifty years.

Before describing and analyzing his work, it will be useful to dispose of the question of his sources. For obvious reasons Mukařovský made much of the local antecedents, since he resented a view that would reduce his work to a simple transfer of the Russian Formalist methods to Czech materials. I do not think that he succeeded in his attempt to find his ancestry in his Czech predecessors. There is nothing in the work of Otakar Hostinský, the first Professor of Aesthetics at the Czech University, a fervent propagandist for Smetana and Wagner, or in the writings of his successor, Otokar Zich, who wrote on the aesthetics of music, dramatic space, and types of poets—always from a psychological point of view— which would anticipate the doctrines of Mukařovský. No doubt, these two scholars established a tradition of aesthetics in Czech which could ultimately be traced back to Herbartian Formalism. It had, for somewhat obscure reasons, a strong tradition in the universities of the Austro-Hungarian Empire in the nineteenth century: Robert Zimmermann was a Professor at the (then still bilingual) University of Prague when he wrote his *Geschichte der Aesthetik* (1858). But one of the main points of the structuralist doctrine is precisely the rejection of a Formalism which conceives of form as a set of relations between materials. Besides, Mukařovský shows hardly any interest in music or the aesthetics of music, and, in the crucial stages at least, he rejected psychology as a valid approach to literary study. There were, of course, even before the twenties, critics in Czechoslovakia such as F. X. Šalda, Arne Novák, and Otokar Fischer who were interested in a study of style, poetic diction, and metrics.[4] Mukařovský is thus right in emphasizing a native tradition of literary criticism and analysis, but in no way did it anticipate the peculiar doctrines of the Circle.

The initial stimulus came from the Russian Formalists and particularly from Roman Jakobson, who arrived in Prague as early as 1920 and met then the later founder of the Circle, Vilém Mathesius, Professor of English at the University. Jakobson brought with him not only a knowledge of the Russian work, but an intimate sense of creative participation in it. He was a literary theorist even in Russia and he contributed importantly to literary study in Czechoslovakia. It would be impossible to disentangle his exact share in the ideas of the Circle as his direct influence on Mukařovský, also through conversation, must have been profound. But Mukařovský is right in stressing his growing disagreement with the teachings of the Russian formalists. In a review of the Czech translation of Viktor Shklovsky's *Theory of Prose* (1934) he points up his rejection of strict formalism which then seemed to him acceptable only if we call form everything there is in a work of art (KP *1*, 346). "Structure" and "structuralism" were terms preferred by him and the other members of the Circle as they avoided the usual implication of empty formalism. As Mukařovský defined structure it is both set off from external form and from such terms as totality, wholeness, *Ganzheit,* or *Gestalt.* "The concept of structure is based on an inner unification of the whole by the mutual relations of its parts: and that not only by positive relations, agreements and harmonies —but also by contradictions and conflicts" (SE 117). It is a

4. See my paper "Modern Czech Criticism and Literary Scholarship," in *Harvard Slavic Studies,* ed. Horace Lunt, *2* (Cambridge, Mass., 1954), 343–58; reprinted in my *Essays on Czech Literature* (The Hague, 1963), pp. 179–93.

dialectical concept while the Russian formalists, at least initially, were somewhat naïve technicians, empiricists with strong mechanistic tendencies.

Mukařovský (as well as Jakobson) acquired a much more sophisticated theoretical and philosophical background mainly by a study of linguistic theory, particularly of Saussure and later Karl Bühler, and an increasing familiarity with the phenomenological movement. Its founder, Edmund Husserl, lectured in the Circle on the "phenomenology of language,"[5] as did the Polish philosopher Roman Ingarden, whose book *Das literarische Kunstwerk* (1931) was the most thorough and faithful application of the principles and methods of his master. Other names should be added: Max Dessoir and Emil Utitz (then professor at the German University of Prague) taught the difference between aesthetics and *Kunstwissenschaft;* Broder Christiansen, in his *Philosophie der Kunst* (1909), drew the distinction between the work of art and the "aesthetic object";[6] and Ernst Cassirer, in his *Philosophie der symbolischen Formen* (3 volumes, 1923–29), pointed the way toward a general philosophy of signs, though Mukařovský never accepted the neo-Kantian assumptions of Cassirer's thought. The confluence of the technical analytics of the Russians with the speculative systematizations of the Germans was the decisive moment. Still, the wealth of sources and antecedents must not obscure the fact that Mukařovský's doctrine has an originality and a systematic coherence and clarity which can rarely be paralleled in the history of literary theory.

Mukařovský began with a thesis, *Some Reflections on the Aesthetics of Czech Verse (Příspěvek k estetice českého verše,*

5. On November 18, 1935. See report in *Slovo a slovesnost, 2* (1936), 64.

6. Hanau, 1909, pp. 41, 49 ff.

1923), which ingeniously distinguishes between the versification of the three main Czech poets of the middle of the nineteenth century: Neruda, Čech, and Vrchlický. He also gives
a psychological account of these differences by relating them
to different methods of composition: the laborious struggle
of Neruda is, for instance, contrasted with the nervous haste
of Vrchlický. The little book shows that Mukařovský has
learned to observe and analyze verse with the methods developed by Sievers and Saran in Germany, but it shows no traces
of his later views.

His next book, an elaborate monograph on the poem *Máj*
by Karel Hynek Mácha (1810–36), the best Czech romantic
poet, reflects the full impact of the Russian Formalists.[7] In
the preface to *Máchův Máj: Estetická studie* (1928) Mukařovský accepts their main concepts expressly. A whole theoretical program is expounded: an aesthetic analysis of a work
of art has to uncover those traits in it which function aesthetically. The relation to the author and to reality outside the
work are irrelevant for that purpose. The usual distinctions
between form and content are untenable. If we consider
images, ideas, and feelings to be content, then the linguistic
elements must be called form. But looking more closely, we
have to come to the conclusion that even the elements of
content have a formal character: thus, for instance, events in
an epic are parts of the content, but the way in which they are
arranged in a plot would be part of the form. The solution
common in German aesthetics of appealing to a concept of
"inner form" is unsatisfactory, as it leaves the boundary between inner and outer form obscure. Mukařovský decides that
it is better to make a distinction between elements of a work
of art which are indifferent aesthetically (which he calls "the

7. Mukařovský translated the lecture Boris Tomashevsky gave
in Prague; see *Časopis pro moderní filologii, 15* (1929), 12–15.

material") and the way in which they acquire aesthetic effectiveness within a work of art (which he calls "form"). Within the "material" he distinguishes the theme (the images, ideas, and feelings) and the language, while form is the organization of these materials. In agreement with the Russian Formalists, Mukařovský considers artistic form as having two main traits: deformation and organization. The term "deformation" has no derogatory implication: it simply means the changes imposed on the original materials, the novelty, for example, of poetic language in contrast to spoken language, the patterning imposed by meter, the tension of a plot, all "devices" (or possibly better "instruments" or "procedures") toward the aim of art which in Mukařovský, as in the Russian Formalists, is conceived as a shock to our ordinary indifference, as a heightening of awareness, as "making strange," *Verfremdung* in a wider sense than Brecht's.[8] But these devices must be applied in a systematic manner, must be organized, must harmonize with each other in order to achieve the totality of a work of art: its structure.

The body of the book on *Máj* first studies, very elaborately, with long lists of examples, the sound patterns of Mácha's poem and then shows how these sound patterns are integrated into the other aspects of the work: how the "melodious style" implies a veiling of the denotative meaning of words and finally harmonizes with the cluster of motifs, the plot, and the manner of telling. In a concluding chapter Mukařovský contrasts Mácha's poem with similar poems of the later nineteenth century, Hálek's *Alfred* and Vrchlický's *Satanella,* in order to point to the dominance of the author's subjectivity

---

8. The term corresponds to what Kenneth Burke calls "perspective by incongruity" and is, of course, a very old motif in the history of aesthetics—e.g. in Wordsworth's famous Preface of 1800 or in Shelley's *Defence of Poetry* (1821).

in Mácha's poem against the objective or rather indifferent attitude of Hálek and the slightly parodistic, ironical attitude of Vrchlický toward his story. Mukařovský sees these three poems ordered in chronological sequence as a proving ground for a study of historical poetics. In the terms introduced by the Russian Formalists he can show how devices become "automatized"—i.e. cease to be felt as aesthetically effective —so that, with the advent of a new poet, they are replaced by new devices which become "actualized," felt to be new, effective, and impressive. *Máj* is Mukařovský's most extensive monograph: it can be rightly described as a model of a systematic structural analysis in which the study of sound patterns, meter, diction, and composition interlocks to form a unified image of a totality which is systematic, harmonious, and hence, we must conclude, aesthetically effective (what we used to call "beautiful").

Mukařovský has applied the same method to other works with some variations and refinements: e.g. he analyzed a descriptive poem by M. Z. Polák "The Sublimity of Nature" ("Vznešenost přírody," 1819),[9] demonstrating how its versification puts certain limitations and demands on the choice of vocabulary; how the vocabulary implies stylistic devices such as extensive periphrasis; and how periphrasis implies always a tension between word and thing: the object is not named but its qualities are enumerated. Stress on qualities implies description, and the particular type of description implies a specific world-view, even an argument: the argument for design in nature, the glory and goodness of God.

Returning to Mácha, Mukařovský in a new paper[10] ex-

9. "Polákova Vznešenost Přírody: Pokus o rozbor a vývojové zařadění básnické struktury" (1934), in *KP*, *2*, 91–176.
10. "Genetika smyslu v Máchově poesii" (1938), in *KP*, *3*, 239–310.

panded his analysis to include all his writings, his total œuvre, which lends itself to a unified treatment, since Mukařovský can show how the same devices recur again and again in both the prose, the poems, and even the diaries, how the whole work from the simplest act of naming to the loosely shifting kaleidoscope of motifs is permeated by the same mood, the same attitude toward reality, so that there is no important difference between linguistic and extralinguistic elements. The new discussion of Mácha shows a shift of emphasis as it abandons some of the earlier rigid exclusions: attention is now turned to such questions as the foreign sources of Mácha's diction and motifs, though always with a regard to their use and to the psychology and experience of the writer: the interaction of life and work.

Other papers elaborate details, defend the position polemically, and slowly expand ideas contained in germ in the early work. Thus "La Phonologie et la poétique" (1931) is a plea for the collaboration between poetics and the new linguistics: an understanding of phonemics (then called "phonology" by the Prague Circle) allows us to distinguish between purely acoustic elements of a work of art—features of its "performance," when read aloud—and phonic elements which are integral parts of its structure. It allows us to study the interaction of the sound stratum of a poem with other elements: intonation, word-limits, and so on, which in turn serve to characterize the rhythm of the poem. This last point is elaborated in a paper "Intonation comme facteur du rythme poétique" (1933). A Western reader can observe Mukařovský at work in these two French papers.[11]

11. "La Phonologie et la poétique," *Travaux du Cercle linguistique de Prague,* 4 (1931), 278–88; "Intonation comme facteur du rythme poétique," *Archives néerlandaises de phonétique expérimentale,* 8–9 (1933), 153–65.

Several papers, early and late, apply such Formalist methods also to an analysis of prose style and the technique of the novel. Karel Čapek's prose style is analyzed most elaborately, its development sketched, and a characterization attempted which, from the observation of small stylistic traits, leads to a definition of his outlook on life: the way in which order is broken up in Čapek's style and technique in favor of the individuality of devices and characters, but how this individuality is, in turn, somehow flattened out, reduced to something universally human.[12] In all of these analytical papers Mukařovský tries to discover a dominant trait *(dominanta)* in the structure which directs or distorts all other traits. A hierarchy is established, since the work is conceived as a stratified structure of sound and meaning.

The Russian Formalists—certainly Jakobson—were closely associated with the Russian Futurist poets, and their theories, in part, were a defense of their experimentation with language. Also Mukařovský established personal relations with the Czech avant-garde of the thirties: particularly with Vítězslav Nezval, who founded a branch of *surréalisme* in Prague, and with Vladislav Vančura, a novelist who can vaguely be described as an "expressionist" and certainly as a bold experimenter with language and form. Mukařovský's analyses of some of Nezval's poetry and Vančura's fiction served as defenses of such "modernist" art, but he never took part in the manifestoes of the different cliques and preserved the attitude of an observer or, at most, an academic ally who lends his prestige to the militant artists. In 1932 the Prague Linguistic Circle organized a whole series of lectures attacking the editing of the journal *Naše Řeč* (Our Language), which advocated the most extremely puristic and archaic

12. Particularly the article "Významová výstavba a komposiční osnova epiky Karla Čapka" (1939), in *KP, 2,* 374–400.

standard of language. Mukařovský gave the lecture on "Written and Poetic Language,"[13] defending the view that poetic language is a special language within language which has its own rights and norms. The sharp distinction between different "functional" languages upheld there was mainly devised to save poetry from the impositions of grammarians judging by norms of correctness and purity from foreign words and neologisms. But it also served as a weapon for a concept of poetry free from any obligation to comprehensibility, logic, and social relevance. During these years Mukařovský was expressly a defender of "modernist" art, even though he recognized the manifold contradictions within the different modernist trends and knew that it reflected a crisis of our civilization and society. But he saw how strong the desire of modern art is for a reconstruction of the world of values and the struggle for order in its apparent chaos.[14]

Mukařovský's main scholarly effort was, however, directed toward the past, toward the construction of a historical poetics. With Jakobson he wrote a "History of Czech Versification,"[15] which he introduced by a theoretical section developing the ideas of Jakobson's path-breaking book *The Foundations of Czech Verse* (*Základové českého verše*, 1926). Also in metrics, Mukařovský takes the principle of totality seriously: the basic unity of verse rhythm, he argues, is not a foot but the whole line and even the whole poem. Feet have no independent status: they exist (i.e. are effective) only in rela-

13. "Jazyk spisovný a jazyk básnický," in *Spisovná čeština a jazyková kultura,* ed. B. Havránek and Miloš Weingart (Prague, 1932), pp. 123–56.

14. "Dialektické rozpory v moderním umění" (1935), in *KP, 2,* 307; also in *Studie z estetiky* (Prague, 1966), p. 265 (hereafter cited as *SE*).

15. "Obecné zásady a vývoj novočeského verše," first in *Československá vlastivěda, 3* (1934); reprinted in *KP, 2,* 9–90.

tion to a whole, and also individual lines are verse only in relation to the whole poem. A poem is characterized by its "melody"—that is, the resultant of the two schemes of intonation: the sentence and the verse intonation. Mukařovský, following the example of Boris Tomashevsky, draws graphs of the verse melody of Czech poems by very simply means. He ascertains the intonation of the sentence by the main word accent (always on the first syllable in Czech) and the verse intonation by the traditional metrical patterns (e.g. five-foot iamb). The divergence between the sentence and the metric intonation can be calculated statistically. For instance, the first syllable of every line of a poem has an accent in 26 cases out of 100, though the syllable in a five-foot iamb should always be unaccented, while the second syllable might be accented in 83 cases out of 100, though the syllable should always be accented according to the metrical scheme. These calculations can be represented by diagrams: on the one axis are entered the numbers of syllables, on the other the percentages, and thus graphs can be drawn which allow us to see the verse melody of a poem at a single glance. By comparing these diagrams for different poems, authors, and periods, we can distinguish between the different schools of poetry which usually are sharply opposed to each other. The new generation reacts against the conventions of the preceding school by systematically violating its conventions and then establishes a new convention which, in turn, will be broken by a new revolt. Mukařovský demonstrates this scheme of action and reaction, convention and revolt, by an analysis of early nineteenth-century Czech poetry: the struggle then occurring between a syllabic and a "syllabo-tonic" system, on the one hand, and a new accentual system, on the other, was not, however, a simple victory of the new system; it was interrupted by the strange experiment of many poets early in the century to introduce a quantitative metrics on the model of Latin which was doomed to fail but served the function of relaxing the rules of exact syllable counting. Mukařovský's history of versification is necessarily abstract and schematic: the material is limited and the clash of metrical systems in the Czech poetry of the time very marked. The whole theory would be difficult to apply, for example, to English poetry, as even the construing of such diagrams would be excessively complex owing to the number of subordinate accents in English words and the variety of metrical devices established in the nineteenth century. But it might prove illuminating for a period such as the English sixteenth century, when a syllabic system inherited from the Middle Ages was replaced by the new freedom of accentual systems and when, as in Czech poetry, some theorists (such as Gabriel Harvey) tried to imitate the quantitative system also in English verse.

Versification represents a historical sequence of devices which can be isolated and analyzed with comparative ease. It is harder to do this with the other elements of a work of art and with the whole development of literature conceived in comparative independence from the history of ideas and society. Mukařovský, following the Russians, put the question of such a historical poetics or of an internal history of literature very radically. He assumes that literature has a "self-motion" (a Hegelian term translating "Selbstbewegung") which is only affected from the outside by the parallel series of the other activities of man: philosophy, religion, the other arts, and society in general. A work of art is not the subjective affair of its author or a mere reflection of the social context, but it is objectively—that is, independently of its author—determined by the evolution of the total structure of a given art. The task of the literary historian will be the construction of an evolutionary series of literary works.

The individual work is valued in relation to this evolution. "A work," to quote him, "appears as a positive value if it in some respect regrouped the structure of the preceding stage, it will appear as a negative value if it took over the structure without changes" *(KP, 2,* 100–01). An aesthetic evaluation either from a subjective point of view or from that of our time is questionable, as we would thus evaluate a different aesthetic object. Since the time of its origin much may have changed in a work (besides its purely physical "thingness"), particularly the language. But Mukařovský does not—as most literary historians would—consider this an argument for the necessity of reconstructing the original historical situation of a work, though he admits this as a possible task of scholarship. He rejects a purely historical evaluation, since aesthetic evaluation "necessarily looks at the structure realized in the work to be evaluated as a fixed and clearly delimited shape while historical investigation must see a poetic structure in constant motion as an uninterrupted process of a regrouping of elements and the permutation of their relationships" *(KP, 2,* 100). Apparently Mukařovský does not reject all evaluation but rather makes a sharp distinction between literary history and criticism. Literary history evaluates only by one criterion: novelty, the violation of tradition. It is not really genuine valuation but the ascertaining of a simple fact: Does or does not this work of art change the direction of the evolutionary series? Mukařovský is committed to science, to an attempt at a value-proof neutral factual literary history as a scheme of evolutionary theses and antitheses, as a "history of art without names."

The whole concept of an internal history of art is extremely difficult. The argument of Croce that a history of artistic devices, procedures, and styles is concerned only with "material things external to art" has much cogency: it is certainly almost impossible to isolate the "literariness" of a work and to order such an abstract quality chronologically. The whole concept of a reaction toward an immediately preceding convention is open to doubt, since a poet can reach into the far past, of his own mind or that of humanity. A concept of time which is less unilinear, which understands the interpenetration of the causal order in experience and memory, makes the idea of a self-propelled evolution seem a mere heuristic device.[16] It raised, at least, the question of literary history, which still is often nothing but a ragbag of encyclopedic knowledge about the past without focus, method, or even clear-cut subject matter.

Mukařovský did not remain content either with stylistic, metrical, and semantic analyses of single works or with placing them in an evolutionary series. He more and more expanded his vision into a general theory of signs: a "semiology" (a term from Saussure) in which poetry appears only a special case. The aesthetic object, he argues, must be conceived not as a material thing but as a system of "autonomous signs." The term seems paradoxical and even contradictory, as "sign" implies pointing to something else which is to be "signified." But "autonomous sign" with Mukařovský is an appropriate formula for what Charles Morris (after C. S. Peirce) later called an "icon." A work of art is not in direct relation to reality; words in poetry have no documentary value; they function only as intermediaries between the members of the "collective"—i.e. the society experiencing the work of art. The concept of "sign" allows Mukařovský to think of all arts as a unity: architecture, sculpture, painting, drama, and the film in particular can be analyzed in terms of

16. See my discussion in "The Concept of Evolution in Literary History," in *For Roman Jakobson* (The Hague, 1956), pp. 653–61; reprinted in my *Concepts of Criticism* (New Haven, 1963), pp. 37–53.

signs. Signs serve functions, impose norms or rules, embody values: they permeate all culture. An enterprise similar to Cassirer's is envisaged.

The pamphlet *Aesthetic Function, Norm and Value as Social Facts (Estetická funkce, norma a hodnota jako sociální fakty,* 1936) provides the best statement of the theory. Any object or event can, in Mukařovský's view, assume an aesthetic function, though in history these objects have been sometimes limited variously in different times and places. The boundaries of art and nonart fluctuate, and the aesthetic function may dominate or be subordinated to others such as communication; it can become a means of social differentiation or it can isolate an object within a society. The aesthetic norm will also vacillate between rigidity and elasticity in different times. Conflicting aesthetic norms often determined by age, sex, or class exist simultaneously in a society. An aesthetic norm accepted in a low social stratum can, in a given context, rise into the highest social sphere and sink back again. Much of literary change can be explained by such a social upward or downward movement. Artistic norms expand, contract in the range of their application, drop out of sight, move from one art to another, compete with ethical, philosophical, and social norms. Value is equally changeable in history, not only in different social strata but also in relation to other nonaesthetic values. But Mukařovský sees that a purely relativistic answer, the acceptance of a "whirligig of taste," is untenable, and he appeals to some "anthropological core," some common human denominator from which the variety of aesthetic values will stand out in agreement or contrast. Many old and well-known questions are reformulated in this scheme of functions, norms, and values. These categories allow Mukařovský to shuffle and reshuffle works of art in ever newer combinations with dazzling ingenuity. But this new social scheme turned out to be ultimately destructive of the very nature of art and the central concern of aesthetics. Mukařovský had come to recognize the limits of "structuralism": the single-minded concentration on relational factors within a single work conceived as a hierarchy of signs, placed within an evolutionary series, and in purely external relations to the other activities of man does not fully take care of the facts. As early as in his article "The Work of Poetry as an Assembly of Values" ("Básnické dílo jako soubor hodnot," 1932), Mukařovský had argued that a work of art is an assembly of nonartistic values dominated by artistic value. But in the new statement, in *Aesthetic Function, Norm and Value,* where the whole culture is dissolved in a huge systems of signs, Mukařovský at a crucial point abandons the concept of aesthetic value altogether. "The work of art," he concludes, "is ultimately an assembly of extra-aesthetic values and nothing but such an assembly." If we asked what happened to aesthetic value, we see that it "evaporated into extra-aesthetic values" and that "it is actually nothing else than a general designation for the dynamic totality of its mutual relations" *(SE,* p. 51). Here aesthetics is asked to commit suicide. Art is merely an arrangement or combination of nonart.

It took Mukařovský many years to realize the consequences of his own position. He actually made surprising concessions to criticisms which pointed out that the focus on the structure of the work of art neglected other legitimate aspects of its study: particularly the relation to the personality of the artist (which must not be confused with biography or with an insistence on experience, *Erlebnis,* or sincerity) and the question of a world view implied in works of art which is not a mere intellectual doctrine or statement. In an article published in January 1935 I pointed out these limitations,[17] and Mukařovský, in several later papers, did try to incorporate these issues into his general scheme. A paper not published till 1966 (though written during the war, 1943–45) discusses "The Role of the Individual in Literary Evolution" and concedes the danger of determinism in his older view *(SE,* p. 232). Another paper, "Art and World-view" (1948, in *SE* pp. 245 ff.) recognizes that there is an epistemological basis to every work of art which must not, of course, be confused with a systematic philosophy. Art implies an attitude toward reality, an answer to the basic questions of human life. At least in his earlier writings, Mukařovský admits that this relation to reality cannot be conceived as mere reflection, a mere image. Rather, "the attitude of the subject realized in the structure of the sign, is projected into reality as its general law. The aesthetic sign shows its autonomy by always pointing to reality as a whole and not to an individual slice of it" *(SE,* pp. 70–71). Something like Croce's "cosmicità" is suggested as a solution to the universalizing effect of art and to its relation to reality.

But in the very same postwar article which contains the most explicit recognition of the problem of world view, Mukařovský decided that the answer to it is contained in Marxism. Soon after the February 1948 Communist takeover, he gave up what seemed to be his attempts, after 1945, to reconcile structuralism with Marxism. In 1948 he hoped for a complete absorption of structuralism by Marxism. In 1951,

17. " 'Dějiny českého verše' a metody literární historie," *Listy pro umění a kritiku, 2* (1935), 437–45. Some discussion in my "The Theory of Literary History," *Travaux du Cercle Linguistique de Prague, 6* (1936), 173–91.

however, he violently denounced structuralism and recanted all his earlier views.[18] His whole work appeared to him an aberration. The only true science, he declared, is Marxism. Structuralism is "a furtively masked and hence the most dangerous idealism." There is no room for an aesthetics which would uphold the autonomy of art and justify modernist trends in art. Mukařovský gave up writing on literary questions almost entirely and threw himself into academic administration and into the so-called Peace Movement. He became Rector of the University of Prague and took a major part in its complete reorganization (i.e. "purging") in the interest of Communist ideology. The small collection of articles which appeared only in Slovak, *Z českej literatury* (Bratislava, 1961), rehearses all the slogans of the strictest Communist orthodoxy. Literary scholarship has only one aim, "to help in the building of socialism" (pp. 56, 234), the only criterion of value is "popularity" *(lidovost),* a term which combines appeal to the broad masses with folksiness and nationality. Mukařovský can now say that "the most popular authors are the greatest authors," and that "a work that is alien to the people, ceases to be a work of art" (pp. 30, 45). All trends of Western scholarship are condemned wholesale as "competing only in the variety of ways in which they cover up truth" (p. 48). Only Marxism solved the division between literary history and criticism. The new Mukařovský was the logical editor-in-chief of the large-scale *History of Czech Literature* (hitherto 3 volumes, 1959–61) published by the Czech Academy, a dull rigidly orthodox compilation which gives an exceedingly simplified, purely ideological

18. "Kam směřuje dnešní theorie umění?" *Slovo a slovesnost, 11* (1949), 49–59 (a lecture dated Nov. 13, 1948). "Ke kritice strukturalismu v naší literární vědě," *Tvorba, 20* (1951), 964–66.

view of the development of Czech literature leading to the glories of Communism.[19]

It thus comes as a considerable surprise that, in 1966, Mukařovský consented to a collection of his *Studies in Aesthetics (Studie z estetiky),* which reprints not only his structuralist writings since 1931 but also adds unpublished papers written during the war years, before his conversion to Marxism. One cannot, however, quite speak of a second recantation. Nothing new is added, except a short note asserting that "the dialectic method of thinking opens the door to Marxist aesthetics" *(SE,* p. 337). Two editors, Felix Vodička and Květoslav Chvatík, provide, however, ample commentary. Vodička's introductory biographical sketch hardly makes a good apology for Mukařovský's repudiation of his own past, unless we consider "the desire to join the creative rhythm of a newly forming society exaggerated and vulgarized the negation of the past" *(SE,* p. 10) a valid defense. Chvatík's concluding study makes much of Mukařovský's then partly unpublished writings of the war years. It tries to minimize the influence of the Russian Formalists and the contribution of Roman Jakobson *(SE,* p. 343) and chides Victor Erlich for ignoring the most fertile period of Czech structuralism, the years between 1941 and 1948. Still, he cannot explain how Erlich could have known these writings at that time or why he should have concerned himself about them in a thesis on Russian Formalism. Chvatík, however, does not hide his disapproval of the orthodox Marxist phase of Mukařovský's career: it is "mechanistic, sociological, sterile, and leads nowhere" *(SE,* p. 363). Chvatík had pub-

19. Cf. my review in "Recent Czech Literary History and Criticism," in *The Czechoslovak Contribution to World Culture,* ed. Miloslav Rechcígl, Jr. (The Hague, 1964), pp. 17–28; also in my *Essays on Czech Literature,* pp. 194–205.

lished a book on *Bedřich Václavek and the Development of Marxist Aesthetics (Bedřich Václavek a vývoj marxistické estetiky,* 1962), in which he exalted this Marxist critic of the twenties and thirties who was also a consistent defender of avant-garde art. Chvatík's attitude is rather odd: any art, even completely abstract art, surrealism or cubism, is acceptable and might even be called "socialist realism" as long as the artist holds the correct—i.e. the Communist—political conviction.[20] In the book on Václavek, Chvatík speaks very condescendingly of structuralism and of Mukařovský in particular, but in the epilogue to *Studies in Aesthetics,* four years later, the praise is almost unreserved, though he holds that Mukařovský's structuralism can somehow be incorporated in a future Marxist aesthetics.

Mukařovský's work must stand and fall with the writings before 1948. The distasteful sight of his public hara-kiri in 1950 and the recent tacit permission to revive his early work must be recorded as symptoms of the time. But they should not influence our judgment of his early work, which seems to me an excellently thought-out, coherent scheme of literary theory which, in its best formulations, guards against the main errors transmitted in history. The emphasis on the work of art as a totality which is conceived as a dynamic dialectical process rather than an organic body, the ideal, however difficult to realize, of an internal history of the art of poetry, the view of literature as part of a general theory of signs in which function, norm, and value interlock seem to me substantially valid conceptions even today. Many of Mukařovský's concrete analyses are superb achievements displaying an acuity of observation and discrimination which can be paralleled only in the writings of a few Russian Formalists or such *Stilforscher* as Leo Spitzer.

20. More on Chvatík in my article, "New Czech Books on Literary History and Theory," *Slavic Review, 26* (1967), 295–301.

The impression of abstractness which this exposition must have made cannot unfortunately be corrected within its limits: it could be modified only by describing Mukařovský's analyses of individual works of art, richly documented by concrete details. But these are almost always confined to writings in Czech and thus closely tied to the peculiarities of the language, its poetic diction and metrics. Mukařovský is, one must admit, resolutely provincial. He quotes some French verse but very rarely, convinced as he must be that the art of poetry cannot be taken out of its linguistic context. Mukařovský constantly moves between two extremes: very large generalizations which we could expound and empirical minutiae which we could not convey successfully. Something between these poles seems to be lacking. Abstraction and induction in Mukařovský are always confined within the framework of an objective scientific ideal. A certain obtuseness and aridity of temper comes out in a curious page *(SE,* p. 236) in which he condemns the rendering of a man's *privatissimum* as impossible and ultimately uninteresting. There is little in Mukařovský of what many critics in history have prized most highly: sensitivity, *Einfühlung,* sensual enjoyment of art or personal involvement in a judgment of value. Possibly a realization of this last need helped to persuade him of the truth of Marxism. But in his early stages he was a first-rate theorist and analyst of texts.

The influence of the Circle and particularly of Mukařovský's doctrines on Czech literary scholarship has been profound and pervasive since the thirties. It would be hard to prove, but even the older established scholar-critics, F. X. Šalda, Arne Novák, and Otokar Fischer, while never subscribing to the exact formulas of "structuralism," showed, in the last years of their careers, an increasing concern for formal problems systematically formulated: Otokar Fischer, in particular, wrote sensitive papers on rhyme and sonnet patterns,[21] and his pupil Vojtěch Jirát (1902–45) produced an elaborate study, in German, of the German poet August von Platen, *Platens Stil* (1933), which is clearly influenced by Mukařovský's work on Mácha.

Even the militant Marxist critics of the thirties discussed the views of the Circle respectfully, recognizing, at that time, that a defense of avant-garde art (then associated in Czechoslovakia with the extreme political left) is useful to their purposes. Kurt Konrad (the pseudonym of Kurt Beer, 1908–41) and Bedřich Václavek (1897–1943)—both to become victims of the Nazi terror—discussed the problem of the relation between form and content, of the idea of literary evolution, and so on, in terms which would have been impossible without Jakobson's and Mukařovský's mediation of the ideas of Russian Formalism. They both, of course, criticized the basic doctrine from their Marxist point of view. Like Lukács, they assert the predominance of content over form and the ultimate determination of literary change by economic forces, but they at least recognized that there are specific problems of aesthetics and hoped that structuralism could be, in a subordinate role, incorporated into Marxism.[22]

The influence of the Circle on Czech literary scholarship since the thirties was also negative. The Circle discouraged, sometimes by harsh reviews of the old-line books, the established genre of literary biography which assumed a comfortably easy and obvious relationship between an author's experiences or psychology and his work and disparaged the usual writing of literary history in terms of external influences

21. Included in *Duše a slovo (The Soul and the Word,* 1929).

22. See Konrad's collected essays, *Ztvárněte skutečnost!* ("Shape reality!" Prague, 1963). On Václavek see Chvatík, *Bedřich Václavek and the Development of Marxist Aesthetics.*

and parallels. But the demand of an internal history of literature was too difficult in practice, and most of Mukařovský's pupils concentrated rather on the one manageable factor in poetic analysis: metrics. Josef Hrabák and Karel Horálek studied Church Slavic, Polish, and Old Czech verse; and in Slovakia, Mikuláš Bakoš traced the development of Slovak verse with the methods of the Formalists.[23] Bakoš went back to the sources and produced a valuable anthology of the writings of the Russian Formalists in Slovak translation.[24]

The most gifted and perceptive of Mukařovský's pupils is Felix Vodička, who wrote a well-considered schematic outline of the problems of literary history[25] and then embarked on studies of the Czech nineteenth-century revival; his *The Beginnings of Modern Czech Prose (Počátky krásné prózy novočeské,* 1948) goes far beyond stylistic investigation. Not only does Vodička solve problems of close analysis of prose rhythm, diction, and sentence structure with rare ingenuity, but he also has a fine insight into the relations of the newly rising Czech literature to developments abroad, a firm grasp of a theory of genres, and a proper concern for the problem of periodization. Vodička decides, rightly to my mind, that Czech literature before Mácha can be best classified as "preromantic" and that the attempts to construe a Czech "classicism" are artificial and forced.

With the enforcement of Marxist orthodoxy after 1948, "Formalist" points of view disappeared. When Mukařovský himself recanted, his pupils embraced Marxism. For years

23. *Vývin slovenského verša (The Development of Slovak Verse,* Bratislava, 1938).

24. *Teória literatúry. Výbor z "formálnej metódy" (Theory of Literature: A Selection from the "Formal Method,"* Trnava, 1941).

25. "Literární historie," in *Čtení o jazyce a poesii,* ed. B. Havránek and J. Mukařovský (Prague, 1942), pp. 309–400.

nothing was produced which, in literary history, would show the influence of the early teachings of the Circle. In 1954 the periodical of the Circle, *Slovo a slovesnost,* expressly dropped articles of literary concern and became an exclusively linguistic journal. The *History of Czech Literature* finally produced by the Academy was a rigidly orthodox Marxist work, though the sections on the Czech revival written by Vodička managed to incorporate some of his earlier findings into the scheme of a social and economic explanation of all literature.

With the thaw new tendencies made themselves felt which allowed, at least, a partial resumption of the ties with the past. In Slovakia, where things eased up more than in Bohemia and Moravia, Bakoš was able to reprint his book on Slovak verse with a preface which deplored its suppression during the "Cult of Personality" and characterized these years as "years of general paralysis and stagnation of thinking in scholarship."[26] Jiří Levý (1926–67) studied the problems of translation from a structuralist point of view and developed methods of statistical studies in metrics which went beyond those originally used by the Russians and Mukařovský, drawing on probability calculus and on the new information theory and its techniques.[27] In a symposium for Mukařovský's 75th birthday he compared Czech structur-

26. *Vývin slovenského verša* (3rd ed. Bratislava, 1966), p. 17.

27. *České theorie překladu (Czech Theories of Translating,* 1957); *Umění překladu (The Art of Translating,* 1963). See also "On the Relations of Language and Stanza Pattern in the English Sonnet," in *Worte und Werte. Bruno Markwardt zum 60. Geburtstag,* ed. Gustav Erdmann and Alfons Eichstaedt (Berlin, 1961), pp. 214–31; "The Synthesis of Antitheses in the Poetry of T. S. Eliot," in *Essays in Criticism, 2* (1952), 434–44; "Die Theorie des Verses—ihre mathematischen Aspekte," in *Mathematik und Dichtung.* ed. Rul Gunzenhäuser and Helmut Kreuzer (Munich, 1965), pp. 211–32.

alism with Western developments, particularly with the theories of I. A. Richards.[28] He also edited a volume of translated papers, *Western Literary Scholarship and Aesthetics (Západní literární věda a estetika,* 1966), for which he wrote a well-informed introduction. Though it ends with a wholesale condemnation of the intuitionist and mythological features of Western scholarship as comparable to alchemy and astrology, Levý was acutely aware of the different trends and the great diversity of approaches in the different countries of the Western world.[29]

Another of Mukařovský's pupils, Lubomír Doležel (born in 1922), is also mainly concerned with the application of quantitative methods to literary analysis. He started out with structuralist work on Czech modern prose and the technique of the novel, paying attention to "point of view," "interior monologue," and other traits hitherto ignored by the Czechs.[30] But recently he has advocated and practiced an application of statistics to stylistics, using the terminology of information theory with its "messages," "codes," and "entropy." The detailed results, proving that sentences in a spoken drama tend to be shorter than sentences in narrative prose, while in the lyric sentence length fluctuates with individual authors, seem to me still unimpressive and hardly worth the effort which the enormous apparatus must have cost.[31] Doležel accepts the dogma of the new social sciences

28. "Československý strukturalismus a zahraniční kontext," in *Struktura a smysl literárního díla (The Structure and Meaning of the Literary Work,* Prague, 1966), pp. 58–69.

29. Prague, 1966, p. 47. The book contains three excerpts from my writings, the first translations into Czech.

30. *O stylu moderní české prózy* (Prague, 1960).

31. "Zur statistischen Theorie der Dichtersprache," in *Mathematik und Dichtung,* pp. 275–94; see esp. p. 287.

that nothing is true until it has been proved by quantitative means. Still, something important may eventually come out of these statistical studies.

These new developments in the direction of mathematical procedures lead away from a humane and humanistic conception of literary study. This has been always the danger of the doctrines of the Prague Circle. Today in Czechoslovakia literary study is divided between such technical research into form, metrics, and style, and ideological debates and historical investigations within a Marxist framework. There is little literary criticism in the sense known to the West and which once also had a fine tradition among the Czechs. F. X. Šalda (1857–1937) was such a critic: sensitive in appreciation and passionate in judgment. Still, Mukařovský in his best writings kept an admirable balance between close observation and bold speculation and propounded a literary theory which illuminates the structure of the work of art, its relation to the universe of symbols, and the history of literature both as literature and social fact.

## Bibliographical Note

I quote from the three collections of Mukařovský's writings as follows:

> *Kapitoly z české poetiky,* 3 vols. Prague, 1948.
> *Z českej literatury,* Bratislava, 1961.
> *Studie z estetiky,* Prague, 1966.

On Mukařovský, in addition to the Introduction and the Epilogue to *Studie z estetiky* by Felix Vodička and Květoslav Chvatík, see:
> *Janu Mukařovskému k šedesátce,* Prague, 1952; and
> *Struktura a smysl literárního díla,* ed. Milan Jankovič, Zdeněk Pešat, and Felix Vodička *(Janu Mukařovskému k 75. narozeninám),* Prague, 1966.

Volume *3* of *KP* contains a bibliography of his work. For some addenda, see *Janu Mukařovskému k šedesátce.*

## Papers by Mukařovský Available in French, German, and English

"Rapport de la ligne phonique avec l'ordre des mots dans les vers tchèques," *Travaux du Cercle Linguistique de Prague, 1* (1929), 121–39.

"La Phonologie et la poétique," *Travaux du Cercle Linguistique de Prague, 4* (1931), 278–88.

"Intonation comme facteur du rythme poétique," *Archives néerlandaises de phonétique expérimentale,* 8–9 (1933), 153–65.

*Estetická funkce, norma a hodnota jako sociální fakty (Fonction, Norme et Valeur esthétiques comme faits sociaux)* Prague, 1936. (French résumé, pp. 77–86).

"K. H. Máchas Werk als Torso und Geheimnis," *Slavische Rundschau, 8* (1936), 213–20.

"L'Art comme fait sémiologique," in *Actes du huitième Congrès international de philosophie à Prague 2–7 septembre 1934* (Prague, 1936), pp. 1065–73.

"F. X. Šalda," *Prager Rundschau, 7* (1937), 198–233.

"L'Individu dans l'art," in *Deuxième Congrès international d'Esthétique et de la science de l'art, 1* (Paris, 1937), 349–54.

"La Norme esthétique," in *Travaux du IXe Congrès international de philosophie, 12,* 3e partie (Paris, 1937), 72–79.

"Dénomination poétique et la fonction esthétique de la langue," in *Actes du IVe Congrès international des linguistes* (Copenhague, 1938), pp. 98–104. English translation in *Review 45, 2* (Winter 1945).

"La Valeur esthétique dans l'art peut-elle être universelle?" in *Actualités scientifiques et industrielles,* No. 851, Publications de l'Institut international de collaboration philosophique III. Les Conceptions modernes de la raison. III. Raison et valeurs (Paris, 1939), pp. 17–29.

"La Langue poétique," in *Rapports du Vme Congrès international des linguistes* (Bruxelles, 28 août-2 septembre 1939; Bruges, 1939), pp. 94–102.

"Karel Čapek. Ein Exotiker aus dem Geiste der tschechischen Sprache," *Slavische Rundschau, 11* (1939), 3–6.

"Standard Language and Poetic Language," "The Esthetics of Language," "The Connection between the Prosodic Line and Word Order in Czech Verse" (English version of No. 1), and "K. Čapek's Prose as Lyrical Melody and as Dialogue," all four in *A Prague School Reader in Esthetics, Literary Structure and Style,* selected and translated by Paul L. Garvin, Washington, 1955.

"Der Strukturalismus in der Ästhetik und in der Literaturwissenschaft," "Das dichterische Werk als Gesamtheit von Werten," "Die poetische Benennung und die ästhetische Funktion der Sprache," "Die Entwicklung von K. Čapeks Prosa," "Zwei Studien über den Dialog," all in *Kapitel aus der Poetik,* translated into German by Walter Schamschula, Frankfurt am Main, 1967.

# A Sketch of the
# History of Dostoevsky Criticism

The effect of a writer on his readers can be analyzed into aspects which are, though interlocking, nevertheless distinguishable: the reputation he acquires (which may assume the proportions of a legend or myth with little relation to reality), the criticism that attempts to define his characteristic traits and debates their significance and value, the actual influence he exerts on other writers, and—finally—the patient scholarship that tries to illuminate objectively his work and his life.

Dostoevsky's reputation—and one main trend of criticism —was established more than a hundred years ago, when Vissarion Belinsky (1811–48), still revered as the greatest Russian critic, welcomed his first novel, *Poor People* (1846), with excited praise: "Honor and glory to the young poet whose Muse loves people in garrets and basements and tells the inhabitants of gilded palaces: 'look, they are also men, they are also your brethren.'" But Dostoevsky's second novel, *The Double* (published only two weeks after his first), sorely disappointed Belinsky. It was fantastic, he complained, and the fantastic "can have its place only in lunatic asylums, not in literature. It is the business of doctors and not of poets." These sentences set the tone of much Russian criticism even to the present day: Dostoevsky is either the compassionate friend of the insulted and injured or the dreamer of weird dreams, the dissector of sick souls.

Dostoevsky's early reputation faded with his ten-year banishment to Siberia (1849–59). It recovered only slowly because he had developed a political point of view similar to that of the Slavophiles and seemed to have deserted the radicals with whom he was supposed to sympathize. In the 1860s Dostoevsky was still treated by the "radical" critics with sympathy and respect, though he now attacked their narrowly utilitarian and political view of literature. Nikolay Dobrolyubov (1836–61) reviewed *The Insulted and the Injured* (1861) very much in the spirit of Belinsky. He welcomed the novel's social pathos and compassion for the downtrodden, but could not bring himself to consider the book a work of art. Dimitri Pisarev (1840–68), the most violent of the "radical" critics, realized that *Crime and Punishment* (1866) was an attack on the revolutionaries. While praising the author's humanity and artistic power, he tried to fend off the implications of Dostoevsky's antinihilistic message by blandly arguing that Raskolnikov's theories had nothing in common with those of the revolutionary youth and that "the root of Raskolnikov's illness was not in the brain but in the pocket."

But after Dostoevsky's return from Germany in 1871, with the publication of *The Possessed* (1871), with his journalistic activity, and finally with *The Brothers Karamazov* (1880), no doubt could be left that he had become the spokesman of conservative religious and political forces. After his speech on Pushkin (June 8, 1880) Dostoevsky, according to his own account, was hailed as a saint and prophet. (" 'Prophet! Prophet!' shouted the crowd.") Soon after Dostoevsky's death his young friend Vladimir Solovëv (1853–1900) delivered three speeches (1883) in which he interpreted Dostoevsky as a "prophet of God," a "mystical seer." In 1890 V. V. Rozanov (1856–1919)—the critic who had married Dostoevsky's friend Apollinaria Suslova—examined

*The Grand Inquisitor* for the first time almost as a religious text and interpreted its bearing on a philosophy of history. The radical intelligentsia, however, necessarily turned against him. The famous "populist" Nikolay Mikhailovsky (1842–1904) found the formula: Dostoevsky is "A Cruel Talent" (the title of his article, 1882), a sadist who enjoys suffering, a defender of the order of things which creates torturers and tortured. Dostoevsky, he declared, is most successful in describing the "sensations of a wolf devouring a sheep and of a sheep being devoured by a wolf." His picture of Russia and the Russian revolutionaries is totally false: he missed "the most interesting and most typical features of our time." Thus two widely divergent interpretations of Dostoevsky had developed in Russia before 1900.

Abroad, Dostoevsky's reputation spread only slowly. He was discussed in Germany relatively early (e.g. by Victor Hehn in 1864), but the decisive breakthrough was made by a French aristocrat and diplomat, Count Melchior de Vogüé (1848–1910), who devoted a chapter to Dostoevsky in his book *Le Roman russe* (1886). De Vogüé offered the Russian novelists as an antidote against the French naturalists, praising Turgenev and Tolstoy in particular. He contrasted the Russians' ethical pathos and Christian charity with the deterministic pessimism of a Zola. But he treated Dostoevsky with an oddly distant, almost puzzled air. "Voici venir le Scythe, le vrai Scythe," are the first words of the chapter, and phrases such as "the Jeremiah of the jail," "the Shakespeare of the lunatic asylum" set the tone of startled apprehension at Dostoevsky's outlandish "religion of suffering." De Vogüé spoke perceptively of *Crime and Punishment,* but all the later novels seemed to him "monstrous" and "unreadable." So strongly did they offend his sense of French form and style that he even doubted they should be called *romans:* he wanted a new word, such as "roussan." Almost simultaneously there appeared an essay (1885; reprinted in *Ecrivains francisés,* 1889) by the brilliant young critic, Emile Hennequin (1859–88), which also concentrated on Dostoevsky's rejection of reason, his exaltation of madness, idiocy, and imbecility, and totally ignored his ultimate outlook. The versatile and influential Danish critic Georg Brandes (1842–1927), whose *Impressions of Russia* (1889) appeared simultaneously in English translation in New York, went no further: Dostoevsky preaches the "morality of the pariah, the morality of the slave."

It was pure chance that the lonely German philosopher Friedrich Nietzsche (1844–1900) discovered Dostoevsky. In February 1887 Nietzsche picked up a French translation of *Notes from the Underground* and immediately recognized a kindred mind: "the only psychologist from whom he had anything to learn" about the psychology of the criminal, the slave mentality, and the nature of resentment. Nietzsche went on to read *The Insulted and the Injured* and *Crime and Punishment,* which had been a success in Germany since its translation in 1882. But Nietzsche was soon to lose his reason: his discovery of Dostoevsky had come too late to make any discernible impression on his thinking. In any case, he saw Dostoevsky only as another decadent and could not perceive the real nature of his religious and philosophical position.

The pattern of Dostoevsky criticism established in the nineteenth century continued, substantially unchanged, into the twentieth. In Russia the main ideological division became even more accentuated. Around the turn of the century the leading Russian symbolist, Dmitri Merezhkovsky (1865–1941), began to elaborate his series of comparisons between *Tolstoy and Dostoevsky* (1901)—Tolstoy, the pagan, "the seer of the flesh," and Dostoevsky, the Christian, "the seer of the spirit." Merezhkovsky argued against the "radical" critics that Dostoevsky is not a realist but a symbolist. Dostoevsky does not describe a social situation but presents tragedies of ideas: he is a prophet of a new religion embodied in works of art. But the image is schematized and conventionalized: the antitheses are drawn too sharply, the features of Dostoevsky assume a decadent and Nietzschean tinge. Nevertheless, Merezhkovsky was the first to realize Dostoevsky's full historical and artistic importance—the first to free him from the simple political judgment of the radical critics and the literal-mindedness of his immediate disciples. Merezhkovsky's book, soon translated into the principal European languages, profoundly influenced all later criticism. His interpretation was supported, but also modified, by Leo Shestov's frequent comments. Leo Shestov (actually Schwarzmann, 1866–1938) made an early confrontation between *Dostoevsky and Nietzsche* (1903), and his later writings proclaimed a radical irrationalism which sought support in *Notes from the Underground*. Shestov's interpretation anticipates that of existentialism: Dostoevsky's utopianism and optimism is ignored in favor of his apocalyptic vision of catastrophe and decay. Both writers exalted Dostoevsky as the representative of a new defiantly antirationalist, antiscientific religion.

The other side, understandably, saw Dostoevsky as an enemy. In 1905 Maxim Gorky (1868–1936) attacked Dostoevsky as "Russia's evil genius," a reactionary and apologist of passive surrender to oppression. After the October Revolution Dostoevsky was dethroned from his position as a rival of Tolstoy and was discussed by Marxist critics with great reservations. During the years of Stalinist orthodoxy Dostoevsky was almost forbidden fare. A comfortable distinction was established which is still used in Soviet Russia: there was the "good," progressive, humanitarian Dostoevsky (up to and including *Crime and Punishment*), and there was the "bad," reactionary, religious Dostoevsky of the later years. The early works were reprinted in cheap editions for mass consumption, while *The Possessed* and *The Brothers Karamazov* were available only in sets or small editions. Soviet writers today can sympathize with Dostoevsky as a critic of Tsarist Russia and a prophet of the Revolution, but they ignore or condemn him for his later political views and dismiss his religion and philosophy as "mysticism" and "irrationalism." They can admire him as a realistic reporter on Russian life and as a creator of social types, but they disparage or ignore his symbolism and his constant deviations from the conventions of nineteenth-century realism. Even so sophisticated a Marxist as the Hungarian György Lukács (born 1885) can, in his essay on Dostoevsky (1943), utilize a simple dichotomy between Dostoevsky's instinctive sympathies and his overt ideology and ignore vast stretches of his work that not only carry his deepest emotional and intellectual commitments but also succeed most triumphantly as art.

In spite of this official attitude, historical scholarship in Soviet Russia has contributed a great deal toward the understanding of Dostoevsky. "Stavrogin's Confession," the suppressed chapter of *The Possessed,* was discovered and published (1922); Dostoevsky's letters were collected and edited by A. A. Dolinin (in spite of all delays put in his way); the writer's notebooks were unearthed and analyzed—even though some of the comment could be published only in Germany. Much was done to shed light on Dostoevsky's involvement in the Petrashevsky conspiracy and his position among his contemporaries and predecessors. Leonid Grossman (born 1888) may be singled out as probably the most eminent of the Russian specialists on Dostoevsky.

The results, though highly valuable, often entail a kind of

immunization, a cold storage of Dostoevsky's meaning. Much in Russian scholarship asks us to accept the view that Dostoevsky belonged only to a specific historical situation, that he represented certain class interests of the time, and that his challenge can today be safely ignored. This also seems to be the view of the few Soviet scholars who, in the wake of the Formalist movement, studied Dostoevsky's techniques and stylistic devices. M. M. Bakhtin, in his ingenious *Problems of Dostoevsky's Poetics* (1929), argued that Dostoevsky developed a special kind of "polyphonic" novel—a novel of many voices, none of which can be identified with the author's own. He comes to the patently false conclusion that "all definitions and all points of view are made part of dialogue. There is no final word in the world of Dostoevsky."

Although the theories of "socialist realism" are obviously not receptive to Dostoevsky's art, almost all twentieth-century Russian literature reflects his influence. Not only the decadents and symbolists, such as Bryusov, but also some prominent Soviet authors, such as Leonid Leonov, show the imprint of Dostoevsky's mind and art.

In recent years Dostoevsky has been reprinted more widely and Soviet scholars have discussed even the later books and the hostile ideology with greater comprehension. A more deliberate attempt is being made to reinstate Dostoevsky among the canon of Russian classics, to assimilate him into the general tradition of realism and social humanitarianism. It can succeed only partially and at the expense of the most original and seminal of Dostoevsky's characteristics, his psychology, his antinihilism, his religion, and his symbolism.

While social, historical, and formal questions were being debated in Soviet Russia, the Russian emigrants adopted Dostoevsky as a prophet of the apocalypse and a philosopher of orthodox religion. Nikolay Berdyaev (1874–1949) and Vyacheslav Ivanov (1866–1949) exalted Dostoevsky to dizzying heights. In *The World View of Dostoevsky* (Prague, 1923) Berdyaev concludes: "So great is the worth of Dostoevsky that to have produced him is by itself sufficient justification for the existence of the Russian people in the world: and he will bear witness for his countrymen at the last judgment of the nations." Berdyaev has an unquestionably profound grasp of the theological and philosophical implications of Dostoevsky's views and is by no means uncritical of some of his teachings: he does not, for example, consider him "a master of spiritual discipline" but, rather, tries to make the concept of freedom, the choice between good and evil, the center of Dostoevsky's thought—as it is of his own thinking. Whereas Berdyaev almost ignores Dostoevsky the novelist, Ivanov— himself an eminent symbolist poet—interprets the novels in his essays (collected in English as *Freedom and the Tragic Life,* 1952) as a new genre: "the novel-tragedy," and tries to define its peculiar norms. Actually, Ivanov's emphasis falls on the myths in Dostoevsky's writings: he sees the novels as vast allegories prophesying the new reign of saints.

While these two great men often forced Dostoevsky's meaning to fit their own purposes, more detached Russian émigré scholars studied his thought and art very closely. The fine scattered work of Dmitri Chizhevsky (born 1894) has thrown much light on the psychology and ethics of Dostoevsky as well as on the relations of the novelist with the history of thought and literature. The essay, "The Theme of the Double" (1929), happily combines an insight into philosophical problems with a knowledge of historical relationships. The same scholarly spirit pervades the work of V. V. Zenkovsky (born 1881), whose ample *History of Russian Philosophy* (1948) compares Dostoevsky's thought with that of his predecessors and contemporaries. Konstantin Mochulsky's *Dostoevsky*

(1946) also keeps close to the actual texts. This long book is enlightened by a warm sympathy for symbolism and orthodox religion and concludes by associating Dostoevsky with the great Christian writers of world literature—Dante, Cervantes, Milton, and Pascal. Mochulsky meticulously interprets figures, scenes, and meanings actually present in the novels. L. A. Zander's *Dostoevsky* (1942), on the other hand, presses Dostoevsky's metaphors and symbols too hard into the mold of myths. Dostoevsky ceases to be a novelist or even a publicist: he becomes the propounder of an elusive wisdom about the good earth and the heavenly bridegroom, a mystic in the Russian Orthodox tradition.

Thus the opposed interpretations of Dostoevsky in Russian criticism remain divided by an insuperable gulf. The compassionate painter of Petersburg misery confronts the product of "the paradise around the corner." The Marxists wrongly dismiss Dostoevsky's central preoccupations, but the émigré writers—who correctly perceive the religious and mystical inspiration of Dostoevsky's work—also misunderstand its nature if they extract a message from it, a system of doctrines and precepts.

There were many religious philosophers and political prophets in nineteenth-century Russia who are almost totally unknown today in the West, though they eloquently expressed many of the ideas which Dostoevsky embraced. But they wrote treatises and dissertations, not novels. Dostoevsky's ideas come alive in his characters: the Christian humility of Prince Myshkin and Alyosha Karamazov, the Satanic pride of Raskolnikov and Ivan Karamazov, the dialectical atheism of Kirilov, or the messianic Slavophilism of Shatov. In Dostoevsky at his best, ideas incandesce, concepts become images, symbols, or even myths. Had Dostoevsky merely presented a picture of Russian slum-life in the nineteenth century or propounded a peculiar version of mystical speculation and conservative politics, he would not be read all over the world today.

In the West, where Dostoevsky is not a political issue, the divergence of interpretations is less marked. It is possible to avoid the fierce commitments of the Russians, to speak of Dostoevsky dispassionately, to make compromises, to combine approaches, to suggest shadings of meaning. Much of the Western criticism has been handicapped, however, by its ignorance of Russian scholarship on Dostoevsky and, even worse, by vague conceptions of the Slavic world and of Russian intellectual and social history. To cite a flagrant example, Thomas Mann's essay "Dostoevsky—in Moderation" (1945) alludes in awe-struck terms to "Stavrogin's Confession" as "unpublished," though it had been available in English since 1923 and in German since 1926. Mann confuses the chronology of Dostoevsky's stories and mistakenly disparages a late short novel, *The Eternal Husband* (1870), as early and "immature." Even more damage has been done by loose generalizations about the "Slavic soul," which Dostoevsky is supposed to represent, and by the determined blindness of many Western writers who insist on seeing Dostoevsky as completely outside the Western tradition—as chaotic, obscure, and even "Asiatic" or "Oriental." Without denying his allegiance to the Eastern Church or his attachment to a nationalist ideology, and without minimizing his powerful originality, one cannot ignore his literary association with the traditions of the European novel: particularly that of Balzac, Dickens, Hugo, and E. T. A. Hoffmann. Nor can his ideology be detached from the Western tradition of Christian and nationalist thought. His tremendous stress on the substantial unity of mankind is a version of Franciscan Christianity that conceives of man and nature—and even animals and birds—

as ultimately united in love and universal forgiveness. The "saint's life" of the Elder Zosima, which Dostoevsky considered his final and telling answer to the blasphemous "revolt" of Ivan Karamazov, descends directly from an eighteenth-century Russian writer, Tikhon Zadonsky, who in turn was saturated with the sentiments and ideas of German pietism. There appear in Dostoevsky versions of Romantic historicism and folk worship that came to Russia with the great vogue of Schelling and Hegel in the generation immediately preceding Dostoevsky's. Even Dostoevsky's depth psychology, with its interest in the life of dreams and the splitting of personality, is heavily indebted to the theories of romantic writers and doctors such as Reil and Carus. Dostoevsky's conscious attitudes toward Europe were often ambivalent; but as an artist and thinker he is part of the stream of Western thought and Western literary traditions.

Still, there have been divergences in Dostoevsky criticism in the main Western countries. In France the early interest was in Dostoevsky's psychology. Only in the changed atmosphere of the twentieth century, when Romain Rolland, Paul Claudel, Charles Péguy, and André Gide rediscovered the life of the spirit, could Dostoevsky become a master. In 1908 Gide (1869–1951) saw that Dostoevsky had taken the place of Ibsen, Nietzsche, and Tolstoy: "But one must say that a Frenchman feels uncomfortable at the first contact with Dostoevsky—he seems to him too Russian, too illogical, too irrational, too irresponsible." Gide himself overcame this discomfort. His own *Dostoevsky* (1923) emphasizes Dostoevsky's psychology, ambiguity, and indeterminism, and seeks support for Gide's own central concern with human freedom, with the *acte gratuit*. Jacques Rivière (1886–1925), the editor of *La Nouvelle Revue française*, voiced his suspicion of Dostoevsky's mysteries in a brief essay (1923): "In

psychology the true depths are those that are explored."
Marcel Proust protested that Dostoevsky's "genius—contrary
to what Rivière says—was for construction"; but in the well-
known passage of *La Prisonnière* Proust confesses that Dostoevsky's "preoccupation with murder is something extraor-
dinary which makes him very alien to me." Surprisingly,
there is little French criticism on Dostoevsky: the early book
by André Suarez (1913) can be dismissed as a flamboyant
rhapsody on Dostoevsky as a mystical sensualist and sufferer.
The attacks on Dostoevsky by Denis Saurat and Henri Massis
must be seen in the context of the "defense of the West"
against the forces of Eastern chaos, anarchy, and irrationalism which Dostoevsky was supposed to represent.

In French existentialism Dostoevsky appears as a forerunner and crown witness. "Every one of us is responsible for
everyone else, in every way, and I most of all": the teaching
of brother Markel, who asked even the birds for forgiveness,
is almost a slogan for these writers. Sartre's *Huis clos* is a
counterpart of Dostoevsky's "Bobok." In Camus' *Myth of
Sisyphus* (1942) Kirilov's dialectic is used to support the thesis
of the absurdity of creation, and in *L'Homme revolté* (1952)
Ivan Karamazov becomes the proponent of metaphysical re-
bellion. Dostoevsky's influence on such diverse writers as
Charles-Louis Philippe, Malraux, Mauriac, Sartre, and
Camus is incalculable. It has hardly begun to be studied. But,
in general, most French writers seem to misunderstand Dostoevsky's final position. The existentialists see only the
"underground" man in Dostoevsky and ignore the theist, the
optimist, and even the utopian who looked forward to a
golden age—a paradise on earth—while disparaging the
socialist dreams of a collective utopia as a monstrous "ant-
hill" or Tower of Babel.

The Germans have produced by far the largest body of

Dostoevsky interpretation and scholarship outside Russia. Karl Nötzel wrote a fully documented *Life* of Dostoevsky (1925), and there are any number of German studies of Dostoevsky's thought. The most conscientious is Reinhard Lauth's *Die Philosophie Dostojewskis* (1950), which thoroughly analyzes Dostoevsky's psychology, ethics, aesthetics, and metaphysics, and treats all his sayings as if they formed a coherent exposition of a consistent system. The basic assumption seems mistaken, but the book is the best and most objective result of a long debate among theologians and philosophers. Eduard Thurneysen was the first (1921) to interpret Dostoevsky with the concepts of the "theology of crisis" deriving from Karl Barth, the Calvinist theologian. But Paul Natorp, a prominent member of the neo-Kantian movement, described Dostoevsky (1923) as a pantheist: "He accepts the world unreservedly: he loves the immediacy of each lived moment. Everything lives, only life exists." Hans Prager, in the well-known *Dostoevsky's World-View* (1925), saw him chiefly as a philosopher of nationalism: God is to Dostoevsky only "the synthetic personality of a nation." Romano Guardini, a German Jesuit scholar of Italian origin, meditated eloquently and sensitively on Dostoevsky's religious characters (1951), deeply worried by his hostility to the Roman Catholic Church. A Lithuanian, Antanas Maceina, gave a careful reading of the *The Grand Inquisitor* (1952) as a scheme of a philosophy of history. Hans Urs von Balthasar, in the second volume of *Apokalypse der deutschen Seele* (1939), discusses Dostoevsky's theology with a profound insight into his extremism, his faith in the *salto mortale:* "Dostoevsky, granting almost everything to the enemy [atheism] in order to defeat him with the ultimate weapon, bets everything on one last card, religion." In rejecting the socialist dream because of his knowledge of man's depravity, Dostoevsky embraces instead the religious dream, which finally fuses with the atheistic dream of a golden age. Urs von Balthasar also understands Dostoevsky's view of a community of guilt. There is no lonely guilt; each man shares in all guilt; and hence the Church is necessary as the redemption from guilt in the incarnation of Christ. No doubt these discussions often attempt to use Dostoevsky as a support for personal convictions, but they contain an insight into the theological and philosophical problems and display a knowledge of Russian intellectual history that is often lacking in the purely literary or social critics in the West.

From central Europe comes another influential interpretation of Dostoevsky: the psychoanalytical method. Sigmund Freud (1856–1939) devoted an essay to Dostoevsky (1928) that derives his epilepsy (or rather epileptoid hysteria) and his gambling mania from the basic Oedipus complex. Much is made of the trauma Dostoevsky suffered at the murder of his father, and of the central theme (parricide) of *The Brothers Karamazov*. But the evidence for Freud's reduction of Dostoevsky's views—even his political ones—to a desire of submission to the Father seems very tenuous: the chronology of Dostoevsky's epileptic fits is totally obscure and no proof can be adduced that Dostoevsky felt guilty for the killing of his father by peasants while he was away in engineering school. Ivan's famous outcry (not cited by Freud) at the trial—"Who of us does not desire his father's death?"—is rather a recognition of universal guilt. Parricide is for Dostoevsky the highest symptom of social decay, a disruption of human ties that contradicts the obligation to universal forgiveness and the promise of resurrection in the flesh with which *The Brothers Karamazov* concludes. The Freudian view elaborated by later writers has favored the reduction of Dostoevsky's novels to autobiographical documents and has emphasized the morbid and even the pathological and criminal themes in Dostoevsky.

Dostoevsky's effect on creative German literature was hardly less than his effect on the French. Rilke's *Malte Laurids Brigge* (1912) is imbued with Dostoevsky. The German expressionist poets welcomed him enthusiastically as a prophet of universal brotherhood. In a curious painting of the expressionist group Max Ernst portrayed himself as sitting on the lap of Dostoevsky. After the First World War Dostoevsky became extremely fashionable: in 1921 alone over 200,000 copies of his novels were sold. But the complete edition of the Piper Verlag in Munich, with introductions by Arthur Möller van den Bruck and other apocalyptic interpreters of the Russian soul, did as much to spread a distorted image of the author as to spread a knowledge of the texts. Kafka certainly learned from Dostoevsky (though he learned more from Gogol and Tolstoy); Jakob Wassermann wrote virtual imitations of Dostoevsky's novels; and something of Dostoevsky's spirit of compassion and universal brotherhood permeates the novels of Franz Werfel. Hermann Hesse (1877–1962) shows the imprint of Dostoevsky in *Steppenwolf* (1927) and elsewhere, though a pamphlet, *Blick ins Chaos* (1920), expresses his fear of Dostoevsky's Slavic murkiness. Thomas Mann expounds the view of Dostoevsky as a combination of criminal-and-saint and asks for "moderation" in one's admiration; but surely Adrian Leverkühn's Devil in *Doktor Faustus* (1947) comes straight and undisguisedly from Ivan Karamazov's shabby visitor.

Dostoevsky was very late in reaching the English-speaking world. *The Brothers Karamazov* was translated by Mrs. Constance Garnett only in 1912, when she began the complete translation of Dostoevsky's novels that is still standard and unsurpassed (in spite of a few errors and a few lapses into

Victorian prudery). *The House of the Dead* had been translated in 1881 (as *Buried Alive*) and *Crime and Punishment*
in 1886. De Vogüé's book was translated in the following
year and seems to have been the source of much early critical
reaction to Dostoevsky in England. R. L. Stevenson expressed enthusiasm (in a letter, 1886) for *Crime and Punishment,* which he had read in French translation—and he remembered some of its details in writing *Markheim* (1885), a
story of the killing of a pawnbroker. In 1882 Oscar Wilde
praised *The Insulted and the Injured* as not inferior to *Crime
and Punishment.* George Moore disparaged Dostoevsky as a
"Gaboriau [an early French crime novelist] with psychological sauce," but oddly enough wrote a laudatory preface to a
translation of *Poor People* (1894). George Gissing noted the
affinity between Dickens and Dostoevsky and was one of the
first to appreciate Dostoevsky's humor. But Henry James
referred to Tolstoy's and Dostoevsky's "baggy monsters" and
"fluid puddings," their "lack of composition, their defiance of
economy and architecture," even while he recognized the
"strong, rank quality" of their genius. Dostoevsky aroused
violent distaste in Joseph Conrad and John Galsworthy.
Conrad called *The Brothers Karamazov* "an impossible lump
of valuable matter. It's terrifically bad and impressive and
exasperating. Moreover, I don't know what D. stands for or
reveals, but I do know that he is too Russian for me. It sounds
like some fierce mouthings of prehistoric ages." Galsworthy,
who could not have shared Conrad's Russophobia, complained about "incoherence and verbiage" and thought Tolstoy and Turgenev far greater. The attitude of academic
critics was similarly hostile. George Saintsbury, in his *History
of Nineteenth Century Literature* (1907), mentions only *Poor
People* and *Crime and Punishment* and finds Dostoevsky
"unattractive and 'such as one could have done without.' " In

the United States William Lyon Phelps, in his *Essays on Russian Novelists* (1911), devoted his chapter on Dostoevsky to lamentations about morbidity and lack of form: he regarded even *Crime and Punishment* as "abominably diffuse, filled with extraneous and superfluous matter, and totally lacking in the principles of good construction." The more serene art of Tolstoy and Turgenev appealed much more strongly to the taste of the time.

Apparently only the experience of the First World War aroused a new appreciation of Dostoevsky, although there were a few murmurs of praise earlier. Maurice Baring's *Landmarks in Russian Literature* (1910) contains the first really perceptive appraisal of Dostoevsky by an Englishman: he sees no absurdity in placing Dostoevsky "equal to Tolstoy and immeasurably above Turgenev," recognizes the relevance of *The Possessed* in the light of the 1905 revolution, and appreciates the religious inspiration of the great novels. Dostoevsky's books are "a cry of triumph, a clarion peal, a hosanna to the idea of goodness and to the glory of God." Arnold Bennett, one of the reviewers of Baring's book, joined in praise for *The Brothers Karamazov,* which he had read in French, as "containing some of the greatest scenes ever encountered in fiction."

But the first full-length English book, Middleton Murry's *Fyodor Dostoevsky* (1916), extravagantly exalted Dostoevsky as the prophet of a new mystical dispensation. According to Murry, Dostoevsky's "Christianity is not Christianity, his realism is not realism, his novels are not novels, his truth is not truth, his art not art. His world is a world of symbols and potentialities which are embodied in unlivable lives." With similar recklessness Murry interprets Svidrigailov as the real hero of *Crime and Punishment* and allegorizes *The Brothers Karamazov*. "It may be there really was no Smerdyakov as there really was no devil, and they both had their abode in Ivan's soul. But then who did the murder? Then of course it may have been Ivan himself, or, on the other hand, there may have been no murder at all." Still, D. S. Mirsky's harsh words about Murry's "Pecksniffian sobstuff" are not justified. Murry is surely right in his principal claim: that Dostoevsky's belief in the regeneration of mankind presupposes a miracle. In his opinion, however awkwardly labored, Dostoevsky "contemplated and sought to penetrate into a new consciousness and new mode of being which he said was metaphysically inevitable for mankind." Murry proudly felt that "the objective 'pattern' of Dostoevsky had declared itself, through me as instrument," though we should recognize the influence of both Merezhkovsky and Shestov. Murry's conception of Dostoevsky as the "archhierophant of intellectual self-consciousness" explains the violence with which D. H. Lawrence, who then lived in close association with Murry, reacted to the worship of Dostoevsky. "I don't like Dostoevsky. He is like the rat, slithering along in hate, in the shadows, and in order to belong to the light, professing love, all love." Lawrence thinks that Dostoevsky, "mixing God and Sadism," is "foul." In two letters to Murry his dislike becomes shrill vituperation of what he considers Dostoevsky's mania to be "infinite, to be God." "The whole point of Dostoevsky lies in the fact of his fixed will that the individual ego, the achieved I, the conscious I, shall be infinite, God-like, and absolved from all relation." The novels seem to Lawrence great parables, but false art. "They are only parables. All the people are fallen angels—even the dirtiest scrubs. This I cannot stomach. People are not fallen angels, they are merely people." When Lawrence received Murry's book, he indulged in a paroxysm of disgust. Dostoevsky "can nicely stick his head between the feet of Christ, and waggle his behind in the air." But when Lawrence had managed to depict Murry and Katherine Mansfield as Gerald Crich and Gudrun in *Women in Love* and to find an antidote to Dostoevsky in the Russian philosopher Rozanov and the novels of Verga, his view of Dostoevsky became more detached and tolerant. The introduction he wrote to a translation of *The Grand Inquisitor* in the year of his death (1930) shows a fine understanding of the argument and its implication, though Lawrence misreads the end when he speaks of Jesus "giving the kiss of acquiescence to the Inquisitor." Surely Jesus Christ does not accept the arguments of the Grand Inquisitor: he answers them in the only way religion can answer atheism —by silence and forgiveness. The Inquisitor is refuted by the silent kiss. Alyosha immediately afterward kisses Ivan, as Christ did the Inquisitor, forgiving him for his atheism, answering his "revolt" by Christian mercy. Ivan knows this when he says: "That's plagiarism. You stole it from my poem."

The Murry–Lawrence dialogue is symptomatic of the tremendous emotional reaction to Dostoevsky in England during and shortly after the First World War. A Dostoevsky cult existed for a few years, and certainly many English novelists show that they have read him and have tried to evoke his mood or draw Dostoevskian characters. The novels of Russia by Hugh Walpole (1884–1941)—*The Dark Forest* (1916) and its sequel, *The Secret City* (1919)—may serve as examples. A figure such as Spandrell in Aldous Huxley's *Point Counter Point* (1928) is inconceivable without Stavrogin and Svidrigailov. But English critical literature on Dostoevsky rather reflects a reaction against the apocalyptic interpretation of Murry and the Russians (Berdyaev and Ivanov) who were then translated into English. E. H. Carr's biography (1931) may be characterized as excessively sober and detached; and D. S. Mirsky's widely read *History of*

*Russian Literature* (1927) treats Dostoevsky very coolly as "an absorbingly interesting novelist of adventure," and accepts, on the whole, Shestov's emphasis on his nihilism. Mirsky was a Russian prince temporarily settled in England, who imported the attitudes of the Russian Formalists: their distrust of all ideology, their emphasis on formal virtues, their love of Pushkin, Lermontov, and Tolstoy. The deft little psychological study of *Dostoevsky and His Creation* (1920) by Janko Lavrin, or the pedestrian survey of *Characters of Dostoevsky* (1950) by Richard Curle, cannot be accused of extravagance. The fine essay by Derek Traversi (1937) may seem even oversevere in criticizing Dostoevsky's mysticism as "baseless and false" and in drawing such sharply critical consequences for Dostoevsky's art from his dualism between spirit and flesh, God and the world. Mr. Traversi sees only the anti-Catholic polemics and ignores Dostoevsky's paradoxical defense of the Orthodox Church. Recently the continental concern with Dostoevsky's theology and what may be called the existential concept of man have begun to appear in English criticism, too. Martin Jarrett-Kerr has expounded Dostoevsky's agony of belief in *Studies in Literature and Belief* (1954); Colin Wilson, in *The Outsider* (1956), used Dostoevsky's heroes as examples of the quest for identity and perceptively linked him with Blake. D. S. Savage brilliantly discussed *The Gambler* (in *The Sewanee Review,* 1950) though oddly enough ignoring the striking figure of the gambling grandmother; and Michael H. Futrell studied the relation between "Dostoevsky and Dickens" (in *The English Miscellany,* ed. Mario Praz, 7 [1956]) with meticulous care and common sense. But, on the whole, Dostoevsky criticism in England has definitely quieted down since the hectic excitement of Middleton Murry's days.

The situation in the United States is somewhat different:

because the impact of Dostoevsky came much later, its greatest effect seems to coincide with the Second World War rather than the First. Dostoevsky's influence on American writers has hardly begun to be explored, partly because it is difficult to isolate it from that of many intermediaries. Dreiser's *American Tragedy* (1925), for example, revolves around the same moral problem of the guilty, guiltless murderer as does *The Brothers Karamazov*. There are echoes of *Crime and Punishment* in Faulkner's *Sanctuary,* and the atmosphere of many of Faulkner's novels may strike us as Dostoevskian. Faulkner himself has acknowledged Dostoevsky's influence. In 1941 Carson McCullers drew the parallel to Southern literature in very general terms: "In this approach to life and suffering the Southerners are indebted to the Russians. The technique is briefly this: a bold and outwardly callous juxtaposition of the tragic and the humorous, the immense with the trivial, the sacred with the bawdy, the whole soul of man with a materialistic detail."

American criticism of Dostoevsky was hardly existent, however, before the Second World War. James Huneker's essay (in *Ivory Apes and Peacocks,* 1915) still echoes De Vogüé and still considers Dostoevsky "infinitely inferior to Turgenev." There was a good biography by Avrahm Yarmolinsky (1934), which was preceded by a study of Dostoevsky's ideology (a Columbia dissertation, 1921). Yarmolinsky tells his story with sympathy, shunning both the raised-eyebrow manner of Carr and the strained hagiographical tone adopted by many Russians and Germans. With E. J. Simmons' *Dostoevsky, The Making of a Novelist* (1940), Americans received a reliable digest of Russian and German scholarship and a clear account of Dostoevsky's career as a novelist rather than a person or philosopher.

Increasingly, American critics have turned to a discussion of Dostoevsky. The three articles by R. P. Blackmur (in *Accent*, 1942; in *Chimera*, 1943; and in *The Hudson Review*, 1948; now collected in *Eleven Essays on the European Novel* [1964], with the addition of three new essays on *The Brothers Karamazov*) are meditations in the style of the later Henry James and progressively lose contact with the texts. George Steiner's *Tolstoy or Dostoevsky: An Essay in the Old Criticism* (1959) brilliantly and sweepingly restates the old contrast between the two writers but spoils its effect by perversely reading *The Grand Inquisitor* as an "allegory of the confrontation between Dostoevsky and Tolstoy." Dostoevsky occurs prominently in many contexts: in Eliseo Vivas' *Creation and Discovery* (1955), in Renato Poggioli's *The Phoenix and the Spider* (1957), in Irving Howe's *Politics and the Novel* (1957), in Murray Krieger's *The Tragic Vision* (1960), and in Albert Cook's *The Meaning of Fiction* (1960). A series of articles by Philip Rahv (in the *Partisan Review*, 1936, 1954, and 1960) are particularly satisfying as they are nourished by a knowledge of the Russian discussions and animated by a central vision. Joseph Frank (in the *Sewanee Review*, 1961) gives a preview of what promises to be a distinguished critical study of Dostoevsky's work.

Since the Second Word War, and with the development of academic studies in Russian literature, Americans have produced an increasing number of papers, articles, and even monographs on specific aspects of Dostoevsky's ideas, techniques, imagery, and use of quotations. Ralph Matlaw's listing of Dostoevsky's recurrent imagery of insects (in *Harvard Slavic Studies, 3* [1957]) and his pamphlet *The Brothers Karamazov: Novelistic Technique* (1957); Robert L. Jackson's *The Underground Man in Russian Literature* (1958), which traces the influence of Dostoevsky's negative hero on subsequent Russian literature, and his *Dostoevsky's Quest for*

*Form: A Study of His Philosophy of Art* (1966); Edward Wasiolek's *Dostoevsky: The Major Fiction* (1964); and the scattered papers of George Gibian—all may be cited as encouraging testimonies to the burgeoning vitality of American Dostoevsky scholarship. Certainly the materials for considered criticism are at hand. Americans are exempt from the dire dilemma of choosing between Marxist and Orthodox interpretations. They can see Dostoevsky for what he primarily is: a novelist, a supreme creator of a world of imagination, an artist with a deep insight into human conduct and the perennial condition of man.

# Stylistics, Poetics, and Criticism

The question of the situation of stylistics among the various disciplines, its exact scope, and its limits has aroused considerable discussion. It seems to me, however, a mere logomachia to argue whether or not stylistics is an "independent" science, a view insisted on, for example, by Helmut Hatzfeld. "Independence" can never be total in such matters: clearly, stylistics studies language and thus must inevitably draw on linguistics, and if we assume that it includes the study of the style of verbal works of art, it is necessarily in contact with poetics or, as I prefer to call it, theory of literature. This term avoids the possibility of being restricted to verse, as is often the case in English, and also any implication of prescriptive poetics. The close relationship of stylistics to linguistics needs no discussion: obviously the student of stylistics cannot get along without a knowledge of grammar in all its branches—phonetics and phonemics, morphology, syntax, lexicology, of course, and hence the study of meaning, semantics.

Stylistics can, for our purposes, be divided into two fairly distinct disciplines: the study of style in all language pronouncements and the study of style in works of imaginative literature. The first is represented by Charles Bally and his followers and aims at an account of all devices serving a specific "expressive" end, securing emphasis or explicitness. It will draw for evidence on all language acts, oral ones or those preserved in print. Bally himself quotes examples also from artistic styles and does not rigidly confine himself to collective usage. This type of study has been carried on since antiquity—since Aristotle, the Greek rhetoricians, and Quintilian—largely in the context of one language and often with prescriptive aims: to define and possibly to recommend or even to enforce "good style," mainly a middle style of exposition aiming at precision and clarity or an oratorical style bent on persuasion and emotional effect.

In more recent times attempts have been made to compare the styles of different languages, to construe something like a "comparative" stylistics, mainly of French, English, and German. Serious scholars such as Eduard Wechssler, Karl Vossler, Max Deutschbein, and even Leo Spitzer have indulged in often loose or arbitrary comparisons and jumped to conclusions on very little evidence. Thus Leo Spitzer considers what he calls "the *fait-accompli* construction in Spanish" "a linguistic reflection of Spanish Utopianism, of the Spanish *plus ultra* will," though in a postscript he himself quotes the same construction found in German.[1] The writings of Benjamin Lee Whorf, who contrasted English with American Indian languages and was able to show that the "structure of a human being's language influences the manner in which he understands reality,"[2] have made a deeper impression on modern linguists, but I do not think we can really speak here of stylistics in any accepted sense when considering the problems raised by Whorf or, with a different philosophical background, by Ernst Cassirer's *Philosophy of Symbolic Forms*. These speculations lead rather to a study of our ways of construing and classifying the world: to a theory of knowledge, to epistemology, to comparative philosophy or *Weltanschauung* which uses linguistic evidence.

1. "Die *fait-accompli* Darstellung im Spanischen," in *Stilstudien, 1* (Munich, 1928), pp. 258–89; quotation, p. 289.

2. *Language, Thought, and Reality*, ed. John B. Carroll (Cambridge, Mass., 1956), p. 23.

Finally, there have been attempts to formulate "general" stylistics: to study the devices presumed to permeate all language pronouncements in whatever language. But I am not convinced that Herbert Seidler's *Allgemeine Stilistik* (1953) is a good beginning. He confines style to the expression of emotion, to the famous German "Gemüt," draws almost exclusively on German examples, and rarely distinguishes clearly between style in any language function and in literary uses. Still, a general stylistics seems a legitimate task, however difficult it may be in practice.

Stylistics in all these senses—as study of a single language or as comparative, and as general stylistics—is, it seems to me, a part of linguistics. I do not see why one should object to this inclusion if one conceives of linguistics generously and widely. Stylistics in these senses laid claims to independence mainly because some schools of linguistics voluntarily abandoned such problems. I remember Leonard Bloomfield bluntly telling me that he had no interest in stylistics or the study of poetic language, and there were theorists who considered the study of style merely a remote possibility.[3] But a vacuum has to be filled; whether we call the study of style in language a special branch of linguistics or an independent discipline, it will attract people who think about language and its uses.

The problem is very different as soon as we narrow our attention to a study of literary style, in the sense of style in imaginative literature, with an aesthetic function, particularly in poetry. We then raise the question of the nature of literature and the nature of aesthetic effect and response. And the study of style then has to come to grips with poetics and the theory of literature. I need not discuss all the various methods of such stylistic analysis. However, some obvious divisions and choices may be mentioned. First there is the

3. E.g. George L. Trager and Henry Lee Smith, *An Outline of English Structure* (Norman, Okla., 1951), pp. 86 ff.

analysis of a single work of art. It may proceed systematically, by elaborating something like a grammar of a work—an exhaustive description of its features working toward aesthetic ends or, more usually, by observing and isolating individual traits which can be contrasted or compared with the traits of nonaesthetic language or may be traced back to the mind of the author to account for their occurrence in genetic terms.

We might refer to such a book as Helmut Hatzfeld's *Don Quixote als Wortkunstwerk* (1927) as an example of a systematic analysis of a single work; we might point to the many recent writers who speak of "ungrammaticalness" or the "counter-grammar" of poetic texts, though I would agree with Edward Stankiewicz that "poetic language need not violate any rules of language and still remain what it is, that is, a highly patterned and organized mode of verbal expression."[4] I can barely allude to Spitzer's early papers, which try to trace stylistic features to the presumed mental dispositions of their authors—sometimes with psychoanalytical assumptions, when he, for instance, investigates the recurrence of such terms as "blood" and "wounds" in the writings of Henri Barbusse, or more often, with an interest in an underlying or implied philosophy, when he shows, that in Charles-Louis Phillipe the recurrent construction *à cause de* points to a personal fatalism.[5]

The analysis of a single work of art easily widens into the analysis of the total work of an author: the traits observable in one work permeate most often all his others. A style such as Thomas Carlyle's or Henry James' can be easily identified

4. "Linguistics and the Study of Poetic Language," in *Style in Language,* ed. Thomas E. Sebeok (Boston, Mass.), p. 70.

5. *Studien zu Henri Barbusse* (Bonn, 1920) and "Pseudoobjektive Motivierung bei Charles-Louis Phillipe," in *Stilstudien, 2,* 166–207.

and described. Franz Dornseiff's *Pindars Stil* (1921), William K. Wimsatt's *Prose Style of Samuel Johnson* (1941), and Viktor Vinogradov's *Stil Pushkina* (1941) are fine examples of a systematic description of the style of a single writer. We can then go beyond the work of a single author and study a group of works, either in a specific genre or a specific period or a historical sequence, in one national language or on an international scale. The combinations and permutations are numerous. Erich Auerbach in his *Mimesis* (1946) analyzes the style of passages selected from Western literature ranging from Homer to Proust in order to use them as a springboard for comments on intellectual and social history, on the changing conceptions of reality and of the human condition. Stephen Ullmann's book on *Style in the French Novel* (1957) combines a selection of examples in historical order with theoretical reflections. Miss Josephine Miles, in many writings, has traced specific devices through the whole history of English poetry.[6] Morris W. Croll, in "The Baroque Style in English Prose" (1929), aims at characterizing a period style in English, while his other papers, "Attic Prose in the Seventeenth Century" and "Attic Prose: Lipsius, Montaigne, Bacon," trace a specific style in three languages.[7] These all seem to be legitimate topics and methods which have succeeded in what must be the aim of such studies: in the characterization of specific works, *œuvres* of a single author, or groups of works or genres or types by an analysis of their verbal style. I cannot see the justice of Louis T. Milic's objections to an attempt by James R. Sutherland to define Restora-

6. E.g. *Eras and Modes in English Poetry* (Berkeley, 1964) and *The Continuity of Poetic Language* (New York, 1965).

7. Now collected in *Style, Rhetoric and Rhythm* (Princeton, 1966).

tion prose.[8] The details of Sutherland's analysis may be wrong, but the enterprise is clearly defensible and even needed, as was the attempt to define and describe the style of Old Germanic poetry undertaken as long ago as 1875 by Richard Heinzel, or the study of German impressionism skillfully performed by Luise Thon.[9]

The claim has insistently been made that such stylistics replaces or rather preempts poetics and literary theory, that stylistics is simply poetics, or even, if we consider stylistics a branch of linguistics, that literary study is a part of linguistics. Roman Jakobson has put the claim forcefully, declaring that "since linguistics is the global science of verbal structure, poetics may be regarded as an integral part of linguistics."[10] Dámaso Alonso, with very different suppositions, declared in *Poesía española* that "Stylistics is the only 'science of literature.' "[11] But this seems to me a mistake. I would be the first to defend the enormous importance of linguistics for the study of literature—for a study of sound patterns, inconceivable without the concept of the phoneme, for the study of rhythm and meter, for the study of vocabulary and syntax, and possibly even for the study of structures exceeding the limits of a sentence, as Samuel R. Levin has tried to demonstrate in his *Linguistic Structures in Poetry* (1962). Still, I fail to see how linguistic procedures can cope with the many features

8. "Against the Typology of Styles," in *Essays on the Language of Literature,* ed. Seymour Chatman and Samuel R. Levin (Boston, 1967), pp. 442–50.

9. *Über den Stil der altgermanischen Poesie* (Strassburg, 1875); *Die Sprache des deutschen Impressionismus* (Munich, 1928).

10. Sebeok, ed., *Style in Language,* p. 350.

11. Madrid, 1950, p. 429. "La Estílistica será la única 'Ciencia de la literatura.' " I am aware that Don Dámaso Alonso uses the term "stylistics" in a very wide sense. See his protest in *The Critical Moment: Essays on the Nature of Literature* (London, 1964), p. 149.

of a literary work which are not dependent on particular verbal formulations.

Let me grant immediately that all our thinking, certainly about literature, is done in language, and that a literary work of art is accessible only through its language. I found Roman Ingarden's phenomenological analysis in *Das literarische Kunstwerk* (1931) very helpful on this point. His concept of stratification allows one to recognize that a literary work of art has a basic sound-stratum out of which the units of meaning arise, while these in turn project a world of objects (not of course identical with objects in the real world) which have a status of their own and can be described independently of the linguistic stratum through which we have access to them. The general history of literature affords ample evidence for this view. Motifs, themes, images, symbols, plots, and compositional schemes, genre patterns, character and hero types, as well as qualities such as the tragic or the comic, the sublime or the grotesque, can be and have been discussed fruitfully with only a minimal or no regard to their linguistic formulations. The mere fact that great poets and writers—Homer, Virgil, Dante, Shakespeare, Goethe, Tolstoy, and Dostoevsky—have exercised an enormous influence often in poor and loose translations which hardly convey even an inkling of the pecularities of their verbal style should demonstrate the comparative independence of literature from language. To condemn research, the staple of literary scholarship, because it pays little or no attention to verbal texture means condemning the majority of serious literary studies. It is simply not true that only impressionistic appreciations or pronouncements of arbitrary opinions or subjective tastes are eliminated. All this seems to me a sufficient argument for the necessity of a poetics on an international scale, but one may strengthen it by adding that some of the problems raised in poetics are problems of general aesthetics (and not merely of literature) which elude a linguistic and stylistic approach. I might refer to pantomime, which can be a part of drama, or to the plot, themes, motifs, and images in the silent film, which is often comprehensible and aesthetically effective without recourse to subtitles. The film may, of course, draw on plots, themes, motifs, and images originally devised in literature. We are aware of the troubles and problems which arise in the filming of novels or dramas, but surely they prove that the devices and techniques of literature can be transferred into a nonlinguistic medium. One may of course, answer that neither pantomime nor film is literature. But the overlapping of such devices and procedures among the arts confirms the view that a literary work of art is not merely a "Wortkunstwerk" or "sprachliches Kunstwerk," to use the title of Wolfgang Kayser's well-known handbook.

One can write a history of narrative forms, as Robert Scholes and Robert Kellogg have done in *The Nature of Narrative* (1966), paying hardly any attention to the language of fiction; one can write a history of such themes or myths as that of Prometheus, as Raymond Trousson has done so impressively;[12] one can trace the image of the earthly paradise through many literatures, as A. Bartlett Giamatti has done recently;[13] or one can discuss the nature of tragedy or comedy without paying particular attention to the style of Sophocles or Shakespeare, Aristophanes or Molière. These seem to me truisms which are now being denied by the propagandists of the laudable cause of stylistics. It seems an oddly restrictive

12. *Le Thème de Prométhée dans la littérature européenne* (2 vols. Geneva, 1964) and his defense *Les Etudes de thèmes: Essai de méthodologie* (Paris, 1965).

13. *The Earthly Paradise and the Renaissance Epic* (Princeton, 1966).

view of literary study to relegate these types to psychology or *Kulturgeschichte*. No doubt some of the questions involved are implicated in these neighboring disciplines. One cannot discuss the nature of tragedy without reference to religion and ritual, or isolate the history of fictional forms from such questions as the status of the teller of the tale or the composition of the audience addressed at a particular historical moment. I have always advocated a sharp focus for literary study on the work itself and have made a possibly oversharp distinction between "extrinsic" and "intrinsic" approaches to literature. Still, there are many genuinely literary problems that go beyond the analysis of style as language. They make up a vast body of knowledge which can be called poetics or literary theory. Such an international, supra-linguistic poetics or literary theory is, one should emphasize, an empirical science, concerned with a historical manifold which does not and cannot yield a system in the sense in which linguistic study leads to the construction of a system. The attempt of Northrop Frye, in his *Anatomy of Criticism* (1957), to devise such a system is *a priori* doomed to fail, however ingeniously contrived his scheme of modes, symbols, genres and myths may be. "A scheme or system which would interpret all literary phenomena as limited internal relations and combinations cannot exist," says Hugo Friedrich convincingly rejecting similar ambitions of the new French structuralism.[14]

I am aware that the term "style" has been used in a sense which goes beyond the conception of style as language, par-

14. "Strukturalismus und Struktur in literaturwissenschaftlicher Hinsicht," in *Europäische Aufklärung, Herbert Dieckmann zum 60. Geburtstag* (Munich, 1967), p. 81: "Ein Schema oder System, das alle Erscheinungen der Literatur als begrenzte interne Relationen und Kombinationen auffassen wollte, kann es nicht geben."

ticularly in the movement that is called *Stilforschung* and has profoundly influenced Italian and Spanish developments. For instance, the late Ulrich Leo argued that anything that makes the "how" (instead of the "what") of a work of art is style—not only the linguistic expression but also structure as totality, the characters, the situations, and even the plot or the action.[15] Style is identical with form or simply with the work itself. This view is substantially that of Benedetto Croce, though Croce, reasoning consistently from his rigidly monistic outlook, could decide that style is simply synonymous with form or expression and hence a superfluous term.[16]

In this concept of stylistics, the term "style," as transferred from its original meaning (derived from a writing *stylus)* and applied to architecture and sculpture, returned to literary studies. J. J. Winckelmann, in his *Geschichte der Kunst im Altertum* (1764), seems to have been the first to describe the different stages of the style of Greek art. In ways which are not entirely clear the terms "Gothic," "Renaissance," "Baroque," "Rococo," and the like were established in art history and thence transferred to literature. I have brought this out in detail in my study of the history of the term "baroque,"[17] and the same could be done with the other terms modeled on art history. The influence of Heinrich Wölfflin's *Kunstgeschichtliche Grundbegriffe* (1915) on literary studies has been particularly strong in Germany. But it is sufficient to refer to books such as Wylie Sypher's *Four Stages of Renaissance Style* (1955) and his *Rococo to Cubism* (1960) or to Roy Daniells' *Milton, Mannerism and Baroque* (1963) to

15. *Stilforschung und dichterische Einheit* (Munich, 1966), p. 30.

16. *Estetica* (8th ed. Bari, 1945), p. 79.

17. 1946; reprinted in my *Concepts of Criticism* (New Haven, 1963), with a Postscript 1962, containing some additions and corrections.

see that this use is still very common and successful, as it appeals to our sense of the unity of the arts, of a unified time-spirit, and the unitary development of the arts, however tenuous some of the analogies and parallels may be if looked at with a critical eye. The linguistic concept of style is here abandoned almost completely. I shall not attempt to discuss questions raised by this use of the term, as I have tried to criticize it before, possibly with excessive skepticism.[18]

In all these discriminations I have assumed that stylistics and poetics are strictly descriptive disciplines aiming at the observation, classification, and characterization either of verbal style or of the verbal devices used in literature. This certainly is the ideal of our scientific age: objectivity, reticence as to value judgment, and abstention from criticism is the dominant mood. Sol Saporta has assured us that "terms like *value, aesthetic purpose,* etc." are not available to linguists.[19] The proliferation of quantitative methods in the study of style, whether statistical or based on computer research, are sufficient evidence. I for one am not disposed to dismiss these methods, though I doubt their adequacy for some problems or refuse to consider them the only panacea. Quantitative relations establish only dependent functions, more or less necessary concomitants in the totality of a work of art but cannot define its central meaning, its historical, social, and generally human import. Other scholars too, even some who could be suspected of an aversion to quantification, have rejected all concern for value judgment. Thus Northrop Frye, in the "Polemical Introduction" to his highly influential *Anatomy of Criticism* (1957), argued that "the study of literature can never be founded on value judgments" and that "criticism

18. See the chapter "Literature and the Other Arts" in my *Theory of Literature* (New York, 1949).

19. Sebeok, ed., *Style in Language,* p. 83.

should show a steady advance toward undiscriminating catholicity."[20] Ulrich Leo, who comes from a totally different background, refers, almost with horror, to the danger that "evaluation" might "creep" into his method of stylistic study.[21] Examples of this kind could be easily multiplied. I believe, however, that the idea of emptying the study of literature, on whatever level, of criticism in the sense of evaluation and judgment is doomed to failure. The mere fact that we select certain texts out of millions for investigation is a critical judgment, even though it may be inherited and accepted without examination. The selection was accomplished by preceding acts of judgment, on the part of readers, critics, and even professors. The study of any work of art is impossible without constantly choosing the traits we are to discuss, the angle from which we are to approach it. We weigh, discriminate, compare, portion out, and single out at every step.

Neither can the practice of ranking be avoided. I understand the dissatisfaction with rankings on a single scale and can sympathize with the ridicule that T. S. Eliot and, borrowing his figure, Northrop Frye have poured on the imaginary stock exchange of literature. "That wealthy investor T. S. Eliot, after dumping Milton on the market, is now buying him again; Donne has probably reached his peak and will begin to taper off; Tennyson may be in for a slight flutter but the Shelley stocks are still bearish."[22] We may indeed balk at the crudity of some pronouncements about first-rank and second-rank writers, about "good," "better," and "best."

20.  Princeton, 1957, pp. 20, 25.

21.  Loc. cit., *Stilforschung,* p. 22.

22.  Cf. T. S. Eliot, "What Is Minor Poetry?" (1944), in *On Poetry and Poets* (London, 1957), pp. 48–49; and Frye, *Anatomy of Criticism,* p. 18.

Nevertheless, it is an illusion to think that we can shirk the problem of what we may call the "canon" of literature. Its historical development has been traced by Ernst Robert Curtius in the main European literatures.[23] In an attempt to refute the historical relativism of such a great scholar as the late Erich Auerbach, I myself have argued that "there is a wide agreement on the great classics: the main canon of literature."[24] There is the irrefutable distinction between really great art and very bad art: between, say, "The Ode on a Grecian Urn" and a poem in a provincial newspaper, between Tolstoy's *Anna Karenina* and a story in *True Romances*. Relativists always shirk the issue of thoroughly bad poetry. Even Northrop Frye has to admit that "Milton is a more rewarding and suggestive poet to work with than Blackmore," and Frye makes frequent value judgments. In the same book he calls Aristophanes' *Birds* his "greatest play" and Robert Burton's *Anatomy of Melancholy* "the greatest Menippean satire in English before Swift."[25]

We have to face the problem of criticism as evaluation, since we should recognize that a work of art is not an assemblage of neutral facts or traits but is, by its very nature, an object charged with values. These values do not merely "inhere" in structures, as the Husserlian phenomenology of Roman Ingarden concludes. The very fact that I recognize a certain structure as a work of art already implies a judgment of value. Literary description and evaluation are inseparable: evaluation not only grows out of description but is presupposed and implied in the very act of cognition itself. Recently

23. *Europäische Literatur und lateinisches Mittelalter* (Bern, 1948), esp. pp. 267 ff.

24. "Literary Theory, Criticism and History" (1959); reprinted in my *Concepts of Criticism*, pp. 18–19.

25. *Anatomy of Criticism*, pp. 25, 44, 311.

E. D. Hirsch, Jr., in his paper "Literary Evaluation as Knowledge," has accepted my view of value and knowledge, though he had earlier disagreed with me about the theory of interpretation, and he has shown how closely this view agrees with Kant's. Value judgments, to use his words, "necessarily subsist in the relationship between meanings and these correlative subjective stances."[26]

Thus we must face the question whether style or any particular style or stylistic device can be considered a criterion of aesthetic value. It can hardly be so considered if we take style in isolation from the totality of a work of art. Descriptions of style have traditionally been governed by criteria of effectiveness of communication: clarity, vivacity, persuasiveness, and so forth—all ultimately rhetorical categories, which cannot by themselves establish the artistic merit of a specific text. In a specific context vagueness and obscurity, illogicality and even monotony may contribute to aesthetic value. Nor can the occurrence of a specific stylistic trait establish the artistic merit of a text. Hyperbole may be tragic or pathetic, grotesque or comic, yet completely ineffective artistically. A dense sound texture does not necessarily establish high poetic quality. Poe's "Raven" has been rightly listed as a prime example of "vulgarity in literature."[27] Its intricate rhyme scheme and sound patterns do not make it a good poem. There are plenty of virtuoso performances in all possible metrical and stanzaic forms in many languages which have only slight aesthetic merit. Nor can a specific choice of vocabulary, figuration, grammatical correspondences, or sentence structure constitute aesthetic merit. I admire the ingenuity with which

26. In *Criticism,* ed. L. S. Dembo (Madison, Wis., 1968), pp. 45–57.

27. Aldous Huxley, *Vulgarity in Literature: Digressions from a Theme* (London, 1930).

Roman Jakobson and Claude Lévi-Strauss analyzed Baudelaire's sonnet "Les Chats."[28] They have demonstrated the
parallelisms, correspondences, reiterations, and contrasts
convincingly, but I fail to see that they have or could have
established anything about the aesthetic value of the poem. I
agree with Michael Riffaterre's view that "no grammatical
analysis of a poem can give us more than the grammar of the
poem."[29] Jakobson himself showed long ago that the supposedly indispensable criterion of poetry, "metaphoricness," can,
on occasion, be dispensed with or can be replaced by metonymic relations, grammatical echoes, and contrasts.[30] Pushkin's "Ja vas ljubil" is Jakobson's example of an imageless
poem, and I may add Wordsworth's "We Are Seven" or
Robert Bridges' "I Love All Beauteous Things. I seek and
adore them," poems to which it would be impossible to deny
aesthetic merit. This type of poetry could be called "poetry of
statement," a term first used by Mark van Doren in defense of
Dryden's verse.[31] One could, however, argue that all poetry is
metaphorical merely by being poetry, language, and *mimesis,*
not life, a view propounded eloquently in the Epilogue to
William K. Wimsatt and Cleanth Brooks' *Literary Criticism:
A Short History*. But this seems to me a very different use of
the term "metaphor": the whole work is seen as such. "Metaphor is a substantive—or mock substantive—universal."[32]

No grounds of total evaluation can, I conclude, be established by linguistic or stylistic analysis as such, though an

28. In *L'Homme, 2* (1962), 5–21.
29. "Describing Poetic Structures: Two Approaches to Baudelaire's *Les Chats," Yale French Studies, 36–37* (1966), 213.
30. "The Metaphoric and Metonymic Poles," in *Fundamentals of
Language* (The Hague, 1956), pp. 76–82.
31. *John Dryden: A Study of his Poetry* (New York, 1946), p. 67;
first published in 1920.
32. New York, 1957, p. 750.

intricate sound texture, a closely knit grammatical structure, or a dense web of effective metaphors may contribute to the total aesthetic value of a work of art. A fortiori, no genetic criterion can establish aesthetic value. Leo Spitzer's perceptive recognition of psychological traits of an author observable in his stylistic quirks does not and cannot establish the aesthetic value of these works. On the contrary, one feels that Spitzer has often overrated authors of ephemeral merit such as Charles-Louis Phillipe or Jules Romains because he has been able to establish such links between mind and word. Similarly, Jakobson overrates poems which lend themselves to an analysis of their sound patterns or grammatical organization or which simply experiment with language, with the result that the perspective on the history of much modern poetry seems distorted. Actually, a very special taste for poetry playing with language is exalted at the expense of the great tradition. Futurism is consistently preferred to symbolism.

We have to become literally critics to see the function of style within a totality which inevitably will appeal to extralinguistic and extrastylistic values, to the harmony and coherence of a work of art, to its relation to reality, to its insight into its meaning, and hence to its social and generally human import. Thus we cannot ignore the meaning given the word "style" used by Goethe in his first paper after his return from Italy, "Einfache Nachahmung, Manier, Stil" (1788). "Imitation," he says, is the lowest stage of art; "manner" arises when the artist expresses himself; "style" is above objective imitation and subjective manner. It "rests on the deepest foundations of knowledge, on the essence of things, so far as we are able to know it in visible and palpable forms." It is the term to designate "the highest stage which art has ever reached and will ever reach."[33] Style in this sense is identical with great art. It is a critical concept, a criterion of evaluation.

33. *Sämtliche Werke,* Jubiläumsausgabe, ed. Eduard von der Hellen, *33* (40 vols. Stuttgart, 1903), 57: "So ruht der Stil auf den tiefsten Grundfesten der Erkenntnis, auf dem Wesen der Dinge, insofern es uns erlaubt ist, es in sichtbaren und greiflichen Gestalten zu erkennen"; 59: "um den höchsten Grad zu bezeichnen, welchen die Kunst je erreicht hat und je erreichen kann."

# A Map of
# Contemporary Criticism in Europe

For many years I have been engaged in writing a *History of Modern Criticism* from the middle of the eighteenth century to the present. Four volumes were published, two in 1955 and two in 1965, bringing the story down to about 1900. A last volume on the twentieth century is still unfinished. Obviously it is a more difficult task to write about the twentieth century than about the eighteenth or nineteenth, as there is no book such as Saintsbury's *History of Criticism and Literary Taste in Europe* (published between 1901 and 1904) which would even give an outline of the subject. There are, of course, some books and articles on developments in individual countries, but even those are not plentiful and, for the most part, not up to date. Still, from the perspective of 1969, it is fairly clear who are the outstanding figures in literary criticism in the early decades of this century: we can hardly hesitate in naming Benedetto Croce in Italy, Albert Thibaudet, Charles Du Bos and Paul Valéry in France, and T. S. Eliot, I. A. Richards, and F. R. Leavis in England. Georg Lukács will appear the most prominent Marxist critic in the East, at least to a Western observer, and Ortega y Gasset seems easily the most conspicuous figure in Spain.[1]

1. Only about Germany may there be doubts. In the early part of the century Germany produced a distinguished group of scholar-critics, including Friedrich Gundolf, who belonged to the circle

If we want to know the state of criticism at the present moment—and such knowledge seems to me indispensible even to a historian of the remote past—our uncertainty grows. The selection of the major figures becomes more controversial as the discord of voices and clash of opinions grows louder and more raucous. The picture in one's mind vacillates and shifts disconcertingly and seems to change almost every year. It would be, I imagine, possible to sit down in a well-stocked library and read as much as one can to form an opinion about the present situation in every country. But this seems not enough. No doubt, one has to know the books and read the periodicals, but besides, I think, there is a need to acquire some sense of the atmosphere, the lay of the land, the relative importance of people, books, and issues by personal contacts.

I have traveled in Europe repeatedly and extensively during recent years, meeting with critics and literary scholars and, without interviewing them in any formal manner (I detest tape recorders), talking freely and frankly. I hope I have thus acquired a knowledge of what I like to call the geography or map of contemporary European criticism. A brief Cook's tour of the main countries might give some feeling of the enormous activity in criticism in Europe today. At least one overwhelming impression I carried away from my travels deserves further reflection: the sense of the gulfs yawning between the different national traditions

---

around Stefan George, and four great experts in Romance Literature: Karl Vossler, Ernst Robert Curtius, Leo Spitzer, and Erich Auerbach (the last two of whom emigrated to the United States). But there was no great public figure comparable to those in other countries. Possibly Walter Benjamin could, in retrospect, assume such stature, although he was isolated and desperately alone in his time.

in spite of all the many attempts at building bridges—that is, of the tenacity with which the main European nations cling to their distinct critical traditions—and, even within one nation, the sense of the almost equally unbridgeable chasms that divide schools, ideologies, and individuals. One may sometimes be disheartened by the worse than Babylonian confusion of tongues that afflicts criticism possibly more than any other comparable human activity. It is often very difficult to understand the terminology and assumptions of much foreign criticism if one starts with any kind of preconceptions and a vocabulary of one's own, as one inevitably does. Acts of mental acrobatics or, put more modestly, of surrender of one's individuality are required to enter into the minds of such diverse men starting from premises which are strikingly different from one's own. Fortunately, I am not entirely unprepared, as my own experience was varied enough during my early life in Europe, largely in Czechoslovakia and England.

England is the country which, for obvious reasons, is best known to Americans. The links in criticism have been particularly strong in this century: two Americans who settled in England, Ezra Pound and T. S. Eliot, were enormously influential also as critics, and an Englishman, I. A. Richards, who moved from Cambridge on the Cam to Cambridge on the Charles River, can be considered the father of the American New Criticism. He was also the teacher of William Empson and, together with Eliot, greatly influenced the early development of F. R. Leavis, who is still, at the age of 74, a dominant force in English criticism.

The many pupils and adherents of Leavis have been extremely active. Among the older men, L. C. Knights, who earned his spurs with the famous attack on A. C. Bradley, *How Many Children Had Lady Macbeth?* (1933), has more recently written *Some Shakespearean Themes* (1959) and *An Approach to Hamlet* (1960); Derek Traversi, a Welshman in spite of his Italian name, has written several studies of Shakespeare; and Martin Turnell, *Scrutiny's* French specialist, has produced a steady stream of books, including *The Novel in France* (1951), *Baudelaire* (1953), and *The Art of French Fiction* (1959). The widely distributed *Pelican Guide to English Literature* is almost entirely written by Leavis pupils in his spirit. John Holloway, in a section of the last volume, proclaims the writings of F. R. Leavis "the outstanding critical achievement of the century in English."[2] Holloway himself, who has made his name by a good book, *The Victorian Sage*, dismisses all philosophical and aesthetic speculation as "abracadabra" in the good antitheoretical manner of Leavis and argues at length against the American New Criticism and its cult of complexity, paradox, and irony as well as against the Chicago Aristotelianism and the ambiguities of William Empson. What remains is an Arnoldian "calm intelligence," "moderation," and "urbanity," along with insights into the implications of literature in life as the ideal of criticism.

W. W. Robson, one of the editors of the *Cambridge Quarterly,* is even closer to Leavis' point of view. His *Critical Essays* (1966) show the same concern for the moral life in literature and for the central role of English studies as a discipline of sensibility as well as the somewhat surprising exaltation of D. H. Lawrence both as a novelist and critic. In a recent lecture defending "criticism without principles," Robson argued that literary criticism is neither a science nor

2. John Holloway, "The Literary Scene," in *The Modern Age,* Vol. 7 of the *Pelican Guide to English Literature,* ed. Boris Ford (Harmondsworth, Middlesex, 1961), p. 90.

a mass of fancies but a personal encounter with the great works: "There is no body of established results which the next critic can build on."[3] There is not even a continuous debate.

The very same point of view is upheld by George Watson, in *The Literary Critics* (1962). Although Watson is, in general, not well disposed toward Leavis—he feels in fact that Leavis has "hurried towards value-judgments without respect to the essential delicacy and complexity of literary values"— he himself dismisses all theory and all evaluation and recognizes only "descriptive" criticism, denying "continuity and intelligibility in the history of literary argument." He sees in criticism only "a record of chaos marked by sudden revolution" and concludes, strikingly, "The great critics do not contribute; they interrupt." For quite mysterious reasons an "anticognitive enthusiasm" is attributed to me, possibly because I have argued against the excesses of historicism.[4]

Historicism is quite comprehensibly the creed of many academic critics in England as elsewhere. Helen Gardner's *The Business of Criticism* (1960) is an eloquent statement and a defense of "intention" as the legitimate and ultimate aim of the critic's quest. But most practicing critics show rather a contemporary social concern. It dominates the books of Raymond Williams, who criticizes Leavis' assumption of a "wholly organic and satisfying past" and advocates a democratic socialism. In *Culture and Society, 1780–1950* (1959), however, he shares Leavis' main worry about the triumphs of a technological civilization destroying the old tradition of humanist culture.

Frank Kermode's *Romantic Image* (1957) was a powerful attack on the whole conception of poetry as imagery and

3. W. W. Robson, *Critical Essays* (London, 1966), p. 34.
4. George Watson, *The Literary Critics* (Harmondsworth, 1962), pp. 215, 221.

symbol. Kermode regarded the idea that Image is "radiant truth out of space and time" as "a great and in some ways noxious historical myth,"[5] which, he argued, entails the equally false myth of the necessary isolation and estrangement of the modern artist. Though Kermode admires Yeats as the culmination of this tradition, he wishes its demise and advocates, surprisingly, a return to Milton. In *The Sense of an Ending* (1967) Kermode construes a tenuous theory of fiction by analogies with man's sense of history and the apocalypse. In his latest book, *Continuities* (1968), he presents himself as a new Edmund Wilson: a social critic who, however, preserves a proper grasp on the nature of art. Kermode becomes quite satirical about the new avant-garde, about pop and op art, the music of silence, and other recent developments in which "the difference between art and joke is as obscure as that between art and non-art."[6]

Theoretical reflections on the problems of criticism have come recently from philosophers—or, rather, the adherents of analytical philosophy deeply impressed by Wittgenstein's criticism of language. John Casey's *The Language of Criticism* (1966) avoids the sterile dismissal of all questions of aesthetics and valuation, which is also the trite conclusion of most descriptive linguists, who try with statistical and quantitative methods to impose criteria of scientific objectivity on the study of literature. Casey sees, to my mind correctly, that "in aesthetics the concept of a personal 'response' is central, while we must at the same time avoid the view which is often taken to be a corollary of that—that aesthetic judgment is ultimately 'subjective.' "[7] But Casey's study moves on a high level of abstraction remote from actual

5. Frank Kermode, *Romantic Image* (London, 1957), p. 166.
6. Frank Kermode, *Continuities* (London, 1968), p. 15.
7. John Casey, *The Language of Criticism* (London, 1966), p. xii.

literary criticism, while the linguists are rather concerned with "taking a poem to pieces," with minute observations on syntax, grammar, and meter. Two books, Christine Brooke-Rose's *A Grammar of Metaphor* (1958), technical and scholastic as it is, and Winifred Nowottny's *The Language Poets Use* (1962), raise genuine problems of criticism. David Lodge's *Language of Fiction* (1966), which offers more than a "Verbal Analysis of the English Novel" promised in its subtitle, bridges the usual gulf between linguistic analysis and interpretative and evaluative criticism very successfully. These recent books contradict the ingrained antitheoretical prejudice of the English strikingly formulated by H. W. Garrod, Professor of Poetry at Oxford, when he said that "criticism is best when written with the least worry of head, the least disposition to break the heart over ultimate questions."[8]

This is precisely what the French are doing. Across the Channel there is a strikingly violent clash of theories and ideologies. A new Marxism is very much alive (while dead in England since the thirties)—sophisticated, sharply aware of Hegel and Lukács—of which Lucien Goldmann may be singled out as the best representative. His book on Pascal and Racine, *Le Dieu caché* (1956), shows how tragedy and tragic vision can be linked with social changes and social groups ("la noblesse de robe") in ways which nobody could have thought of before. Interest in psychoanalysis, Freudian and Jungian, is also flourishing in France. Charles Mauron, who died late in 1966, aroused even academic respect by his studies of Mallarmé and obsessive metaphors. A philosopher of science, Gaston Bachelard produced a psychoanalysis of fire and followed it up, not unexpectedly, with books on air, earth, and water.

8. H. W. Garrod, *Poetry and the Criticism of Life* (Oxford, 1931), pp. 156–57.

But the most flourishing and original movement in French criticism calls itself "la critique de conscience." The group, sometimes referred to also as the Geneva school, reveres Marcel Raymond for his book *Du Baudelaire au surréalisme* (1933) as the originator of the method but actually goes far beyond him in formulating a new way of studying literature. They aim not at an analysis or judgment of a single work of literature but rather at a reconstruction of the peculiar consciousness of a writer. Every poet is assumed to have lived or to live in his peculiar world, which has an interior organization or "structure" which it is the task of the critic to discover and articulate. The emphasis on various aspects differs from critic to critic. Georges Poulet is primarily interested in the attitude to time of poets and writers which he traced in several books—*Etudes sur le temps humain* (1950), *La Distance intérieur* (1952)—with unparalleled ingenuity. In recent publications, particularly *Les Métamorphoses du cercle* (1961), Poulet has moved toward generalizations about Renaissance, baroque, and romanticism, viewing consciousness as an all-embracing spirit of the time. Romanticism, for instance, is described as an effort to overcome the opposition of subject and object, or center and circumference, in a personal experience.

Jean-Pierre Richard, a much younger man, is concerned rather with analyzing the perceptual life of the authors he discusses. Thus for Flaubert love is like drowning, with the lover losing his bones, becoming like plastic paste. *Littérature et sensation* (1954) is Richard's aptly titled first book. In all his works he uses sentences and observations, metaphors and scenes from all books, diaries, letters, and jottings, without regard to context, to build up the scheme of the mental life or the imaginary universe of a poet such as Mallarmé, organized by leading motifs, obsessive metaphors, or recurrent stylistic devices. Richard's perspective is resolutely anti-formal. He considers his approach superior to what he calls "Anglo-Saxon criticism," as it does not concern external form and linguistic surface but establishes "a connection, an immediately felt echo between the forms of its expression (syntactic, rhetorical, melodic) and the shapes (thematic or ideological) of the deep experience it expresses and incarnates."[9] Richard conceives of literature as an imaginary universe in which individual problems or "projects" move toward their solutions.

Another member of the Geneva group, Jean Starobinski, is very close to Richard in theory, though his particular interests stress the Enlightenment and its "invention of freedom." His book on Rousseau (1957) is actually a psychological study which describes Rousseau as searching for "transparency," for a communion of human hearts and, when rebuffed, erecting a subjective "obstacle" within himself. Language, as in Bishop Berkeley, is conceived of as an impediment to direct vision because it throws a "veil" over reality. Raymond's successor, Jean Rousset, is much more interested in form and has tried in his books on the baroque in France and in *Forme et signification* (1962) to bridge the existential criticism of his training and a grasp of literature as art. The "living organism" and "focus" of a work of art are terms which are to connect form and meaning.

Among the so-called critics of conscience Albert Béguin and Maurice Blanchot stand somewhat apart. Béguin who had written an excellent book, *L'Ame romantique et le rêve* (1939), on German romanticism and the French writers who followed in the exaltation of the life of dreams—Baudelaire, Rimbaud, Mallarmé, and Proust—turned in his later writings

9. Jean-Pierre Richard, *Onze Etudes sur la poésie moderne* (Paris, 1964), pp. 9–10.

to Catholic mysticism. Maurice Blanchot, a most difficult and even obscure writer, discussed, in *L'Espace littéraire* (1955), such questions as "whether literature is possible?" or the "space of death," using Kafka, Mallarmé, and Hölderlin as examples. Blanchot arrives at a strange nihilism: silence is the ultimate significance of literature. The ineffable is the only thing left to express. Fortunately, there are more articulate and rational critics in France.

Although Poulet, Richard, and Blanchot are sometimes referred to as structuralists, their approach has nothing to do with "structure" as understood by linguists and literary theorists, who have always used the term to refer to the pattern or totality of a language or a work of art. Roland Barthes appeals to the linguistic and anthropological concept of structure and speculates about an all-inclusive theory of signs which he has illustrated by a study of feminine fashions. But his little book *Sur Racine* (1963) draws on Freudian psychoanalysis and a Jungian concept of archetypal myth rather than linguistics. The situation of every drama of Racine is reduced to a formula: "A has complete power over B. A loves B, who does not love A." A kind of abstract thematology emerges, enlivened by references to solar myth, Oedipal relations, and a parallel in historical events. No wonder that he was violently attacked by an exponent of the historical method, Raymond Picard. Barthes defended himself, in *Critique et vérité* (1966), by pleading for an almost complete freedom of symbolic interpretation for what seems, in practice, an arbitrary "creative" criticism duplicating the work of art.

In general, what is today called "structuralism" in France and what has attracted much public attention through the success of the work in anthropology of Claude Lévi-Strauss is a bafflingly diverse and even contradictory set of doctrines with the most diverse philosophical affiliations: the mood of Sartre's existentialism, the techniques of Husserl's phenomenology, the fanciful pseudo-science of Gaston Bachelard, modern linguistics ultimately derived from Saussure, and, sometimes, Marxism or Marxist motifs. It provides a rich hodgepodge of methods which—whatever the interest and stimulation afforded may be—suffers from the constant tendency to direct attention away from what I must consider the central concern of criticism: the analysis and evaluation of a work of art in its integrity.

If we cross the Rhine in imagination, we find a very different situation. In Germany one also hears of existential criticism, and no doubt the vocabulary of Heidegger is omnipresent, but actually German criticism today engages rather in a variety of "close reading." This obviously reflects a reaction against the speculative excesses of *Geistesgeschichte*, a general revulsion against literary history and the grandiose constructions of the historians of the German spirit who often succumbed to the not so spiritual ideology of Nazism. Emil Staiger, a Swiss, is the leading practitioner of "interpretation"; he is sensitive and learned but, as a recent speech indulging in a wholesale attack on modern literature shows, narrowly limited in taste, confined to the German classicist and romantic tradition. Staiger also tried his hand at theory in *Grundbegriffe der Poetik* (1946), a surprisingly schematic application of some of the oldest ideas about the distinctions between the genres: the lyrical mode is supposed to relate to the past, the epical to the present, the dramatic to the future. But Staiger is only one among the many sensitive readers of German poetry: his three-volume study of Goethe and his new book, *Stilwandel* (1963), show his return to the problems of literary history. He and his many academic followers can hardly be called critics in a strict sense.

Criticism is either carried on in the newspapers or by a few militant new Marxists who might be better called left Hegelians. They appeal to the work of Walter Benjamin, who perished in 1940, an obscure, allusive writer who formulated a Marxist view of literature but was, unlike the Eastern Marxists, responsive to avant-garde tastes and modern feelings. Theodor Adorno, a music critic and sociologist in Frankfurt, edited Benjamin and is the acknowledged high priest of the new left Hegelian criticism. He sets himself sharply off from eastern Marxism, chiding Lukács for his old-fashioned realist and bourgeois taste, and emphasizes the difference between art and reality: the work of art criticizes reality by the very contradiction between the image (which is the object received by the subject) and the reality outside. Valéry, Proust, Kafka, and Beckett are his concern. Recently the new Marxism has been strengthened by emigrants from East Germany. Among them Hans Mayer is the most versatile and productive. Mayer has managed to follow the sinuosities of the party line in the East: quite easily changing, for instance, his interpretation of Georg Büchner from a forerunner of expressionism to a forerunner of socialist realism. But after his flight to the West, he has adhered to a basic unorthodox Marxism in lively comments on Thomas Mann, Hesse, Gerhart Hauptmann, and almost every figure of recent German literature.

Compared to the left-wing group, the right is weak—if "right" means critics committed to a religious and conservative outlook. Hans Egon Holthusen is a genuine critic who argues from a Protestant bias for a literature which creates a reality fraught with the need for decisions and thus eminently ethical. Holthusen has criticized Rilke and Thomas Mann severely for their ideas and has welcomed the position of the later Eliot.

When we go south and cross the Alps into Italy, we are again confronted with a very different cultural landscape. In Italy Croce and his followers dominated criticism for decades, and they are still strong in the universities. Croce offered taste and great learning, but his discarding of literary history and formal analysis left Italian criticism, like English, with a choice between impressionism and antiquarianism. Croce's dominance has been on the wane since his death in 1952, however, and most Italian intellectuals seem to have gone over to one or the other variety of Marxism, often oddly combined with the aesthetic doctrines of Croce or with a revived Aristotelianism. Galvano della Volpe, author of a *Critica del gusto,* who died last year, was a critic of this kind. Fortunately, some Italians discovered that there are other choices available than an option for either Croce or Marx. The great German scholars of stylistics, Leo Spitzer and Erich Auerbach, made a profound impression on academic criticism, and there is now much fine analytic work which resumes the tradition of close reading, by scholars such as Gianfranco Contini, who ranges from the earliest Italian sonneteers to the most "hermetic" modern poets. Besides, there is considerable interest in existentialism of the French variety, of which Luciano Anceschi and his review *Aut-aut* in Milan are most fervent propagandists.

I know least about Spain. There is no public figure alive comparable to Ortega y Gasset or Unamuno, and I doubt that there is much criticism. A new book by Emilia de Zuleta, *Historia de la crítica española contemporánea* (1966), lists many fine scholars and essayists but hardly any critics. Among the scholars Dámaso Alonso stands out as the practitioner of "stylistics" in the wake of the Germans, but he has, unlike them, a mystical streak. In his sensitive and ingenious book on

Spanish poetry, *Poesía española* (1950), he comes often to conclusions which seem to me mere gestures toward the ineffable and mysterious. Among his followers Carlos Bousoño produced a well-argued *Teoría de la expresión poética* (1952).

I have reserved the Communist world for the last portions of this map. It is a very different world, where an official creed of criticism is imposed and enforced relentlessly. For a time there was some hope for a thaw, but even this is gone. The dogma of Socialist realism rules supreme. Sinyavsky attacked it cogently for its blatant contradiction between the recommendation of faithful realism and the exaltation of an ideal socialism, and he is in prison. Still, during the thaw some liberalization was achieved, and in Russia some interest in the Formalists active during and after the First World War was allowed to revive. The book by Mikhail Bakhtin, *Problems of the Poetics of Dostoevsky* (1929), was reprinted in 1963, and at least some scholars show the influence of the Formalist school even if they profess a general Marxism. For example, Dmitri Likhachev, who is a specialist in Old Russian literature, has written well on the unity of form and content, on the tasks of comparative poetics, and on chronicle time in Dostoevsky, topics which are taboo in orthodox Marxist criticism. Comparative literature, long a subject on the black list, is again admissible, though restricted within the limits of the Marxist dogma. In Czechoslovakia there was an even more far-reaching loosening: for example, a book by Květoslav Chvatík on the prewar Marxist critic Bedřich Václavek praised the avant-garde of the twenties and published pictures by such nonrealists as Picasso and Léger. It slyly advocated the view that any and all kinds of modern styles may be practiced and even called "socialist realism," provided the writers are committed to Communism. It is symptomatic of the changed atmosphere that in 1967, before the advent of Dubček, Jan Mukařovský, the most prominent theorist of the Prague Linguistic Circle, who had abjectly recanted in 1950, republished his early Formalist writings. In Poland for a time a more liberal outlook was possible, and several active scholars, such as Henry Markiewicz, combined a commitment to Marxism with a genuine interest in literary problems. But Jan Kott, the interpreter of Shakespeare as our contemporary, of Shakespeare as an ancestor of Beckett, of *King Lear* as anticipating *Endgame,* stays prudently away from Poland.

Emigration has not been possible for the most prominent of all Marxist critics, Georg Lukács in Hungary. He is by far the most influential Marxist critic in the West, as he writes in German and on German and French topics. Although in the fifties he was branded a "deviationist," and in 1956 became Minister of Education in the short-lived government of Imre Nagy and was deported to Rumania, he was allowed to return to Budapest and write and publish in retirement. His new two-volume *Aesthetik* seems, however, a monument of the past, an attempt to reconcile Marxism with German classicism and to combine it with Pavlovian "conditioned reflex" physiology, hampered by its doctrinaire framework and a basically nineteenth-century taste which lets Lukács admire Thomas Mann but disapprove of everything more modern, whether it be Kafka or Joyce, Eliot or Valéry. In Hungary Lukács, who is now 84, remains on the sidelines. Orthodox Marxists are in the saddle, and there as well as in all the other Communist countries much scholarship (I don't say genuine criticism) is produced that manages, within its rigid framework, to reintroduce considerations of aesthetics and criticism at least in a subordinate position to its generally social and political concerns.

The map I have sketched is, I hope, multicolored and, I fear, also sadly flat. An airplane flying at great height affords a wide view but also flattens out the landscape. Still, one has seen many things one would not see if one stayed on the ground. For some purposes airplane travel is the right way of locomotion. I hope it was for this hurried trip to Europe.

# Bibliography of the Writings of René Wellek

(supplementing the list in
*Concepts of Criticism*)
from January 1, 1963, to December 31, 1969

## *A. Books*

2a.   New ed. with "Preface to the Paperback," New York, McGraw Hill, 1966.

3j.   Third rev. ed. of 3a, Madrid, 1962.

3k.   Up-dated reprint of 3e, Frankfurt am Main, Ullstein, 1963.

3l.   *Literaturteori,* Danish translation by Elsa Gress Wright, Copenhagen, Munksgaard, 1964.

3m.   New ed. of 3c, with new Premessa, Bologna, Il Mulino, 1965.

3n.   *Teorija književnosti,* Serbo-Croat translation by Aleksandar Spasić and Slobodan Dordević, Preface by Nikola Koljević, Belgrade, Nolit, 1965.

3o.   *Theoria logotechniae,* modern Greek translation by Stavros G. Deligiorgis, Athens, Diphpor, 1965.

3p.   *Litteraturteori,* Swedish translation by Maj Fresch, Foreword by Thure Stenström, Stockholm, Bökförlaget Aldus/Bonniers, 1967.

3q.   *Torat Hagifrut,* modern Hebrew translation by Jonathan Ratogh, Tel Aviv, Yachdav United Publishers, 1967.

3r.   *Teoria Literaturii,* Rumanian translation by Rodica Trinis, introductory study by Sorin Alexandrescu, Bucureşti, Editura Pentru, Literatură Universală, 1967.

3s. *Kirjallisuus ja sen teoria,* Finnish translation by Vilho Vik- sten and Matti Suurpää, Helsinki, Helsingissä Kustannu- sosakeyhtiö Otava, 1969.

4d. *História da crítica moderna,* Vol. *1:* Século *XVIII,* Por- tuguese translation by Livio Xavier, São Paulo, Herder, 1967.

5d. *História da crítica moderna,* Vol. *2: O Romantismo,* Por- tuguese translation by Livio Xavier, São Paulo, Herder, 1967.

7. *Concepts of Criticism,* edited with an Introduction by Stephen G. Nichols, Jr., New Haven and London, Yale University Press, 1963.

   7a. *Grundbegriffe der Literaturkritik,* German translation by E. and M. Lohner and others, Stuttgart, W. Kohlhammer, 1965.

   7b. *Kritički Pojmovi,* Serbo-Croatian translation by Aleksan- dar I. Spasić and Slobodan Dordević, Beograd, Vuk Ka- radžić, 1966.

8. *Confrontations: Studies in the Intellectual and Literary Rela- tions between Germany, England and the United States during the Nineteenth Century,* Princeton, Princeton University Press, 1965.

   8a. *Konfrontationen. Vergleichende Studien zur Romantik,* German translation by Rolf Dornbacher, Frankfurt am Main, Suhrkamp Verlag, 1964.

9. *A History of Modern Criticism 1750–1950,* Vol. *3: The Age of Transition,* New Haven, Yale University Press, 1965; London, Jonathan Cape, 1966.

   9a. *Storia della critica moderna,* Vol. *3: L'Età di transizione,* Italian translation by Agostino Lombardo and Ferruccio Gambino, Bologna, Il Mulino, 1969.

10. *A History of Modern Criticism 1750–1950,* Vol. *4: The Later Nineteenth Century.* New Haven, Yale University Press, 1965; London, Jonathan Cape, 1966.

    10a. *Storia della critica moderna,* Vol. *4: Dal Realismo al sim- bolismo,* Italian translation by Agostino Lombardo and Rosa Maria Colombo, Bologna, Il Mulino, 1969.

11. *The Literary Theory and Aesthetics of the Prague School,* Michi- gan Slavic Contributions, edited by Ladislav Matějka, Ann Arbor,

The University of Michigan, Department of Slavic Languages and Literature, 1969.

### B.  Contributions to Books

1. Reprinted in A8.
3. Reprinted (with some corrections) in *Sir Gawain and the Pearl: Critical Essays,* ed. Robert J. Blanch (Bloomington, Indiana University Press, 1966), pp. 3–36.
8. Reprinted in A7.
11. Reprinted in A6.
58. Reprinted (in part) in A6.
60. Reprinted in A7.
61. Reprinted (considerably expanded) in A9.
63. Reprinted in A6.
65. Reprinted (expanded and revised) in A10.
66. Reprinted in A6.
    66b. Hungarian translation in *Helikon, 10* (1964), 42–49.
    66c. Partial Czech translation by Jiří Levý in his *Západní literární věda a estetika* (Prague, Československý spisovatel, 1966), pp. 323–31.
71. Reprinted in A6.
72. Reprinted (revised) in A9.
74. Reprinted in A6.
76. "Romanticism Re-examined," in *Romanticism Reconsidered,* ed. Northrop Frye (New York, Columbia University Press, 1963), pp. 107–33. Also in A6.
77. "French Criticism between 1815 and 1850," in *Studi in onore di Carlo Pellegrini* (Torino, Società Editrice Internazionale, 1963), pp. 649–82. Reprinted in A9.
78. "Preface" to Leo Spitzer, *Classical and Christian Ideas of World Harmony.* ed. Anna G. Hatcher (Baltimore, Johns Hopkins Press, 1963), pp. v–x.
79. "Some Principles of Criticism," in *The Critical Moment: Essays on the Nature of Literature* (London, Faber and Faber, 1964), pp. 40–47; also New York, McGraw Hill, 1964.
    79a. German translation by Lothar Fietz, in *Von Oxford bis Harvard: Methoden und Ergebnisse angelsächsischer Literaturkritik.* (Pfullingen, Neske, 1964), pp. 38–46.

79b.  Serbo-Croatian translation by M. Borojević and Lj. Jojić, in *Razlog, 3* (1963), 777–83.

80.  "Recent Czech Literary History and Criticism," in *The Czechoslovak Contribution to World Culture,* ed. Miloslav Rechcígl, Jr. (The Hague, Mouton, 1964), pp. 17–28. Before in A7.

81.  "The Literary Criticism of Frank Raymond Leavis," in *Literary Views: Critical and Historical Essays,* ed. Carroll Camden (Chicago, University of Chicago Press, 1964), pp. 175–99.

  81a.  Italian translation by Fioretta Mandelli, in *Nuova Presenza, 6* (1963), 23–40.

82.  Introductions to Turgenev's *Fathers and Sons* and Henry James' *Aspern Papers,* in *World Masterpieces,* rev. ed. Maynard Mack, 2 (New York, W. W. Norton, 1964), 658–62. Supplementary to B62.

83.  "Discussion of Mario Praz's Paper 'Historical and Evaluative Criticism,' " in *Literary History and Literary Criticism: Acts of the Ninth Congress, International Federation for Modern Languages and Literatures,* ed. Leon Edel (New York, New York University Press, 1965), pp. 77–83.

84.  "The Term and Concept of Classicism in Literary History," in *Aspects of the Eighteenth Century,* ed. Earl R. Wasserman (Baltimore, The Johns Hopkins Press, 1965), pp. 105–20.

  84a.  Also in *Actes du IVe Congrès de l'Association Internationale de Littérature Comparée, Fribourg, 1964;* (The Hague, Mouton, 1966), pp. 1049–67.

  84b.  German translation in *Schweizer Monatshefte, 45* (1965), 154–73.

  84c.  Hungarian translation by Szabó Ákosné, in *Helikon, 11* (1965), 328–45.

85.  "What is Reality? A Comment," in *Art and Philosophy: A Symposium,* ed. Sidney Hook (New York, New York University Press, 1966), pp. 153–56.

86.  "Vernon Lee, Bernard Berenson and Aesthetics," in *Friendship's Garland: Essays Presented to Mario Praz on his Seventieth Birthday,* ed. Vittorio Gabrieli, 2 (Roma, Edizioni di Storia e Letteratura, 1966), 529–47.

87.  "Irving Babbitt, Paul More, and Transcendentalism," in *Transcendentalism and Its Legacy,* ed. Myron Simon and Thornton H. Parsons (Ann Arbor, University of Michigan Press, 1966), pp. 185–203.

87a. Reprinted in Ann Arbor Paperbacks, 1969.

88. "Masaryk, Tomáš Garrigue," in *The Encyclopedia of Philosophy*, ed. Paul Edwards, 5 (New York, Macmillan, 1967), 176–77.

89. "French 'Classicist' Criticism in the Twentieth Century," in *The Classical Line: Essays in Honor of Henri Peyre. Yale French Studies, 38* (1967), 47–71.

90. "The Poet as Critic, the Critic as Poet, the Poet-Critic," in *The Poet as Critic,* ed. Frederick P. W. McDowell (Evanston, Ill., Northwestern University Press, 1967), pp. 92–107.

91. "Genre Theory, the Lyric and *Erlebnis,*" in *Festschrift für Richard Alewyn,* ed. H. Singer and Benno von Wiese (Köln, Böhlau, 1967), pp. 392–412.

92. "The Name and Nature of Comparative Literature," in *Comparatists at Work: Studies in Comparative Literature,* ed. Stephen G. Nichols, Jr., and Richard B. Vowles (Waltham, Mass., Blaisdell, 1968), pp. 3–27.

    92a. Italian translation by Rosa Maria Colombo, in *Belfagor. 22* (1967), 125–51.

    92b. My German translation in *Arcadia, 2* (1967), 229–47.

    92c. Slovak translation by Zdeněk Pištek, in *Slavica Slovaca, 3* (1968), 121–41.

93. "A Reply to Mario Praz, Concluding Remarks at the Sixth Congress of the International Association of Professors of English," in *English Studies Today: Fourth Series, Lectures and Papers Read at the Sixth Conference of the International Association of University Professors of English Held at Venice August 1965* (Roma, Edizioni di Storia e Letteratura, 1966), pp. 13–20.

94. "Introduction" to Thomas Warton, *History of English Poetry, 1* (New York, Johnson Reprint Corporation, 1968), v–vii.

95. "The Supposed Influence of Vico on England and Scotland in the Eighteenth Century," in *Giambattista Vico: An International Symposium,* ed. Giorgio Tagliacozzo and Hayden V. White (Baltimore, The Johns Hopkins Press, 1969), pp. 215–23.

96. "The Term and Concept of Symbolism in Literary History," in *Proceedings of the Vth Congress of the International Comparative Literature Association, Belgrade, 1967* (Amsterdam, Université de Belgrade, Swets Zeitlinger, 1969), pp. 275–92.

    96a. Hungarian translation in *Helikon 14* (1968), 202–20.

97. "Czech Literature: East or West," in *Czechoslovakia: Past and*

*Present,* ed. Miloslav Rechcígl, Jr., *2* (The Hague, Mouton, 1969), 893–902.

C.   *Articles in Periodicals*

2.  Reprinted in A7.
3.  Reprinted in A7.
4.  Reprinted (greatly expanded) in A7.
6.  Reprinted in A7.
9.  Reprinted in A7.
    10c.   Partial reprint in *Modern Criticism; Theory and Practice,* ed. Walter Sutton and Richard Foster (New York, Odyssey Press, 1963), pp. 257–61.
13.  Reprinted in A8.
14.  Reprinted in A8.
15.  Reprinted in A7.
16.  Reprinted in A8.
17.  Reprinted in A8.
18.  Reprinted in A7.
19.  Reprinted in A6.
23.  Reprinted in A6.
    23b.   Partial reprint in *Romanticism: Problems of Definition, Explanation, and Evaluation,* ed. John B. Halsted (Boston, Heath, 1965), pp. 45–52.
    23c.   Partial reprint in *The Romantic Movement,* ed. Anthony Thorlby (London, Longmans, 1966), pp. 28–34.
26.  Reprinted in A5.
    28b.   Croat translation by M. Borojević and L. Jojić, in *Razlog* (Zagreb) *4* (1964), 836–67.
29.  Reprinted in A10.
30.  Reprinted in A10.
31.  Reprinted in A6.
32.  Reprinted in A10.
33.  Reprinted in A10.
35.  Reprinted in A6.
    35c.   Reprinted in *The Practice of Modern Literary Scholarship,* ed. Sheldon P. Zitner (New York, Scott, Foresman, 1966), pp. 14–26.
36.  Reprinted in A10.

37. Reprinted in A6.

    37a. German translation in *Begriffsbestimmung des literarischen Realismus,* ed. Richard Brinkmann, Wege der Forschung, *211* (Darmstadt, Wissenschaftliche Buchgesellschaft, 1969), 400–33.

    38a. Italian translation by Maria-Luisa Spaziani, in *Convivium, 33* (1965), 225–51.

39. Reprinted in A6.

    39c. Polish translation by Maria Traczewska in *Życie literackie, 15,* No. 682 (21 lutago, 1965), 6; No. 683 (28 lutago, 1965), 4.

    39d. Slovak translation by Vincent Šabík, in *Slovenské Pohľady, 83* (1967), 78–88.

40. Reprinted in A10.

41. Reprinted in A9.

44. "Philosophy and Postwar American Criticism," *Comparative Literature Studies,* Special Advance Issue, ed. A. Owen Aldridge (College Park, Md., 1963), pp. 1–16. Printed before in A6.

45. "German and English Romanticism: A Confrontation," *Studies in Romanticism, 4* (1964), 35–56. Printed before in A8.

46. "The Classics and the Man of Letters: An Arion Questionnaire," *Arion, 3* (1964), 89–92.

47. "Comparative Literature Today," *Comparative Literature, 17* (1965), 325–37.

48. "New Czech Books on Literary History and Theory," *Slavic Review, 26* (1967), 295–301.

49. "Why Read E. T. A. Hoffmann?", *Midway, 8* (1967), pp. 49–56.

    49a. Reprinted, in shortened version, as "Foreword" to *Selected Writings of E. T. A. Hoffmann, 1,* ed. and trans. Leonard J. Kent and Elizabeth C. Knight (Chicago, The University of Chicago Press, 1969), 1–4.

50. "On Rereading I. A. Richards," *Southern Review, 3* (1967), 533–54.

    50a. Italian translation in *Umanesimo, 2* (1968), 62–81.

51. "The Literary Criticism of Friedrich Gundolf," *Contemporary Literature, 9* (1968), 394–405.

51a.  Also in *Criticism: Speculative and Analytical Essays,* ed.
      L. S. Dembo, Madison (University of Wisconsin Press,
      1968), pp. 120–31.

*D. Review*

74.  Renato Poggioli, *The Spirit of the Letter,* in *Yale Review, 55*
     (1966), 429–32.

*E.  Miscellaneous*

Before 1.  "Czechoslovak Literature" Correspondence, *New York
Herald Tribune Books* (February 1, 1929), p. 18:XI.
     11a.  German translation by Annette and Ulrich K. Dreikandt,
           in *Begriffsbestimmung des literarischen Realismus,* ed.
           Richard Brinkmann, Wege der Forschung, *211* (Darm-
           stadt, Wissenschaftliche Buchgesellschaft, 1969), 448–52.
13.  *Czech Literature at the Crossroads of Europe,* Toronto, The
     Toronto Chapter of the Czechoslovak Society of Arts and Sci-
     ences in America, 1963.
15.  A Letter addressed to Robert L. Kahn on Josef Körner, in Robert
     L. Kahn, "Some Recent Definitions of German Romanticism or
     the Case against Dialectics," *Rice University Studies, 50* (1964),
     20–22.
16.  Foreward to *American Comparative Literature Newsletter,* ed.
     Alain Renoir, No. 1 (Berkeley, 1964), pp. 1–2.
17.  "Alexander Veselovsky," remarks preceding translation of his
     "On the Methods and Aims of Literary History as a Science," in
     *Yearbook of Comparative and General Literature, 16* (1967), 33.
18.  "Reply to Bernard Weinberg's Review of my *History of Modern
     Criticism,*" in *Journal of the History of Ideas, 30* (1969), 281–82.
19.  "Eighteenth Century English Criticism," introductory remarks to
     *English Literary Criticism of the Eighteenth Century, A Collec-
     tion of 208 Original Texts Printed in Facsimile* (New York,
     Garland Press, 1969), pp. 7–9.

# Index of Names

# Index of Topics and Terms